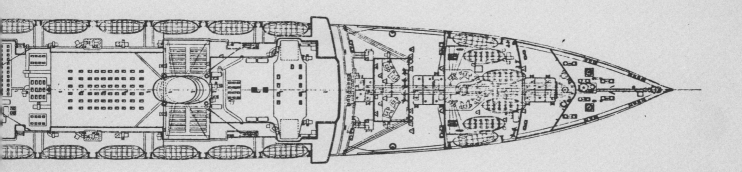

"World's Greatest Ship"

Vol. 1

The Story of the LEVIATHAN

By FRANK O. BRAYNARD

This book is dedicated to Albert Ballin and also to William Francis Gibbs and his brother Frederic, and to the Robert L. Hague Merchant Marine Industries Post and to two generous LEVIATHAN engineers: "Eddie" Jones and Harry Wright and to the LEVIATHAN Veterans Association with sincere gratitude.

Published by the South Street Seaport Museum, 16 Fulton St., N.Y. 10038 — 1972

TABLE OF CONTENTS

PREFACE

Aside from all the exciting moments, the many "firsts" and the stream of adventure that makes the VATERLAND/LEVIATHAN story interesting, there is an intangible attraction that has drawn me to her. It is the pathos enshrouding her life. So human, so like a living thing she was, and so transitory, so much a creature of fortune, a setting for contrasts. Even in her great moments, and there were many, she was a target of sarcasm. Even in her days of white-elephant neglect, she was a thing of awe, a loved presence. A creature of mass and beauty, she was an extraordinary entity. Like the Great Pyramid or Chartres she represented much more than the total of her parts. Unlike these architectural masterpieces her span was brief. This perhaps, above all, impells me to attempt to document her short appearance on life's sea.

As the VATERLAND her detractors were loud, although in size and in many features she was an advance over other ships. In Germany she was looked down upon by anti-Jewish high society as an ostentatious bauble of the newly-rich. Abroad she was disparaged as tubby, big-but-slow, hard to handle and garish. One high purpose behind her introduction into Atlantic service in mid-1914, her owner's determination to give substance to his conviction that peace between Germany and England could be maintained, went unrecognized and, to my knowledge, never before has been brought out. Then during her years of internment the deteriorating queen took on a new character. To some she was the center of spies where bombs were being made and plots hatched. Or she was a symbol of the embattled, blockaded homeland, a rallying point for fund raising for starving German war victims.

With America's entry into the war she was the victim of one of history's most pitiful rapes, her rich adornments were despoiled both by outright and by legalized thievery. During the war she was denounced as a potential death trap for troops, as top heavy, as unsafe—all hogwash. But it was as a troop carrier that she came to win her most undisputed appreciation. In 1919 the Secretary of War ebulliently described her as "the greatest ship in the world," a phrase her peacetime owners picked as her slogan. When all the boys were home, the LEVIATHAN endured a three-year eclipse and was the subject of many misadventures. Despite valiant efforts by William Francis Gibbs, she was pictured as being allowed to fall into disrepair. She became the target of political attacks. While foreign ships were returned to service, she sank into the Hoboken silt. Newspapers invented stories about giant rats aboard. There was even a cry that she should be taken out and sunk. America couldn't operate her and shouldn't try.

Then it was determined to recondition her. This was done magnificently and with sparks in all directions. In her career as the American sea queen, largest liner ever to fly the U.S. flag, before or since, she reached heights of success on many fronts and plumbed the depths of failure. Genius and stupidity, brilliance and ineptitude, dedication and indifference—the gamut of high mindedness mingled continually with flagrant evidences of human weakness in the hectic happenings that befell the LEVIATHAN—each spotlighted by the press. She was both one of the finest examples of how a government could run a utility and a profligate display of all that's bad in government control. She was the world's largest ship and yet she wasn't. She was the world's fastest ship and yet she wasn't. Her inexperienced management was attacked by private U.S. shipowners who opposed government operation. They were also run ragged by nationalistic foreign rivals boasting eons of experience and the finest crews and who were not bothered by Prohibition. But the LEVIATHAN probably did have the world's finest cuisine, and she really was the "in ship" of her era. She carried an average of 995 passengers a crossing over 12 years of service, the highest average list of any of the six largest ships afloat. James J. Callahan, one of her engineers, summed up her career:

"She was many things to close to a million people, all good things. To an extraordinary degree she inspired affection. If there is such a thing as the inanimate having charisma, she had it."

That I am not alone in my affection for the LEVIATHAN is shown by the 800 who have been reading my "LEVIATHAN Newsletter" in the years this book has been in preparation, and by the following list of friends who have advanced $100 or more to permit the publication of this volume:

C.S. Ashdown	George Staehle	A.B. Crummy	W.S. Billings
Alfred Miller	Victor Scrivins	R.L. Hague Post	Earl L. Artz
James Callahan	Harry Wright	Kenneth Harder	Richard W. Berry
Albert Boyce	Anselmo Dappert	Clarence McKee	R.W. Morrison
Roland Haines	Louis A. Gabrielli	Mrs. G.L. Raynor	William Hood
John Morgan	Neal Farwell	Mrs. A.M. Vanderhaak	F.J. Jones
H.W. Peters	A. Cunningham	S.H. Schluter	Rix McDavid
J. Maxtone-Graham	Arthur Van Dyck	Philip Franklin	Forrest Cummings
Norman Morse	Joseph Coyne	N. Vernicos-Eugenedes	George Weber
William Morris	Irving Jones	Mrs. Arthur Tode	H.M. Booker
Robert Morton	R.L. Hedlander	Deloss A. Grant	B. Branch
Dudley Martin	Hugh Platt	Mrs. Mary R. Godfrey	Ray Brown
John Mulligan	Louis Varrone	Randall LeBoeuf	James Wilson
Edward Mueller	Douglas Curtis	M.P. Iverson	Mrs. V.O. Poure
Everett Northrup	Irving Ariel	Frederic H. Gibbs	Harold J. Jonas
Harry Manning	Claire Gonska	Francis Barry	John Bull
Leslie Veader	Terry Donais	Robert Parkinson	Malcolm Bell
E.J. Farr	G.E. Applegate	John Gronan	S.S.H.S.A.
Albert Engel	Howard Whitford	George Tamaro	Everett Viez
Rebecca Dallas	John Dondero	William Oman	James M. Stewart
Ernst Glaessel	D.W. Hurley	Donald Ringwald	

These names do not include those who advanced sums under $100. The formula is that each of the $100 sponsors will get copies of each volume for which his money is used at no cost and will then get his full contribution back. It was only in this way that an effort of this depth could be undertaken. I am also grateful to many others, notably Marg Burns and Walter Hamshar, who proofread this first volume and Charles Hurley, who contributed the title page and gave many other encouragements and to Harvey Brouard of the Adams Group, my printers, who solved countless problems. Above all, a special thank you to the hundreds of LEVIATHAN stalwarts who gave me their memories for this volume and for the three volumes to follow.

Frank Braynard

HAPAG model featuring the VATERLAND contrasted with a clipper ship, the paddle-wheeler BRITANNIA, the BORUSSIA, ARIZONA and OCEANIC. Below that the grand IMPERATOR, with eagle figurehead and original tall stacks. Photo courtesy Harry O'Donnell. A portrait photo of Albert Ballin courtesy A. Kludas—bottom left) and the keel is laid (courtesy Blohm & Voss).

Chapter I

BEFORE THE BEGINNING

t was a momentous thing that happened on that September day in 1911. It was an event filled with great portent when the first rivet joined together the first two keel plates and the new ship began her life as an entity. The keel plates were 33 feet long, 78 inches wide, and 1.36 inches thick. They were made of high toxic, non-corrodible chrome nickel steel. To the riveter and his fellow workers in the island shipyard of Blohm & Voss in Hamburg harbor, the new monster was Hull #212. A number of people already knew her as the EUROPA, but a year and a half later she would be christened VATERLAND. The world would come to know her best as the LEVIATHAN, one of the grandest and most storied ocean liners of all time.[1]

It was a momentous thing because this was the physical beginning of a ship that would mean much to millions of people. She was to be the world's largest ship, a title she would hold for eight years.[2] Only six other liners have surpassed her in gross tonnage, and in all probability no more big ones will ever be built.[3] She could well be called the world's saddest ship, for she lay idle for nearly half of her relatively brief twenty-four-year life. A ship of great promise she was, too—at first for the proud Germans; then for American doughboys eager to get "over there" and, later, even more impatient to get home; and finally for the American Merchant Marine, whose flagship she was for a decade. She was a ship of purpose and inspiration for men like Albert Ballin, who conceived her; William Francis Gibbs, who rebuilt her to fly the American flag as a luxury liner; and countless others of genius who were caught up in her orbit. She was also a ship of controversy, a ship of turmoil, a ship that was perpetually on the front page.

Before zoom-lensing in on the actual physical beginnings of the great liner, we will scan what was going on in the world of shipping in 1911 and then train a magnifying glass upon this Albert Ballin, shipping genius *par excellence*. History has almost forgotten him; yet he strove to—and almost did—change history.

Virtually unrestricted immigration to America, coupled with rapid advances in naval architecture and marine engineering, had produced an astonishing leap forward in ship size, speed, and luxury during the 19th century. The first vessel with a steam engine to cross any ocean was the 1819 SAVANNAH. Of 300 tons, she had a 98-foot hull and was driven by a 90-horsepower, paddle-wheel engine. At mid-century the largest Atlantic liners had grown to 5,000 tons and could make speeds of 16 knots on 5,000 horsepower.[4] The largest ship in the world in 1900 was the OCEANIC, of 17,000 tons, and the fastest was the DEUTSCHLAND, of 23 knots on 35,000 horsepower. In 1907 Britain broke all records for size and speed with the flying Cunard Line sisters LUSITANIA and MAURETANIA, of 31,000 tons and 26-knot speed on 70,000 horsepower. As the keel for Hull #212 was being laid two British lines were building ships to exceed 40,000 tons, although they would make no claim to being speed record-breakers. Albert Ballin's goal was three mammoth liners of over 50,000 tons each. He was head of the Hamburg-American Line, the world's largest shipping enterprise. The first of these had already been under construction for over a year when Hull #212 was begun. So much for the ocean liner picture as of 1911.

Now for a look at Albert Ballin, the man who might have altered the course of history had his efforts to ward off World War I been successful.

Born on August 15, 1857, in Hamburg, barely 100 feet from the waterfront, Ballin was the youngest of ten children. As a child he was beset with all sorts of maladies and constitutional weaknesses, according to his friend and biographer Bernhard Huldermann.[5]

He was educated at a private day school. Music was his favorite hobby, and he played the cello. It was apparent early in his life that he was a gifted boy. He had a prodigious memory, and he became a passionate reader of books on history and politics, gaining a great store of knowledge.

Just as he was finishing what formal education he was to have, his father's death shook him free from his home attachments and placed him, at 17, in the competitive world of business. He succeeded to his father's small emigration agency, Morris & Co., which had been founded in 1852. None of his older brothers showed any interest in the business or in helping support the family. Actually the break was not as abrupt as might be thought, for both home and office occupied the same building, and Ballin had for years done his school homework right at his father's side. He knew the business by heart.

Emigration from Germany to America was one of the products of the Napoleonic wars. At first the emigrants had embarked in Antwerp or Le Havre, but then Bremen began to attract more and more of those on the move. Eventually Hamburg, too, came to share in the profits sieved out of this flow of humanity. For a time the poor emigrant was more a victim than anything else, being mistreated in shameful fashion every step of his long route to the New World. In due course laws were passed, corruption was restrained, and the way was made somewhat smoother.

When Ballin became the chief executive of his father's little agency, his work was exclusively with foreign ship lines. Morris & Co. routed most of the emigrants it handled via the American Line's services between Liverpool and Philadelphia and New York. Ballin's earliest and most important connections were those he adroitly cultivated with the English representatives of this line. He made frequent trips to Great Britain and learned to speak English fluently. The agency did not send emigrants via Hamburg's own great transatlantic line, the well-known Hamburg Amerikanische Packetfahrt-Actien-Gesellschaft (known to all as Hapag), for that company did not deign to deal with agents; it had its own passenger offices.

Ballin's agency concerned itself almost entirely with the emigrant or steerage traffic. Most of the emigrants sailed with tickets that had been prepaid by relatives in America. Between 1875, the year Ballin took over Morris & Co., and 1881, the annual number of emigrants from Hamburg rose dramatically from 25,000 to 123,000. This was due in large part to better times in the United States, but young Ballin's zeal must have helped, too. His tireless efforts and his friendly personality could not help but pay dividends. Things were really booming for his agency.

Such was not the case with the Hamburg Amerikanische company, coming to be known widely as the Hamburg-American Line, or Hapag. This pioneering Atlantic line was suffering from poor management and had allowed the North German Lloyd, its younger rival, to get ahead of it. The latter's service from Bremen to New York took only nine days and was maintained by newer and much finer ships than the best Hapag could offer.[6]

Albert Ballin was aware that his own company had to have a better way to handle the growing horde of emigrants. Routing them to England and thence across the Atlantic via the American Line was becoming too complicated. He turned to a small Hamburg freighter company, the Carr Line, and worked out with them an agreement whereby that company would equip two new freighters to carry emigrants. Ballin would become their passenger agent. The Carr Line was owned by Edward Carr, a nephew of Robert M. Sloman, Jr., whose short-lived Sloman Line of paddle steamers had been an early Hapag competitor.[7] The two freighters which caught Ballin's eye were named AMERICA and AUSTRALIA. He proposed that their upper decks be fitted to carry from 650 to 700 passengers. This was done, and in their first year of operation, Ballin delivered 4,000 emigrants to them. He increased this to 11,000 the next year, by which time the Carr Line was offering passenger space on six erstwhile cargo ships. In addition to substantial improvement in convenience and routing for Ballin's emigrants, the Carr ships could offer more than even the best Hapag ships in one important particular. Because they had no first or second class, their passengers had the run of the ship. Word of these better conditions was quick to get back to the "old country," and by 1883 Carr was carrying 16,000 emigrants, more than a quarter of what the giant Hapag was carrying.[8]

By 1885 a somewhat frantic Hamburg-American Line was seeking a rate-setting agreement with Carr. There were protracted negotiations between the two companies, with young Ballin speaking for Carr. He impressed the Hapag executives more and more. A rate agreement was reached in 1885, but that development was overshadowed by what happened the next year. The mighty Hapag absorbed Albert Ballin and the Carr Line. As one source put it on the 100th anniversary of his birth: Hapag, the Goliath, was wise enough to come to terms with the forward-looking, purposeful, and able David, young Ballin.[9] As another source noted: "This recognition of Albert Ballin by the Hamburg-American Line was one of the most astute moves" they ever made, for "he proved his worth almost at once, and within a few years became one of the greatest personalities ever known in the long history of North Atlantic and, indeed, world shipping."[10] It was in May, 1886, that Albert Ballin went to work for Hapag as head of their North American passenger division. He had arrived.

Ballin's Early Ships

In the world of passenger shipping there have been many enterprising men. None have had more ability, push, zest, and foresight than Albert Ballin. None have had higher goals or exerted greater influence in their homelands than Ballin. None have had more involvement in non-shipping matters than Ballin. None have had so much riding on their success or failure in these "extracurricular" activities as Albert Ballin.

Because of his early associations with British shipping men, Ballin had developed many close ties in England. The English banker Sir Ernest Cassel became a lifelong admirer of his. Sir Ernest was a transplanted German with the highest connections in British royal circles, society, and business. He was an ideal point of reference for Albert Ballin. The mutuality of interests and ideals of these two men foreshadowed what they hoped would be cooperative relations between their two countries. This link became more and more portentous as the power and influence of the two men grew. They could claim the closest of ties with their respective monarchs—those unhappiest of relatives, Kaiser Wilhelm I and King Edward VII.[11]

On May 31, 1886, when Albert Ballin first sat at a joint meeting of the Board of Trustees and the Board of Directors of Hapag, he had many more immediate concerns than a dream of three monster 50,000-ton palace liners. But even as far back as that, a few of the men who were to be leading actors in the story of Hull #212 were already on the scene. Since their lives are of interest in the emerging diary of this great ship, a quick glance around the world to spot a few of them on this day in 1886 might be good.

The first master of the VATERLAND would be Hans Ruser. He was 24 in 1886 and well into a distinguished career at sea. Rudolph Blohm and Ernst Foerster, who would design the great ship together, were babes-in-arms that year. Rudolph Blohm was the son of Herman Blohm, co-founder of the Hamburg shipyard of Blohm & Voss, which would build the VATERLAND. Willy Schreiber, to be the ship's interior decorator, was a lad of 16. The first commander she had as an American troopship, Captain J.W. Oman, was a boy of 14 in 1886. Her navigator during the troopship period and later one of her most famous peacetime American masters, Harold Cunningham, was one year old.

Later on, during Hull #212's period as an American luxury liner, she had her most famous American master, Herbert Hartley. In 1886 he was a boy of 11, learning to sail on Lake Oswego. Albert Borland Randall, her last American master, was six years old and learning to wonder at and love the sea from his home on Long Island Sound, in Connecticut. Finally, the man who was to have more to do with her than any other American, and who, with Albert Ballin, is the co-hero of this story, William Francis Gibbs, had just been born.[12]

To say that Albert Ballin was a dynamo would be an understatement. When he became Hapag's North Atlantic manager, the company ranked 22nd among great ship lines of the world.[13] It had been surpassed by its younger rival, the North German Lloyd, and had only one first-class steamship in the Atlantic passenger trade, the 3,969-ton HAMMONIA, a ship that was "inferior both as regards her efficiency and her equipment," according to Huldermann.[14]

Ballin's forceful approach to things became evident in his first year with Hamburg-American. It was not long before he persuaded Hapag to order two new ships that would be pioneers in many ways and were designed to contend for the transatlantic speed record. He had watched closely the experimentation with twin screws and realized what great security they would bring to ocean liners.[15] When he learned that the Inman Line was building two new twin-screw liners, he decided that this was what he wanted for his new ships. It was the introduction of two propellers by Inman and Hapag that finally and for all time ended the dependence of ocean liners on sail, for now if one propeller shaft broke, as often happened, there was another to bring the ship home. With the elimination of sail, the modern silhouette of the liner was at last possible. Tiered decks and high superstructures could not evolve as long as masts had to support working sails. And Ballin, in his first year with Hapag, was one of the chief pioneers here. Mechanically, the new German liners were innovators in other ways. They adopted forced draft as a feature of their power plant. They were the first German ships to have three smokestacks. They were Germany's first true express steamers.[16]

Ballin's pair of new liners would also be trailblazers in other ways. They would have electric lights in steerage as well as in first and second cabin class. Ballin was still very conscious of the needs of emigrants. There would be a few single-berth cabins in steerage, a marvelous selling point and an unheard-of luxury for emigrants. Finally, the new vessels would be over 7,000 tons, nearly twice the size of any earlier Hapag ships.

In selecting the shipyard for this fine pair of vessels, Albert Ballin adopted several procedures that were to become policy with him. He had developed a distrust of naval architects and never had one as such on his staff. He evolved the plan of going from yard to yard, from naval architect to naval architect, picking and choosing ideas and never staying with one yard or man for long. He played one yard against another. The first of his express steamers he built in Germany, giving a tremendous boost to national pride, but the second he handed to the famous Scotch Laird yard at Birkenhead.

The year of 1888 was a year of great change and events of high portent in Berlin. The first Kaiser, brilliant old King Wilhelm I of Prussia, who with the help of Count Otto von Bismarck had unified Germany 17 years before, suddenly died. He was succeeded by Frederic III, who also died in the same year. In turn Frederic was succeeded by Kaiser Wilhelm II, that sad monarch whose good points often have been ignored because they were so overshadowed by his weaknesses. The new Empress, his wife, was Auguste Victoria.

Although only 31 years old, and a veteran of only two years with Hapag, Ballin could think big and did. What higher honor could he pay the new Kaiser than to name the first German express liner ever built in a German yard after the new Empress? This gesture may have been the foundation stone in Ballin's long friendship with the Kaiser. It may also have been the beginning of an unfortunate animosity that Empress Auguste Victoria bore toward Ballin. When the new liner was launched in December, 1888, it became apparent that one of the most ludicrous errors in all maritime history had been made, something almost unbelievable in light of Ballin's reputation for attending to even the most minute detail in everything he did. The ship's name was misspelled, appearing in large metal letters as AUGUSTA VICTORIA! Ballin apparently chose to ignore the error, and this was the name under which the ship sailed until 1897, when she was taken into a British shipyard, Harland & Wolff, at Belfast, and enlarged. She emerged as the AUGUSTE VICTORIA.[18]

Because she was built in Germany, the construction of the AUGUSTA VICTORIA received the widest publicity in the fatherland. Here at last was proof that German yards could compete with British in a field in which, until then, the English had had no peers. The British-built COLUMBIA followed with comparatively little drumbeating. Aside from the name fiasco, both ships were truly outstanding Atlantic liners and did much for the reputation of Hapag and Albert Ballin. An elaborate company brochure published in New York heralded the AUGUSTA VICTORIA's success on her first visit to the New World. She was visited by 30,000 people, "who expressed their admiration of her beautiful appointments in unmeasured terms."[19]

Ballin's two express steamers immediately took the speed record for runs from Channel ports to New York, but were unable to beat their Cunard and Inman rivals for the overall Atlantic Blue Ribbon.[20] Their ornate public rooms put them right in step with the period's taste for sumptuous décor. For plush, rococo elegance, the first-class music room and the ladies' saloon on these twin liners were unsurpassed. The ornate cupola of the dining saloon, a room that extended through two decks, had to be seen to be believed. Even the French Line steamers of this time could not outdo the gilt and plush that Ballin lavished on his first big-time luxury liners.

Ballin followed this first pair with two other prestige ships, the NORMANNIA and the FÜRST BISMARCK. The first was built in Scotland and the second in Germany.[21] Ballin personally showed old Prince Bismarck over the liner while she was being built. The old warrior remarked that he would not live to see it, but that a world war was coming and that it would start in the Near East.[22] The Kaiser, his Empress, the Prince and Princess, and their large entourage sailed in the FÜRST BISMARCK from Hamburg to Heligoland and Wilhelmshafen in 1890. They carefully examined the ship, and again and again expressed their delight and pleasure with the "magnificence of the interior, the comfortable arrangements, and the mighty and ingenious machinery," a Hapag brochure proudly noted.[23] The Emperor presented the company with his picture and conferred the Order of the Crown on Captain Albers, commander of the new ship.

One of the first steps Albert Ballin took after becoming a director of Hapag was to visit New York and name Carl Schurz the company's American representative. Typical of Ballin's unconventional approach to problems, this move brought credit on Hapag, particularly in the eyes of new Americans of German extraction, the people who paid for the prepaid emigrant tickets. In 1848 Schurz had tried to create a liberal democracy for Germany. He had been defeated by reactionary Prussianism and had been forced to flee. His reputation as a German patriot never died, and, in fact, was enhanced by a brilliant career in America. He became a leader in the anti-slavery movement, was named to the Cabinet of President Rutherford B. Hayes, and then earned a high reputation as a writer.[24]

Ballin loved to travel, and, as a top Hapag executive, he spent almost half of his time on shipboard or in foreign lands. He often sailed on ships of rival lines to see how they treated the passengers. He moved around the world establishing new offices, inspecting agencies, and keeping in close touch with everything that might have a bearing on his worldwide operations. But his first concern was always the passenger facilities on his own ships. As his biographer Huldermann put it:

"Those who saw the finished products of his imagination, the beautifully appointed floating hotels, hardly realized how many apparently insignificant details—which, after all, in their entirety make what we call comfort—owed their origin to his own personal suggestions. Each time he made a sea voyage he brought home with him a number of new ideas."[25]

Jottings from his trip notebooks include such items as:

"Toast to be served in a serviette (hot)."

"Notices on board to be restricted as much as possible, those which are necessary to be tastefully framed—sailing lists and general regulations to be in passengers' lists."

"State cabin on board KAISER FRIEDRICH: key, latch, drawer; no room for portmanteaux and trunks."

"DEUTSCHLAND: soiled linen cupboard too small; steward's white jackets, celery glasses — butter dishes too small — large bed pillows, consommé cups — playing cards."[26]

In addition to an endless passion for passenger comfort, Ballin had a practical nature. He improved freight rate structures and spent much time working out ways to handle cargo. He built four large freight ships, beginning with the 13,300-ton PENNSYLVANIA in 1897. They could carry 2,400 persons in steerage as well, and went full on most westbound crossings. These "P" ships also carried a few in first and second class. They were outstanding ships, and, for a brief time when she was new, the PENNSYLVANIA was the largest ship in the world. The ship which took away her title of "largest in the world" was the famous North German Lloyd luxury liner named KAISER WILHELM DER GROSSE, the first Atlantic liner to have four smokestacks.[27] Not only was this new Lloyd queen a beautiful ship, but she finally captured for Germany the coveted transatlantic speed record.

Albert Ballin recognized the challenge and rose to the occasion. He went to the same yard which had built his own AUGUSTA VICTORIA and the new Lloyd flyer and ordered his own four-stacker. She was to be 34 feet longer than the KAISER WILHELM DER GROSSE and would be named DEUTSCHLAND, the same name as the first ship in the Hamburg-American Line fleet.

The new DEUTSCHLAND came out in 1900 and captured the Blue Ribbon, but, unfortunately, her added length seemed to produce a most serious vibration problem, particularly at the high speeds she had to maintain. She also suffered from the fact that Ballin built no sister ships to sail with her. To have maintained a weekly service from New York to Hamburg, with one ship leaving each side on the same day, would have required four first-class liners of the DEUTSCHLAND's speed.[28]

Ballin the Man

t the turn of the century, Albert Ballin was firmly established. He was ready to build some new first-class liners, and Hapag needed them. The company treasury had been filled when the older COLUMBIA and NORMANNIA were sold to Spain as auxiliary cruisers in her war with the United States, a move that America never forgave Ballin for making. Hapag could claim to be the largest steamship concern in the world. It owned more tonnage than the entire merchant marine of any nation in Continental Europe except Germany. Ballin, who had in effect run the company since 1888, had been made its managing director in October, 1899[29] He was at a high point in his career, but his goals were by no means all achieved.

In appearance, the 42-year-old Ballin was not prepossessing. He was becoming bald. His nose was large and his features had a rubbery look. A heavy mustache and thickish lower lip could be said to balance a large, lined forehead. He often wore *pince-nez* glasses, always dressed with elegance, and invariably had a pearl tie pin whenever photographs were taken.

If anything, his head, which always seemed to be tilted deferentially to left or right, had a slightly comic touch to it.

Ballin's voice and manners, however, were commanding, and his eyes were a striking, piercing feature of his otherwise lack-luster face. They were dark eyes, sharp and wise, eyes that spoke, that could be stern and yet were always candid. They were the doors opening out of a brilliant mind, spellbinding and dominating when they locked with the eyes of another.

How much of Albert Ballin's drive was due to the fact that he was Jewish in a society where anti-Semitism was strong will never be known. It must have been a factor. His passion for success took him far, and as he rose into the highest business, social, and political arenas his demeanor became more highly polished and more cultured. Marianne Rauert, his wife, was a gentile from a middle-class Hamburg family. Slightly taller than Ballin, she could not match his energy and was not cut out for the life he brought her; but she rose to the challenge as well as she could. Married in 1883, they adopted a two-year-old orphan girl the next year.

Ballin had a large and handsome office overlooking Hamburg's harbor in the five-storied Hapag-House on Dovenfleth. There were potted palms, souvenirs of his trips around the world, and a feeling of elegance. Here he presided over company affairs, mixing his interest in detail with an impulsive delegation of power to hand-picked executives. His associates were happy that he traveled so much, for his passion for work and his eagerness to solve even the smallest problem himself frightened them.

On shipboard he was "somewhat imperial, moving from passenger to passenger with a word of greeting for each, while an anxious crew stood nervously at attention. Or he could be a capricious autocrat, commanding changes of course or speed in order to suit his convenience."[30]

Ballin's penchant for face-to-face negotiations had established a working relationship with his company's greatest German rival. The concept of a system to eliminate costly competition between all Continental steamship companies serving America was evolving in his brain. His talents made him a natural leader in settling disputes between rival ship lines, and his conscience and foresight led him into the more complicated field of diplomacy. He became the leading cosmopolite of Germany, but he remained first, last, and always a German. This duality of purpose was to be both a great asset and cause of growing personal guilt feelings and frustration.

Facing the new century and its many world-encompassing problems, Ballin concluded that the only way to overcome temporary business dips in one area was to have many different enterprises in many areas. Drops in emigration to America, cholera epidemics, and other relatively localized problems called for a long-range self-insurance policy that only new and even more varied global operations by Hapag could provide. Out of this came the Hamburg-American Line's major expansion effort into the Orient and into the Persian Gulf. In both these drives the new German enterprise provoked frowns and growing alarm among British interests. Ballin's support of German shipbuilding had been another policy step that had hurt Britain's pocketbook, for shipbuilding was one of her major industries.

Ballin played a part in the lengthy international negotiations that resulted in the creation of the International Mercantile Marine, an American-dominated world shipping combine that shook British maritime pride to its foundation. With money provided by J.P. Morgan, the huge trust swallowed up a long list of famous British companies: Atlantic Transport Lines, Leyland Lines, Dominion Line, and—who would have believed it?—the great White Star Line! There was fear that Cunard might be gobbled up too, and, to keep it loyal, Parliament authorized a subsidy that resulted in the twin flyers MAURETANIA and LUSITANIA, of 1907. Ballin was right in the middle of all this, and as the Red Star Line, of

Belgium, and the Holland-America were drawn into the consortium, he must have given serious thought to putting the fortunes of Hapag on the line. He made frequent trips to America to meet with Mr. Morgan, and, in 1902, reached an agreement that in the long run proved unfortunate for his company. He agreed to pay the Morgan trust a share of any Hapag earnings above 6 per cent, in return for a guarantee that Hapag would have a 6 per cent dividend each year. Ballin, like everyone else, was overly impressed by the huge proportions of the combine. Between 1903 and 1911 Hapag paid more than 1,500,000 marks to I.M.M., which turned out to be a financial white elephant.[31]

Although the Kaiser had inspected the FÜRST BISMARCK and made a brief voyage on her, his real friendship with Albert Ballin did not begin until 1895. In that year Ballin had shown himself and his company off to great advantage by participating in the historic ceremonies held at the opening of the Kiel Canal, which linked the North Sea with the Baltic. Hapag was very much present on that occasion, and, because he was able to offer the hospitality of his commodious liners to the Kaiser and his guests, Ballin was soon well known to the German monarch.[32] When Mr. and Mrs. Ballin sailed for the Orient on Hapag's new METEOR, the Kaiser came down to see them off, inspecting the ship in the process. The connection between the two men bloomed, with Ballin receiving numerous signs of the Kaiser's growing friendship. They exchanged Christmas cards, and notes on their respective anniversaries. The Kaiser visited Ballin's mansion in the Feldbrunnenstrasse so often that it came to be known as the Little Potsdam, after the Royal Palace at Potsdam. On one occasion the monarch recommended his personal physician to Ballin, who was having acute neuralgic pains. Ballin was often invited to important dinners given by the Kaiser, and would frequently sit next to him; and they had long, unattended walks together. They both loved ships, and the Kaiser even submitted drawings and sketches he had made himself of new features for Hapag ships. They both loved pageantry, and Ballin's great express liners were superb settings for sumptuous parties on such occasions as the Elbe yachting regatta each summer or the annual Kiel celebrations.

Unfortunately, there was a dark side to the relationship. The Empress grew more and more displeased with Ballin because he was a Jew. She and others of the Prussian aristocracy criticized the Kaiser for his friendship with Ballin and others whom they lumped together in the newly-rich category. She was able to keep Ballin out of the most intimate palace gatherings and to make him aware of the barriers she was setting up against him.

More Ships

The DEUTSCHLAND's vibration problem deepened Ballin's distrust of naval architects. Although he built many fine intermediate liners, there were no sister ships for the famous four-stacker. The North German Lloyd, however, had added a sister to their most successful KAISER WILHELM DER GROSSE, and she was named the KRONPRINZ WILHELM. Two more were projected. Hapag had to look to its laurels.

On one of his visits to England, when dining at the Ritz-Carlton, Albert Ballin had been introduced to Charles Mewes, noted interior architect now recognized as the father of modern hotel design. Mewes had done the Ritz in Paris and the famous Automobile Club building in London, as well as the Carlton House Restaurant, also in London. Ballin invited him to make a voyage on the DEUTSCHLAND with an eye to planning improvements in the interior. The ship that came out of this planning was the AMERIKA, completed in 1905, and she marks a turning point in ocean liner interiors.[33]

The AMERIKA was built at the well-known Northern Ireland yard of Harland & Wolff at Belfast. Ballin knew the yard and was on the best of terms with its chief executive, Mr.

W.J. Pirrie, who in 1906 would be raised to the peerage.[34] He had an understanding with Harland & Wolff that there should always be a building berth reserved for Hapag. The yard was famous for its Union Castle Line ships, which served from England to Africa, and, above all, for the long list of White Star Line ships it had built. The AMERIKA, in fact, was a slightly larger version of a series of big White Star ships, each the largest in the world when new. Externally there was little to set her apart from these fine vessels, the CELTIC, CEDRIC, BALTIC, and ADRIATIC.

On the inside, however, the AMERIKA was revolutionary. Her passenger accommodations and public rooms were "far ahead in luxury of any preceding ship," according to Bonsor, in his *North Atlantic Seaway*, the most respected study to date of Atlantic liners.[35] She had suites with private bathrooms; she had the first electric elevators on a ship; and she had the first Ritz-Carlton restaurant ever put on a liner, where passengers could order *a la carte*. There were other previously unheard-of features, such as electric medicinal baths. A major change was the large windows that looked out on deck from her public rooms. They were real windows, inside and out. On earlier ships, where the lounges and smoking rooms were much lower down and closer to wave action, these windows looked real on the inside but were actually only round ports on the outside. In a sense, this was a bonus resulting from the shift from single screw to twin screw. The interior of the AMERIKA had a new feeling of clean-cut, airy bigness. Running with the DEUTSCHLAND, she kept Hapag in the forefront of the Atlantic competition. A second liner was ordered. She was to be named EUROPA. Both the AMERIKA and the EUROPA were much larger than the 16,000-ton DEUTSCHLAND. The AMERIKA had a tonnage of 22,225, and the EUROPA was to be even larger. A third ship of 30,000 tons was contemplated. Ballin had abandoned the idea of building speed record-breakers and had adopted the White Star policy of operating very large, very commodious ships.[36]

A serious depression cut Atlantic travel while the AMERIKA and her larger sister, the EUROPA, were being built, and the idea of a four-ship weekly service had to be abandoned for the moment. The 30,000-tonner was never built, and Hapag had to be content with an odd assortment of liners on its premier service to New York.

As the time neared for the launching of the EUROPA, Albert Ballin decided to make one more effort to ingratiate himself with the Kaiserin. Not only did she dislike him, but, being an Anglophobe, she resented his many ties with England.[37] Ballin decided to try to please her by changing the name of his newest liner, which would be the world's largest ship when she was completed. Instead of the EUROPA, the new ship would be called the KAISERIN AUGUSTE VICTORIA. There is no doubt he made sure the "e" was correct this time. The 24,600-ton K.A.V., as the new liner was quickly dubbed in shipping circles, was Ballin's last big ship before he plunged into the biggest liner program ever attempted before or since—the construction of three monster ships of more than 50,000 tons each, the trio that would give him his long-awaited weekly service.

Before coming to this Ballin dream fleet, a few words on his activities between 1906 and 1910 and then a close look at his efforts to keep the peace between England and Germany.

On one of his visits to New York Ballin inspected the nine-story Aldrich Court office building at 45 Broadway. Its tower had an unbroken view of the harbor and it was a showplace of downtown Manhattan. Visitors came in a steady stream, and its four Otis hydraulic elevators were a marvel of the day. Emil L. Boas, resident director and general manager of Hapag in America since the death of Carl Schurz, recommended the purchase of the place, and Ballin agreed. It was reopened as Hapag's headquarters and advertised as "easily front rank in magnificence and elegance among ornate places of business in the Western Hemisphere."[38] Into the tiled floor of the lobby was worked the Hapag motto: "Mein Feld Ist Die Welt." All office interiors were paneled in mahogany, and potted palms abounded. The red brick exterior, with its huge, rough-cut granite stones as a base and its heavy, low-arch main entrance, fitted the exuberant mood of the day.[39]

Early in 1907 Albert Ballin sat down to a series of sessions that would produce the first Atlantic Steamship Conference organization. The meetings were held at Jena, Austria, and Ballin headed a nine-man delegation from the Hamburg-American Line. There were six from the I.M.M. and five each from North German Lloyd and Cunard. The French Line had three men, and there were others from Canadian Pacific, Donaldson, Anchor, Allen, and Red Star lines. It was a fine example of hard, peaceful international bargaining. Out of this session came a body of rules to govern Atlantic rates and shipping practices, many of which still stand at this writing. A headquarters was set up in Brussels and has continued to this day.[40] There can be little doubt that Ballin and the others relaxed after the meetings and listened with eagerness to the discussions by Cunard people of their two new liners to go into service that very year—the superb LUSITANIA and MAURETANIA, each of 31,000 tons and of 25 knots or more. There must also have been hints from the White Star group of their new trio of 45,000-ton ships to be named OLYMPIC, TITANIC and GIGANTIC.[41] In passenger liner construction, particularly, there seemed no limit to what man could do. It was a heady climate and one that was just suited for great plans. How far Ballin had gone at that point with his own thinking about his three great ships would be most interesting to know. Certainly he must have already had many conferences about them, and their basic design points must already have been established. Every indication suggests that he planned to have at least the first two, and probably all three, built at Belfast by Harland & Wolff. They were to be the largest ships in the world, of course, and perhaps he would break with the White Star/Harland & Wolff tradition and attempt to make them the fastest as well.

Efforts for Peace

Politically Albert Ballin was a conservative and a monarchist. At the turn of the century, when the German government began a propaganda campaign for a big navy, Ballin supported it. However, as this evolved into a bitter naval race with Britain, he tried to cool the situation off and to "circumvent its disastrous consequences," as his biographer Huldermann remembers it. Ballin realized how Britain felt about a big navy. He recognized that as a nation that dominated a third of the inhabited world, Britain was determined to maintain naval predominance. He realized that England would fight for this dominance. He concluded that an Anglo-German meeting of the minds on the naval question had to be achieved to keep peace between the two nations, despite whatever else might happen in the powder keg of Eastern Europe. From 1908 on, this was his goal, and he did not admit failure until the actual outbreak of war in 1914.[42]

From the Franco-Prussian war on, newly-unified Germany came to be regarded more and more as a threat to Great Britain. The German merchant was a keen rival of the British trader all over the world. Germany's late start in the colonial sweepstakes only keyed her up to greater efforts. Her tariff system proved a challenge to Britain's long-time policy of free trade. All these matters were alarming to the British, but the real issue was naval rivalry. For Britain, having a navy stronger than that of her two closest rivals was a matter of national survival.

Ballin was recognized by the forces of moderation in both England and Germany as the man who could negotiate a settlement on this basic naval problem if anyone could. His success in winning a meeting of minds again and again in international commercial matters had won renown. It was natural that in the summer of 1908 Sir Ernest Cassel should come to him with a challenge that was by far the greatest of Ballin's career. Much has been written on what Albert Ballin did between 1908 and 1914, and major portions of both the Huldermann and Cecil biographies are devoted to this subject. The Ballin goal was in line with one of his basic business tenets—get both sides to sit down together and talk, and any problem can be solved. The Ballin technique was to move back and forth between the two nations, talking with the highest naval and political personages, sometimes directly and sometimes through Sir Ernest. Ballin reported every conversation to the Kaiser. Ballin believed he was making progress.

The death of Edward VII in May, 1910, removed one problem and created another. Wilhelm II had never approved of his uncle's rather free style of living, and, although the two monarchs had often visited each other, their relationship was not the best. This problem was solved when George V took the throne. But the death of Edward caused a sharp decline in the influence of Sir Ernest. For a time Ballin was fearful that his own value was so reduced as to negate all his future efforts; but, after a few months, Ballin and Cassel were again the key men in the effort for peace.

A grave crisis over Morocco fanned the flames of enmity between Germany, France, and England in 1911. With Ballin deeply involved almost from the beginning, the furor was finally resolved when all sides realized how close to war they were and how relatively unimportant were the stakes. The peaceful settlement inspired men of good will in both England and Germany to hope that a happy conclusion to the naval race might also be achieved. This hope was bolstered by the 1912 mission to Germany of Viscount Haldane of Cloan, the British Minister of War. Ballin was instrumental in the planning of this mission, and he involved his friend Huldermann, by then general manager of Hapag, as well. It began with Ballin proposing to Sir Ernest that he come to Germany and bring Winston Churchill, the new First Lord of the Admiralty. Churchill suggested instead that King George V make a state visit, with both sides agreeing to limit new naval construction. At long last, things seemed to be on the right track.

As an opening move, Britain sent Sir Ernest to Germany and Ballin arranged to have him meet the Kaiser for an informal round of talks. At the first get-together there was a wholesome exchange of ideas looking toward a recognition by Germany of England's superiority at sea in exchange for England's approval of certain of Germany's colonial ambitions. Germany would not increase its existing navy, and both nations would agree to refrain from joining any coalitions against each other. It seemed at the moment as if these understandings had created the basis for a long-range settlement. However, a major hitch developed when it became clear that Germany wanted the new squadron of warships she had been planning to be considered part of her existing navy. Cassel warned that this way of thinking would mean trouble. More exchanges took place, more modifications were made, and the two sides drew slowly farther and farther apart. This preliminary exchange, which had begun with such promising progress, disintegrated and fell apart.

But there still remained the long-awaited official visit to Germany of Lord Haldane. Again, and largely through Ballin's efforts, there was a face-to-face meeting with Kaiser Wilhelm II. Again there were the beginnings of a compromise and a brief show of good will. Over the objections of Admiral von Tirpitz, Germany's naval champion, the Kaiser agreed to some modifications of the navy's new construction tempo in exchange for political concessions by Britain. At this point, strange to relate, both Ballin and Cassel were ordered by the Kaiser to leave Berlin. Tirpitz, Chancellor Bethmann Hollweg, and the Empress had objected to their presence from the beginning. The Chancellor had spoken out against what he called meddling by private well-wishers. It was he who finally engineered the dismissal. This step marked the beginning of the end of the Haldane mission. It slowly withered to a negative conclusion and Haldane went home completely pessimistic and disillusioned.

Ballin continued to be active, but now he was struggling against the publicly acknowledged dislike of the Kaiserin, who was completely under the influence of Admiral von Tirpitz. In the final analysis, Ballin blamed Tirpitz even more than he did England for the failure of this and his other peace efforts. Even the Kaiser had some hesitancy about fully accepting the thinking of Tirpitz. Ballin believed the Kaiser was afraid of Tirpitz. He told the Baroness Spitzemberg, a prominent member of the court circle and a diarist, that the Kaiser "has a sort of superstitious dread of letting Tirpitz go, out of remembrance of the disaster which Bismarck's dismissal brought in its wake."[43]

During the next two years Ballin continued his private efforts, reporting continually to the Kaiser and keeping in close touch with Sir Ernest and others in England. Up through the summer of 1914 he tried, and his last plan was to get Tirpitz and Churchill together. The Kaiser agreed to welcome Churchill to the June, 1914, festivities during Kiel Week, but insisted that the British government make the first overtures. The meeting never took place.

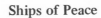

Ships of Peace

erman advocates of a big navy frequently attacked Ballin, saying that the commercial rivalry stirred up by his merchant ships was causing more bad feeling between England and Germany than was the navy issue. This was Tirpitz' theme. William Freyer, an old enemy of Ballin's, was an exponent of this charge. He had been the head of a Hamburg ship officers' union and had long been distrusted by Ballin. The feeling was mutual, and so it was natural that Freyer should make Ballin the villain in his 1914 novel called *Napoleon of the Sea*. In the yarn an unscrupulous shipowner brings Germany and England to the brink of war because of his commercial ruthlessness. By suing Freyer for libel, Ballin only publicized the charge. Even one of Ballin's friends, however, discussed with him the risk he ran by building larger and larger liners in the face of growing British jealousy. Years later this friend said that Ballin had agreed there was a risk, but declared that it was impossible to bring technological developments and successful competition to a halt.[44] Ballin would never admit that economic competition would really alienate the two countries; he believed they knew their prosperity was based on commercial association. This commercial relationship was the most direct avenue to long-range improvement of political relationships, Ballin maintained.

During the period between 1908 and 1914, while Ballin was doing his best to bring about a mutual understanding on the naval issue, he was creating his crowning achievement. Each of the three 50,000-ton liners he was planning would be ten times the tonnage of the largest Atlantic liner of his father's era. Despite his heavy chores in the diplomatic area, Ballin lavished intense personal care on his new creations. They were more than the culmination of his career. They were his $30,000,000 money-on-the-line display of confidence in a peaceful future. Who but a firm believer in the probability of peace would make such an investment of genius, time, and capital in luxurious peacetime liners? These great ships were his gesture of confidence in his own ability to keep the peace. They were ships of peace.

Hull #212, in particular, was his way of contradicting those who said war was inevitable. Her keel was laid as Lord Haldane's mission was being activated with Ballin as the catalyst. As she was launched, Ballin was commuting back and forth to England as Chancellor Bethmann's agent in some cases.[45] As she was about to sail on her maiden voyage, Ballin was seeking to bring Churchill and Tirpitz together. Ballin had to keep the peace. His three super ships could serve only during peace. They were designed strictly as peacetime liners, despite statements that would be made in the heat of war that they were planned as troopships. They had no deck strengthenings for gun emplacements, as did several major

British liners. They had very limited fuel capacity. They were too large and bulky for commerce raiders.

It was not only his training that led both British and German peace factions to look to Ballin in 1908 as their negotiator in the anti-war effort. It was not only that all knew of his admiration for the British and his personal friendship with many in England. For Albert Ballin, peace was vital to the fruition of everything he had worked for all his life. For him, everything depended on peace, even his own life.

Hamburg. Riesendampfer „Vaterland" im Hamburger Hafen.

S. S. "Vaterland," Hamburg-American Line
Largest Steamer Afloat
58,000 tons, 950 ft. long, 100 ft. wide.

Chapter II

HULL # 212

"It is known," stated a Cleveland, Ohio, news item in May, 1910, that the Hamburg-American Line has been in the market for two new steamers and that the vessels "are of mammoth proportions."[1] Strange as it may seem, this is the first printed reference the author has found to the actual construction of the subject of this work. She is the second of the two ships mentioned. The news story continues: The first will be ordered from the Vulcan works shipyard in Hamburg. The second will be built by Harland & Wolff, Belfast. The two new sisters will be 800 feet in length, with a tonnage of between 45,000 and 50,000 and a speed of 20 knots. They are to be powered by conventional reciprocating engines instead of the newer turbines so successful in the MAURETANIA and LUSITANIA.

In June the same Midwestern American source confirmed the word that Hapag's second new liner would be built in Belfast. It was added that she would be able to carry 4,800 passengers and would cost $6,250,000.[2] In giving the second ship to a British yard, Albert Ballin was playing Belfast against his native German shipbuilders. His strategy may have been even more devious. He may never have intended to let Harland & Wolff really make a start with construction, despite his long association with them. He knew that legislation was being planned to require that German ships having mail subsidies must be built in Germany. Nevertheless, he went ahead with the Belfast plan, to twist the screws a little tighter on Hamburg's other famous shipyard, Blohm & Voss. With the first Hapag monster ordered from Vulcan and word that the second was to be built in Ireland, Ballin had Blohm & Voss in a vise.[3] They had to create something dramatically new in ship design so that they would at least get the third ship everyone knew Ballin would need. Ballin and Hapag were the winners in this game, for the naval architects employed by Herman Blohm and Ernst Voss created an improved design and won the contract to build not only the third 50,000-tonner but the second as well. The contract with Harland & Wolff was canceled and the two ships became Hulls #212 and #214 with Blohm & Voss. Just how they won and the impressive new thinking that got them the contract can wait to be told. The first of Ballin's three great ships is well worth a glance. A great and wonderful ship in her own right she was, and her design caused excitement throughout the world of shipping.

"About once in a decade a new fleet of ocean liners is launched, setting a new standard for size, luxury and safety at sea. The great ships which are thought to express the last word in boat building are soon greatly exceeded by their new sisters, and relegated to a second place. The new fleet now under construction in turn surpasses all the great ships which have gone before. To do them justice, we must find a new vocabulary of adjectives for these super-leviathans."[4]

This is what the *Scientific American* had to say about the new Hapag monster ships. The article hailed the first, which at that time Albert Ballin was planning to name EUROPA. The original EUROPA had been renamed KAISERIN AUGUSTE VICTORIA, and the name EUROPA had been assigned to the 30,000-tonner that was never built. For a time the new Vulcan ship would have the name, only to pass it on to Hull #212, as will be explained below. Ballin and his ship names!

Not only was the new Hapag giant ship to be the first vessel ever to surpass the 50,000-ton mark, she was to be the first with a length of over 900 feet. And here was a grand example of the competitive spirit of liner building in those days. Everyone apparently agreed that the new Hapag ship would be the largest in tonnage, but as to length—that was a different story. Cunard's new super ship, to be named AQUITANIA, was to be 901 feet long, but they kept this statistic a closely-guarded secret. The first Hapag monster's length would be 909 feet, but so eager was Albert Ballin to earn the title "world's longest" that he commissioned Berlin sculptor Dr. Bruno Kruse to design a bronze and gold figurehead for his new ship. It turned out to be a fearsome German eagle astride a globe boasting the old Hapag motto: "Mein Feld Ist Die Welt." This creature was fastened to the prow of the new ship and made her 919 feet long. Although it was damaged by a big wave on an early crossing and had to be removed, this 919-foot length remained part of the ship's vital statistics throughout her long career.[5]

The tone of the rivalry can be judged from the following quotation from a book by British author F.A. Talbot written in 1912.

The new Hapag ship "will not hold the record for long, as she is being matched by the new White Star liner on the stocks, which represents a very marked advance upon the German competitor in length, displacement and every other respect."[6]

Talbot was speaking of the third big White Star liner, the ship which was to have been named GIGANTIC but would emerge as the BRITANNIC. In point of fact, none of the three White Star ships came near equaling the first of Hapag's trio in length, tonnage, or speed.[7]

Despite all the competition between British and German public relations staffs, the first of Ballin's new ships was more than just a bigger version of the Cunard and White Star ships that were being built. She would have public rooms with much higher ceilings. Her Pompeian swimming pool would be three decks high, for example, and would completely outclass anything offered on any other ship. Even more striking would be her silhouette and stacks. Throughout the previous century, as ships had gotten bigger thay had had more smokestacks. The new Hapag liner would be the first great ship to break this tradition. Instead of four she would have only three, and the third would be a dummy. For years, emigrants had been known to favor the ship with the most smokestacks, assuming that the more funnels the bigger and safer the ship. From the LUSITANIA of 1907 to the AQUITANIA of 1914, all six of Britain's newest big liners would have four stacks. Hapag was bucking the trend. From here on, the naval arhitect would think of smokestacks more as esthetic elements, reducing their number and cutting them down in size until at this writing, the newest Atlantic liner has only one thin pipe arising far aft.[8]

Ballin would break with tradition in another major way with his 50,000-tonners. He planned them not only as the largest but as contenders for the speed crown. If three instead of four ships were to provide a weekly service, they had to be fast. To win this speed, Ballin chose turbine propulsion instead of reciprocating engines. Whereas the OLYMPIC-class liners were driven by a combination of old-style reciprocating and low-pressure turbines, the new Hapag ships would be all turbine. Still another mechanical advance was the water-tube boiler that Ballin picked over the old-style Scotch boilers used in the White Star ships. He was commended by *Scientific American* for "breaking away from a too long entrenched practice by adopting this more modern and efficient" boiler type.[9]

The part played by Ballin in the creation of his three dream ships can not be overstated. As Huldermann says: "The big passenger boats of the Hapag have been described as the outcome of Ballin's imaginative brain. This they were indeed, and in many instances it is scarcely possible to say how far the credit for building them is due to the naval architect and how far it is due to Ballin."[10]

Ballin's well-trained publicity men in America worked hard to make the first 50,000-ton Hapag ship well-known. Typical of the news stories they released was a note that first appeared in the Portland *Morning Oregonian* on December 21, 1910. It described the German freighter OMEGA and the last lumber cargo of the year which she carried out of

Portland. The cargo included 47,444 pieces of Oregon fir for the decking of the new EUROPA. Only clear, vertical-grain wood was chosen and it was dried for months before shipping. It was sent "in the rough" so it could be finished to fit.[11]

The First EUROPA

wo things happened before the May 23, 1912, launching of the first EUROPA. Sometime in the winter of 1911-1912 the Kaiser suggested that she should be named IMPERATOR instead.[12] Ballin was quick to acquiesce. He had done it before and it would only mean a postponing of the name's use. He would give it to Hull #212. But Ballin could not let the opportunity pass to ask a favor in return: Would the Kaiser officiate at the christening? He would.

The other event was the sinking of the TITANIC. This world-shaking disaster came five weeks before the launching of the IMPERATOR, and it brought some substantial design changes for the new ship, as might be imagined. Instead of the widely-spaced row of boats on the top deck, there would be lifeboats everywhere—83 in all, enough to carry all her 2,496 passengers and crew of 1,180. By means of this design change, provision was made for the first time on any ship to stow lifeboats below the main promenade in pockets along the side of the ship. They would be closer to the water and easier to launch. This would cut into the space normally used for the finest first-class cabins, but Ballin thought it worth it. Special launching arms that swung out from under the pockets where the boats were stored were invented for these lifeboats. Only Ballin's big three, among all the great liners ever built, had this advanced safety feature, although several smaller passenger ships built years later would boast it.[13] For safety against icebergs an inner skin five feet in from the outer shell was fitted into the half-built IMPERATOR from the bow to the after end of the engine rooms. Throughout the center two thirds of the ship, this inner bulkhead extended twenty feet above the waterline. It was even higher towards the ends.[14]

A near-disaster marred the launching of the IMPERATOR and presaged a string of unlucky accidents that were to befall this fine ship. A section of steel chain, possibly the forward anchor chain, snapped and flew around in the vicinity of the Emperor's launching platform.[15] However, the rest of the launching went without a hitch and must have satisfied both Ballin's and the Kaiser's love for pomp and ceremony. The great hull was quickly taken to one of Vulcan's fitting-out berths so that all the new safety features inspired by the TITANIC's loss could be incorporated into its structure.

Each June the Kaiser attended the Elbe regatta and then journeyed through the Kiel Canal, now called the Kaiser Wilhelm Canal, for Kiel Week, the German navy's annual review. In 1912, as always, there was a fine turnout of German liners. One of them was the former Hapag DEUTSCHLAND, renamed VICTORIA LOUISE. Her vibration had been just too much, and she had been reduced in power and speed and assigned to cruising, with a new name. On this occasion the Kaiser was a guest aboard. He was particularly pleased with the way the VICTORIA LOUISE was illuminated at night. A young electrician named Eberhardt Wulff won a nod of praise from Albert Ballin for this work. The famous old four-stacker was literally covered from bow to stern, from masts to stacks to deck, with electric lights.[16]

For a century, ever since the earliest steamships, the hull and its passenger spaces had been obstructed right up through by great squared-off smoke uptakes. On emerging from the upper deck these became the ship's smokestacks. Blohm & Voss offered something different for their Hull #212 design, and this new idea must have been one of the selling points that helped them win the contract from Harland & Wolff. Given Ballin's predilection for passenger comforts, the idea of having split uptakes from the engine room was a master stroke. They would set the new ship apart from any other ship ever built. In fact, the design was so costly that it was only rarely to be used again, notably in Hull #212's sister ship, in two smaller Hapag ships built a little later, and on the NORMANDIE.[17]

Split Uptakes

ith split uptakes, the public rooms on B Deck, which were large on the IMPERATOR, could be made even larger on the new EUROPA. The connecting passage between the Wintergarden and the Social Hall would not have to be two side alleyways, but could be one broad, open foyer flanked by shops on either side. With no central uptakes, Hull #212 could have a sweep of 300 feet of unobstructed space for public rooms. Those who are interested may compare A Deck on the EUROPA with A Deck on the OLYMPIC, the finest ship afloat at that time, to see the advantages of this design feature offered Ballin by Blohm & Voss. Looking ahead to the time when Hull #212 would be a ship, Ballin could imagine himself standing at the forward end of the Social Hall, on the stage. He would be beneath Stack #1. Looking aft he could see all the way through to the Ritz-Carlton ballroom, under Stack #3. On C Deck this feature would permit him to walk the same distance, amidships via a wide central passageway straight down the middle of the first class area. Split uptakes were a daring departure and a dramatic example of the lengths to which Ballin went to make his new ships the high point of ocean liner evolution.

The underwater design offered by Blohm & Voss for the new ship's stern was another departure. From the waterline up, the stern would appear to be a traditional counter stern, with the top of the rudder at the cutwater (where the waterline is) and rising into a widening flair upward and outward into a full fanshape stern. In reality what appeared to be the top of the rudder, as on the older OLYMPIC trio design, was the top of a rounded cruiser stern, later to become the almost universally adopted stern hull form. The rudder post, from which the massive rudder would swing, was well inside or forward of the bulbous end of this new cruiser stern.[18]

The use of forced draft ventilation in Hull #212, an early form of air-conditioning, was still another design breakthrough. It would eliminate the need for most of the long-familiar deck air funnels. Clusters of air funnels had taken up valuable deck space and encumbered the ship's silhouette since earliest steamship days. With the new Blohm & Voss design, they just weren't there, except for a few on the bow deck and a couple at the far stern.[19]

A novel strength feature of the hull plan was special deck reinforcement just forward of the bridge. Looking like a child's slide, it consisted of massive steel plating descending from C Deck to D Deck from Frame 234 to Frame 242, widest at the top.[20] Hull #212 would be formed of 316 seven-deck-high frames, narrow V-shaped at the bow and broadening to a wide U-shape amidships. This was standard hull design, but never before had there been so many frames of such size.

The new hull would have all the safety refinements of the IMPERATOR and a power plant somewhat more powerful. She would also have an iceberg warning device on her main control board in the engine room which would sound an alarm if any ice came near her hull. Among other minor innovations would be a "reverse steam whistle" on the after side of Stack #3, to be sounded when she was going backwards.[21]

The Blohm & Voss design for Hull #212 was conservative in one most important particular. The superstructure height from keel to top deck was less than on the

IMPERATOR. A composite drawing of the hull and superstructure of Hull #212, superimposed on that of the IMPERATOR, to a scale of 1 to 300, shows a difference of one eighth of an inch. Not only did the IMPERATOR rise higher out of the water, but she was slightly narrower than Hull #212. The composite also shows that there was a very slight V in the bottom line of the IMPERATOR, whereas the bottom of Hull #212 was flat. On all counts, the newer vessel was designed to sit better in the water, and history would prove Blohm & Voss right, for Hull #212 had no top-heavy problem, while the IMPERATOR did.[22]

Specifications

The paperwork involved in planning a great liner is staggering. Even before the blueprints and detailed plans there are the specifications by which the owner of the ship sets forth his requirements. Five such books of specs were printed for Hull #212.[23] These printed specs were bound with blank pages interspaced for notes. When Hull #214 was being planned, draftsmen carefully inked out certain words in the Hull #212 specs and wrote in new specs, using green ink in all cases.

The thickest of these volumes has 242 pages, excluding the blanks, of detailed engine requirements not only for the main power plant but also for the countless steam-powered auxiliaries. Since in later ships most of the auxiliaries were electrically powered, it is safe to say that the assembly of steam-producing and -using units here is the largest ever installed in any ship. The table of contents of this volume takes four pages of single-spaced type and there is a 22-page index.

The biggest volume, from the point of view of page size, is the companion book to that, giving the machinery specs. It is also clothbound and finely printed. It contains 30 pages of 12- x 14-inch engine diagrams, beautifully done—in fact, works of abstract art. The titles of these drawings are hand-lettered in beautiful script. There are words of "breathtaking" length, such as the caption on page 10: "Entwasserungsleitungen fur die Turbinen."

Another volume, from Hapag's Ship Construction Division, gives overall facts about Hull #212.[24] The ship's principal dimensions are given first, in millimeters and in English feet:

LENGTH BETWEEN PERPENDICULARS	277,975 mm or	912' 0"
BREADTH: MOLDED BREADTH	30,478 mm or	100' 0"
DEPTH: from top of keel to side of upper deck	19,507 mm or	64' 0"
MAXIMUM DRAFT	10,820 mm or	35' 6"

The vessel was to be built as a four-screw steamer on a straight keel, with straight forward rake, rudder-shaped stern frame, and elliptical stern.[25]

Then, next to the names of the ship's eleven decks, is a most interesting notation in the margin at the left. It reads:

"As per Belfast plans."[26]

This shows that Harland & Wolff had gotten far enough along in their preliminary work on Hull #212 to have projected her in her full size, eleven decks and all.

The minimum deck height is shown as 7 feet 4 inches, and the maximum, that of the Social Hall, is given as 22 feet, 3 3/4 inches. This does not take into consideration the dome over the Dining Saloon, which reached a height of 31 feet above the deck. The tallest room on the OLYMPIC was 12 feet, 3 inches.[27]

The ship was to be made of "mild Siemens Martin Steel, best shipbuilding quality. . . ."

Next comes a section dealing with the frames, and the distances between them. For example, the first 25 frames from the stern were 680 millimeters apart (about 27 inches), while the last, frames 295 to 316, were only 570 millimeters separated from one another. The widest spacing was the 915-millimeter spread between frames 31 to 291.

On the subject of coal, the specs show a capacity of 8,220 tons, barely enough to get over to New York at the anticipated rate of more than 1,000 tons per day. The book states that to move the coal inside the ship a "complete rail plant is to be provided and rail trucks are to be supplied according to further particulars."[28] There would be 25 coal chutes and openings on either side of the hull.

Three bridges were called for, the commander's forward, a 'midships bridge for supervising the launching of lifeboats, and an aft bridge for docking. The forward bridge "will be surrounded with a bulwark (teak) 1,400 mm. high and will on both the ship's sides have guard corners of teak for square windows."[29] On the forward bridge there "shall be erected or fitted the chart, wheel and navigation house, the telegraphy, compasses, steering arrangements, voice tube, teak holder for life belt for one, sailors' and stokers' watch flags, telegraph, etc. Gratings in deck. Everything to be arranged to the particulars and plans of the H.A.L."[30]

Two pages later there are comments about the masts, the last of which will bring into focus the length of time that has passed since their writing:

"The two masts shall be made high enough for wireless telegraphy. The mast trucks [topmost end piece] are to be made of maple, gilt and with two bronze sheaves as on the IMPERATOR. *The masts are not to be adapted to carry sails.*"[31]

Many liners were still using sails when Hull #212 was designed.

For the benefit of those old salts who call the famous clipper ships the "tall ships," it should be noted that it would be 248 feet to the keel from the truck of the foremast.[32]

There were to be five bells and "they shall be cast in the best bell metal, turned and polished and shall have the ship and home port name engraved thereon."[33] Three "loud bells" of 600 mm. in diameter were to be placed on the foremast, below the lookout, on the docking bridge aft, and at the forecastle. The fourth, of 350-mm. diameter, was to be placed on the commander's bridge. The fifth, of 800-mm. diameter and 240-kg. weight, was to be the fog bell.

"They shall be suspended quite freely so that the sound is not held back on any side. The bell to be hung on the foremast below the lookout is to be covered by a securely fixed sounding board beaded by 26-mm. round iron."[34]

The bow and stern ornamentation was to be tastefully carved and gilded and fitted with suitable guard rails.

The ship's name at the bow must be made of polished brass letters screwed on. The letters were to be 450 mm. high (18 inches), and the letters of the name at the stern were to be 300 mm. high (12 inches).

Although the masts were not to be fitted for sails, the ship still had a sail room. Its floor was to be covered with fir gratings, and it was to be well lit and ventilated by side windows. The ship's 83 lifeboats would each have sails and these would be repaired here, along with canvas hatch covers and many other canvas items. Two sail hooks and two palms (a palm is a sail-making utensil) were on the list of Bos'n's Stores "and various." Also on this list were 12 American brooms. And 5,500 life jackets. And 20 lifebuoys.[35]

One of the coppery items was 12 teak buckets with brass hoops. They had galvanized chains and brass padlocks. They were designed to last. Under Carpenter's Gear there was a request for a dozen pairs of police pattern handcuffs. Under Gunnery Items, one mortar rocket apparatus, with cage line 1,500 feet long complete to American regulations, was called for. Also: 22 cartridges, 12 rockets, 12 red lights, and 12 blue lights.[36]

The fourth and fifth volumes of specifications cover passenger accommodations. One is devoted entirely to first-class cabins and public rooms. The other deals with second-, third-, and fourth-class spaces.

Drawings

he next step in the creation of Hull #212 was the making of contract drawings. The Hapag specs book has a whole section just on how this was to be done. The drawings were to be made on linen, and "in the making less importance is attached to beauty of drawing than to exact agreement with the finished ship."[37] A complete set of handmade plans, mounted and framed, was required, along with various duplicate sets. Do the Hapag archives still shelter these framed treasures, or were they destroyed in the bombardment of Hamburg? One set of clear white prints on thin paper was to be furnished before construction began. There were to be the longitudinal section and rigging plan, all deck and double bottom plans, the hold plan and layout of coal bunkers, and various "classification drawings with scantlings of material and riveting." "Scantlings" is shipyard parlance for size and thickness of steel plates.

A long list of additional drawings that were to be supplied after construction began was included. These were all to be made to a scale of 1 to 50 millimeters. Among the drawings produced for approval before the ship was begun was the "Langsschnitt" or outboard profile, which was in reality a huge picture of the ship from bow to stern, from keel to truck. The original must have been very large, but for convenience copies were made on a sheet 20 inches long and 16 inches wide.[38] Also on this same sheet are an air view looking down on the full ship, plans of the officers' deck, and plans of decks A, B, C, and D. A companion sheet of the same size shows the seven lower decks.

The outboard profile (see end papers) would have been the first reasonably definitive view that Albert Ballin had of his second great ship. The drawing is delicate and yet precise. It is done in a transparent way, with the hawse pipes for the bow anchors showing through, as it were, the boiler rooms and split uptakes, and with the engine rooms dotted in within the hull. Also shown is all the rigging. The four wireless antennae strung all the way from the foremast to the mainmast must have challenged the imagination of all who saw the drawing. In later years, when Hull #212 became an American ship, it was decided that such a span was just too long, and the wireless was given an antenna from Stack #1 up to the foremast. The three smokestacks were evenly spaced and the distance was exactly the same from the first stack to the bow as from the third stack to the stern. The fine sweep of the Boat Deck is shown minus all the air funnels that cluttered the decks of other liners of the day.[39]

Three much larger diagrams are numbered 407, 408, and 409. They show the entire superstructure from E Deck up, both side view and deck plan. The originals of these have survived down to this writing.[40] Plan 407 goes from the extreme stern forward to the awning over the aftermost curve of B Deck. Also shown on this plan is another, smaller, plan of the open deck areas at the end of E Deck. Shown here is the open area where a massive tiller could be fitted at the top end of the rudder post so the ship could be steered manually if all other steering devices failed. Some forty men or so would have been needed in such an eventuality, and the job would have been back-breaking. Five possible rudder positions are laid out on the plan.

The E Deck superstructure, beginning at Frame 23, ends the small deck area. These plans are so large and so detailed that it is possible to refer, as has been done, to their spread by using frame numbers, as the officers of all liners pride themselves on doing. The D Deck part of Plan 407 extends from the aft flagpole to Frame 69, showing a profusion of bollards (heavy steel posts rounded at the tops to which the huge mooring lines would be fastened), lifeboats, steam-powered winches to lift the cargo booms that were slung from the main mast, hatches, companionways, and deck equipment.

Blohm & Voss had never built a ship anywhere near as large as Hull #212, and the yard's naval architects must have felt a sense of exhilaration as they drew these plans. The originals must have been drawn full size on the huge, flat, molding loft floor of the shipyard, and then reduced and transferred to scale print drawings such as these plans.[41]

Deck Plan 408 is ten feet long and two high. It is five two-foot squares glued together. It carries the ship from Frame 60 to Frame 290, including all the amidships superstructure. Ballin's AUGUSTA VICTORIA could have sat on the top deck, with her sister ship COLUMBIA alongside. Their combined width would have overhung only six feet on either side.[42] Both a side elevation drawing and a "look down" deck plan are part of this huge drawing. The pride in craftsmanship that the Blohm & Voss draftsmen felt in making these plans can be seen in many little extras. Each glass window pane and each porthole is shaded carefully with several dozen delicate vertical lines covering the upper left-hand corner, as if the sun were shining from high up over the stern. The sheer (gentle rise of the ship's hull at the bow and stern) is shown to perfection, and the perspective of the rounded veranda deck at the after end of B Deck is exactly right. There was much love in this labor.

The notations on the plans are in script, and are not easy to read. In the "look down" plan the viewer is placed directly overhead and the three stacks are shown with their rake aft clearly delineated. The 16 guy lines supporting these tall stacks fan out to their proper deck fastenings, and even the deck-level turnbuckles are shown with precise skill. Every pane of glass in each skylight is shown, rounded where it should be or square where the panes were square. Beneath it all, dotted lines identify the frames like an X-ray showing a skeleton. The large fog bell is located amidships between #2 and #3 stacks. In reality it was placed abaft the third funnel.

The lower plan or "look down" view is cleverly done to show the Boat Deck on the port side aft, where there is a wonderfully broad promenade, and is cut away to show C Deck on the starboard side aft. Here can be seen the seven C Deck lifeboats in their recesses. A good view of the specially-designed swing-out lifeboat davits can be had, while, above, the same davits may be seen as if from the outside looking in. They are among the innovations in Ballin's big-three design, and show how his special features carried over even when two different yards were involved.[43]

The plan shows three great oval-topped windows letting light into the Social Hall. These were eventually changed, probably for the sake of strength, to three tall vertical windows. The original curved window idea was suggested on the inside by the use of a single frame for the trio of openings and through hanging draperies.

The forward end of the superstructure begins like a two-step pyramid, with D Deck extending farther out than C Deck. Decks B and A are flush, supporting the pilothouse and bridge. The side elevation reveals that the pilothouse extends forward several feet out over the façade of A and B decks, giving the navigators a better vantage point. Open walks athwartships (from one side to the other) on B and C decks are shown. The starboard "lighthouse" is drawn just around from the forward face of C Deck, and, to make sure the viewer knows what it is, the draftsman shows a spray of dotted lines coming from the green light opening, another little extra that adds life to this plan.

Finally, this ten-foot-long drawing is finished off with a diagram of the impressive bridge and forward stack seen from the bow. Ever since the elimination of sail and the gradual rise of the ship's superstructure, the bridge had been evolving more and more into an impressive point of identification with great ships. Here is the climax in liner evolution, with the forward face of five and a half decks rising in an imposing façade. Only steerage-class passengers, who used the deck area immediately below the bridge, and the crew, who could relax in the forward tip of the bow deck, could see this most impressive forward bridge superstructure.

The forward face of D Deck has four portholes on either side and two doors. The plan is so detailed that it shows the port door's hinges on its port edge and the starboard door's hinges on its starboard edge. Both doors are shown slightly ajar. Two immense bollards are on either side just forward of the end of D Deck. The face of C Deck has four doors leading out onto its athwartships promenade. A glass-enclosed promenade makes up the forward end of B Deck, with doors at either side to permit access to the athwartships promenade. The face of A Deck rises a deck and a half and encloses an athwartships promenade outside the Smoking Room, whose very tall windows look out forward under the commander's bridge. The bridge tops it all, with each end extending some six feet out over the widest part of the hull. These extensions bring the extreme width of Hull #212 to 112 feet. Above the bridge is a flying bridge, with braces for an awning. The forward stack rises to its full height amidships, supported by eight guy wires at its first rib halfway up and eight more at the second supporting ring three quarters of the way to its top.

The third large diagram shows the bow deck. Numbered 409, it is rich in detail. It shows a track leading down the middle to the point of the bow on which the huge "bower" anchor chain clanked along from the chain locker below to the cast-iron hawse pipe and out through the very stem of the ship. This stem anchor was another new feature of Ballin's 50,000-tonners. The OLYMPIC-class-ships design had a stem hawse pipe, but no anchor was ever fitted to it. The plan shows the hawse pipes for the port and starboard anchors. A wide V-shaped wave brake just before the forward deck house is shown. Six sets of nested lifeboats are drawn atop the deck house, the designers assuming that there they would be safe from the pounding sea. After all, wasn't this sixty feet above water level and more than that distance abaft the bow? Express cargo, passengers' trunks, and mail would be loaded through Hatch #1, forward of the deckhouse, and Hatch #2, between it and the bridge. Three booms to lift the heaviest sling of mail pouches are drawn attached to the sturdy trunk of the foremast, rising out of the deckhouse forward. Two king posts stand in the well deck, each with two smaller booms attached to serve Hatch #2.

Rivets

 o doubt countless smaller drawings supplemented these main plans, show-ing in the greatest imaginable detail the most insignificant-seeming corner, part, or fragment of the vast new complex, for the most careful guidance is necessary in translating an idea from a flat surface to a three-dimensional creation. Unlike an ordinary building or land facility, Hull #212 had to be solid and secure, for she would move, lift, heel, sag, twist, and tremble when finally in her element. And the complexity of it all was beyond the ken of most people, for she was to be the largest moving object ever created by man.

Hull #212 was built on an inclined ship way facing downsteam toward Cuxhaven and the world. Blohm & Voss's island yard is where the North Elbe curves below the main part of Hamburg. Giant foot-square blocks of wood formed the base of the way on which the flat-lying protective keel, with its continuous-center-girder double bottom, was laid. The way was surrounded by steel scaffolding. Over the top were connecting girders that supported tracks for moving hoists. The assembly of steel and the making of plates was a major job and took many months before the actual keel was laid in late 1911. Some 34,500 tons of rolled steel would be used in the new ship, plus 2,000 tons of cast steel and a like amount of cast iron. The wood that would go into her would weigh an additional 6,500 tons.[44] The riveting together of these plates and frames and girders was the key operation of the whole construction process, and the specifications were most exacting in their demands on this count:

"The riveting is to be done throughout the ship in the most careful way and when in any way possible, hydraulically."[45] Blohm & Voss had the latest hydraulic riveting devices. They looked like huge magnets, twice the size of a man, and were suspended by cranes over the plates to be riveted together. A worker would guide the device into place.

"The riveting holes, particularly for more than two thicknesses, must be thoroughly reamed and full hammered," the specs add.[46] Despite these directions, in 1922 when the ship was being rebuilt as an American luxury liner, it was found that rivets had been omitted in several of the bulkheads where holes had been provided for them.[47]

A quaint story about the rivets for Hull #212 was told in a Hapag publication of the day. The publicity department had flooded Germany with stories about the new ship and her three million rivets. Each rivet was described as weighing five pounds, and some "honest locksmith living in the country far from the sea" became greatly excited about what he thought was a gross exaggeration. He wrote an indignant letter to the company saying that "it was all very fine what the newspapers managed to write about the building of the new ship, but they ought not to be allowed to lie so abominably, it was indeed too ridiculous, as the bragging was laid on so thickly that any blacksmith apprentice could take it up with the tongs. They ought to be ashamed to try and gammon the public so outrageously."[48]

The new liner's double bottom was 5½ feet thick. After the TITANIC disaster, the public was most interested in such safety features, and Hapag didn't neglect to tell all about this one on Hull #212. A brochure goes so far as to picture the ship "in the midst of the greatest danger. . .the hull, having come in contact with the ground, has been ripped open, and the floods rush into the hold through the enormous gaping rents." The passengers "need not be in any anxiety, for, indeed, they are traveling in a double ship. The keel on which the steamer floats is higher than a man, and, fastened on both sides of it, 300 steel floor-timbers form a second immense bottom and it is only from this that the side-walls of the ship begin to ascend in mighty curves. On this second, inner foundation. . .the ship can calmly pursue her way through the waves."[49]

Just above the double bottom were the anti-rolling tanks designed by Hermann Frahm, a Blohm & Voss naval architect. So confident was Frahm that they would work that he designed no bilge keels for Hull #212 or her sister ship. Bilge keels are long, narrow fins that protrude from the hull about halfway between the keel and the waterline on either side and slow down a ship's roll. The IMPERATOR had both Frahm tanks and bilge keels. Hapag had been one of the first to adopt the Frahm anti-rolling tank, using it on their CORCOVADO in 1907. The Cunard Line was the first to have them on the Atlantic, with their LACONIA, of 1912.[50]

At the time that Albert Ballin was completing his plans for the maiden voyage of the IMPERATOR and for the launching of Hull #212, America's two largest liners on the Atlantic—America's only liners on the Atlantic, for that matter—were the 12,000-ton twins ST. LOUIS and ST. PAUL. Built way back in 1895, they were far outclassed by most other passenger ships, but they remained the flagships of the American Line.

A tall, bespectacled young American aristocrat from Philadelphia who had been inspired as a boy by the drama of the launching of the ST. LOUIS back on November 12, 1894, was still passionately fond of ships as the year 1912 came to an end. He was William Francis Gibbs. He was studying law at Columbia University, and no one at the time could know how important he was going to be in the story of Hull #212.

On the same day that the ST. LOUIS was launched, a young Pennsylvania Schoolship cadet was asked to ride down the ways aboard her to help drop her anchor. The young cadet was Herbert Hartley, who, next to Gibbs and Ballin, was to be more important in the story of Hull #212 than any other man. That these two men should have such an involvement with the ST. LOUIS shows how small the world of shipping really is. And it was the American Line with which Ballin had worked in the days when he directed emigrants on the indirect route from Hamburg.

The sturdy little ST. LOUIS, so ably christened that day back in 1894 by Mrs. Grover Cleveland, had seen yeoman service during the Spanish-American War, and had continued on the Atlantic afterward under one of America's most famous master mariners, Captain John Clark Jamison. Her young first officer at the end of 1912 was none other than Herbert Hartley, who, thanks to Captain Jamison, had risen through the hawse pipe, as sailors say of a man who has worked his way to officer's standing from the position of a lowly unlicensed seaman.[51]

American ships and the American Merchant Marine were of great interest to Ballin when on October 23, 1912, he stepped ashore at New York from his company's flagship named in honor of the Kaiserin.[52] His association with J.P. Morgan and the I.M.M. had been far from happy, but, now, there was another project on the horizon which really appealed to Ballin. He had watched with great interest the planning and construction of the Panama Canal, recognizing in it great implications for worldwide shipping. He had watched, too, while Bernard N. Baker, president of the Atlantic Transport Company and a leading figure in the I.M.M., had tried and failed to raise money in America for a fleet of passenger liners to operate from the East to the West Coast via the Canal. Mail subsidies were available, but powerful rail interests were said to be blocking the project. Ballin stepped forward and offered to subscribe one half of the needed capital, about $7,500,000. If necessary, he would contribute up to $30,000,000 if an equal amount of American money was forthcoming. He proposed to build ten liners in American yards. They would fly the American flag and be manned by Americans. Ballin asked for assurances that he would not be accused of violating the Sherman Anti-Trust Act. Unfortunately, Congress could not give the guaranty Ballin wanted and the project languished.[53]

Back in Germany, Ballin found himself once more involved in matters political. Ever since the founding of greater Germany in 1871 there had been unhappiness among the Bavarians because a Prussian Hohenzollern was head of state. Prussia and Bavaria were the largest of the twenty-six kingdoms, grand duchies, ordinary duchies, principalities, and independent cities that had merged to form the fatherland. Citizens of Bavaria (Bayern) still viewed the nation as a confederacy. This political situation was a major problem to the Kaiser and he was always looking for a way to bring the House of Wittelsbach, which ruled Bavaria, more snugly into the fold. As the time approached for the launching of the EUROPA (Hull #212), Ballin's fertile brain, searching for a way to be of service, once again came up with a plan that combined his company's fortunes with the Kaiser's. Again he would defer the use of the name "EUROPA" in favor of a name that would have real purpose. The new ship would be named VATERLAND, in honor of united Germany, and she would be christened by Lewis (Ludwig), of Bavaria, the Prince Regent. Bavaria would thereby be paying homage to the one-fatherland concept. The Kaiser liked the idea, and the plan worked out, with one exception, as will be seen below. As a final fillip, the change in name would not be announced until the last minute, adding impact to the significance of the sponsor's identity.[54]

To help make sure that the Bavarian Prince would come, the Kaiser agreed not to attend the launching. The day would be Bavaria's, and it would honor both the House of Wittelsbach and the new VATERLAND.[55]

Chapter III

TWO FIERY WEAPONS

espite his efforts for peace and his cosmopolitan attitude, Albert Ballin must have had some knowledge of the writings of Nietzsche. He must have absorbed some of this philosopher's pride in the German nation. He may have felt in his own accomplishments some of the exhilaration of Nietzsche's superman. Certainly he did allow his publicity men to outdo even Wagner's Nibelung in the use of flowery language. Here is a paragraph from a Hamburg-American Line brochure about the IMPERATOR and the VATERLAND:

"The Hamburg-Amerika Linie has forged two fiery weapons of highly tempered steel, two sharp, gigantic, gleaming swords. Though the Company has so firmly established its name and reputation, yet from year to year it aims at still higher and more splendid achievements, for the higher the crowning pinnacle of the mighty building rears itself, the more vociferously does multitudinous Life roar all around it, demanding either defense, or the accomplishment of some end. But life is conflict, and a strong man must always be armed for battle, either in order to ward off aught that might hinder him in his course, or in order to advance victoriously along hitherto untrodden paths and thus attain his goal. This is the duty of the strong. Then Life, ever-increasing, immeasurably rejoicing Life, will follow his leading hand, and impetuously yield to his direction. And that will bring the strong man to his goal and his happiness. This is the reason why the Hamburg-Amerika Linie has forged two sharp, glittering, gigantic swords."[1]

The IMPERATOR and the VATERLAND, of course, were the two swords.

In early 1913 the VATERLAND was being readied for her launching while the IMPERATOR was getting her final touches before her maiden voyage.

The high-flown language of the Hapag brochure is certainly not Ballin's, despite his flair for the dramatic. The speeches at the launching would have very little of such Wagnerian bombast. There certainly was nothing of this spirit in a pleasant little exchange between two ships on the Atlantic in February, 1913. The ships were three days out of New York. They had sailed at the same hour from their Hudson River piers. Aboard the KAISERIN AUGUSTE VICTORIA was Captain Hans Ruser, who was slated soon to take command of the new IMPERATOR. The other ship was the ADRIATIC, of White Star, with Captain Bertram Hayes on the bridge. Little did he realize that one day he would be master of the BISMARCK, the third of Ballin's great trio. The K.A.V. and the ADRIATIC were quite similar, each with twin stacks, each with four masts. All through the past three days they had sailed within sight of each other, but now they would part company. The Hapag liner was bound for the Azores, while the White Star beauty was heading for Madeira. Both were making Mediterranean cruises. When some of the passengers on the British ship learned that the two liners would be parting company they composed a wireless message and asked Captain Hayes to send it to Captain Ruser.

"It is pleasant to see two fine ships steaming together in friendly rivalry," the message said.

Captain Ruser replied with a similar friendly greeting.[2]

Meanwhile the VATERLAND grew. Twenty of the new-style water-tube boilers were hoisted into the depths of her hull while she was still on the ways. Blohm & Voss's pride, a 250-ton-capacity Hammerhead electric crane, did the lifting. There would be 46 boilers in all and they would operate at 235 pounds of pressure per square inch. Ten would be in the forward boiler room, followed by twelve each in three other 75-foot-long boiler compartments or stoke holds. That was where the hundreds of firemen would stand and shovel a thousand tons of coal a day into the furnaces under the boilers.

The ship would be driven by four propellers, each 19 feet, 7 inches in diameter. They would be powered by a high-pressure turbine in a port engine room, an i.h. pressure turbine in the starboard room, and two low-pressure turbines on the inner-shafts in the central engine room. The turbines would have 760,000 blades of varying lengths, and their installation would be one of the most massive and time-consuming projects in all shipbuilding history. They would turn the propellers, or wheels, as shipping people call them, at 180 revolutions per minute at full speed, at which point they would be developing a total of 61,000 effective horsepower.[3]

One part of Ballin's plan to use the naming of Hull #212 as a political device didn't come to pass: the man who was supposed to christen her, the Regent, Prince Ludwig (or Lewis), could not attend. In his place the honors would be done by his son, Prince Rupprecht. Prince Ludwig "stood godfather," as the Hapag house organ put it, and sent a congratulatory message. It read:

"In connection with tomorrow's festivities where my son Rupprecht will represent me, I send my warmest wishes. May this powerful ship be always worthy of its name, which it will carry on all voyages at all times, where the German flag will take her and always bring honor to its beloved Fatherland."[4]

The Launching

pril 3, 1913, a Thursday, was a gala day for Hamburg. In the town all public and private buildings were decorated with flags. In the harbor all ships were "dressed" (flag bedecked). Even rival shipyards adjacent to Blohm & Voss joined in the mood and put up bunting and decorations. Blohm & Voss, of course, was a sight to see. Flags flew from every high point.

The day began early for the official party headed by Prince Rupprecht and Albert Ballin. They first went to the Vulcan Works yard and inspected the resplendent new IMPERATOR. She was due to begin her maiden voyage May 24, only weeks away. Showing her off must have been most gratifying to Albert Ballin and was a fitting beginning for the greatest day in his life. The white marble bust of the Kaiser was in the Social Hall, and the magnificent painting of him hung on the main stairway. When Prince Rupprecht came to that point in his inspection, Ballin certainly must have paused to tell him that an equally fine portrait of his father would hang in a place of honor on the VATERLAND.[5]

Within sight of the Elbe ferries taking people over to grandstands along the Steinwerder to watch the launching, there lay the 12,335-ton Hapag liner BLEUCHER. Her black hull and white superstructure glistened with fresh paint and her two yellow-buff stacks rose in a maze of pennants, signal flags, and streamers. Built in 1901 for Hapag's Mediterranean service, she was a spare boat in 1914, sometimes filling in on the Hamburg to New York run, sometimes on the Boston line, and now and then on her old Mediterranean route.[6] She was the scene of busy preparations, for, after the IMPERATOR tour, the launching party boarded her for a "festive breakfast." Her main dining saloon, into which Ballin graciously escorted the Prince and others, was three and a half decks high, rising from the promenade deck through two upper levels and on up into a glass cupola that emerged forward of the first stack. At breakfast Ballin rose to extend formal greetings "and a warm welcome" to the Prince, who in turn "hailed the occasion and expressed his pleasure in having witnessed the German efficiency so well illustrated by the Hamburg-American Line." So the moment is

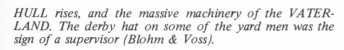

HULL rises, and the massive machinery of the VATER-LAND. The derby hat on some of the yard men was the sign of a supervisor (Blohm & Voss).

STOUT, moustached Ernest Voss (left) and goateed Herman Blohm, escort Prince Rupprecht around the VATERLAND's huge hull before the launching. Framed between Voss and the Prince may be seen a smiling Ballin (Blohm & Voss).

THE LAUNCH – a magnificent sight. Hapag now had two of its 50,000-tonners afloat. One to go (top 4 photos courtesy Blohm & Voss, bottom picture from N.Y. Tribune file).

IN DRY DOCK at Hamburg *(top left, Blohm & Voss), and the rudder and propellers (Gibbs & Cox).*

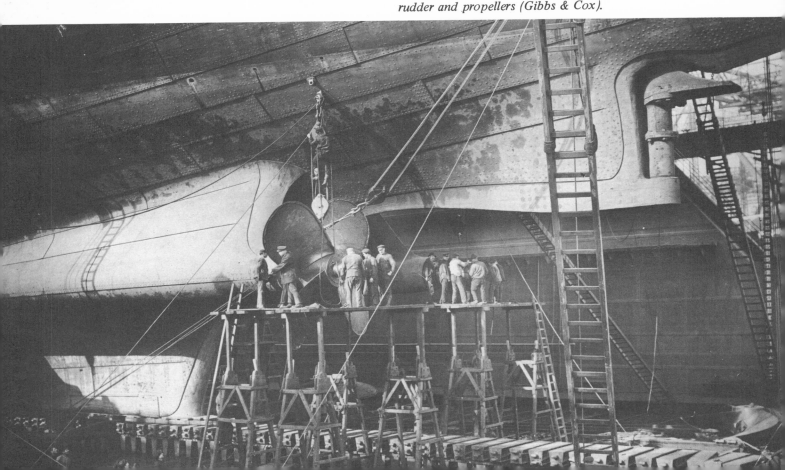

PROUD DAY, leaving the yard and heading down the Elbe (Blohm & Voss).

described in the company's 1913 house magazine.[7]

Ernst Voss and Hermann Blohm, founders of the yard, met Prince Rupprecht and Ballin when they reached their island plant. They took the party in tow and escorted them down to the stern of the great new liner and back. Stout, mustached Voss walked with a cane, his great coat open showing a gray vest. He had a high, winged collar and a light tie. The Prince was in a long army coat which almost hid a sheathed sword, which could be seen hanging out of the bottom. It must have made walking awkward. He wore a spiked iron helmet, emblasoned, had a dark band on his left arm, and looked very sober. To his left hurried Hermann Blohm, goateed and wearing a dark coat buttoned up tight. Both shipyard officials wore high silk hats, as did all those in the rest of the party, who kept about ten paces behind. As they walked past the gleaming new steel hull, a photographer caught the three leaders, with Albert Ballin framed between Voss and the Prince. He was in the group in the back, but, even at that distance, a broad, happy smile can be seen on his face. This was the high point in his career—no question!

High above, on the unfinished stern superstructure of the VATERLAND, a single figure in uniform can be made out in the photo. He is looking down at the official party, assuming a deferential, hands-behind-him air even at that distance.

When the party reached their position of honor under the huge prow of the vast new ship, looking even more the world's largest with her entire bulk out of water, the crowd hushed. There she rose, Hull #212, the EUROPA, the VATERLAND, the LEVIATHAN. Her months of pre-natal life were finished. She was about to leave the stolid German motherland that had been her cradle; she was soon to be released into her predestined element—the sea.

It was a dramatic, thrilling event for the thousands who jammed the yard and the land across the Elbe and on the city side, and for those in grandstands, on roof tops and on the highest rung of the scaffolding all around. The new leviathan, as many newspaper descriptions had called her, was gaily decorated.[8] Five loops of heavy, dark garlands swung from either side of her prow. Her hull was painted black except for its top deck (E Deck), which was white. Her partly finished superstructure was white, except for the massive red, boxlike erections of still unsculptured deck housing. There were no smokestacks or masts. A huge German flag flew from the stern flagpole, and two jury-rigged poles fore and aft also boasted large German flags. Strings of code flags hung down on either side of these temporary masts. A big Hapag houseflag whipped from a staff at the prow. It had a quartered design, diagonally divided, with white on top and bottom and blue on either side. On top was superimposed a yellow shield with the letters H.A.P.A.G. in black. A black anchor was under the shield.[9]

The moment was at hand.

Charming young Olga Schaetz sang the German national anthem to start the ceremonies.[10] The band played. Mayor Dr. Schroder began his address.

"Imperial Highness!

"It was in May of last year when several thousand people assembled at the Vulcan shipyard to participate in the christening by His Majesty Emperor Wilhelm II of the ship he named IMPERATOR. . . .We are here today assembled to witness the hull of her sister ship with enormous dimensions and beautiful lines. . . .Hamburg can be proud, all Germany can be proud of this giant, an accomplishment of German technique, but we must also admire the spirit of the Hamburg-American Line for its courageous step to add not only this giant vessel but also a third one in the not-too-distant future to her fleet. . . ."

The Mayor expatiated on the rise of Hapag, concluding that it had the right to say, "My field is the world." Looking back into the past, he noted that it was the hundredth anniversary of the burning of Moscow and the halting of Napoleon. Tired of slavery, the people of Prussia had risen up in answer to the call of their king.

"With God—for King and Fatherland" was the call, and it became the living slogan for young and old "as far as the German tongue will ring and God in heaven sings."

Warming up to the occasion, he continued:

"In defense of this Fatherland they drew their sword and God brought victory. As the sun rays overcome the winter storms, as the morning sun frightens away the shadows of the night, so did the German people break the yoke of France."[11]

With a brief reference to the victory over another Napoleon in 1870, the Mayor turned toward the great hull before him.

"Even though always prepared for war, our country concerns itself only with peace in friendly competition with other nations. And so shall you, YOU PROUD SHIP, true to your spirit of the Fatherland, serve in a peaceful way and bring together the friendship of the peoples of this earth. Now go forth toward your element! If storm and bad weather overtake you, you will defend yourself with courage, always aware of your heritage, your homeland, and the deep embedment of your name in our hearts."

Prince Rupprecht came forward.

He was within arm's reach of the bottle of champagne with which he was to christen the huge ship. All around, the crowds of dignitaries and workmen were silent as he spoke a few words of reply to the Mayor. He called attention to the "high service this ship will perform in joining together Europe and America."

Then he reached for the champagne, raised the bottle, and, without hesitation or fault, smashed it against the hull.

"I christen you VATERLAND."

There was a moment of tension, and then Mayor Dr. Schroder broke the stillness with a call for all to hail the Prince. Down below, the hydraulic launching machines had begun their thrusting and then, imperceptibly at first, magically, wondrously the 36,000 tons of steel so long planned and so carefully assembled began to move.[12] Her hull alone was eight stories high, and it seemed as if a monster building had suddenly been put into motion. Slowly at first, and then with increasing speed and amid a roar of hurrahs the VATERLAND broke forever from the earth and glided down the ways. A halo of steam rose round her keel, blocking part of the ways from sight. A line of tiny figures waved hats and arms from her foredeck. More clustered around the rails along her stern as her rudderless after portion, with its four propellerless struts, went down and out of sight under the splashing of foam and the bobbing of debris. The sun shone on her starboard hull face through the overhead steel girders, making a criss-crossed pattern of swiftly moving shadows as the speed of her progress down the ways increased. On either side heavy manila cables from her foredeck swooped down from her prow to the massive piles of heavy chain placed at intervals on the ways. These hawsers became taut, and up rose the chains in writhing, snakelike tendrils, keeping her in check. Two forty-foot-high wooden cradles reached up from the ways on either bow, moving down with the ship like twenty-fingered hands stretched upward, firmly holding her upright. And then the air was filled with din, with clanging bells, with horns, with deep whistles, piercing, shrieking sirens, and with a babel of voices.

When the VATERLAND first knifed into the water, the harbor seemed deserted. Immediately it was crowded with little craft that seemed to have come from nowhere. There were tugs galore, one with a white funnel and black top, one with red stripes on white, and one with two gold stripes—and others. There were small steamboats and naphtha launches loaded with derby-hatted people. One had a colored awning with a crinolated edging. She was named WESTPHALL. In no time the VATERLAND's hull seemed to come to a stop—"wonderful control, wonderful planning," the spectators exclaimed smilingly to each other. The German flag stood straight out from its jury pole on the foredeck, and everyone aboard a large white steam yacht cheered as the sleek craft passed under the new liner's prow. The flat, gray-green waters around her hull were littered with timbers, boards, a painter's stage, and odd floating objects. Three tugs took her in tow, one, the little KIRCHWAEROSA, pulling so hard she heeled far over to starboard. No one minded; it all added zest to the occasion. Soon the VATERLAND was safely in her berth just below the ways. But the day was by no means over.

A festive dinner was held that evening in the Hall of Emperors in the Hamburg City Hall. It was given by the Senate in honor of Prince Rupprecht. Everyone was there: the Chairman of the Senate, the Mayor, special representatives of the military and of the local civic organizations, and many prominent citizens. The Prince was again hailed by the Mayor and he in return hailed the Senate and all the citizens of Hamburg.

But still the program continued. After dinner Director Eggers, of Hapag; Director Frahm, of Blohm & Voss; and a Mr. Bischoff, of Bischoff and Mewes, joined in a lantern slide show about the wonders of the new liner. They showed "still pictures" of the hull, engines, safety features, and interior.

Around the world the marine press wrote about the launching. The New York *Herald* began its story by stating that the name had been changed at the "last moment from EUROPA to VATERLAND."[13] Three quarters of the story was about the safety features of the new sea titan. It was within eleven days of being the first anniversay of the sinking of the TITANIC. An American technical journal noted that the exact tonnage of the VATERLAND had not as yet been disclosed, adding that she was supposed to be about 4,000 tons larger than the IMPERATOR, and that she would be able to carry 5,250 persons: 4,050 passengers and a crew of 1,200.[14]

There was considerable confusion about her length; in fact, the Hapag house organ for summer 1914, written before the launching, listed her in one place as being 919 feet long and then later gave her length to be 911 feet. They apologized for the 911 figure, saying that the 919-foot-long IMPERATOR "is not really any longer, for her measurement includes the figurehead, the mighty bronze eagle with its imperial crown."[15] A British publication gave her correct length, 950 feet, but was way off on the number of her rivets and their weight, saying there were 1,500,000 and that each weighed two pounds.[16] A contemporary book about liners by the English author R.A. Fletcher displayed an amusing bias:

"All that is known at the moment of writing of the new Cunarder AQUITANIA is that she is larger and expected to prove faster than the IMPERATOR, but whether the AQUITANIA will be larger and faster than the IMPERATOR's sister, the VATERLAND . . .is at present undivulged. The BRITANNIC, yet to be launched, is expected to be faster and will certainly be larger. . . ."[17]

Britain's *Shipping World* cited the VATERLAND's record size of 54,000 tons but added that the AQUITANIA would dispute her premiership in tonnage.[18] The Hapag 1914 house organ estimated her tonnage as being 58,000 tons. Actually her tonnage was yet to be measured at the time of her launching. Her tremendous hull was still a year away from her completion. She was a great point of interest, however, to passengers on Hamburg harbor sightseeing boats. One such visitor to the port took a photo:

"Looking up at it from the water level it sure was a hill of steel," he wrote years later.[19] George F. Weber, another sightseeing boat passenger, was especially interested, for in a few months he would sail for New York on the IMPERATOR. A year later he would stand and cheer as the VATERLAND made her maiden arrival at that port.[20]

The next few months were hectic ones for Albert Ballin. Not only was he getting nowhere with his peace efforts, but all sorts of headaches vexed him with the IMPERATOR. On her delivery trip down the Elbe to Cuxhaven, where that famous river flows into the North Sea, the world's first 50,000-tonner stranded on a sand bank. Every effort was made to lighten her, including the lowering of all her lifeboats. It was found that only 17 seconds were required to drop a boat the 80 feet to water level, a fact that the company publicity men pounced on as one cheering facet of the embarrassing episode. They made the best of it.[21]

The IMPERATOR was pulled off the sandbar and a careful check showed that she had suffered no damage. She continued on her way, only to be halted again by an explosion in one of her engine rooms. Several engineers were killed.[22] Her maiden voyage had to be postponed from May 24 to June 10.[23]

The First Fiery Sword

The IMPERATOR was repaired at Cuxhaven and sent out on her sea trials. One interesting device aboard was the first Sperry gyrocompass ever installed on a liner, and aboard to run this new facility was Eberhardt Wulff, Ballin's young electrical genius who had illuminated the DEUTSCH-LAND at Kiel the year before.[24]

The IMPERATOR's master, Commodore Ruser, was born June 2, 1862, in Burgauf Fehmarn. Trained to the sea at an early age, his entire life had been spent in the service of Hapag except for a brief exploratory voyage in 1903 to the Antarctic. He had served as master on the MOLTKE, the BLUECHER, and the KAISERIN AUGUSTE VICTORIA, among other ships. His jump to the IMPERATOR, twice the tonnage of the K.A.V., must have given even this doughty mariner some qualms.[25]

J. Bernard Walker, a writer for the *Scientific American*, was one of the American press representatives aboard the new ship when she began her first crossing. Matthew Claussen, Hapag public relations man in New York, was well aware of the importance of giving free trips to members of the fourth estate. Walker's account of the maiden voyage of this first 900-foot ship is filled with superlatives.

"At the first sight of such a ship one fails to grasp its magnitude. The first thing that strikes the visitor on going aboard is the unusual height between decks, which in the case of several is from 11 to 12 feet....If the ship were to be placed in Broadway it would be necessary to cut 18 feet beyond the building line on each side of that thoroughfare for a length of four city blocks, and the roof of the topmost tier of staterooms and assembly halls would extend far above the roof-line of the six- and seven-story buildings erected in the pre-skyscraper period."

Walker hailed the Hamburg-American Line for adopting the water-tube boilers, which he called "an innovation in big ocean liners." With them, he noted, she had reached a maximum of 23 knots on her trials. He said she could probably do 23.5 under full pressure. At the start of the maiden voyage the IMPERATOR showed her sea qualities in a strong head sea and high wind conditions. Two days out, under pressure of strong winds, the "ship assumed a slight angle of heel." As if to make sure that his hosts didn't think he was being critical, Walker quickly added that she moved "parallel with the waves with a steadiness that was remarkable even in so huge a vessel." He praised the absence of vibration and laid it to the placing of the two outboard or wing propellers far out and away from the hull, "with the result that they rotate in comparatively quiet water, and well away from the belt of water which is drawn along by the skin friction of the hull and is now known to be a prolific cause of vibration." He concluded by pointing out in a highly scientific fashion that the "movement of the expansion joints in the uppermost deck was only between a quarter and three eighths of an inch."[26]

Others on this first trip were not quite so generous in discussing her strange roll; in fact, some of her passengers became alarmed at the way she tended to "hang on to the roll," as was said. Another comment on this problem was made by the Sandy Hook pilot assigned to her when she approached New York. He was Captain George Seeth, Sr., and he noticed that she had a list to port. By the time he had climbed aboard and been ushered up to the bridge, the ship was about to make a right-angle turn into the new Ambrose Channel. Most pilots take it in two 45-degree stages, but on large ships it is done in one gradual swing. For the first half of the turn, Captain Seeth ordered easy right rudder. The ship started to swing very slowly to the right, and as she did she gradually assumed an upright position on an even keel. Captain Seeth noticed that everyone on the bridge heaved a sigh of relief. The great ship would enter New York looking trim. Then, suddenly, over she went to starboard, as much as she had been listing to port. Anything that was loose fell, and a number of passengers lost their footing. Something was definitely wrong.[27]

Virtually all photographs of the IMPERATOR taken during her trials and maiden voyage show her listing. It was finally concluded that she was "deficient in initial stability"—top-heavy, to use the blunt language of the sailor. When she got back to Cuxhaven some drastic changes were made in her upper works to reduce their weight. Nine feet were cut off the top of each smokestack. Heavy paneling in her top deck public rooms was replaced with light sheeting. Her marble and mahogany grill room far aft was done over completely, becoming a garden restaurant with light cane furniture and see-through lattice columns. It worked. With proper ballasting she lost her list, although her reputation for being "tender" remained.[28]

The maiden voyage welcome at New York was a brave one, none the less. There were quips, true, about the bronze eagle. The *Herald* metaphorically equated the rattling of the IMPERATOR's anchor chain at Quarantine with the shrieking of the great bird at her prow, as if the eagle were getting ready to fly. But this paper's story also said that the new ship bore her bronze eagle in triumph to the pier.[29]

"There is little of the old-fashioned steamer to be found on the IMPERATOR except the brass ports and the striking of the ship's bell," wrote the *Times* reporter.[30]

A second incident while the IMPERATOR was in New York drew added attention to the stability problem. There was a small fire aft, and so much water was poured into the ship by fireboats and land fire equipment that she almost turned over. A *Herald* photographer, with an eye for the garish, made a picture from an upper story of a building across the street from Pier 1, Hoboken, where the IMPERATOR was berthed. He aimed his camera straight at the huge eagle, which was tilted away from the pier at a frightening angle because of the ship's list.[31]

Two extracts from the 1914 Hapag house organ show how the home office reacted to the voyage.

The first completes the analogy of the first fiery sword:

"When, for the first time, one was brandished, thousands of twinkling sparks flashed from the variegated, gold-veined Damascus blade, and shone far over the earth, into the human eyes raised so expectantly to follow its upward curve, and when from that first joyful stroke it descended with a rushing sound, it awoke clear, sonorous echoes, like the cheery ringing of bells over land and sea, and over all the earth where German hearts were beating, and German blood was coursing through the veins, there was breathless listening for a whole week to that clanging melody. And for seven days did that young gigantic weapon cleave with mighty blow through the Ocean's foaming billows, and like the bright flourish of trumpets came the wild rhythm of the echoing waves: IMPERATOR!"[32]

Another item in the same issue, much more restrained, could almost have two meanings, although that was certainly not the intention of the author:

"The whole civilized world seemed to draw a long breath of relief" when the IMPERATOR completed her maiden voyage at 10:30 p.m. that June 18th. The item then explained the press's reaction to the Elbe grounding and explosion, the stability problem, and the fire at New York as "betraying malicious pleasure in the spiteful exaggeration of the IMPERATOR's actual or invented mishaps." Trying to make the best of the situation, the Hapag house organ added that the ship's first voyage created a feeling of suspense "so profound and universal concerning the success or failure of this enormous venture that when it was over, nothing could at first diminish the general feeling of gladness, which indeed among the Americans was so hearty and unrestrained that it rose to almost frenzied, jubilant applause."[33]

The same source hailed the reaction of our "American cousins," because of their "absolute and unreserved fairness in recognizing and admiring excellent deeds by whomsoever performed." In what was clearly a gentle reproof to the British for their tongue-in-cheek sympathy for the IMPERATOR, Ballin's journal hailed the Americans as being "entirely free from all illiberal narrow-mindedness." Americans "recognized quite justly the eminently peaceful significance of the Hamburg-Amerika Linie's new weapon of warfare which, though aimed against the hostile powers of Nature, was nevertheless designed for the safety and protection of friendly intercourse and peaceful traffic between nations, and for the blessings and prosperity arising from their interchange of goods."[34]

An early voyager on the IMPERATOR, identified by Hapag as "the well-known writer E. Naeck," praised the cuisine on the new ship. He described the many things to choose from at table, the variety of fruits, jams, honey, marmalade, milk-foods; the many dishes prepared with eggs and flour, and the fish of all sorts, with potatoes "in their skins or mashed, tossed or made into pancakes," and the truffles, and the meats, and "amid the homely ham and sausages, venison-pies, poultry, pickled herrings, and other kinds of fish, in oil, in mushroom sauce, and all sorts of different cheeses. . . ." And all this long sentence just for breakfast! He went on to say that after the third day of such epicurean banquets, he asked for a bit of plain herring and potatoes and some sauerkraut, and got it.[35]

Not all the reactions were so favorable.

A Prussian general referred to the "sumptuous Hamburg-style meals" and the "whole get-up" of the IMPERATOR as being a "typical manifestation of the new Germany, with its huckstering, obtrusive manners more a snobbism than a symbol of true German ability."[36]

The Seventh Wonder

 contest in Germany to determine the seven wonders of the 20th century placed the IMPERATOR as the seventh. The others were: wireless, the Panama Canal, the dirigible, the flying machine, radium, and cinematography. Taking full advantage of this honor, the Hapag publicity people released a photograph with caption showing the IMPERATOR and the dirigible HANSA, passing overhead. The HANSA was slightly more than 500 feet long and made regular air cruises over Germany. She was owned by the Hamburg-American Line and could make over 60 miles an hour. The caption noted that flights of over 1,000 miles had been made without "alighting." Albert Ballin was still reaching out to the new and the promising.[37] Count Zeppelin, inventor of the ship which bears his name, was predicting even then that a dirigible crossing of the Atlantic might be attempted before the year was out. It would take three days, and German warships would be stationed at intervals to render assistance if necessary.[38]

After her first teething troubles the IMPERATOR settled down to a most successful year, making seven voyages and carrying more than 50,000 passengers. She had brought more than 3,014 on her first crossing. Two of her next five westbound trips surpassed the 3,600-passenger mark. Eastbound crossings were always much smaller, since there were fewer returning third-class passengers.[39]

On one of her westbound trips the IMPERATOR brought to America a huge model of herself, complete with uncut smokestacks and golden eagle. It was put on display at the 45 Broadway headquarters.[40] This model was to have a long history in America and would for years be palmed off on the public as a model of the LEVIATHAN.

The eagle figurehead was damaged during a storm on one of the IMPERATOR's crossings in 1913 and had to be removed. Had it not been for this accident, it is probable that the VATERLAND and later the third Ballin super ship would have had ornate eagle figureheads. After it was removed, it was replaced with a large gilt decoration embodying the winged eagle design used on so many German postage stamps, a much more tasteful emblem.

On October 22, 1913, the day the IMPERATOR sailed from Germany on her last voyage of the season, a 24-year-old sailor named Christian Wilhelm Schultz won his master's papers. Young Captain Schultz, a veteran officer even at that age, was to become second officer on the VATERLAND eight months later and would live on to assist in the preparation of this book.[41]

With 87 westbound crossings in 1913, Hapag carried 162,600 passengers on the New York run, considerably more than its nearest rival, the North German Lloyd. Ballin anticipated that his three 50,000-tonners would be able to carry the entire traffic by themselves, making only 36 crossings. This would leave 11 good smaller liners to be used on other routes.[42] And he would have his long-cherished three-ship weekly service—the finest, by far, on the Atlantic or any ocean.

The Second Sword

hile the IMPERATOR was establishing herself, the VATERLAND was being completed. Imagine a great hotel measuring 2,743,975 cubic feet superimposed on a 950-foot hull. That is what interior architects Bischoff and Mewes, of Cologne, and interior decorators Schneider & Hanau, of Frankfurt-on-Main, had to work with. Charles Mewes has been introduced. His counterpart on the interior decorating team was Willy Schreiber, who was briefly mentioned in Chapter I. Schreiber had designed the interiors for Hermann Blohm's home in 1905, and in 1911 had done the same for a Albert Ballin mansion. A traditionalist, he had to his credit the Palais Hammerschmidt in Bonn, home of the chancellor. He had also done the foyer of the Frankfurt Opera House and many famous hotel interiors. In the marine field, Schreiber had to his credit the two lovely Hapag twins CLEVELAND and CINCINNATI.[43]

The Mewes-Schreiber specialists were working on the VATERLAND with a superstructure area especially constructed to produce vast public rooms. The upper decks were quite different from the rest of the ship. Instead of being supported by columns from within, they employed the principle commonly used in new American skyscrapers: Their strength was in the shell, with bridgelike roof girders spanning the huge open spaces. These roof girders were hinged to side supports, for the whole superstructure had to have give. The side supports rose at close intervals from a row of hull pillars riveted to the frames. This is doubtless why the three large windows originally planned for the Social Hall had to be altered to three groups of three tall windows each. The side supports rose right up through these windows.[44]

Not only were the roof girders hinged to permit some element of twist, but three expansion joints were provided, giving longitudinal flexibility. They ran right across the ship from side to side and actually permitted the ship to expand as she rose on a huge wave amidships, with bow and stern hanging. The three joints would permit a total expansion of slightly more than one inch. One was just abaft Stack #1. The second was forward of Stack #2, and the third was aft of Stack #3. All three ran from B Deck up through A Deck and the Boat Deck. Each was an actual break in the deck with a metal lip on either side, the forward lip overlapping the after, so that no actual opening could be seen no matter how wide the momentary separation of the joint.[45]

The most noteworthy difference between the IMPERATOR and the VATERLAND interiors was due to the split uptakes to the two forward funnels. The June, 1914, *Shipbuilder*, noted British marine journal, called this an "innovation" that "has made possible the adoption of a central entrance to the dining saloon and central galleries between the public rooms, which, besides their novelty, add greatly to the decorative features of the ship."[46] Fine praise, and from the British. The Hapag brochures of the day were not backward in describing this feature, either. A superb 1914 folder published in New York said it this way:

"The funnels pass through the decks at a point near the hull instead of through the center of the ship. By removing this obstruction it has been possible to have one great salon open directly into another, thus giving the ship a remarkable effect of artistic spaciousness."[47]

Moving from the after end of B Deck forward, the last rooms to be finished were the Ritz-Carlton Restaurant, the Social Hall, and the Library and Smoking Room. Their spaciousness and style made a great impression, and even to this writing they have not been exceeded in size or beauty.

The Ritz-Carlton was described as an exact copy of the restaurant under the same management in New York.[48] Here the most wealthy passengers would be able to eat in exclusive luxury and yet be seen by the ordinary first-class travelers six steps below in the Palm Court. The Ritz-Carlton was exquisite, with its low dome, fluted doric columns, pilasters, and two-deck-high wall of decorated windows on either side.

The Palm Court, also to be known as the Wintergarden, came next and boasted a 21-foot-high ceiling. It was "adorned with a rich display of flourishing palms, and the foliage of thriving plants and flowers," according to a contemporary description.[49] Gilt latticework and plaster of Paris walls followed styling of the Louis XVI period. One great center window, curved on the top and bracketed with tall side windows, made up the port wall and the starboard wall. Both the Ritz-Carlton Restaurant and the Palm Court were decorated by the firm of Ph. Remon, of Paris.[50]

"Through a glass door of monumental appearance, one reaches the principal vestibule, with its elevators for passengers, and means of egress to the deck," a company brochure said.[51] On either side of the vestibule the staircases wound up in three stages, with wrought-iron banisters adorned in bronze. These twin flights of stairs rose through the six-deck section devoted to first class on the new ship. From the vestibule another large glass and iron door led into the Social Hall, a room that was 75 feet long, 56 wide, and 23 high. The central figure in the room was the bronze head and bust of Kaiser Wilhelm II, similar to the marble bust on the IMPERATOR. The Social Hall's walls were of oak, with "costly carving in the Louis XVI style." These carvings were the work of Willy Schreiber's Frankfurt plant.[52] Years later, when the ship was scrapped, a small secret panel was found leading into a compartment in the after wall on the starboard side.[53] A huge glass ceiling, decorated with delicate designs in wrought iron, suggested a vast overhanging dome. A wide white edge to the ceiling highlighted both the beautiful paneling and the delicate vastness of the glass work. It gave the impression that the glass-and-iron ceiling was floating in distant space. Beautifully carved wooden pilasters separated the paneling and framed the huge windows on either side and the doors at either end. Between the three windows on either side were four oil paintings measuring 13 feet in height (without their frames) and 12 feet in breadth.

These paintings had been given to the ship from the personal collection of the Kaiser. The artist was a Flemish painter and engraver named Gerard de Lairesse. Born in 1641, he had studied under the German architect Johann Gregor, and his paintings show his love for arches, large buildings, and deep perspectives. Painted around 1670 for some wealthy family in Amsterdam, these works are allegorical in style and show four scenes from the myth of Pandora.[54] The Kaiser also presented Ballin with a bronze statue of Marie Antoinette done in 1780 by the French sculptor Houdon for use on the VATERLAND.[55]

Early photographs made before the maiden voyage of the VATERLAND show that the Kaiser's bust was at first placed on the small half-moon stage between the two doors forward. Later it was moved down in front of the mass of palms and flowers between the six steps leading up to the stage on either side.[56] This gave more room for performers to cluster around the grand piano, a huge instrument of deep-grained oak decorated with a carved band of roses.[57] Singers facing an audience from the stage would have had their back to the Kaiser's bust, so moving it down was another mark of Albert Ballin's patriotic sensibilities.

The last public room on B Deck was the Library, occasionally called the Ladies' Saloon. One wall was occupied by a large glass-faced bookcase. Opposite, over a handsome dummy fireplace, was a large oil painting of Ludwig, the Bavarian Regent. It showed him in an army uniform and was continually being mistaken for a portrait of the Kaiser. On the floor was a large oriental rug, its light blue color set off by a pattern of reds and deep blues. A piece of this rug later became an heirloom for a family on Long Island[58]

The Smoking Room on A Deck forward was a gem. Its tall, three-part windows looked out over the long bow deck. Done in the Flemish style, it had superb oaken wainscoting and a beamed ceiling with hanging brass lanterns. Sixteen brilliantly colored stained-glass panes were set in the upper third of the windows on either side. They showed shields and ancient German heraldic designs. A great white stone fireplace was a centerpiece on the after bulkhead, its heavy wooden mantel supported on two thick columns carved to represent women, their heads bent under the load. Handsomely carved panels above and below the mantel added distinction. Heavy, crowned andirons added to the realistic appearance of the fireplace, and, for publicity purposes, it could be illuminated at night to suggest a burning fire. One such scene was photographed, with eight models in evening clothes all sitting in massive, high-backed chairs in a circle around the "fire." Another special feature in this room were the four "Old Salts." Carved by F. Heit of Flensburg, they are said to have been done with an adz, an old-style hand cutting tool having its blade at right angles to its handle.[59] They are full figures, 27 inches tall and done in oak.[60] These four hunched-over statuettes were among the most beloved decorative items on the ship and lasted through to the day she sailed for the scrapyard. All four have been saved.[61]

The VATERLAND's Dining Saloon for first class "is the largest space ever provided hitherto on board ship," the Hapag 1914 house organ said proudly.[62] It rose two stories high, with a balcony around the second level on E Deck. A cupola rose through most of D Deck, giving the room a height of 28 feet. A grand central staircase brought diners down from the deck above to make their entrance at the after end of the saloon. Two other entrances were forward on F Deck. Tables seating from two to eight were spaced around the room from side to side—100 feet across. Two private dining rooms were on either side of the forward end of the room. Over 700 people could eat at one sitting, the full complement of first class. A balcony for the orchestra was on E Deck forward. Tall white pilasters with gold tops supported six bays on either side of the ceiling. The bays in turn merged into the base of a great oval dome. A vast single mural by Kolmsperger was painted on this large curved area. It showed a gay combination of hunting scenes, gardens, costumed sportsmen and women, troubadours, apple pickers, and fishermen. A deep, richly piled rug was on the floor, and the chairs were upholstered with rich fabrics. The high point in the dome was 31 feet off the floor, three times the height of the dining room on the OLYMPIC.[63]

The last of the major VATERLAND public rooms was her swimming-bath, as it was called then. Forward of the dining room and one deck lower, it could be reached via a pair of lovely twin marble staircases leading down from a curved balcony overlooking the pool on F Deck. The pool proper had an area of 69 square yards. Its greatest depth was eight feet, so with its balcony area it extended through three decks. Adjoining it were "dressing-boxes, hygienic baths, places for massage and shower baths, and a hall for gymnastic exercises." A full-sized statue of a winged young man stood on a fluted column, a stream of water arching from his nude loins as if to fill the pool. The statue was of black marble. Twelve free-standing fluted columns vaguely Doric in style supported the high ceiling. White marble benches lined the sides.[64] The style was Pompeian.

Brass Door Knockers et cetera

irst class staterooms were on an equally sumptuous scale. Their richness gave new point to the old joke about the meaning of H.A.P.A.G. This was, of course, an abbreviation for Hamburg Amerikanische Packetfahrt-Attien-Gesellschaft. Wags loved to say that it really stood for "Haben Alle Passagiere Auch Geld?" or "Are all passengers well supplied with money?"[65]

Everywhere could be seen the little extras that were the trademark of Ballin. For example, all first-class cabins had brass door knockers. About 4½ inches high and 2½ inches wide, they incorporated the number of the cabin as well as a place for a card to be inserted with the name of the occupant. They were in the shape of old spice urns. Two have survived in a collection of door knockers owned by a Brooklyn man.[66]

Little bronze lighthouse lamps were another unusual yet functional item in many suites. They were 12 inches high and fitted with an electric bulb that got brighter, brighter, went off, then lit again. Or the light could be made to remain steady. "Blohm & Voss, 1914," was stamped on the bottom of these pieces, evidence of the company's pride of workmanship.[67]

Care was taken in the selection and mounting of the thousands of color prints hung in great profusion in the staterooms. The scenes were from all over Europe, often bearing captions in both English and French. Two of these, by a British artist with bilingual captions, have been preserved.[68]

All the bedsteads in first class were of brass, and there were no cabins with upper bunks. Each first-class stateroom had its marble washstand with running fresh water, hot and cold. Front and side mirrors, twin outlets for electric plugs, brackets for glasses, shelves for water pitchers, soap trays, and even a built-in flower holder were part of each room. A curtained porthole and brass wall fixture to hold on to when the ship was rolling were the only suggestions that one was on a ship. There were 136 staterooms with private bath and toilet or shower and toilet, almost unheard-of luxuries; on other liners, everyone used common toilets and tub baths. In all, there were 220 tub baths aboard, a few even for steerage. All rooms had electric lighting, heating, bells to call stewards, and ventilation.[69] The average size of a double room on the VATERLAND was 172 square feet. Compare this to the 43-square-foot average on a Hapag ship of 1886. The two imperial suites on the new ship covered 247 square feet each. They were on either side of C Deck, just forward of the main foyer. Each had nine rooms, including a private veranda looking out over the ocean and fitted with cane furniture, potted palms, and elaborate drapes.[70] In one of these was a special upright piano for the Kaiser. It was made of light woods inlaid in a beautiful design and set within a frame of highly polished darker woods. Both this piano and the grand from the Social Hall turned up in Norfolk in 1919.[71]

Before leaving first class, a word about an oddity: the Tea Room aft on B Deck. It does not appear on the preliminary deck plans made up for travel agents, but is shown on some of the earliest Blohm & Voss deck plans. The room was done in simple style, suggesting that it was not a part of the original plan furnished by Charles Mewes.

So much for first-class public rooms and cabins. Some 700 people at the most would enjoy more than three quarters of this vast ship, for this was the day of conspicuous consumption. On ships, particularly, it was the rule for the rich to act as though they were all princes and princesses. Such was the atmosphere that ship lines tried to create, and most of those in second, third, and steerage classes seemed quite content to envy and gawk. After all, they were going to America, where someday they would become princes and princesses, at which time they would relish lording it over their less fortunate relatives.

Second class could accommodate 600 and its public rooms at least had the pretense of quality. There was a smoking room and a ladies' lounge on D Deck aft. Second-class passengers had an elevator, too, something most unusual. They even had their own gymnasium. A few second-class cabins were on C Deck aft, and there were blocks of rooms on E and F decks, but the bulk of the second-class cabins were aft on G and H decks. For the most part, they were four-berth cabins, but some were cabins for two. Many were inside and none had toilets. The second-class dining saloon was aft on F Deck, and was far from pretentious. Long tables with 12 seats fixed to the deck were standard. There were a few with only four chairs. Two small areas of enclosed deck space and the top of the after deckhouse were all there was of promenade space.

For those going in third cabin there was even less room, although 1,050 could be accommodated. Two cramped little public rooms, one a smoking room with bar and the other a ladies' cabin, were all there was in the shape of public rooms, except for a huge dining saloon. The staterooms were on F, G, and H decks, and the few that were outside were all so low in the hull that the outer bulkhead slanted at a striking angle to conform to the stern shape of the ship. All the cabins were directly over the four propellers, and if there was to be vibration it was going to be here. There were two small deck space areas at the stern.

For steerage it was the bow section, with two small general rooms where people could sit; and what little deck space there was, was forward of the bridge. The dining saloon was on F Deck. It was functional in the extreme, with long wooden tables without tablecloths, and fixed wooden benches. Heavy soup bowls, handleless drinking mugs, wicker bread baskets, and all sorts of condiment bottle holders were set out on the table in posed photographs made for publicity purposes. Neatly uniformed waiters, white napkin over each hooked left arm, stand in the picture. For most steerage passengers, the dining saloon was heaven on earth, despite its lack of luxuries.

But there were luxuries for steerage class. A special feature on the VATERLAND was a compartment where emigrants could wash their clothing. Six large white enamel tubs lined either wall, with hot and cold water faucets over each. This was where Ballin was advancing ahead of what others offered in steerage. Four-, six-, and eight-berth rooms were the rule on G and H decks, and this was another improvement. The space on I Deck was used for open bunks in three large compartments, one for women. This lowest passenger area was about at waterline level. While there were portholes, they could never be opened; in fact, most of the time they had to be covered on the inside by round steel lids known as "deadlights." Normal steerage capacity could be increased from 1,200 to 1,700 by using this I Deck area. With every bunk filled, she could carry 4,050 passengers, which made her the largest passenger carrier ever built.[72] Her lifeboat capacity of 5,300 persons just exceeded her maximum passenger capacity plus her maximum crew of 1,200 persons.[73]

Steerage business was very important to Albert Ballin and to the success of the VATERLAND. Great attention was paid to every item of merchandising. The business was complex and rules had been developed for all phases, many of which came to sound outlandish in later years. Those buying through tickets and using steerage on a ship had to use fourth class on the railroad. Those using third class on the ship could go only in third class on the railroad. Russians were not be booked in third class, but were to go steerage. Children under one year of age were charged $2.50 in steerage, and the agent's commission for them was 25 cents. Steerage rates from Hamburg to New York were $29.50, except for Russians, who had to pay $1.25 extra per adult and 65 cents extra per child for board and lodging at Hamburg and transfer from railroad to steamer. A Steerage and Third Class Circular issued January 1, 1914, shows a painting of the IMPERATOR with the name "VATERLAND" on the bow.[74]

Electricity on the VATERLAND was one of her most talked-about features. The quaint language of the Hapag 1914 summer house organ says that the ship's five "turbo-dynamos render it possible to illuminate the ship with the dazzling brilliance of 10,000 electric lights," and that there was a "motor-dynamo" on the uppermost deck for emergency use. Even the lifeboat winches were worked by electricity.[75] The 32-page VATERLAND booklet put out by Hapag's New York office upped the number of electric lights from 10,000 to 15,000, and said that "in no other ship, probably, is electricity so generally employed."[76] Hoists, derricks, operating machinery, elevators, and kitchen machinery of all types were also electrically operated. Staterooms and public saloons were heated by electricity, and fresh air was forced to every part of the ship by an electric ventilating system.

In addition to the forced air ventilation, the VATERLAND had an even newer feature in its "ozone system." As described by her electrician, Eberhardt Wulff, it was used to purify the air in the first-class Smoking Room and in all first-class cabins and bathrooms. Fresh "ozone," an almost pure oxygen, was stored in a large "ozone room" forward in the superstructure. Each morning at 6 a.m. it was pumped into the Smoking Room and other places. Wulff said it smelled the way air smells after a big storm. The 50,000-volt machine that did the pumping gave Wulff headaches. Wulff also said that the American-made heating elements in the electric heating units in each cabin gave him much trouble. Passengers could control the temperature in their cabins with a panel of buttons.[77]

Electricity also ran the submarine sounding signals "that in fog listen to the approach of ships and in the proximity of coasts to submarine bells."[78]

This device led the Hapag publicity men to wax eloquent:

"Should a ship be threatened by the proximity of a coast, which is not seen, but which the ship hears, the electrically-worked sounding machines immediately send their unending spiderlike fingers down into the depths of the water and thereby make it more easy to ascertain the ship's location."[79]

Wireless, another wonder, was of great interest to the public, and the installation on the VATERLAND was the largest of its day. Three operators were required, and the ship was "almost always" in communication with some shore station, Hapag proudly said.

Finally, the pride and joy of the Hapag publicity men was the huge searchlight. It was mounted on the crow's nest up the foremast. The "Two Fiery Swords" brochure is magnificent in its descriptive language:

"And then the gigantic, Cyclopean eye of the ship!

"As in the legendary Polyphemus of the *Odyssey*, it is situated in the middle of the Ocean-Giantess's brow. A wonderfully clean, uncanny eye, for it not only looks straight ahead, but also sideways and backwards, and in fact just wherever the brain on the

Commander's bridge chooses. With a luminosity equal to that of 34,000 candles, it pierces the fog, looks all around, searchingly, scrutinizingly, and commandingly, as if to say:

" 'Here am I! Come to me, all who seek my protection; away from me, all who have cause to fear me; let me conjure up the enemy that would threaten me, that I may behold him in due time.' "[80]

Another colorful electric device was the great bell on the upper deck forward of #2 Stack. It struck the hours with an ingenious arrangement of twin hammers, one on either side. Larger than any of the bells called for in the Hapag specifications, it was decorated with a belt of embossed three-masted galleons on its upper third. The bell was suspended over the deck by an arrangement of twin iron horseshoes, open ends down.[81]

In the category of tidbits, it is interesting to note that much of the joiner work, stateroom partitions, and bulkheading was made of a new type of composite wood in which Germany had been pioneering called "plywood."[82]

There can be no doubt that the VATERLAND was a substantial improvement over the IMPERATOR, and she was well ahead of her British rivals in size and refinements. There was even talk, as the time came closer for her trials and maiden voyage, that she might make a serious try for the Atlantic speed crown.

Chapter IV

SHE SAILS

lbert Ballin had often suffered from severe headaches. As the year 1914 was born, his nights were long and he must have been driven to distraction by inner conflicts and forebodings. There was the continuous political tension in Central Europe and the Middle East. The German military was becoming more powerful and Ballin, in anguish, saw naval policies widening the gap between Germany and England. Despite his conviction that Tirpitz was the enemy of peace, Ballin began the new year by pressing Cassel for a meeting between the Admiral and Churchill.[1]

In between his nightmares about war and his efforts to lay a groundwork for peace, and despite fears that his own mercantile successes were contributing to the tensions, there must have been periods of reflection when the Hapag chairman took pleasure in his own accomplishments. A company brochure was issued at about this time. Its heading suggests a moving picture title of the 1970s:

"Wonderful Progress of the Line During a Period of 67 Years, Beginning in a Small Way and Now Operating Ships Which Are Masterpieces of Human Achievement."[2] The brochure describes the VATERLAND as "nearly 100 times the size of the company's first transatlantic passenger vessel," adding that she and her sister the IMPERATOR and a "third sister ship will complete the extra-ordinary trio of ships, the greatest the world may ever see." Hapag had 194 ocean steamers of 1,307,000 aggregate tons, the folder noted, while its closest rival, North German Lloyd, had 136 ships of 911,000 tons. Two other well-known Atlantic lines, White Star and Cunard, had only 487,000 tons and 350,000 tons, respectively. Hapag ships made 2,218 ocean voyages in 1913, covering 8,986,000 nautical miles (6,080 feet is one nautical mile), or 415 times around the earth. The company employed 25,000 persons and had many socially-advanced ways of helping them and their families, such as an invalid, widow, and orphan's pension fund, free medical treatment, old age pensions, sick benefits, and savings funds.

The year began with a serious dispute between Ballin and the Trans-Atlantic Conference. Although Hapag's share of the 1,427,000 emigrants who had gone by ship to the United States in 1913 was very large, he apparently felt that it was not large enough in light of his three new 50,000-tonners. He knew his big three would be tremendously expensive to operate and that they had to run full. He called upon the Conference to increase Hapag's quota of the steerage trade based on the capacity of these new ships. The Conference refused, pointing out quite logically that only the IMPERATOR was actually in service and reminding Hapag that the pool-sharing ratio was made up on the basis of past carrying performances. Ballin ought to know—he had hammered out this agreement himself—but he was adamant, demanding. So was the Conference, and on January 31, Ballin withdrew his company from the body. It was a drastic step and one that suggested the possibility of a rate war. Some interpreted his action as at least in part a result of the tremendous strain he was under.[3]

One quick result of Hapag's exit from the Conference was a new agreement with North German Lloyd. Announced February 23, it created a "community of interests" between the two lines. Both would share equally in the North American passenger trade and its freight business. It is said that Emperor Wilhelm II had personally intervened to bring about the new "peace treaty," as it was called.[4]

World interest in big liners continued at a high level as the White Star Line launched its new BRITANNIC, 46,000 tons, on February 25 and the French Line announced plans for a large liner to be named the PARIS. Both Cunard and Hapag were rushing their newest super liners to completion. No dates had been announced at this time for the maiden voyages of the AQUITANIA and the VATERLAND, but it was known they would sail very close to each other in the early spring.

The crew of the VATERLAND were assembling. Commodore Ruser was already on hand, as was electrician Eberhardt Wulff. These men have been introduced. There were to be 1,232 others. Besides the Commodore, the ship would have four full-rank captains and seven other deck officers. She would need a chief engineer, three first assistants, and 35 assistants and electricians. Her boilers would be operated by 12 chief firemen, 15 oilers, 187 stokers, and 189 trimmers. This was the famous "black gang," the men who would feed the coal into the 46 boilers. This was a rough job, but Hapag had plenty of men to choose from because everyone was eager to get a berth on the VATERLAND. In the eight kitchens there would be three chefs, 52 cooks, five pastry bakers, 36 waiters, and 350 stewards. The ship would have three physicians and three medical assistants as well as one trained nurse. Also there would be three telephone operators, a stenographer and "typewriter," meaning a typist, a master of the bath, a bookseller, a cabinetmaker, several masseurs, and a gardener, not to mention a social director, according to a 1914 VATERLAND brochure.[5] There was also an interpreter, who was named Maurice Mueller.[6] The total crew numbered 1,234, compared to 1,180 on the IMPERATOR. The White Star's OLYMPIC had 860 in her crew. The new Cunarder, AQUITANIA, would have 970.[7]

The task of stocking the ship's pantry and linen closets was grist for the publicity writer's mill. There were 12,250 large and small pillowcases and coverings for the eiderdown quilts and bolsters. There were 9,700 sheets and 1,225 counterpanes, not to mention 3,000 hand towels and 950 "roller towels." In the dining saloons the VATERLAND needed: 13,800 table napkins, 6,870 tablecloths, 4,400 finger napkins, 2,530 dish cloths, 800 glass cloths, and 700 dusters. For the bathrooms there were orders for 4,900 bath towels, 2,500 bath sheets, 600 bath mats, and "150 bathing mantles."

The finest polished silver and cut glass were needed, "not only to meet all imaginable demands of the most fastidious passengers, but if possible to surpass them, if that which is offered is not to be thrown miserably into the shade by the style in which it is served," wrote the Hapag publicity office.[8]

The food that had to be bought and carried aboard the brave new liner was good copy too.

This included 45,000 lbs. of fresh meat for the three upper classes and 24,000 lbs. of pickled and tinned meat for the crew and steerage.

The list seems interminable, with great orders of oysters, lobsters, crabs, and fish, cases of lemons and oranges, and even 1,500 boxes of ice cream. For staples there were 100,000 lbs. of potatoes and 350 barrels of flour. Again for the crew and steerage there was an order for 18,000 lbs. of rice and leguminous food.

To satisfy those with a sweet tooth, 10,000 lbs. of sugar, treacle, and honey, 400 lbs. of chocolate and cocoa, and 250 bottles of fruit syrup were lugged aboard.

For vegetarians, the ship took on 5,200 tins of preserved vegetables; 2,400 lbs. of cucumbers, beet root, and pickles; 5,000 lbs. of pickled cabbage and French beans; and 1,200 lbs. of dried vegetables. There were also 25 barrels of herring, each barrel holding 650 fish. What German ship could sail without herring?

The wine cellar for each voyage consisted of:
    700 bottles of luncheon wine
    5,000 bottles of hock
    4,500 bottles of claret
    3,000 bottles of French champagne

2,100 bottles of German champagne
2,200 bottles of liquer, brandies
13,000 litres of best quality beer
15,000 litres of Hamburg beer
5,000 litres of wine and spirits for crew[9]

A Beautiful Ship

er slide down the ways into Hamburg harbor a year before had been the VATERLAND's first motion. Then she was towed to the fitting-out pier, where her superstructure was completed, her remaining boilers installed, and her great smokestacks and masts erected. She now had her full silhouette, and she was a beautiful ship! She was quite different from the IMPERATOR in a number of small but distinctive particulars. Her bridge front was her most impressive new feature. The bulkheading on the Boat Deck under the bridge was stained mahogany, as were the sweeping bridge and pilothouse on the deck above. On the IMPERATOR the whole forward end of the superstructure had been white. The two-deck-high Smoking Room windows on the VATERLAND were recessed under the bridge, leaving an open walkway athwartships and adding a feeling of depth and impressive bigness to the whole bridge front. The corner supports on port and starboard were massive, suggesting that the officers who walked that bridge must be almost superhuman. The two masts were tall and tapering. Just below the pilothouse level on the foremast was the great searchlight, all wrapped in new, dark canvas. The lower crow's nest was above the level of the bridge; and an upper crow's nest was high up near top of the mast, just above a "spreader" for the long wireless antenna.

The three 64-foot-high smokestacks measured 200 feet in width and were 30 feet long.[10] The two working stacks forward each had four vent pipes, two on either side, rising on the outer face. They would have looked better inside the stack. The dummy funnel, used for galley smoke exhaust and for ventilation, was cut open at its base with a row of tall, rounded air intakes forward.

As the last of the linens were being taken aboard and touch-up paint jobs were being completed, the 950-foot hull was taken into tow once again and put into "Das grosse Schwimmdock." Her rudder and propellers had to be put on, and a final coat of paint had to be given to her bottom after it had been cleaned of the first few thousand barnacles that had affixed themselves to her new steel plates in the months since her launching. There was no single dry dock in the world large enough for her, but, as had been done with the IMPERATOR, ordinary-sized dry docks were spliced together and used.[11] Their water compartments were filled, and the double dock sank down to the proper depth, and in slid the monster ship, settling slowly on the blocks especially placed. When it had been propped into a perfectly balanced position by side supports, the water was pumped out and the dry docks rose, lifting the great new ship completely out of the water.

The installation of the 50½-ton rudder made of forged steel was a delicate task, as was the fitting of the four 18½-foot wheels. Cranes mounted on the upper sides of the dry dock lifted the rudder and propellers and held them in place while the last of the rivets and bolts were secured. The three bow anchors were also installed. The VATERLAND's bow ornamentation, a substitute for an eagle, was marked on in white chalk and then riveted to the hull plates. It looked like a pennant, the straight edge at the stem and the wavy tip stretching about 20 feet aft. Within the gold-edged emblem was a white and gold shield featuring the German eagle. Plumed curlicues made up the rest. A very similar decoration went on the bows of the IMPERATOR after the eagle fell off.[12]

In March the IMPERATOR began her second season. Her first voyage was a rough one and she lost some lifeboats forward in the gale. Her master, Captain Kier, was hailed by his passengers on March 19 when she reached New York safely.[13] There were no more stability problems.

On April 10 the VATERLAND, which had moved out of her dry dock for a while, went back in for her last docking before the yard trials. She was virtually complete, and every effort was made to avoid the embarrassments which had beset the IMPERATOR in her first days.

On April 25, the VATERLAND's career really began. Excursion boats surrounded her and yard whistles blew as she headed down the Elbe for the first time. It was 5 p.m. when she started. Since it was a Saturday, it was possible for large crowds to be on hand to see her sail. Six tugs were alongside and ahead to help in case of any emergency. As she moved away from the yard, workers on the new liner CAP POLONIA, being built for the Hamburg South American Line, waved and cheered. This luxurious three-stacker had been ordered only a year before and launched in March.[14] She was something of a miniature VATERLAND.

The run to Cuxhaven was not an easy one because of the many shallows. The VATERLAND drew fully 37 feet, 18 inches more than the IMPERATOR, and so the voyage was made with the greatest caution. She had taken aboard only enough coal for the short trip. Twice on the way she had to stop, and on both occasions she was passed by a four-masted bark, the VALKYRIE. Everyone aboard this lovely relic of the past piled out on deck to see the new queen of the seas, none with more enthusiasm than a young ordinary seaman named Charles Rosner, who was to be one of America's best-known marine artists in years to come. Watch Officer Barthold aboard the sailing vessel later became an officer on the VATERLAND. The VALKYRIE was under tow herself.[15]

New York newspapers kept close tabs on the new Hapag giantess. The *Herald,* in its account of the run to Cuxhaven, took occasion to note that her steerage passengers were accommodated in rooms for from two to six instead of in dormitories. This source also was impressed by her fire brigade, composed of experienced fire fighters from the fire departments of German cities.[16]

Eberhardt Wulff, electrician, was settled aboard the great liner. A photographer snapped his picture as he posed in his cabin, pretending to be making a telephone call; or perhaps he really was calling someone. All officers had phones in their cabins, as did all first-class passengers. Wulff wears his fine uniform, with its high, starched wing-collared shirt. His cabin is not very large, but it has many luxuries. There is an electric fan on the bulkhead. An upholstered couch extends the length of the room on the right side, and a high, polished-wood bunk with a decorative curtain is at the left. Below the bed are some long drawers for gear. Between the bed and the couch is a fine-looking chest of drawers, each drawer with its brass keyhole and two inset brass handles. Wulff is paid 2,200 marks a year (about $500), plus room and board. It is the finest job he has ever had.[17]

Blohm & Voss ran their yard trials on April 29 and 30, taking the VATERLAND out into the open sea for the first time. She was put through her paces along the coast of Norway, "with most gratifying results for the owners as well as the builders," the New York *Journal of Commerce* reported.[18] The engines performed beautifully and an average speed of 25.84 knots was achieved. The transatlantic speed record at this time was held by the Cunarder MAURETANIA with an average of 26.06 knots.[19] With the wind in her favor, the new VATERLAND got up to 26.3 knots for a period, developing 90,400 shaft horsepower, far above her guaranteed 60,000. This naturally provoked considerable talk of trying for a record on her first run, although Commodore Ruser was steadfast in his refusal to make any predictions. Nevertheless, the VATERLAND was hailed as having "exceeded even the sanguine expectations formed about her."[20] It was also said that "in respect of manageableness and vibration, the huge vessel also proved throughly satisfactory."[21]

The trial trip showed that there was positively no stability problem with the VATERLAND, something that the yard people were most concerned about. The ship's easy-rolling characteristic was due to her negative g.m., or metacentric height, it was explained. This was designed into the vessel to make her more comfortable for passengers. It produced a longer, more gentle roll, instead of a quick flip-flop. Tug men didn't like it because it made the ship rather hard to handle. She would lean longer on the tugs that were up close to her.[22]

Also tested on the trial trip was the ship's wireless. Her call letters were "DVD" and her equipment was operated and controlled by Deutsche Betriebsgesellschaft fur drahtlose Telegraphie, of Berlin.[23] On May 2 the New York *Times* reported that the possibility of a race between the MAURETANIA and the VATERLAND was being widely rumored in Germany. The new ship's maiden voyage, set for May 14, coincided with the departure of the MAURETANIA.[24] But the next day this same paper had a story discounting predictions of a race and saying that such rumors could not be confirmed.[25]

Meanwhile, back at Cuxhaven, Albert Ballin was making the most of his new liner. A reception was held aboard for the members of the Reichstag and the Bundesrat. Frantic preparations were being made to receive royalty on the official trials of the new liner. The Bavarian Regent Ludwig had been invited to be aboard, but he could not be present. He sent in his stead Prince Franz, a brother of Prince Rupprecht, who came with a large suite of courtiers.[26]

She sailed on Monday, May 10, with the Hapag houseflag at the truck on her main mast for the first time. She had been the property of Blohm & Voss on her first trial, but now she had been accepted by Hamburg-American and was their ship. As she headed toward the North Sea she passed a tiny coastal schooner, whose white-tipped mast tops barely reached up to her superstructure. The schooner's crew cheered. So did the passengers on a white-hulled paddle-wheel excursion steamer that followed close astern. Those aboard the VATERLAND waved back. There was a distinguished list of passengers aboard, all guests of Albert Ballin. In addition to the Prince and his friends, there were representatives of the Hamburg Senate, leaders of the German military, and men in high civil and other public positions. At dinner the first night out, Ballin made an eloquent speech, welcoming all and expounding on the progress Germany had made in the past 44 years. He particularly noted Bismarck's famous remark that Germany must export either goods or men. Shipping services were one way of exporting, and thus the new VATERLAND. Ballin then paid tribute to the Kaiser's contributions to German sea power:

"It was, and is, the Kaiser's high and noble mission to increase, promote, and protect Germany's power at sea—the merchant marine not less than the navy. The Kaiser has set himself to this great task with unfailing devotion."[27]

Maiden Voyage

 will just point the VATERLAND toward America and let the ocean blow by," Commodore Ruser said to a New York *Herald* reporter at Cuxhaven on Thursday morning, May 14, as the maiden voyage was about to begin.[28]

All the major New York papers had men on hand and many were to make the voyage as guests. It was a great day for Cuxhaven and for all Germany. The sailing was set for 2 p.m., but most passengers boarded the new liner in the morning. A special boat train had brought many important voyagers down from Hamburg, and most of the ship's list were aboard by noon. Luncheon was served in all four of the great ship's dining saloons. Only one sitting was necessary, for there were only about 1,000 passengers. Another 600-plus would board the ship at Southampton and Cherbourg, but still the total would be well under half her capacity.[29] People were rather scared of maiden voyages.

A slight drizzle dampened the enthusiasm a little but there were big crowds just the same at the long dock, or Steubenhoft. The VATERLAND lay port side in to the planked pier as last-minute passengers hurried aboard and visitors departed. Some homeward-bound Americans were already poring over the 58-page passenger list, looking for the names of friends aboard. The booklet had a superb painting of the VATERLAND on the cover, showing her majestically tied to the pier ready to sail, wreaths of light-colored smoke rising from her tall yellow stacks. This passenger list, printed in German and English, told how letters and telegrams could be sent, what to do with valuables, and all about the wireless service. The next five voyages of the VATERLAND through September were given, as were the sailings on Hapag's other principal lines around the world. There were advertisements for the many cruises Hapag was offering and two full-page notices of "Zeppelin Airship" trips the company was running out of seven major German cities. Two more full pages listed the officers of the VATERLAND, from Commodore Ruser to the sauce chef, H. Friis.

On the bridge Commodore Ruser said goodby to his wife and young son Hans. The four captains selected to assist him wore their finest uniforms to have their picture taken with the Commodore. They were H. von Maibom, V. Bernholdt, Th. Koch, and R. Karbiner. There were three second officers, as many third officers, and one fourth officer. The chief engineer was O. Wolf.[30]

A crowd of beshawled emigrants were in the well deck forward. In order to be seen by friends on the pier far below, some perched atop the canvas-covered lifeboats on the forward deckhouse. A ship's photographer took their picture when the sun came out a few minutes before the last lines were let go. He was pleased because he caught a white-coated miss wearing a jaunty automotive cap and holding up a bottle in her right hand.[31] Then the ship was moving, the heavy bow hawser still held by twelve men on the pier. Slowly it was brought aboard and all contact with the shore of Germany ended. The sun went back under the clouds. It began to drizzle again. Umbrellas went up on the dock, but aboard ship all was gay and lighthearted. Now at last the VATERLAND was really on her way.

The New York *Times* man aboard jotted down in his notebook that the departure was so quietly maneuvered that many of the passengers who were still eating were unaware that the ship had started. He also reported in his first story from the ship that there would be no race on the VATERLAND's first eastbound voyage, although she and the MAURETANIA would leave New York on the same day. Their departure was to be scheduled ten hours apart so there could be no racing. Both captains had been given explicit instructions "to engage in no speed competition."[32] These jottings appeared on page one of the *Times* the next morning.

Four directors of the Hamburg-American Line were aboard, but Albert Ballin himself did not make the trip. The Hapag men were in high spirits because the VATERLAND had beaten the AQUITANIA into service. The Cunarder completed her trial trip on the day the new Hapag liner began her first voyage. A short final paragraph in the *Times* story about the VATERLAND mentioned that the new Cunard ship had realized her owner's highest expectations, adding that there was a "remarkable absence of vibration."[33]

Vibration was an important problem in those days. The New York *Tribune's* man aboard the VATERLAND said she had no perceptible vibration at speeds of up to 22 knots. He called her "Herr Ballin's latest marvel" and said she was "as steady as a rock."[34] The New York *Sun's* correspondent wrote that "a striking feature about the voyage so far is that there is absolutely no vibration and the passengers find it difficult to realize they are on board a fast steamship."[35] This same *Sun* man, in something of a flight of fancy, added that "a ball was in progress in the gorgeous ballroom at the time the aerogram was sent." New word for wireless—"aerogram." Actually, all three stories were sent by wireless via the much more powerful facilities of a shore station at Scheveningen Haven.

Thursday finally ended. The graceful VATERLAND thrust her way at a steady 22 knots through the dark waters toward Southampton. Among the 300 first-cabin passengers who would board her there would be a few more Americans to join the 16 who had sailed from Cuxhaven.[36] Perhaps some of these Americans smiled quietly at the rather quaint English in the "Handbook for Passengers" which everyone found waiting for him on his cabin bureau. A handsome little 76-page booklet with a red, white, and black tassel, it contained many sentences whose structure was a bit Teutonic:

"Passengers will please inform their room steward regarding the manner in which they wish to have made up their beds."

Or:

"Mattresses, bolsters, pillows, blankets, and quilts can be had at any time, so there is no necessity of using the bed as it is found made up."

Is it possible that this latter sentence reflects a trace of inferiority complex on the part of Albert Ballin's passenger department? There really should have been no such complex for Hapag was junior to Britain's Cunard Line by only seven years.

Mustache-curling cost 10 cents in the barber shop, while beards were trimmed for 15 cents. The most expensive thing a man could ask for was a 75-cent manicure.

Under "Drinks" there appeared this admonition:

"Passengers are requested not to give wine, beer, or liquors of any kind to any member of the crew, unless special permission of the captain has been obtained."

No children could use the gymnasium unless accompanied by an adult. Women had special hours and during these periods a nurse was always in attendance. For 50 cents, ladies could have an "undulation" treatment—whatever that was—at the hairdresser's. Probably a hair wave.

The booklet noted that the Library had books in English and French as well as in German. Passengers were asked to take care of them and "it is especially requested not to leave them lying on deck."

Tipping was left to the discretion of the passengers, with this one exception:

"The Bandmaster has permission to circulate a subscription list towards the end of the voyage, but only once, on a day to be fixed by the chief-steward," and "if employees importune passengers for gratuities, they should be reported at once."[37]

On Friday the VATERLAND reached Cowes, where her huge bow anchor rattled out of its hawse pipe and held her while her contingent of Southampton passengers came aboard from two tiny tenders. The red and gold castle flag of Hamburg flew from the staff far forward, and fifteen brand-new code flags flew from the fore and main masts, whipping off with abandon toward the shore on the starboard. The tenders unloaded on the port side, one aft and the other forward under the bridge, the passengers climbing aboard through side ports on G Deck. A large sloop, probably the pilot's, lay close under the port bow, her main sail furled. A tremendous German flag whipped and flattened in the breeze from the staff at the VATERLAND's far stern.[38]

Her noontime pause at Cowes was over and the VATERLAND headed across the Channel toward France. At Cherbourg she would make an even shorter stop and then be off for America.

Next came one of those delightful coincidences, those rare twists of fate. The weather was calm in the Channel as the VATERLAND passed the lightship off the Isle of Wight and headed toward the French coast. It was a beautiful early summer day. At the same hour the small American steamship ST. LOUIS, christened so long ago by Mrs. Grover Cleveland but still the flagship of the American Line, came into the English Channel, approaching Southampton. Here is how her first mate remembered it:

Great Moment

ar ahead off the starboard bow a streak of smoke showed over the horizon. I raised my binoculars. What I saw was enough to take the wind out of any sailor's canvas. There she stood out to sea, her three great funnels towering proudly above her upper deck. I didn't say a word. I just stood there and looked. She was the biggest ship that had ever sailed the seas."[39]

First Mate Herbert Hartley was speaking, and he was talking to Captain John Clark Jamison. Both would live to be master of the VATERLAND later, when she was called LEVIATHAN.

"Sir. The captain of that ship must indeed be a proud man," Hartley said.

Jamison shifted his pipe, pulled at his goatee, spat to leeward, and said: "Let him try to get up the English Channel some dirty night when he doesn't know where he is and he won't feel so damn proud."

This was Jamison's way, but he knew and admired Ruser. It was a moment that those two Americans never forgot.

And still another tap from the wand of coincidence:

The world of the sea is really a small world, and seamen are all brothers. Aboard a Royal Mail Line ship, the AMAZON, there was a young seaman named Reynard. He had served aboard the IMPERATOR the year before and was on the lookout for the new VATERLAND. Reynard's ship entered the Cherbourg roadstead just as the VATERLAND was leaving, and they passed "dangerously close," as he remembered later. The German liner had stopped briefly to pick up her Cherbourg passengers and was heading out to sea. Reynard had also served aboard the ST. LOUIS and he knew First Mate Hartley well. Years later they both served together again aboard the LEVIATHAN.[40]

Back aboard the VATERLAND, people were getting to know each other. Most passengers had become familiar with the beautiful public spaces. Some had explored the Georg Stilke bookshop on C Deck by the elevators, "C Deck Square" as it was known. The Stilke shop was managed by a well-known Berlin bookseller and offered souvenirs, magazines, and the latest newspapers. One deck above, there was another little store. This one sold "the best known brands of candies and chocolates." Opposite the confectionery was a flower stand supplied with fresh flowers grown in the stained-mahogany and glass house on the top deck, aft of the last funnel on the starboard side.

As evening of the first full day aboard came, one of the four Hapag directors aboard, none other than interior designer Willy Schreiber, was becoming better known to other passengers. He was continually being congratulated on two counts. First, for his splendid work on the interiors of the great public rooms, and second, because it was his wedding anniversary.[41]

After dinner, with Cherbourg behind them and nothing but the great dark Atlantic out in front, the first-class passengers gathered in the Social Hall for the evening's "Musik-Programm." An off-white program with a delicate blue decoration on top was passed out. Seven selections were offered, beginning with a march by Fetras entitled "Der Wandervogel."[42]

At ten that evening a cold buffet was offered in the Main Dining Saloon, and what a choice: Pork Chops in jelly, Duck a la Montmorency, Leg of Pork with cole slaw, Beefsteak Tartare, Roast Beef, Roast Veal, Smoked Ox Tongue, Smoked Ham, Boiled Ham, and all sorts of sausages. The gilt-edged menu, with the Hapag anchor and shield embossed in gold and with gold lettering, was impressive. It was in German on one side and English on the other.[43]

A few late strollers could be spotted as the VATERLAND left the Channel far behind and set out for New York. Some braved the tearing, blasting wind under the bridge in the dark walk just outside the tall windows of the Smoking Room. Others remained inside, watching through these same windows of "that vast and lofty room whence once viewed, as though from Olympus, the awesome spectacle of the monstrous ship thrusting her knifelike bows into the relentless Atlantic seas," as one of her officers put it.[44]

The weather got worse and people were sick. Forward in one of the glory holes (a glory hole is a large cabin with bunks for a dozen or more men) young Fred Hecker, a steward, lay in an agony of seasickness. He had been sick, in fact, ever since the ship had left Cuxhaven. A veteran of service on the IMPERATOR, he had been almost continuously sick aboard her too, but he still loved the sea. He was a veteran of three years in the German army and hated to hear all the talk of a war between Germany and England.[45]

In steerage there was much sickness, but not all from the waves. Young Zelda Danielevitz, from Gozovo, in Minsk, Russia, recalled afterwards that many of her fellow passengers had eaten too much. They had never dreamed there would be so much food and that it would all be free. Her mother had given her a supply of zwieback just in case. But instead there were tables loaded down with delicious edibles and there was tea between meals and more food set out in the evening. She relished every minute and wasn't sick herself. Zelda was under 13 but had given her age as 17 so she could travel to America alone. She had a bunk in one of the large cabins for women on J Deck.[46]

Another passenger's experience on that maiden voyage made a paragraph years later in a new book on liners. She was telling an officer how she always got sick, but how wonderfully smooth this crossing was. The officer took her by the arm, saying, "Well, there's a bit of a gale on now; if you care to come with me I will show you."

They went down five decks in the elevator and looked out through one of the lower portholes. Great waves were smashing up against the thick glass, turning it dark green and then foamy white.

"You see, a big sea is not much to look at from the height of a cliff," he said.[47]

By Sunday the crossing was half over. Down in the hold the VATERLAND's seapost was busy. This was a carefully locked room where mail was sorted. Two men, one American and the other German, were employed. The American was in charge on the westbound voyage, the German would run things on the way back. Started in 1891 on the North German Lloyd, the seapost system was a way of speeding the delivery of mail from abroad. Only the largest ships had seaposts aboard.[48]

In New York the readers of the Sunday *World* learned something about the fine art aboard the VATERLAND. The four De Lairesse paintings in the Social Hall were described, and it was noted that the Smoking Room featured two marines by Prof. Schnars-Alquist. The Kilmsperger mural in the Dining Saloon dome was listed. Two landscapes by Giovanni Battista Pittoni in the main companionway were mentioned, along with the portrait of Regent Ludwig.[49]

As the VATERLAND drew closer to America, her wireless came within range of the station on Sable Island off Nova Scotia. The *Times* man sent three successive stories which were published Monday, Tuesday, and Wednesday. They told of the entertainment aboard, of the well-to-do passengers, and of the ship's fine qualities.[50]

The *Herald's* reporter, in his story printed Wednesday, May 20, provided a fact that his copy desk in New York stretched into a scare headline:

THE *VATERLAND* BARELY MISSES ICEBERG
AS PASSENGERS, UNCONSCIOUS OF PERIL, DANCE

MAIDEN departure, steerage passengers wave from well deck forward. Who said the third stack never smoked? It is exhaust from the galley (Gibbs & Cox).

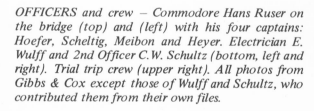

OFFICERS and crew — Commodore Hans Ruser on the bridge (top) and (left) with his four captains: Hoefer, Scheltig, Meibon and Heyer. Electrician E. Wulff and 2nd Officer C.W. Schultz (bottom, left and right). Trial trip crew (upper right). All photos from Gibbs & Cox except those of Wulff and Schultz, who contributed them from their own files.

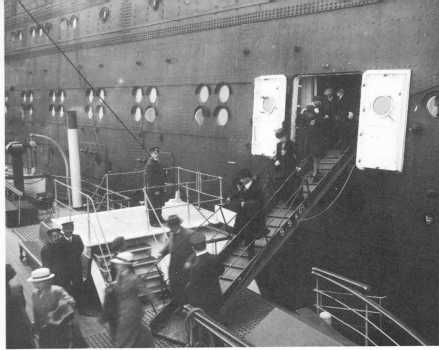

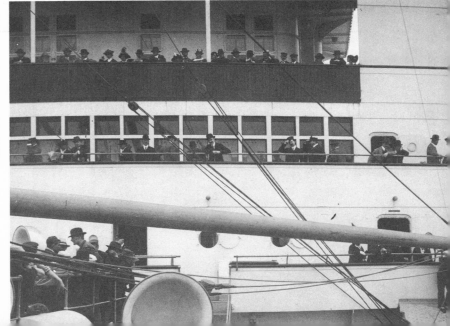

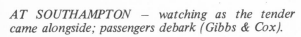

AT SOUTHAMPTON — watching as the tender came alongside; passengers debark (Gibbs & Cox).

DECK SCENES—a fancy hat (top left) and the third stack's air vents were open (above). Wonderful deck game scenes (Gibbs & Cox).

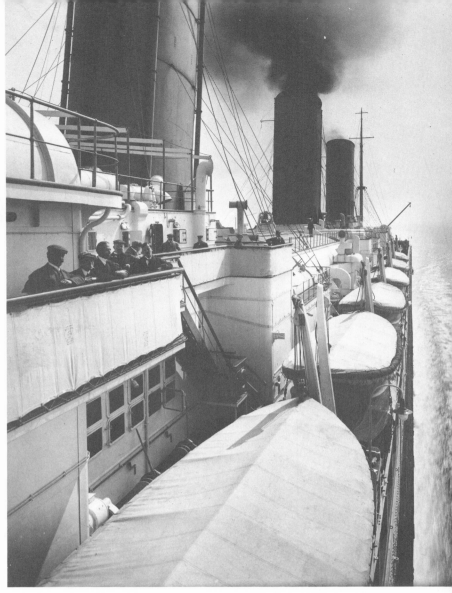

FLOWER SHOP - top deck, starboard; and dog kennel, to port. Two top deck views and the enclosed promenade (Gibbs & Cox).

THIRD CLASS (top and left) deck scenes, and passengers in Second Class playing shuffleboard (Gibbs & Cox).

NEW YORK *for the first time, off Quarantine (top), pilot coming aboard (bottom left); customs and press arrive (Gibbs & Cox).*

DOCKING—crowd at pier waiting (top left), tugs in place, heading toward pier, trouble (top right), more power, she finally heads into slip (Gibbs & Cox).

INTERIORS—Library (top left), Regent of Bavaria's portrait (2nd left), two of the "old salts" and three other views of Smoking Room (Gibbs & Cox).

SOCIAL HALL—the carved clusters on the paneling were a trademark of Schneider & Hanau, interior decorators. Note in upper left picture Gerard de Lairesse's oil of Pandora, shown in full below. It was done around 1670; was presented to VATERLAND by the Kaiser, whose bust is at bottom right (Gibbs & Cox.)

RITZ CARLTON—one of the most magnificent rooms ever built into a ship. The Palm Court (below left) and (below right) one of the Giovanna Battista Pittoni oils aboard. Painted in 1720, this painting and its twin across the foyer were known aboard as the mirror paintings because of their frames. Lord Kenneth Clark discovered this work in a Bristol wine shop. It has survived as has the other Pittoni (Gibbs & Cox).

DINING SALOON—so soon to be the mess hall for American soldiers—as seen in its full magnificence. The mural was done by a German artist named Kolmsperger (Gibbs & Cox).

SWIMMING POOL—looking smaller than it really was because of the crowd of happy VATERLAND voyagers. An arched stream of water from the cherub's penis curved into the pool (below left). The gym (right-Gibbs & Cox).

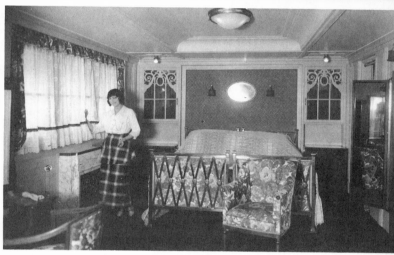

IMPERIAL SUITE—veranda and sitting room (upper left), and a "double lavatory" in a deluxe cabin (below), a cabin deluxe (upper right), bedroom of Imperial Suite (above), and cabin deluxe (below right—Gibbs & Cox).

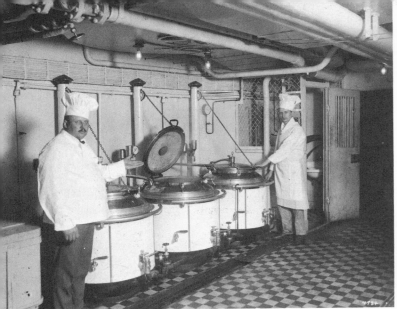

CHIEF COOK and steam soup kettles and the pantry (top–Gibbs & Cox); 2nd Class Dining Saloon (Blohm & Voss) and 2nd Class Lounge (Hapag); 2nd Class Smoking Room and 3rd Class Lounge (below–Gibbs & Cox).

STEERAGE—pride of Albert Ballin—pantry and dining room (top left and right) with kitchen (middle left) and steerage cabin (above). Large and clean washing facilities (below) were provided.

SAFETY had a high priority, with lifeboat drills (left) and exotic fire fighting equipment (middle left), not to mention the finest in radio facilities (bottom left). Commodore Ruser's clerk is using an American typewriter (Gibbs & Cox).

The story said that a "brilliant ball" was going on when warnings came by wireless that ice was drifting "perilously near" the ship's course. Commodore Ruser changed course 30 miles to the south and "remained up all night, personally overseeing every possible precaution," the story said.[51] It was illustrated by a four-column map showing the North Atlantic and charting the course of the VATERLAND to show how she had turned south. The warnings came from the Coast Guard cutter MIAMI, and Commodore Ruser sent a radio "thank you." The *Herald* reporter quoted him as saying that "everything during this voyage has been up to the fullest expectations."

Dr. Ernst Foerster, of Blohm & Voss, designer of the VATERLAND, was one of the passengers the *Herald* man had interviewed about the iceberg. He said that a berg like that which has sunk the TITANIC would not injure the VATERLAND "vitally." The TITANIC's designer, who was also aboard, said that the VATERLAND was the finest ship in the world. He was Alexander W. Carlisle, and he was also known as a great supporter of votes for women, the *Herald* story added.

The *Herald's* story had only one other brief reference to icebergs. It said the VATERLAND's great searchlight made it impossible for a good-sized snowball to escape detection.

In addition to the standard comments about the ship's spaciousness, her steadiness, and her "splendid ventilation," this account took particular note of the tub baths. In steerage these baths provoked great wonderment and were apparently considered too fine for practical use. So far only two "daring travelers in the steerage have utilized them, and each of these on one occasion only." The ventilation in the stoke hold, where the black gang shoveled at the rate of 1,100 tons of coal a day, was so good that it was described as "no hotter than the subway on a warm day." No attempt was being made to set a speed record, it was added. The run Tuesday was 580 miles. During the day the IMPERATOR passed, headed toward Germany.[52]

Water polo and other sporting events were enjoyed daily, and the voyage was enlivened by "deck tangos" with music by the ship's band. "Some striking dresses have been seen on board," the *Herald* correspondent continued, and he went on to talk of how charming Mrs. Wyvill was, in her "early Victorian dress of turquoise taffeta with a shadow lace pelisse. Ruffled tunic effects and accordion pleated skirts are features of the smartest costumes. . . . Mr. W.B. Cooke, who has made a reputation aboard as a deck dancer, has busied himself taking moving pictures and says the ordinary camera is a back number." Little Melissa Yille won the children's shoe race. A contest was held for a name for the third Hamburg-American monster ship, Hull #214. It had not as yet been decided to name her the BISMARCK. Passenger A. J. Baldwin, a lawyer from New York who was said to "lapse into poetry when dwelling upon the beauties of the VATERLAND," suggested that her sister ship be named WESTERLAND. He was sure he would win the Kaiser's 1,000-mark prize.

On Wednesday, the last full day of the maiden voyage, the VATERLAND was so close that the wireless messages from reporters aboard were sent via Siasconset, Massachusetts. There was a celebration in the Social Hall presided over by James A. Hart, from Chicago. Prizes to the winners of the deck sports competitions were given out, and addresses of congratulations were made. Magazine editor John A. Sleicher hailed Commodore Ruser "and his splendid associates on the bridge, the engineers, the pursers, the stewards, and those in every other department who have contributed to our safety and comfort." He hailed "this historic first trip," adding: "The timid and superstitious are fearful of the first voyage of a great steamship. Every ship must have its first voyage, and its first voyage has every reason to be one of its most delightful ones. The ship is always in perfect trim on its maiden voyage. The Commander and all his associates are eager to make the best record; the voyagers have a sense of fellowship peculiar to such a rare occasion, and let us not forget that on its first trip the newcomer from across the sea is assured of a reception on landing that few ever receive."[53] Mr. Sleicher praised Albert Ballin: "No matter what our flag may be, we take off our hats to that which flies over the VATERLAND and we take it off again to the virile, vigorous, earnest, commanding personality that has led the German Empire to its foremost place in the commercial and industrial world. Our country might well emulate his patriotic example."[54]

There were many other famous people aboard.

Paul J. Rainey, noted African hunter, told one reporter that he was sure that Col. Roosevelt had discovered that new river in Africa. He added that he had the fullest confidence in the truth of Roosevelt's statements.[55]

Adolph S. Ochs, of the New York *Times,* headed a group of distinguished passengers who sent a wireless to Albert Ballin late Wednesday night when the great ship was steaming along past Fire Island. She had just made her best distance in one day—592 miles. The message congratulated Ballin on the new ship, calling her "the greatest" and "the best ship afloat" and "a monument to your company's intelligent direction, its courage and enterprise."[56]

The *World* not only published a story sent Wednesday from the ship, but ran with it a lead story about her arrival, with a large photograph of the new liner. She "will swing imposingly but obediently into her berth in Hoboken at about 11 a.m. today, it is expected," the story began. The city desk man who handled this feature must have had at least some knowledge of the ways of the sea to make him attach that qualification "it is expected." And perhaps he was glad later that he had, for the docking of the VATERLAND was to turn into one of those horrible misadventures that were to plague her distinguished yet hectic career. It was one of the most awkward experiences of her life, and a sad ending to an otherwise successful maiden voyage.[57]

The Arrival

$6,000,000 SEA MONSTER *VATERLAND* TO MOVE MAJESTICALLY INTO THIS HARBOR TO-DAY

nder this imposing four-column headline the *World* ran its story of the "expected" 11 a.m. docking. Besides a picture of the new ship taken on her trials, the story included four to-scale silhouette drawings of the VATER-LAND, IMPERATOR, AQUITANIA, and LUSITANIA, showing their respective lengths of 950, 919, 901, and 790 feet. The story compared the tonnages of the VATERLAND and AQUITANIA, which up to then had been thought to be close rivals on this score. The German ship was described as being of 58,000 tons, while the new British liner "which will claim New York's attention within a few days" was only 47,000 tons.[58] Both figures were exaggerated, but the ratio was about correct. The final accepted tonnage of the VATER-LAND was 54,281.718.[59] The AQUITANIA's tonnage was 45,647.[60]

It was still dark on the Atlantic not far from Ambrose Lightship when a tiny pilot yawl left the Sandy Hook pilot boat and headed toward a monstrous black bulk of a ship ablaze with thousands of lights. Aboard the pilot yawl it was assumed that she was the VATERLAND, and Pilot John F. McCarthy was in turn for her, so off he went. As the yawl approached the dark hull, Pilot McCarthy saw that she was not slowing down very much. She was the VATERLAND all right, and her speed would make it what pilots called a "hot pickup." The yawl approached and came close up under the starboard side, with young George J. Madigan and another apprentice pilot pulling furiously on the oars to get into position. An oblong of bright yellow opened up quite high in the vast hull. It was the G Deck side port forward, and its great steel doors swung out, showing a passageway straight across the ship. The port was three decks above the splashing waterline, and out of it a German sailor leaned with a coil of rope in his hand.

The most dangerous part of the whole operation was lashing this rope around the yawl's "span." A span was a sturdy crosspiece of wood used to hoist the little craft aboard the pilot boat. Taking the line, George Madigan deftly made a couple of lightning turns around the span. It took him a couple of seconds, but there was grave risk of losing a hand in the process if he wasn't nimble, for once the rope was secure, it carried the whole weight of the yawl.[6 1]

Then a rope ladder came slapping down, smelling tarred and new. Eager hands helped Pilot McCarthy up, and he disappeared through the yellow port. The line was let loose and the yawl drew away, fast! The great steel doors clanged shut and the VATERLAND continued on via Ambrose Channel into the Upper Bay and toward the Narrows. She passed Sandy Hook to port and a few scattered lights marking Coney Island and Gravesend Bay to the starboard. It was now getting light fast, and as the proud new liner neared the Narrows, small crowds of people could be seen on either side. Fort Hamilton, on the Brooklyn shore, was dotted with watchers. Fort Wadsworth, too, on the Staten Island side, had many people looking, including an excited Army corporal and his family. The corporal was of German stock and he had been talking of nothing but the VATERLAND for days on end. Everything had stopped that morning in the six-family house in the fort where Corporal Miller lived with his wife and son Alfred. Young Alfred never forgot how close the liner seemed as she moved slowly past one of the fort's old 10-inch gun emplacements.[6 2]

The VATERLAND dropped anchor at Quarantine just inside Fort Wadsworth, and a large cutter from the Battery came up alongside to let Customs inspectors, company officials, and ship news reporters aboard. They did it through the same side port that Pilot McCarthy had used, but instead of a rope ladder, the cutter's wooden ladder was employed, much safer. It was 8 a.m. and the brilliant morning sun glistened on the thousands of ink-black rivet heads in the huge, towering hull. Uniformed Hapag officers stood in the port to help as the good-sized party climbed aboard. An American Press Association photographer stood back a way on the cutter's top deck and snapped a photo of the officials boarding. It was used the next day in the New York *Times*. The same photographer hurried aboard and busied himself making other pictures. He found a charming young lady passenger from Brooklyn and photographed her with her German police dog. Commodore Ruser was smiling when the photographer took his picture on the bridge.[6 3] After the medical formalities were completed and the Quarantine launch had gone back to its Rosebank station on Staten Island, the huge ship, now bedecked with flags from bow to stern, began her stately progress up the Lower Bay toward the Battery and Hoboken. It was 8:50 a.m.

A large fleet of small boats surrounded her, and others were approaching. One of the most interesting of these was a little vessel owned by John A. Nernoff. She was called the JOHNNY N., and was only 16 feet long. But she had a steam engine in her and a brave smokestack. Mr. Nernoff, a steam engineer, ran her himself. She had a soft coal bunker forward and he had to sit on one side, steering with a side tiller so he could feed coal into the boiler with his free hand. The JOHNNY N. led the parade down to meet the new VATERLAND—the smallest steamboat in the world and the largest. When her shrill, screaming little steam whistle saluted, someone on the VATERLAND's bridge heard, or perhaps someone saw the puff of white steam from her thin little stack, but anyway the huge whistle on the forward stack of the new liner boomed out a reply. It was a great moment for Nernoff. He had made the steam engine in his tiny craft by himself, using a section of seamless sewer pipe with its top riveted on for his boiler. She could make six knots, but very soon was left behind in the VATERLAND's wake as larger, faster harbor craft took up the saluting on up the Bay towards New York's skyline.[64]

Approaching the Battery, where waited the largest crowd ever to see a new ship arrive, the VATERLAND was saluted by her companion liner, the gaily dressed PRESIDENT LINCOLN, outward bound and with her rails lined with passengers and her band playing "Die Wacht Am Rhin." The VATERLAND's passengers echoed the strains of this stirring anthem as the two ships passed.[65] One of the throng at the Battery was George F. Weber, who had sailed past the ship's stern after her launching in Hamburg harbor a year before.[66] Perhaps some of the Hapag people aboard were seeing the Woolworth Building, the world's tallest, for the first time. They had repeatedly used illustrations of it with the VATER-LAND rising alonside it on her stern to show her great length, for the new liner would have been 200 feet taller if stood on end. And on went the procession up to the flag-decorated Hoboken, New Jersey, terminal just this side of the high land on which Colonel John Stevens had built his mansion after the American Revolution. All went well, and the great ship turned and was slowly maneuvered into position for docking. A fleet of 14 tugs were in position and helping. At nearby piers were the Hapag liners AMERIKA and BATAVIA, also bedecked with flags and crowded with cheering figures. The sun shone and everything was going magnificently. It was 9:30 a.m.

The Docking

early four hours later, after experiencing the most difficult docking operation the port of New York had ever seen, or ever would, for that matter, the new liner was finally tied up at Pier 2, Hoboken. And all her detractors had just what they wanted to bolster the public impression that, like the IMPERATOR before her, the VATERLAND was ungainly, too big, poorly handled, and in no way equal to the sleek British sea queens like the MAURETANIA, the OLYMPIC, and the forthcoming AQUITANIA. And they made the most of it:

"The VATERLAND. . .was an unhappy bumbler from the start. . . .

"On her first visit to New York, the grandeur of her carefully planned introduction was marred considerably when she barged all over the harbor like a drunken sailor. Her intractability gave rise to a spate of charges and counter-charges among the steamship fraternity [and] New York City harbor officials, and hilarity in the press."

So wrote the noted shipping publicist and marine artist William Seabrook in his as-yet-unplublished book on ship news reporters entitled "The Seven O'Clock Cutter."[67] The New York *Herald's* story of what happened was a trifle kinder:

"The Hamburg leviathan had the longest and hardest docking in fair weather the port every saw."[68] Several other news stories used the descriptive noun "leviathan" on this occasion.

The New York *Tribune's* story was kinder, and fairer:

"Under trying circumstances which called forth to the fullest his splendid seamanship, Captain Hans Ruser put his 54,000-ton charge in to her dock in Hoboken yesterday without a scratch."[69]

What actually happened was in no way the responsibility of Commodore Ruser or Hapag. Every precaution had been taken to insure an easy docking, even to the construction of several high-powered tugs by Hapag and the addition of an extension onto the pier itself.[70] The slip to the south of Pier 2 had been deepened by weeks of costly dredging. Commodore Ruser had years of experience in docking ships at New York, and, of course, had been on the IMPERATOR for her seven successful arrivals in 1913. The pilot, John F. McCarthy, was one of the ablest of Sandy Hook pilots and knew the currents inside and out, but his responsibilities ended when the tug docking pilot came aboard. Unfortunately, this gentleman's name has been lost, or perhaps fortunately, for the docking pilot is the man who actually directs the placing and use of the tugs and orders what assistance he needs from the ship's own propellers. The main channel into New York and up the Hudson had been deepened to 40 feet for the arrival of the MAURETANIA and LUSITANIA seven years before. The Hudson River is continuously depositing vast amounts of silt along this channel and continual dredging is necessary. The VATERLAND's draft of 36½ feet gave her only 3½ feet of clearance in the deepest part of the harbor, if it was as deep as it was supposed to be, which is unlikely. But outside the channel there were shallows all over the port.

When the VATERLAND had entered misty New York harbor early that morning, she had been met by an outbound tide, which was made doubly troublesome by the current of the outward-flowing Hudson and by a stiff wind blowing downriver. The arrival had been planned to coincide with the slack tide, the point at which the tide has stopped and has not yet begun to run the other way. This would have taken place at 10 a.m., the time Commodore Ruser specified in a wireless to the New York *Herald* that he expected to dock.[71] As it was, the ship was ready, in position, heading into Pier 2 with just a hundred feet to go at 9:30 a.m.

At this juncture, and apparently from out of nowhere, there appeared between the VATERLAND and the pier a small tug laboring upstream with a tow of barges. As the VATERLAND began to move very slowly in toward her pier, the tug suddenly lost her headway and began to drift toward the bow of the new liner. To avoid a collision the docking pilot stopped the VATERLAND's propellers. The tug and her barges were saved and got out of the way. Later the tug's captain insisted that he had not caused the VATERLAND's problem, but rather that she had nosed into the mud "through extreme caution" and had had to go astern on that account.[72]

Whatever the cause, and everyone else agreed it was the tug, the huge liner lay there dead in the water, without headway and at the mercy of the last vestiges of the outgoing tide, the Hudson currents, and the tremendous wind. Imagine a sign board nearly 1,000 feet long, the bulk of it rising twelve stories high. This was the surface that the VATERLAND presented broadside to the gusty force of the Hudson wind. She began slipping sideways downriver. The 14 tugs at hand were divided into three fleets: five were pulling with hawsers from the ship at the bow. Three were on the starboard side guiding her. Six were along her port holding her against the tide, current, and wind. More tugs quickly joined her until there were 15 on the port side, but still she slipped, her stern edging around downstream and her bulk moving slowly in toward the 27-foot-deep Lackawanna ferry channel.

Time seemed to stand still. The waiting crowds on Piers 1 and 2, the white-jacketed stewards lining the rails of the other Hapag ships, the gay groups of welcoming dignitaries on the excursion boats and other surrounding craft, the crews of the laboring tugs, and the hundreds watching from across the Hudson—all could see that the VATERLAND was in trouble. Dock Commissioner R.A.C. Smith, who had gone down with the Customs cutter, was aboard the VATERLAND. He was agreeing with ship news reporters and others who were saying that there ought to be more regulation of harbor traffic. New York's tug population numbered well over 300 boats in those days, and some had so little power that they could pull barges only if they went with the current. They were continually getting in the way of incoming liners. Then there were another 500-odd craft of all sorts, some self-propelled and others without power, crisscrossing and being towed up and down the harbor day and night.[73] It was a nightmare for liners.

The VATERLAND was finally brought to a stop after she had drifted stern first so that half her length was below the first of the three Lackawanna ferry slips. Her propellers had been churning up great swirls of dark black mud, for she was barely feet away from the mounts of silt that might have trapped her for hours. Just how many tugs came to her aid is uncertain. The lowest figure mentioned is in a *Times* report which says there were 25 "employed." Other reports say 50 tugs came to help. Slowly the huge hull was given headway against current and wind. The tide had changed a long time back and its incoming thrust helped. By 12:15 the VATERLAND was again in position to dock, not an easy maneuver for such a large ship, for by their nature New York piers are hard to get into. They are of the so-called "finger" type. They jut out from shore at right angles, in contrast to the marginal piers found in most seaports. In 1914, with 5,000- and 10,000-ton ships still the rule, the slips, or spaces between piers, were often very narrow, and, when another ship was in the slip of the next pier, the maneuvering space for a 100-foot-wide, 50,000-ton liner was very limited. The tugs on the pier side as the VATERLAND approached had to be very cautious not to become trapped between the ship and the pier. They would have been crushed like matchwood. The tugs on the outer side had to be careful that their propellers and stern didn't scrape against the 10,500-ton BATAVIA, across from which the VATER-LAND would tie up. The much larger AMERIKA was berthed on the north side of Pier 2, safely out of reach. Tugs on the bow could stay there until the great hull was almost in the slip, but then would have to back away so as not to be knifed up against the shore end of the slip. The stern of the VATERLAND overhung the lengthened end of Pier 2 and stuck out into the Hudson by 25 feet. This left her four propellers, which were not very far below the surface, in a position of potential danger. Should a tug or barge edge past too closely, the tips of these 18½-foot propellers might be bent, a most costly event. To protect them, Hapag had ordered several lighters to stand by. When at 1:20 the great new liner was finally made fast, these lighters were hurried into position by tugs to serve as a buffer around the ship's stern and protect her wheels.[74]

The MAURETANIA, arriving the same day, docked without difficulty at her pier in lower Manhattan.

But the day was not over for the VATERLAND, and not lost, either. Charming Olga Schaetz was there to sing the German national anthem as she had done at the launching. She had come over especially for this and would remain to become an American and establish a dancing school in the Yorkville section of New York City.[75] The positive accomplishments of the maiden voyage made headlines. She had averaged 23.2 knots from Cherbourg to Sandy Hook, taking 5 days, 17 hours. During the trip she consumed 1,157 tons of coal a day.[76] Long columns on the wonders of the new ship appeared in all the papers, and some facts turned up that even the Hapag publicists had not included in their advance publicity. For example, it was noted that buckwheat cakes were turned and browned by an electrical device in the VATERLAND's all-electric galley; that the center alleyway running through the ship was 391 feet long; that there were 800 water jets for use in case of fire; that she was equipped with fireproof glass doors that would stand a temperature of 1,000 degrees; and that on her return voyage her passengers would be able to telephone to Hamburg "from a distance of 100 miles at sea" via the ship's wireless.[77]

Alexander Carlisle, who was continually being asked for quotations by the press because of his association with the TITANIC, summed it up by saying:

"The VATERLAND is the most wonderful ship afloat and she won't be surpassed in my time."[78]

Perhaps the most glowing tribute, however, came from outside New York. The *Germania-Herold,* of Milwaukee, carried a front-page article hailing the new ship in extravagant terms. The editor of the German-language paper wanted more than just a picture of the VATERLAND. He instructed his artist to cut out a photo of the Statue of

Liberty and superimpose it on the VATERLAND's foredeck between her mast and bridge, and this is how it appeared, with an artistically decorated frame around the whole.[79]

It had been an exciting day back in Hamburg for Albert Ballin and Marianne, his wife. They had entertained the Kaiser and his entourage at a gala luncheon at the Ballin mansion in the Feldbrunnenstrasse. Afterwards Ballin joined the Kaiser aboard the imperial yacht HOHENZOLLERN and sailed for Kiel. It may be that he received news of the VATER-LAND's unfortunate arrival experience while still in the Kaiser's company.[80]

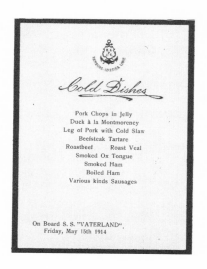

Chapter V

SIX MORE CROSSINGS

hese boys, of course, will never have a ship like this," said Commodore Ruser, speaking in German so a group of young American lads from the New York State Schoolship NEWPORT would not understand what he was saying. But one did, and it became a prime motivating factor in a career that was to be one of the most brilliant in American maritime annals. The schoolship boys were on the bridge of the VATERLAND, among the first to get a tour on Friday, May 22. The 17-year-old who understood Commodore Ruser had been born in Germany of a German mother and a British father. Nine years later he would be second officer of this very ship, and later her staff captain. He would also become famous as Amelia Earhart's navigator, and would climax his career as master of the super liner UNITED STATES on her maiden voyage in 1952 when she broke all existing speed records. He was Harry Manning.[1]

The VATERLAND made a great impression during the five days of her first visit. Virtually everyone knew, for example, that if she was placed on Fifth Avenue she would block 42nd, 43rd, 44th, and 45th streets. Perhaps for the city's sake it was fortunate that all the good pier locations on the Manhattan side of the Hudson had been taken by British, French, and American ship lines and that the VATERLAND had to be over in Hoboken. Otherwise she would have been overwhelmed with visitors. As it was, there were always crowds aboard her and watching whatever went on around her. While the schoolship boys were aboard, ten patented DeMayo System coal-loading devices were brought alongside and in 21 hours they loaded 8,500 tons of coal "automatically." Although billed as "foolproof" and a great advance over coaling by hand, they were cumbersome at best. Ten enclosed elevators were rigged over three wooden coal barges. A conveyer belt-drum combination lifted the coal about 30 feet and dumped it into a wide-mouthed chute leading down to the ship's side ports on H Deck. The elevators were suspended over the barges by wooden booms fitted into the VATERLAND's side along D Deck.[2]

On Saturday a luncheon was held aboard for 500 steamship agents and V.I.P. guests. Two comments made at that luncheon have come down through the years.

Dr. Karl Bünz, Hapag's New York representative, urged the agents to help make the VATERLAND a commercial success, driving his point home with a quaint concluding plea: "You need not be afraid of ever feeding her for she has great capacity and an excellent digestion." The New York *Tribune's* reporter scribbled these words down and they appeared in his story the next day.[3] The *Times'* story missed this quote but carried an interview with the VATERLAND's designer Foerster. It was not until shortly after World War I had ended that the second conversation came to public notice, and it may be somewhat suspect on this account. Admiral Albert Gleaves was at that lunch and he sat next to one of the officials of Hapag. Being of a military mind, the Admiral asked this German how many troops the VATERLAND could carry.

"Ten thousand, and we built her to bring them over here," came the reply as Admiral Gleaves remembered it. The German smiled as he said this, the Admiral also noticed.

"When they come we will be here to meet them," Admiral Gleaves replied, also with a smile.[4]

Admiral Gleaves was head of the Brooklyn Navy Yard. Later he would head the United States Navy's Transport Service. Even before he put his "10,000 troops" story on paper, he must have told it many times, and one person who heard it made it a part of a 1919 newspaper article. As evidence of how such word-of-mouth stories tend to grow in the telling, this account has the German starting the conversation and saying after one of the speeches extolling the VATERLAND:

"And the best thing about her is her ability to carry 10,000 troops."

This version came from Captain W.W. Phelps, one of the ship's Navy commanders during the war, but to it he added one important paragraph:

"But there was no evidence anywhere in the VATERLAND that, in her design or building, special adaptations or fittings were provided with a view to any abnormally rapid transformation from the passenger-carrying steamer into the transport. No stateroom bulkheads were fitted so as to be removed in any other way than by ruthless destruction. No magazines for powder and shell and no ammunition hoists were built in. No gun emplacements were fitted and structurally strengthened. All of these things we had to do."[5]

Despite the few such seeds of enmity that some planted during the VATERLAND's first stay in New York, there was a warm flowering of good will. German-Americans were proud of the new ship and came in droves to see her. Henry Minke was an example. A saloon keeper from Yorkville, he brought his nephew, Ralph Pontifex. Although Ralph was only nine, he was impressed by the contrast between the luxurious suites and the barren steerage facilities. He liked the ship's band, but he remembered best the enormous anchors.[6] Mr. Minke and Ralph were among the 17,000 people who came aboard on Sunday. They paid 50 cents each for the benefit of widows and orphans of German seamen.[7]

Trouble was brewing, however, among the crew members. The possibility of a strike became more and more evident. The day after the ship arrived the stewards and firemen held a grievance meeting in Hoboken, and on the next day another. Sunday night they met aboard the ship, and on the following day their story was in all the papers. The stewards were earning 50 to 60 marks ($12 to $14.40) a month and demanded 80 marks ($19.29). The firemen, who were getting 83 marks ($19.92) were asking 110 ($26.40). The men were also complaining about their quarters. As many as 50 had to sleep in one compartment and the ventilation was bad, they said. The ship was due to sail at 10 a.m. on Tuesday and there was talk that the firemen and stewards might refuse to work.[8]

Meanwhile, on Monday, the last full day in port, another luncheon was held aboard. Although Hoboken's Mayor Mitchell missed the lunch, some 60 more than the 500 who had been invited showed up and the affair was a great success. The German ambassador, Count von Bernstorff, spoke, as did Commodore Ruser. When cornered by the press after the meal, the Commodore was asked about the possible strike. He said that the problem would be settled in Hamburg, adding that anyone who walked off the ship would be considered a deserter.[9]

Another Black Eye

s if the very difficult docking had not been enough, the VATERLAND was to endure another humiliation that was even worse. As a prelude of things to come, the Monday evening *World* had a story filled with nerve-titillating problems for the VATERLAND's cheering section.

Problem I — The *World* let it be known that the MAURETANIA was "crammed with coal" and that the Liverpool Irishmen in her stokeholds were "grasping their shovels with determination and fire in their eyes," eager to show the VATERLAND that they could catch and pass her. The Hapag liner had been ordered to sail eight hours ahead of the Cunarder, and this, it was figured by the *World*, would give her a handicap of 180 miles over the Britisher.

Problem II — William E. Cleary, "a crusty old-line New York harbor barge operator," complained that liners like the VATERLAND should not be permitted to "invade the

Hudson" to endanger small craft. They ought to dock in Bay Ridge. Commodore Ruser, asked for a response, condemned the lack of control of small craft in the port and emphasized that in Hamburg the harbor boats were cleared out of the path of big ships.

Problem III — The crew dispute on the VATERLAND continued right up to 8 p.m. the night before her departure, and it was settled only after the Commodore had given his pledge that the differences would be adjusted when the ship got to Hamburg.[10]

The 10 a.m. sailing time had been determined by the tides and by the fact that the MAURETANIA was sailing on the same day. It was not a convenient time for a big ship's departure, particularly one with 2,307 passengers. Everyone who was sailing had to be up early. Many chose to be late, and the scene aboard was "almost of panic proportions," one reporter wrote. Two women fainted in the main saloon because of the crush. Another passenger was overcome by the heat and had to be carried to his stateroom. Many who had planned to see friends off never made it, because the ferry from Manhattan was all snarled up by long lines of autos on the New York side. Even some passengers were caught in these lines and several had to abandon their cars and go aboard the ferries on foot. Some even had to leave some of their baggage in their cars, hoping it could be brought over by friends. Two automobile loads of passengers arrived at 10:10. They stood forlornly on the pier and watched the ship leave. What they saw was a disaster.

No one except a very few on the VATERLAND's bridge and in her engine room ever really knew what happened. When she pulled away sternfirst from the slip at Hoboken, she did so with a burst of speed, and she continued right across the Hudson. She did not slow down until her stern ran into the mud and silt of the slip between Piers 50 and 51 at the foot of Jane Street in Greenwich Village. The Morgan Line, a coastwise passenger and freight company serving between New York and New Orleans, occupied these piers. The pier ends, the slip between, and the bulkhead at the end of the slip were crowded with barges and assorted small craft. At the piers were the Morgan steamers TOPILA and EL VALE. Finally the VATERLAND's propellers seemed to gain control, and as they sucked in the shallow water in a powerful effort to reverse the ship's motion, both Morgan liners were literally torn loose from their piers, their hawsers snapping with loud reports. The tremendous suction of the VATERLAND's great power pulled them from their berths. The barge ULSTER, with 799 tons of coal, was swamped in the upheaval, her captain jumping to the pier just in time. The railroad tug FREEPORT, also caught in the backwash, was almost overturned, and one of her engineers fell overboard and could not be found.[11] Finally the two Morgan ships were thrown back onto their piers, smashing bulkheads, rails, and stanchions like matchwood.

"Both vessels looked as if they had been toyed with by a typhoon when the VATERLAND finished paying her parting respects," said the *World*.[12] Only two tugs had been ordered for the undocking, as it had been felt that this would be a simple operation requiring little help. They tried valiantly to halt the liner as she raced sternfirst across the Hudson. Finally, as she came to a halt amid a pool of wreckage, they managed to turn her and head her down river. After this performance, the reading public was probably ready to accept almost any exaggeration as fact, and the *World's* man didn't let it down.

"Captain Hans Ruser of the VATERLAND had sworn an oath that he would not be passed by the MAURETANIA. The VATERLAND sailed at 10 o'clock, and the MAURE- TANIA is to go out at 6 this evening. With such a handicap to overcome, Captain Ruser figures that the MAURETANIA will never overtake him, but he is not taking any chances and he started the VATERLAND out of the harbor, crowded as it is with ferryboats and tugs, at a speed of 18 knots." This was an exaggeration, and the reporter compounded the felony by saying a few paragraphs later that a tug came alongside off the foot of Liberty Street and took a man off who had not heard the "All Ashore" warning. This was done "while the VATERLAND was going 18 knots," he repeated. For the liner to get up to such a speed in that distance was an impossibility, but it would have been even more impossible for a tug to come alongside with safety, let alone make a transfer, at 18 knots. Adding insult to injury, the *World's* headline must have turned Albert Ballin's hair white:

BIG LINER VATERLAND
SMASHES SHIPPING IN
GETTING OUT OF PORT
She Runs Amuck, Sinks Two Coal
Barges, and Her Wash Slams Two
Morgan Line Freight Steamers Up
Against Piers, Crushing Bulkheads,
Rails and Stanchions.[13]

The headlines in the New York *Tribune* for the next morning were equally damning:

VATERLAND TERROR
OF NORTH RIVER

Big Liner Sinks Coal Barge
And Causes Panic In
Sailing From Port[14]

Whereas the *World's* estimate of the damage had been $20,000, by the following morning the estimate had dropped to only $5,000.

Aboard the VATERLAND there was little excitement, because relatively few people were on deck and saw what was happening. There was some brief alarm but no panic, and once the ship was back in midstream and heading in the right direction, the near-disaster was quickly forgotten. Earl Grey, a British diplomat, was a passenger. It was he who, three months later, would utter the famous words: "The lights are going out all over Europe."[15] Completely ignorant of what had happened, large crowds watched at the Battery and other vantage points as the VATERLAND sailed. A 9½-year-old boy waited for nearly an hour on an elevated station platform in Brooklyn to see her sail past Governors Island. John Carrothers' mother waited patiently with him, and neither had any notion that this ship would be his home for a good part of his early working career.[16]

The New York *Herald's* story on the following day maintained that there had been a misunderstanding between the bridge and the engine room, adding that the representatives of Hapag would not even discuss the matter except to say it would be investigated in Hamburg.[17] The possibility that there might have been a steering fault rather than an engine mistake was suggested years later when it was discovered that the telemotor, which controlled the steering gear, was not properly wired. This problem had existed since the ship's first trials and had been a continuous troublemaker in her navigation.[18] Whatever the cause, it is certain that the precipitate dash sternward across the Hudson resulted in serious damage to the VATERLAND's astern turbines, the beginning of a problem that bothered her for much of her career. If Commodore Ruser or someone on the bridge, in a moment of alarm, ordered full ahead while the ship was going full astern, and if the engineers attempted to carry out this abrupt change, the resulting crisis situation would have stripped her reverse turbine blades. By the end of her seventh crossing they were damaged beyond repair. It seems likely that on the last six of these Atlantic crossings she was driven with little or no reverse capabilities.[19]

Sometime very early in the morning on Wednesday, May 27, the VATERLAND's printer made a mistake. He ran off the English menu for breakfast under the heading "Fruhstuck" and, on the other side he printed the German menu under the heading "Breakfast." Disgruntled, he tucked the mistake behind his press. Three years later, almost to the day, it was found by an American bluejacket and stashed away as a souvenir.[20] The menu was a one-fold affair on light-colored cardboard. It had a thick gold edging and the Hapag seal in gold on the top over the large script "Breakfast." It offered 78 different items under 11 headings: five kinds of fruit, six egg or omelet dishes, four types of fish, 11 roasts, six types of potatoes, eleven cold dishes, and three cheeses.

Homeward Bound

A s the VATERLAND sped toward England, many people aboard were conscious of the MAURETANIA somewhere astern doing her best to catch up. Stagger the sailings, warn the captains, do what you could but this still was a race, with the newest luxury liner and the world's largest ship pitted against the famous greyhound of the Atlantic and holder of all ocean speed records. On Friday, May 28, three faraway events happened, all of which had unfortunate repercussions for the new liner. The least of them was a newspaper report in New York that said Hapag was considering building a landing stage for the VATERLAND north of the Hoboken piers. This was an echo of her sad docking and undocking experiences.[21] On the same day, off Sandy Hook a pilot yawl picked up the body of the tug *Freeport's* engineer, lost when the VATERLAND's suction nearly sank his craft.[22] Also on the same day, the 15,857-ton Canadian Pacific liner EMPRESS OF IRELAND was struck and sunk by a Norse freighter in a bad fog. She took down with her 1,387 lives, only 115 fewer than had been lost on the TITANIC. No one on either the VATERLAND or the MAURETANIA was told about the tragedy, but virtually all newspaper talk of a race between the two liners suddenly was dropped.[23]

During the night of May 30 the VATERLAND, the tops of her yellow funnels smeared with black coal soot from the windy Atlantic passage, passed the four-stacked AQUITANIA. Since she was on her maiden voyage too, the new Cunarder's orange-red and black stacks were still clean and her thousands of lights shone as she headed westward out over the Atlantic. What a sight it would have been if some Jules Verne had been in a balloon over the two wonderful ships, and what a sad comparison their careers were to provide—the German doomed to a controversial, rough-and-tumble life of ups and downs, the Britisher headed for a life of phenomenal success and service. Readers of that week's *The Sphere*, a popular British picture magazine, saw a full-page drawing comparing the two new giantesses in point of size, and here everything favored the VATERLAND. The page showed a huge set of scales with the VATERLAND on one side and the AQUITANIA on the other, with the little ST. LOUIS sitting next to her. The caption noted that the tonnage of the German liner "approximately equals the tonnage of the AQUITANIA plus the well-known American liner ST. LOUIS."[24]

The London correspondent of the New York *Tribune* cabled home on June 2 that the race had been won by the MAURETANIA. The Cunarder's passengers were in London at 5:45 p.m. on June 1, while those from the VATERLAND did not arrive until 8:30 p.m. But the London story did add that the VATERLAND had covered a longer distance "and, moreover, stopped at Cherbourg" as well, while the MAURETANIA had made no other stops. Working backward it would seem that the two ships maintained about the same time separation all the way across the Atlantic. The MAURETANIA unloaded her London passengers at Fishguard, Cunard's stop on eastbound crossings, at about 2:45 p.m.[25] The

VATERLAND reached Southampton at 6 p.m., having spent five hours coming from Cherbourg, at least two hours at that port unloading her France-bound passengers, and another five hours getting to Cherbourg after passing St. David's Head, near Fishguard. Although this might even be made to look like a possible victory for the VATERLAND, the only known report of her average speed for this first round trip indicates she made 22.4 knots, somewhat below the normal average maintained by the MAURETANIA.[26] The *Tribune's* report said there were many bets on the race and that both "boats" had good weather coming across.[27] Out of it all, however, came the realization that the VATERLAND was not just a big ship, but that she might be a contender for the speed crown. As if to support this idea, the IMPERATOR reached New York June 3 having averaged 23.20 knots. Dock Commissioner Smith went down to meet her in a police launch and escorted her up to her pier. The *Times* took occasion to boast that "this was the result, it was said, of the article in the N.Y. *Times* commenting on the four hours' delay in docking the VATERLAND and calling attention to the fact that New York had no harbor master or any authority afloat to see that the big liners got the right of way."[28]

The AQUITANIA had her day on June 5. Her average speed of 23.65 showed that she too must be considered a potential record-breaker. Captain William Thomas Turner, who would next command the ill-fated LUSITANIA, was on her bridge as she slipped easily into Pier 54, at the foot of 11th Street. With the VATERLAND's docking disaster fresh in everyone's mind, the *Sun* seemed to delight in describing how the Cunarder did it in only 20 minutes, hailing the "marvelous celerity" of the maneuver. Captain Turner "brought her in like a duck paddling up to a float in a placid lake and put her in like a canoe. . .ship-shape and Bristol fashion," the afternoon paper said.[29]

Maritime publicist and author William Seabrook is even harsher:

"In sharp contrast to the VATERLAND's clownish behavior in the port, the AQUITANIA's handling was a model of quiet efficiency. . . .Cunard has taken great pains to ensure that this would be so. She was like a floating stately home of England, which was indeed the theme of her decor. An aura of dignified exclusiveness surrounded her throughout her career.[30]

As if to rub it in, the AQUITANIA sailed without using a single tug. The "whoops of self-satisfaction" in England could be heard all the way across the Atlantic, British marine historian Leslie Reade wrote.[31]

Back in Cuxhaven the VATERLAND on June 6 boarded 1,863 passengers and sailed on her second voyage. She arrived in New York on June 13, docking in an hour and a half without incident. The only excitement was the echoes of a shipboard brawl between card-players. It had been serious enough to make Commodore Ruser radio ahead for detectives to meet the ship at Quarantine. It all started when eight passengers become involved in a game called Rocky Mountain Bill. Five of them, headed by a lanky Texan, suspected the other three of being professional gamblers. There were rumors that one of the players had lost $1,500 in the game and another had dropped a thousand. The Texas was determined to thrash someone and stood in wait for one of his opponents in D Deck Square near the elevators. One of them appeared and the Southerner jumped him, struck him and knocked him down. They were pulled apart. When two of New York's "finest" arrived, it turned out that the three suspects were quite legitimate passengers. The Texan and his friends quieted down and no one pressed charges.[32]

Bookings for the next eastbound crossing were excellent, and Hapag's New York office began to settle back in anticipation of the best summer in many a year. Their advertisements proudly showed a pen sketch of the VATERLAND framed in a long, hull-shaped outline, their trademark. It looked like a ship, with the pointed bow at the top. The sketch showed the VATERLAND with all three of her stacks throwing out smoke in a most impressive, if untruthful, way, for the third, of course, was a dummy. There was no thought of air pollution in those days. Smoke meant power. The ads all boasted about Hapag being the largest steamship company in the world, and they offered a variety of interesting cruises as well as the transatlantic service. For $75 a voyager could make an 18-day cruise to Cuba, Jamaica, and the Panama Canal, with meals *a la carte.* Many decades later this concept was introduced as brand new. Defying the conservative tradition of most ship lines, the Hapag advertisements even listed the company's phone number. It was "1900 Rector."[33]

Adverse winds and tide delayed the second eastbound departure by an hour on June 16, but no one worried because she had a grand, big passenger list—3,151 voyagers.[34] Also sailing the same day were the North German Lloyd's KRONPRINZESSIN CECILIE and the MAURETANIA. These two racy four-stackers together carried fewer than 3,000, good evidence that the VATERLAND's glamour had not been tarnished much by her first-trip troubles. One famous lady on the VATERLAND's celebrity-studded list was Madame Schumann-Heink. She was sailing with her two children and would say only three words to the press:

"No more husbands!"[35]

Ambassador Count Bernstorff was aboard with many of his staff, among them his young and dashing aide, Captain Karl Boy-ed. Also sailing was international trader Frederick S. Haas with his family. A few moments after the ship left her pier, when all the cheering and flag-waving had died down, the Haas family bumped into the Count, somewhat to the annoyance of Mr. Haas. Some weeks before, the German had tried to rent the Haas home in Cedarhurst, L.I., as a summer embassy. Mr. Haas had not liked the hand-kissing and other attentions that Count Bernstorff had showered on Mrs. Haas, and he had deliberately set such a high rent that Bernstorff had gone elsewhere. And now again Mrs. Haas was being greeted by the hand-kissing and heel-clicking routine. The two older Haas daughters, Sarah and Helen, who secretly admired the tall, blond Boy-ed, took it all in with great pleasure.[36]

Sarah and her sisters (the youngest was Edith) had a cabin to themselves with a couch and two large beds. Their Irish nurse was aboard, but no governess. Their stateroom was fitted out in French walnut with rose velvet drapes. The girls were heading for school in Switzerland. Sarah, who spoke what she called "stage German," had no trouble getting along with the waiters and stewards. She had a marvelous time, one continuous "gala." She resented being invited to the children's parties, which were held daily, and was flattered to be the only girl member of a group of boys ranging in age from 14 to 18. For some reason they called themselves the "White Rats." They played cops and robbers all day, chasing among the lifeboats and around the great yellow stacks, and stayed up late each evening, singing and skittering around the upper deck, with a little smoking on the sly. Once they paused long enough to let someone make a snapshot of the group on the prom deck, Sarah in the center.[37] Among the club members were George Schumann, son of Mme. Schumann-Heink; Frank Hoffman, son of the famous singer's accompanist; and Gerald Haxton, later to be a close friend of Somerset Maugham and still later to commit suicide. For the adult passengers a high point of the voyage was the concert by Mme. Schumann-Heink.

On Saturday, June 20, as the VATERLAND was approaching England, the third of Albert Ballin's gigantic liners was launched at Hamburg, and again bad luck seemed the order of the day. The Countessa Hanna Bismarck, granddaughter of the German leader, had been invited to christen the new ship to be named in his honor. She was on hand with a distinguished throng which included Albert Ballin and the Kaiser. The Countessa was given the signal to go ahead; she shouted out the ship's name and hit the hull with the champagne bottle, but it failed to break. This was long before the easy-breaking bottle had been devised for such occasions. Aware that such a failure was believed by many to be a bad omen, the

Kaiser himself grabbed the bottle from the flustered countessa and flung it at the ship's bulk as it began to move. The bottle broke, and Ballin had three 50,000-tonners in the water. Unfortunately, he would not be alive when the BISMARCK made her first voyage, a short trip from Cuxhaven to Southampton.[38]

Third Voyage

ne thesis of this book is that the VATERLAND marks the zenith of ocean liner evolution in terms of luxury for passengers in first class. The lower classes were squeezed into small areas in the bow and stern. As a fascinating slice of the rich living that is now forever lost to us, the daily doings of a typical first-class passenger on this superb ship may be reconstructed. Let the reader imagine a German passenger sailing from Hamburg on the June 27 voyage. Give him the name of one of the real passengers so as to be as close to reality as possible and, using all the documents, deck plans, and odd printed memorabilia available, picture what he might do on the first full day at sea. Call him Herr S.A. Goldschmidt.[39]

Yesterday, being a methodical individual, Herr Goldschmidt read the "Handbook for Passengers" carefully. He noticed that an early breakfast is available from 6 to 8 a.m. "to anybody who wishes to partake"; and so, after a brisk walk around the promenade, he goes down below, five decks down, to the Main Dining Saloon, which is almost empty, and has coffee and delicious freshly baked rolls. Back up on D Deck Square he studies the souvenirs in the still-not-open bookshop. He thinks of the Library—he saw it just briefly yesterday—and goes up a deck, passing the cut-flower shop and the display of candies and chocolates on B Deck Square. He walks almost reverently through the empty Social Hall with its glistening De Lairesse paintings and forward into the Library, also known as the Ladies' Saloon. He feels a bit out of place, but the room is empty and he leisurely examines the specially bound books behind the glass doors of the wall-size bookshelves. He will get a catalogue of the books in English, French, and German when the library steward is on duty. His wife will enjoy browsing here.

At 9 a.m. he escorts his wife, Frau Goldschmidt nebst Bedienung, to the Dining Saloon for a real breakfast, after which she returns to their cabin and he spends half an hour on one of the new Swedish-Zander-system apparatuses in the spick-and-span gym on the top deck next to the Wireless Room. Then he spends ten minutes or so in the deck chair he has rented, waiting for his wife. His chair costs four marks—one dollar, rather, for he reminds himself to use American money terms to get used to them. The chair is on the promenade deck near the large windows looking in to the Palm Court. He spends another dollar on a rug for his wife and is enjoying the morning band concert when his wife appears. It seems she got lost.

Taking her by the elbow, he guides her up to the gym, where there is a nurse on duty between 10:30 and 12:30 when it is open exclusively for women. He would love to see his wife on that mechanical horse, but men are barred. He leaves her and goes to check with the Hapag passenger department office on D Deck Square about through-checking his baggage to Milwaukee. But passing the A Deck darkroom, he remembers that he has his camera around his shoulders and that it is a gorgeous day for snapshots. He photographs several of the smokestakes, monstrous things whose upper rims are already becoming sooty even though they were freshly painted yesterday at Cuxhaven. Only a few wisps of smoke are coming from their tops; good combustion, he thinks, knowledgeably.

This afternoon he will have the steward take his tuxedo to the ship's tailor to be cleaned and pressed for tonight's dinner. His wife noted that it was wrinkled when he took it out of his suitcase and hung it in his highly polished wooden wardrobe. The charge for cleaning and pressing is two marks—no, 50 cents; reasonable enough. He is now in the Wintergarden, or Palm Court, and he realizes he has missed the morning bouillon and sandwiches on deck—but you can't do everything. It is nearly noon and there are still people sitting in the elegant Ritz-Carlton Restaurant. No breakfast is served there after 11 a.m., but you know how some people are. He is happy that the Ritz-Carlton is run on a strict system, and that no games, cards, or even dominoes are permitted, let alone the making up of the ship's pool. He does not approve of betting on the distance made each 24 hours. Thinking again about the people in the Ritz-Carlton, he decides that they must have ordered breakfast at the last minute. The handbook notes that drinks will be served only if meals are ordered at the same time, and those people have drinks.

Before picking up his wife at the gym he decides to take a quick look at the swimming pool. It is open only to ladies between 10 and 12:30, but he is able to look down at them from the balcony at the forward end. He spends nearly 30 minutes examining the pool in all its vastness and beauty, with many a quick glance at its attractive users. He thinks for a moment of signing up for an electric bath, but it costs one dollar. Unfortunately he did not bring a bathing suit, but according to the handbook, the Barber Shop has a supply for sale. Back in his deck chair for a sweet moment of salty air and then up to the gym. He and his wife change in their cabin and just make it to the 1 p.m. luncheon. While waiting for the Holsteiner Schinken (smoked ham), Herr Goldschmidt wonders casually why luncheon is served half an hour later on eastbound than on westbound crossings. The chief steward, C. Herrmann, bows to them as they leave after their sumptuous repast. Trying to think of something to say, Herr Goldschmidt asks when Bandmaster P. Instinsky will circulate his subscription list to permit passengers to show their gratitude for his music. Herr Herrmann says it will be done tomorrow. Herr Goldschmidt notes casually that they would like to have their names on the list.[40]

En route to their cabin, the couple stop at the Purser's Office on D Deck to buy stamps. For the first time they buy American stamps, as mail bound for America and mailed on the ship westbound has to have U.S. postage. Before dropping their letters in at the Post Office they both carefully examine the red two-cent stamp with its profile of George Washington. "Much less elegant than our German stamps," Herr G. thinks, as he relaxes on his brass bedstead and looks at the reflection of the waves far below—they show on the freshly painted deadlight hooked in an open position in front of his porthole.

He doesn't rest long; there are just too many interesting things to do. He hurries up to the top deck photo shop and buys several rolls of film, each with six exposures. Each roll costs a mark. As he comes out he sees several engineer officers lounging on their deck under the third stack. One is Oberingenieur O. Wolf, and Herr Goldschmidt takes his picture. He would like to get a snapshot of the commodore or one of the five captains, and this reminds him of the paragraph about storms in the handbook:

"In stormy weather or whenever the captain deems it necessary for the safety of the passengers and the steamer, the passengers, upon request, must leave the decks at once and repair to their respective cabins."

He almost hopes the commodore will have to do this once during the crossing; it would be exciting! Little does he know that at this very moment a finger is on a trigger and an Archduke is about to die. Tomorrow the ship's newspaper will have the story via wireless, but few will realize the implications.

The weather is anything but stormy now, and the VATERLAND is forging bravely toward Cherbourg and Southampton. Everyone is gay and carefree, or seems so to Herr Goldschmidt. He watches a game of shuffleboard on A Deck just where the row of six lifeboats comes to an end. One chap is leaning against the rail. He has white shoes, white trousers, and a white African explorer's hat, not to mention a stiff winged collar. Down on the prom deck Herr Goldschmidt pauses long enough to allow the ship's photographer to include him in a group photo of seven men and one lady, friends he has made aboard. His ankle-length overcoat is very much in vogue, as is his derby. The sun shines through the port prom windows. No one smiles, except the lady.[41] Can any of these eight dream that this very deck will be crowded with sleeping American soldiers, four deep in tiered metal bunks, just four years and a few hours from this moment?

Frau Goldschmidt is having her hair dressed and undulated (75 cents), despite her husband's suggestion that it is a bit extravagant. He must meet her precisely at 3:45 so they can be in their deck chairs at 4 p.m. in time for coffee and tea, with cakes. Making the turn at the after end of B Deck promenade, he looks up at the massive mainmast. It rises 146 feet from C Deck. He gazes up at its shimmering newness, and sees it moving against the blue sky. He becomes dizzy and quickly looks down toward where some happy second class passengers are dancing. A girl's hair blows in the breeze as she is waltzed around by a well-dressed chap under a huge golfing cap. Goldschmidt is reminded of how shocked he was at reading in the handbook that passengers in first class can not use the prom decks and public rooms of second class. It is quite right that they can not come up to first, but who ever heard of the rule being the other way around?

There is also confusion in his mind about the hours when the band and the orchestra will play. The band is supposed to play each morning on the promenade deck—he has already heard it. It plays in the first-class Dining Saloon during dinner and from 9 to 10 p.m. in second class. The orchestra has already performed from 1 to 3 p.m. in the Ritz-Carlton; he missed that. They are tuning up to play again from 4:30 to 5:30, and from his deck chair he can hear them. While he is enjoying the band at dinner, the orchestra will be playing in the Ritz again, from 7 to 11 p.m., with a half hour's break at 9 p.m. It is all rather complicated, and to make it worse the band is not permitted to play during these evening hours except when the orchestra is playing, so as "to avoid annoyance to passengers," the handbook says. But the handbook also says that the band will be playing between 9 and 9:30 p.m. in second cabin! Eureka, that is when the orchestra takes its half-hour break. He has caught Hapag in an error! His precise mind finds pleasure in this utterly unimportant little discovery. Somehow this all reminds him to stop secretly at the flower-stand and get a corsage for his wife before going down to dress for dinner.

Dinner is wonderful! The band plays from its balcony. Everyone is beautifully dressed, in formal attire, of course. His own tuxedo is as good as anyone's, and his wife is pleased with her flowers. They have gold-plated knives and forks! After dinner they taste more sheer elegance in the Wintergarden. Palms, growing live in their own huge tubs, rise majestically and bend over gracefully, well above a man's head height, to give a feeling of romantic luxury to the beautiful white and green room. Someone plays softly on the piano. This will be their most vivid memory of the voyage. Although a rounded glass shield stands at the top of the six richly carpeted steps leading into the Ritz, those seated there can still be seen as, of course, they want to be. What style! There is a main table under the huge room's dome, and Herr Goldschmidt counts. He counts again! There are 16 people at this huge center table. They aren't a bit crowded, either. All around them the fluted mahogany columns rise, polished, shimmering, their elegance heightened by six rows of delicate white ivory inlay at about a waiter's-head height. Behind the columns are walls with equally handsome pilasters. The gorgeous room is dominated by its leaded-glass dome, resting on a finely decorated, Roman-style circle of gold swirls on polished mahogany. What other ship ever had such a room in all the world or such a pair of rooms as the green and white Wintergarden and the mahogany, red and gold Ritz-Carlton?

When he bought the flowers for his wife, Herr Goldschmidt indulged himself in two fine

93

cigars. Now, after escorting her below through the luxuriously wide central companionway to their cabin, he raffishly decides upon a stroll alone. He wants to see the smokestacks at night. He wants to smoke one of his new cigars, and smoking is not permitted in the cabins. He will have his smoke and a beer in the manly solitude of the Smoking Room Bar, open until midnight!

The VATERLAND is doubly magnificent at night out on deck. She is beginning to pitch slightly; it was quite noticeable in the companionways and on the stairs. He looks down at the water and then up to the top of the funnels. From where he stands on A Deck the water is 58 feet below. He paces off the 144 feet between each smokestack; he is in a daze of wonderment and inner pleasure. Germany has much to thank Albert Ballin for in this great ship.

Stepping inboard he enters the Smoking Room and is quickly brought back to reality by a framed warning:

"Professional gamblers frequently travel by the Atlantic steamships for the purpose of engaging their fellow passengers in games of chance. It is, of course, desirable to discourage these individuals as much as possible, and the Hamburg-Amerika Linie, therefore, beg to advise their patrons to exercise the greatest care in this respect."

Herr Goldschmidt walks far forward and sits in the port alcove under the two statuettes of "old salts." He wanted beer for dinner but knew it was not served—"no draught-beer will be served at dinner," the handbook says—but now he can have it, and his cigar. A feeling of security and well-being wells up strongly. He is glad to be aboard the VATERLAND, happy to be going to America and content with the world.

One Down, Eight Million to Go

n June 29, the third day out, the ship's newspaper reported without fanfare that Archduke Francis Ferdinand, the Crown Prince of Austria, had been shot by an assassin at Sarajevo, capital of a place called Bosnia. Few dreamed that this would lead to the death of eight million others in the First World War. Least interested of all, perhaps, at least aboard the VATERLAND, was an eight-year-old lad named Felix J. Tomei, Jr. He had sailed with his family for a European vacation and was now returning. He enjoyed the new VATERLAND very much and remembered the trip across on the IMPERATOR because everyone had said she was top-heavy.[42] With the boy were his two sisters, Felice and Novella, and his parents. The Tomeis and the Goldschmidts would not have met, for the Tomeis were in second class.[43]

On July 4 the VATERLAND reached New York and docked with precision and ease.[44] While it was in port many visitors crowded aboard, none more struck by the ship's beauty than a young Hoboken belle named Helen Fleming. She had a girl friend whose uncle was a steward aboard and so she was invited to visit the ship. She loved the excitement of River Street, Hoboken, and remembers with awe all the great ships of Hapag and the North German Lloyd and the countless beer gardens where their seamen sat and drank. Hoboken was a melting pot in 1914, about half German and half Irish.[45]

There was another large passenger list for the eastbound VATERLAND, 3015 persons in four classes, and an expeditious departure. Even if her reverse power was totally gone, as some believe, she could be eased out quite easily by tugs with no one the wiser. To be on the safe side, however, an incoming Red Star Line ship with a very similar name, the VADERLAND, of 11,000 gross tons, was careful to hold up her Hudson River docking so the two ships would not pass while either was maneuvering in the stream. The German liner's departure had been set for 10 a.m., but was postponed an hour to accommodate a heavy mail shipment.[46] As it worked out, the two ships passed each other off the Battery, each saluting. The smokestacks of the Red Star liner came up to about the lifeboats of the big new sea queen.

The VATERLAND's passenger list for this voyage is a fascinating document. This time the zeppelin ads contain not only a picture of Hapag's airship but a combined view of the zeppelin passing over the IMPERATOR. A 48-page booklet, the list includes many ads for Ballin's cruises, including an announcement of something offered by no other line before or since: two around-the-world cruises by the same company leaving 15 days apart. The CINCINNATI would sail on January 16 and the CLEVELAND on January 31, both from New York and both through the new Panama Canal. The Hapag passenger men were not overly modest in describing their cruises. The ad notes that these voyages "have rapidly approached perfection through the frequent introduction of fresh itineraries and the judicious use of all newly gained experience."[47] In the ad for the VATERLAND and the IMPERATOR, the former's tonnage is still given as 58,000 gross.

Count von Bernstorff was again a passenger, with his "manservant." Another was Joseph Clark Grew, secretary of the American embassy in Berlin. He would later be the ambassador to Japan at the time of Pearl Harbor. Every 10th name on the first-cabin list is accompanied by "manservant" or "maidservant." One name which meant very little then and which had no servile adornment is that of Frank B. Kellogg, who was shortly to be elected senator from Minnesota. Fourteen years later Kellogg would be welcomed home with blimps, Navy destroyers, and harbor salutes when he returned on the same ship with a peace pact named in his honor. Also named in this booklet is someone who would help link the German and American careers of the ship, her second chief steward of first class. Shown on the page listing the ship's officers, the name is H. Schussler. A big, outgoing person, he would serve later as chief steward in third class.[48]

The passenger list announced a special new facility to make things easier for all passengers, except those in steerage, who were going to Hamburg. Hapag had made special arrangements with German Customs to have officials board the VATERLAND at Cherbourg. All baggage examinations could be done aboard ship en route to Cuxhaven. There need be no waiting around on the pier. It was also noted that the ship's wireless was in "almost daily communication with all parts of the world, either directly through the shore-stations, or indirectly by means of passing ships." The names of the ships with which communication might be expected would be posted every morning in different parts of the ship for the convenience of passengers wishing to send greetings to travelers on other ships. In reality the VATERLAND and the IMPERATOR were outdoing even the most extravagant claims made for their wireless capability. Their Telefunken transmitters were experimenting with very long distance transmission, and in 1914 the radio operator of the LUSITANIA, Robert Leith, told C.D. Guthrie, an American shipping man, that one day out either German superliner was able to reach the rest of the way across and "would send traffic," evidence of the "terrific kick in their transmitters."[49]

On July 20, while international tensions were boiling and bubbling in the most horrendous fashion, a new second officer was assigned to the VATERLAND. He was only 24, but he already had master's papers and also had his wireless telegrapher's certificate. For this latter document he had passed a test proving his ability to send 20 words a minute. His name was Christian Wilhelm Schultz, and as a stripling he had signed on the four-masted barque PETSCHILI. Later he had been privileged to serve on the great POTOSI, possibly the fastest sailing ship of all time. She could make 23 knots, and he remembered her passing steamships with the greatest of ease. With five masts, the POTOSI was the pride of Hamburg.[50] Then Schultz became third officer of the 5,000-ton Hapag passenger liner RHAETIA.[51] Several photos taken aboard the VATERLAND before her last sailing from

Cuxhaven were preserved by Captain Schultz. One shows his cabin, filled with bits of sailing ship memorabilia. Another pictures him on the flying bridge above the pilothouse with his sextant (an instrument with which ship's officers find their position at sea). A third shows him lounging on a rich sofa beneath an oval-framed painting of naked cherubs. But the fourth really tells a story. It was taken just before sailing on July 22. The second officer is posing with a young lady who has been more or less selected as his future wife—selected, that is, by her family. Christian Wilhelm apparently is having some second thoughts on the matter, for he is shown sitting as far from her as he can and still have his arm around her shoulder. With him on the bench are three other women, all stern-faced and richly dressed. With cane and derby hat, a sixth person, possibly the bride-to-be's father, sits on the edge of the bench.[52]

On the day the VATERLAND called at Cherbourg a new agent's bulletin for steerage and third class was put out in New York. A 16-page affair, it featured a Fred Pansing oil painting, reproduced in black and white, showing the VATERLAND arriving in New York. A tiny tug the size of the ship's anchor is at the right, and two others are on her starboard. Apparently artist Pansing still did not have good plans to work with when he made the painting, for the bridge structure is clearly that of the IMPERATOR. In the caption the VATERLAND's exact tonnage is given for the first time. She measured 54,190 tons gross.[53] On the same day Austria-Hungary, with German support, sent a stiff ultimatum to Serbia, claiming that that country was responsible for the murder of the Archduke. On July 28, two days before the VATERLAND was due to reach New York, Austria-Hungary declared that Serbia had failed to accept the ultimatum and declared war on her little neighbor, despite frantic last-minute efforts by Germany to restrain the tottering old empire. The VATERLAND, with a somber passenger list, tied up quietly on July 30 at Hoboken. The war was on everyone's lips.

Chapter VI

HOBOKEN IDYLL

unard's sleek LUSITANIA came into port on July 31, and at her rail was fourteen-year-old ship lover John W. Dunn. He was already a veteran traveler, having gone abroad on the CAMPANIA nine years earlier. His interest in ships had been recognized even then, when that old liner's Captain Pritchard had solemnly taken him to the ship's bridge and pointed out the noontime position on a chart. As he arrived on the LUSITANIA, young Dunn spotted the three thick buff funnels of the new VATER-LAND, rising high against the low background of the Jersey shore. He thought back to another Wednesday 28 months before at Southampton, when he had seen the world's largest ship of that day about to sail—the TITANIC. Had he been able to look forward in time, he would have known that for 24 more years he would be able to see the same VATERLAND outline at the same pier, and that he would be one of the many to watch her sail out on her voyage to the scrapyard.[1]

Dunn had no idea of the chaos that was to break out that day aboard the VATERLAND. Steam was rising faintly from her stacks. Masses of baggage were aboard, being distributed to cabins. More than $225,000 in passage money had been collected from her 2,700 passengers for the next eastward crossing. Mail for Europe was aboard and being sorted in her seapost. And then a cable from Germany arrived! It warned that British and French cruisers were waiting off New York to seize her if she sailed. Her sailing was to be cancelled. War was on the horizon. The VATERLAND must remain in New York port.

By the same cable Hapag's 45 Broadway office was told to wireless the PRESIDENT GRANT and order her to return. The International Postal Service, which ran the ship's seapost, ordered all the ship's mail returned to the Morton and West Streets Foreign Station.[2] The company began to make frantic efforts to head off those passengers who were not already in New York City. The task of returning the quarter of a million in fares was begun. The next day Germany declared war on Russia, and the New York *Times*, in an editorial, put the stamp of history on the VATERLAND's situation.

"Probably nothing could have made Americans in general and New Yorkers in particular more clearly realize their own intimate involvement in the geographically remote cataclysm which is shaking Europe than does the cancellation of the VATERLAND's sailing, today, and the indefinite withdrawal of the world's greatest ship from movements that we had come to consider of almost sidereal regularity."[3] For the fourth time in four months the VATERLAND was front-page news. She had begun to exhibit that amazing fact of coincidence in her history, her facility for being where the action was and for somehow becoming a focal point of public involvement. Repeatedly in the years to come the sizzling heat of publicity's magnifying glass would find her at the heart of major news stories, whether it was through her wartime use as a troopship, her sale by the government to a private line, her part in the drama of Prohibition, or one of her many other adventures. Her life would be one continuous procession of page-one appearances.

"The VATERLAND in the popular imagination represents all seagoing transportation and communication," the *Times* editorial continued.

"That she could be tied up, therefore, is more impressive than is the similar action taken with other vessels here and abroad." When war broke, Hapag alone had 83 of its ships, valued at 200,000,000 marks, in neutral ports around the world. The VATERLAND, worth 36,000,000 marks, was the most valuable of the 35 ships interned in American ports. Seven more of Germany's largest ocean liners were in Hoboken. They were the PRINZESS IRENE,

FRIEDRICH DER GROSSE, PRESIDENT LINCOLN, PENNSYLVANIA, BARBAROSSA, PRINCE JOACHIM, and GEORGE WASHINGTON; there was also the Austrian liner MARTHA WASHINGTON.[4]

The *Times* concluded its editorial by saying that it was not entirely by accident that the VATERLAND "enters upon her terribly expensive rest" in New York, for "there is nowhere even a suspicion that the United States can be drawn into the savage quarrels" of Europe.

Things began happening in pell-mell fashion. A mass meeting of German seamen, oilers, and machinsts from all the Hoboken liners was held at the Atlantic Gardens restaurant to discuss the war.[5] On Sunday, August 2, there was talk of a conspiracy to blow up the VATERLAND.[6] On August 3 Germany declared war on France. The next day Great Britain declared war on Germany and the lights were going out all over Europe. On the same day Germany invaded neutral Belgium.

And now the war hysteria had arrived full-blown. A police launch with a large searchlight and 50 policemen were sent to keep watch on the VATERLAND.[7] The *Tribune* stated wildly that eight to ten thousand German reservists had somehow sneaked aboard the great liner and that the Kaiser had ordered her to make a dash for home and that, what's more, she was being coaled for the journey under the cover of darkness. There were three German cruisers, and the *Tribune* named them, waiting outside the three-mile limit to escort her home. As if this weren't enough, it was further reported that once the VATERLAND had been met by the cruisers they would transform her into a cruiser and that she would be the fastest of her type in the world. The conversion would be done at sea, since the Germans were equipped "with armament and other things" to make the changeover while under way in the Atlantic. French and Russian secret agents, the *Tribune* added, were the ones who were trying to blow up the ship, and their purpose was to keep her from being restored to German control.[8]

There were stories each day in the newspapers, but underneath all the passion and sensationalism, there was one trend that might have been discerned. The VATERLAND's crew began to slip away, a first sign of her decay and despoliation. Fred Hecker, the boy who was always seasick, went ashore and became a butler. He did not want to be repatriated because he didn't want anything more to do with the German army.[9]

On August 5 port officials denied that the VATERLAND was being coaled at night.[10] New rumors were circulated that the battleship FLORIDA and the cruiser TENNESSEE were lying in wait for the liner in case she tried to leave port without clearance papers.[11] On the following day, while the *Times* came out with a factual story that the VATERLAND was being watched to prevent shipment of contraband or loading of German reservists, the *Tribune* again relied on sheer gossip and imagination for its story. The Kaiser's agents had decided not to risk the ship in a sea dash. Instead she would "hug her pier here." That much was reasonable; but then the newspaper asserted point-blank that "German agents yesterday began to unload the excess coal she had previously taken aboard." As a source for this, the paper naively cited "the authority of laborers, who helped in the unloading, or said they did."[12]

There were some who feared for the VATERLAND's safety and to make sure that no small boat could come up to her and attach a bomb to her hull a big net was stretched across her stern. Stewards from all the German ships gathered at night on River Street and with the VATERLAND's band sang patriotic songs and listened to speeches. There were no signs of disorder.

Sir Bertram Hayes of the ADRIATIC was spending the weekend with friends in New York. For five days the White Star Line debated whether to send his ship or the giant OLYMPIC back to England, loaded with all the passengers booked for both. Finally it was decided that the ADRIATIC, older and only half the tonnage, should go, and, when her pilot came aboard, Sir Bertram was astonished to be told that the VATERLAND was also sailing. With only a 17½-knot speed, Sir Bertram was concerned. He would try to get off first, for he half believed the rumors that the German ship had guns aboard, and he certainly didn't want to be her first prize of war. Then it turned out that the pilot had meant the little Red Star VADERLAND.

"We were the first British passenger steamer to leave New York after the declaration of war, and the send-off that we got from the other ships lying at the piers and from the people of New York is something I will never forget," the British sea dog wrote a decade later.[13] The piers and the ships on the Manhattan side of the Hudson were crowded with people all singing "God Save the King" as the ADRIATIC sailed past. On the other side were the Germans, and many of them were watching too, but there was never a sound from them and "we rather wondered what thoughts were passing through their minds."[14] There was plenty of spirit on both sides, and on the same day that the ADRIATIC sailed, 10,000 German reservists stormed the German consulate in New York to demand that they be sent back to Germany to join their regiments. And they wanted the VATERLAND to take them home.[15]

There had been no exaggeration in the statement about British cruisers prowling the Atlantic, however, and this fact was brought home on August 8 when the Hapag liner CINCINNATI arrived at Boston convinced that she had evaded traps set for her by the enemy.[16] Two days later a British warship captured the Hamburg South American liner CAP ORTEGAL with a gold shipment aboard.[17] The war at sea had begun and the British had first blood.

And then slowly the VATERLAND retreated into the darkness of newspaper disinterest. On August 15 the *Times* noted that Hapag officials in the United States now had power of attorney, adding that this was given them so that they could try to sell the VATERLAND and other idle ships in New York.[18] It was admitted the next day that such a sale was being considered.[19] And then the German government offered any of the idle passenger ships at Hoboken to the United States government, for use in bringing home the thousands of American tourists stranded in Europe.[20] Meanwhile the tug DOLPHIN was stationed off the VATERLAND's pier to maintain a 24-hour vigil. The tug's searchlight played on the huge stern which protruded out into the Hudson, both to protect her against careless harbor traffic and to reassure the public that she would not attempt to slip away under cover of darkness. And the VATERLAND "loomed there, still and silent, a monument to creative forces suddenly gone destructive," the *Times* said.[21]

And Time Passed

 ootnote to the VATERLAND's brief period of service as a German luxury liner, Lloyds Register of Shipping for 1914, published at this time, listed her as having a service speed of 24 knots.[22] This was considerably better than she had averaged on her first three voyages—22.4 on the first, 21 on the second and 20 on the third—and was doubtless based on the high speeds she had made on her trials.[23]

Many of the VATERLAND's crew went home in the first few weeks after her August 1 sailing was canceled, but for thirty-two months after that, she remained a bit of Germany afloat at Pier 4. Commodore Ruser and more than half the ship's company remained. The Commodore's wife and son came over from Germany. They eventually settled in Morristown, New Jersey. Everyone had the highest respect for the Commodore, including American port officialdom. He did his best to keep his ship and crew in tip-top condition, having no idea how long they would be there but well aware that he had to maintain appearances and morale. The crew stood regular watches and discipline was maintained. Pay continued, although as the months went by it was reduced several times. As the queen of the German liners interned in America, the VATERLAND became a headquarters for German sympathizers. Many meetings were held aboard her, her well-stocked wine cellar being a special attraction. Wine was also sold to her officers at very low prices, and this is one reason why they were invited to dinner in German homes in Hoboken. Champagne was five marks a bottle.[24] The VATERLAND's famous swimming pool and her gymnasium were other reasons why she was a popular center for German officers and others in the area. For a time spirits were high; and then came the first battle of the Marne and a general German retreat.

Now little was heard of the great silent ship. In late September a small story reported that the marine insurance firm of Waring & Gillow had attached her for $1,845.72, the writ of attachment being served by James Clark, Under Sheriff of Hudson County.[25] A month later Mr. Clark withdrew the attachment when Julius P. Meyer, a Vice Director of Hapag in the United States, denied that the VATERLAND would be sold and assured him that she would not be moved.[26] "It is true that the VATERLAND is a big source of expense to us," he said. "Besides the interest charges on her lying idle, we also pay the wages of the crew of 800 and look after their families in Germany." He added that Hapag had paid out more than $3,000,000 to satisfy claims for passenger tickets and freight not delivered since the ship had been idled. But, he said, "the Hamburg-American Line is going to keep its American friends. It will meet all its obligations."[27]

In November there was another brief series of small news items. This time it was a crew problem. Some of the men refused to accept a cut in pay, and police were sent to guard the VATERLAND. The *Times* had a feature story about the plight of the idle German sailors at the Hoboken piers. A wage compromise was worked out and the crew lost another round with Commodore Ruser. He struck 200 men from the ship's crew list and had them transferred to the much smaller and less comfortable PENNSYLVANIA. They were to be fed and given quarters but were to receive no pay.[28]

Winter came and the VATERLAND was covered for the first time with snow and ice. In early December there was a rumor that a new company was being formed to take over all the idle German ships and use them in trade to South America.[29] A month later Albert Ballin cabled a denial that he planned to start a neutral shipping line between Hamburg and the United States.[30] Ballin's open opposition to the war had ended after Germany's involvement, but he remained cold to the conflict and to those he felt were responsible for it. How separate and apart he was from the German navy is shown by an amusing thing that happened when war began.

Ballin's old pride and joy, the graceful four-funneled speed-record-breaker DEUTSCH-LAND, was taken over by the navy and commissioned as an active naval vessel in the belief that she could make 23 knots. She had been renamed VICTORIA LOUISE in 1911 by Ballin and put into cruising service, but no one in the navy seemed to know that her power had been drastically cut down at that time, and Ballin didn't tell anyone. She could make only 18 knots at best. When this was discovered she was immediately paid off ("retired").[31]

Eberhardt Wulff, the electrician, remembers that every third day he had to stay aboard the VATERLAND on watch. He got to know Hoboken well, and the neighboring counties also, for he often went for rides with friends out into the country. There was one trip he was glad he didn't make. The car with several VATERLAND men in it had a bad accident and everyone was killed. Wulff remembers the lovely old German-style restaurant on River Street across from the VATERLAND's dock. The head waiter, Max Schuman, later became owner, and in the days when the LEVIATHAN sailed from the same pier the place was known as Schuman's Hoffbrau House. In due course the bar of this establishment would have as its chief decoration the 21-foot-long name board from the port side of the LEVIATHAN's bridge deck, which still later would become the author's prize artifact from this ship.

The VATERLAND's two bands occasionally took part in shoreside concerts and also frequently played aboard the liner on weekends and holidays. The PENNSYLVANIA had a Japanese band made up of men from Germany's colonial outposts in the Japanese area. They stuck together and were very popular. Despite all of Commodore Ruser's morale-building efforts, however, discipline and even loyalty began to diminish. A number of the crew came to spend much of their time ashore in the homes of friends, and they liked to bring presents. Bits and pieces of the VATERLAND began to disappear. One of the ship's carpenters, a man named Heidenreich, was particularly known for his ability to whisk things off the ship. Years later, when he had his own home ashore, it seemed that half his possessions had come from the VATERLAND.[32]

A big celebration was held aboard the liner on Saturday, January 25, 1915. It was in honor of the 250th anniversary of the founding of the Hamburg Chamber of Commerce. Almost any occasion was worth a party. A message from the Kaiser was received and read aloud to crew and guests.[33] But the rough edges were beginning to show. Another crew dispute arose, this time over food. Early in February sailors from the VATERLAND and other interned ships complained to the New York Board of Health. They said the food was no good, but their claim was rejected as the Board ruled it had no authority over food in "German territory."[34] Talk continued about the possibility that the interned ships might be put on some kind of neutral-flag run.[35]

Meanwhile the long-threatened submarine blockade of the British Isles was finally put into effect by Germany. Admiral Tirpitz had won.

In the United States, life went on only faintly changed by the European war. The Panama Pacific Exposition celebrating the opening of the Panama Canal was a great success. Hapag's lovely twin liners CINCINNATI and CLEVELAND were not there, of course, but the Holland-America Line had a fine exhibition, featuring full-sized reproductions of cabins and public rooms, even deck areas, aboard their new 35,000-ton luxury liner STATENDAM.[36]

March came and with it more rumors that the VATERLAND might try to slip away. Collector of Customs Dudley Field Malone's so-called neutrality squad made a complete investigation of all the interned German liners and reported that there was no evidence of any intention to break the rules and flee.[37] Nevertheless, two destroyers were assigned to join the tug DOLPHIN in patrolling the Hoboken pier area.[38] The horrors of the European war were gradually becoming known in America at about this time, and the first use of poison gas in warfare by the Germans set off a shock wave that reached across the Atlantic. Again Hapag's J.P. Meyer felt it necessary to deny rumors that the VATERLAND would violate the American neutrality laws and flee for home.[39] But these and other more bizarre tales multiplied. The sinking on May 7, 1915, of the LUSITANIA by a German submarine created a new surge of anti-German feeling. The widely believed reports that VATERLAND seamen knew about the sinking before news of the disaster reached the United States by cable added fuel to the feelings of general suspicion. On May 12 the big liner and her companions in Hoboken were searched for explosives.[40] Two weeks later the *Times* reported that several of the VATERLAND seamen had been driven insane by the confinement and emotional stresses.[41]

The sinking of the LUSITANIA was a psychological turning point in the war. The world had lost its faith in endless and uninterrupted progress when the TITANIC went down; now the loss of the LUSITANIA projected Americans into the conflict, and it was no longer a European war. Any possibility that the United States might sympathize with Germany was now a thing of the past. German vessels in American waters now were looked upon as enemy vessels by a large majority of the public. On May 30 the *Times* published a suggestion that the German liners should be seized in reprisal for the LUSITANIA.[42]

But there were still many Germans and some German supporters in Hoboken, and, on July 7, Commodore Ruser announced a campaign to raise one million marks for the relief of war orphans and widows in Germany. His plan was to cut the VATERLAND's immense German flag into thousands of tiny squares and sell each for $3.50. A list of all the buyers would be put into a great album and sent to the Kaiser. The album would be entitled "The flag of the VATERLAND."[43]

A report from Sweden at about this time stated that the once-great Hamburg-American Line had failed. It was promptly denied.[44] A month later the North German Lloyd, which was in better financial position, offered to buy Hapag's idle ships, including the VATER-LAND.[45] And then, as the summer neared its end, there was an outbreak of cholera on the PRESIDENT LINCOLN and she was quarantined.[46]

Trying to keep up appearances, the crew of the VATERLAND on October 22 celebrated the 500th anniversary of the reign of the Hohenzollern family in Brandenburg. A news story about the affair led harbor wits to dub the idle German ships "the Hohenzollerns of Hoboken."[47]

American war hysteria was reaching new heights, and, in late November, Karl Boy-ed, handsome young aide of Count von Bernstorff, was made the villain in a purported plot exposé published in the *Times.* The VATERLAND and her German sisters were described as "local war offices" of the Germans. It was said that Boy-ed had spent $2,000,000 in his spy work.[48] Several weeks later the Navy boarded Hapag's liner BULGARIA and sealed her wireless to prevent the sending of secret messages.[49]

As 1915 drew to a close, strange as it may seem to us today, there were those in Germany who thought the war itself might be near an end. The Russians had been driven back on the eastern front and many Germans thought that the submarine blockade was having the desired effect on Britain's morale. Perhaps Albert Ballin was hoping that some kind of compromise settlement was in the wind when he urged around Christmastime that in any forthcoming peace treaty Germany's freedom of the seas should be insured.[50]

Those on the VATERLAND knew better, however, and from practical experience they knew that England's surface-vessel blockade of Germany was very effective. Except for a few raiders, the seas had been swept clear of German ships. It was more and more difficult for Germans to get home from the United States. The few VATERLAND crew members who made the attempt had to devise all sorts of ruses.

With the help of friendly Norwegian skippers, some succeeded. They would build a false partition in a closet in the captain's cabin to hide behind when the British searched the vessel.[51] In this way a trickle of Hapag officials were able to come to America, and when they came they went straight to the VATERLAND. Plans were continually being made to get the ships home. The difficulties seemed insurmountable, and they were. The ships remained at their piers, becoming more and more sad-looking inside and out. The decay of idleness was taking its toll.

From many sides came the cry that the ships should be used to help the Allies or to send relief to the Belgians or to begin new sea services under the American flag.[52] Ships of all kinds were in great demand. Anything that would float was worth her weight in gold. Even old sailing ships were hauled off mudflats, patched up, and put into service.[53] The International Mercantile Marine decided that it should buy all the German liners, and it made overtures to Washington, seeking help with the financing. William Gibbs McAdoo, President Wilson's Secretary of the Treasury, turned the proposal down. It is safe to say from this vantage point in history that had this effort succeeded the career of the

VATERLAND might well have continued on the same highly successful plateau that it had reached under Hapag.[54]

Albert Ballin was one of those behind the idea of using his liners in America to transport relief cargoes for Belgium. He met a young American named Herbert Hoover, who was in Belgium trying to find food for the starving citizens. Hoover proposed that 40 Hapag ships be chartered to the Belgian Relief Committee for this purpose. They would fly the flag of the Royal Dutch Lloyd for the trip across and would then be returned to Hapag. Lengthy debate over freight rates and over security for the ships from both British warships and German submarines brought the negotiations to an impasse. Hoover, with what was to become one of his most famous statements, groaned that "stupidity is an essential concomitant of war" and went to other sources for ships. Ballin blamed the German Admiralty.[55]

Ballin was also behind the I.M.M. proposal to buy the VATERLAND and other German liners. In his view, it was again the German naval authorities who torpedoed the proposal. Their feeling was that the submarine would eliminate all ocean tonnage from the high seas, and that therefore German tonnage should not be sold to foreign interests because it would only add to the number of ships available to the enemies of Germany.[56]

Ballin for Peace

To friends and associates, Ballin over and over again described the war as stupid. To him the conflict between Austria-Hungary and Serbia was meaningless. At a personal interview with the Kaiser on January 10, 1916, he tried to convince the Emperor that the submarine could not destroy England and should not be viewed as way to end the war.[57] He realized the danger of American hostility better than most Germans did, and in the same month he wrote to a friend that "the American danger seems to be averted for the moment at least." He added that a break in relations with the United States would be nothing short of fatal to Germany. He believed England and Germany were in the last stage of a war of exhaustion. The entry of America into the war would change all this, and would stiffen the "obstinacy of our enemies."[58]

The day after the Ballin meeting with Emperor Wilhelm, port officials in New York sealed the aerials on the VATERLAND and disconnected them from her wireless shack. It had finally dawned on them that the VATERLAND was able to transmit all the way across the Atlantic, and could receive from Germany as well. The aerials on all other German ships in the harbor were physically removed.[59] The only possible explanation for the more gentle treatment afforded the VATERLAND is Commodore Ruser's reputation for integrity. The Commodore, in his efforts to maintain discipline aboard his ship, had two of his seamen arrested for violating the contract labor law on January 18. After a series of hearings they were allowed to become American citizens, something that they had apparently been hoping to achieve all along.[60]

The news of Britain's withdrawal from Gallipoli in the Mediterranean sparked rejoicing among Germans all over the world in January, 1916, and the Hamburg-American Line announced that the company was preparing for a big rush of emigrants after the war.[61] In February the OLYMPIC's sister ship, named BRITANNIC, White Star's third monster ship, was lost in the Aegean Sea while serving as a hospital ship.[62] The Cunard Line announced that the Dutch liner STATENDAM, the one so proudly introduced at the Panama Pacific Exposition a year earlier, would replace the lost LUSITANIA and would be renamed NEURETANIA. This name, and, in fact, the ship herself were to be very short-lived, and her sinking would be closely associated with the story of the LEVIATHAN.[63]

While the Battle of Verdun was raging in France, in New York the VATERLAND's officers held a giant bazaar for the relief of war sufferers back in Germany. The affair is said to have earned $85,000 and it lasted from March 11 to the 23rd. The original Madison Square Garden at 4th Avenue and 26th Street was crammed with exhibits, including many models of German warships and liners. There was one of the VATERLAND and also one of the commerce destroyer EMDEN, whose exploits had so heartened Germans the world over. An eight-page catalogue of the models was published. Many were raffled off as a climax of the show.

A hit of the show was a 42-foot-long model of a German zeppelin, which was hung from the rafters and moved around. It had three propellers that worked. They consisted of electric fans inside the body of the craft whose propellers protruded and buzzed around in a very realistic fashion. This was the work of electrician Eberhardt Wulff. The VATER-LAND's second engineer, H. Deelwater, and two of her fourth engineers, O. Plath and C. Gernand, also helped with displays.[64]

Finding ways to raise money for war relief was the major occupation of Commodore Ruser and his crew. In June, just two weeks after the Battle of Jutland ended in a permanent retreat by the German High Seas Fleet, the VATERLAND's master announced that the fund raised by the "Reisenfahne VATERLAND" had passed the 50,000-mark point. Some $5,000 had already been sent to Berlin, he said, adding that the Steneck Trust Company of Hoboken was handling all contributions.[65] Years later the U.S. Navy's history of the LEVIATHAN, probably repeating a wartime rumor, said that the money raised was used to support the German spy system "through the craftiness of a high functionary." As if this weren't bad enough, this same source added that some of the money had been used by this same gentleman "for private speculation."[66]

Regardless of how it was spent, the ingenuity of the VATERLAND's crew in raising money was very real. A favorite way was to create a design requiring some 500 brass hobnails, and to charge a mark for each hobnail. The most popular design was an iron cross, with ribbon, imperial crown, and the initial "W" for Wilhelm. Often the years 1914, 1915 and 1916 would be added—to use more hobnails. It was done on a red velvet background and appropriately framed. A very large design like this was always on display in the ship's lobby. Captain Christian Schultz helped make several.[67]

Another money-raising item was a decoration made of lignum vitae, the hard, close-grained wood that looks and feels like iron and is almost as heavy. It was used in many places on shipboard, and there was a stock of it in the carpenter's shop, although it could not be cut with anything but the finest of cutting tools. From this substance oval-shaped decorative pieces were laboriously made, with a rope-design border and the letters "G," "D," and "V" intertwined, to stand for Grosser Dampfer VATERLAND. Each two-by-four-inch piece, fitted into a foot-long section of the ship's teak rail, weighed 15 pounds. They made outstanding paperweights.[68]

The Madison Square Garden effort had been so successful that in September another fund-raising party was held, largely supported by VATERLAND crew members. It took place Saturday and Sunday, September 23 and 24, at the German gathering place known as Schuetzen Park, in Union Hill, New Jersey. Count von Bernstorff was listed as the "Protektor" and top man of the affair, and the special guests included Victor F. Ridder, owner of the famed *Staats Zeitung*. Hapag's American Manager, Dr. Karl Buenz, was another participant, as were Hapag's Director Dr. O. Ecker and Secretary Julius P. Meyer. August Thiele, provision manager of the VATERLAND, was one of the three officials running the festival. Eberhardt Wulff served on a committee, as did Dr. Seidel of the VATERLAND. In two days the affair raised $24,495.01, a good part of which came from the advertisements in the elaborate 40-page program, which was wrapped in a heavy cardboard cover decorated with a red, gray, and black German flag and a sepia-tone picture of a sailing ship.[69] Among those who took ads were the Kaffee Hag company, whose slogan "95 per cent of the caffeine removed" was one of the few English lines in the booklet; the Pilsenser Brewing Co.; Ebling's Bottled Beers; and J. Schmitt, importer of Rhine wine. The Atlantic Basin Iron Works, of Brooklyn, also had an ad.

Albert Ballin, almost at the end of his rope, had come under fire in Germany for his efforts to end the war. He was accused of seeking a settlement in the interest of preserving his company. In answer to this charge, he defended his stand in a letter to a high official which was published in part in a page-one story by the New York Times on October 2, 1916.

"I always thought the world had room enough for ourselves and England, also for America, and for a few other powers besides," he wrote.

"Still I believe that this insane war might have been avoided if the English statesmen had acted wisely.

"Now that war has come rumor imputes to me the idea that by yielding and abstaining from victory we might achieve that for which we worked during the last peaceful years. This is a most absurd idea which ought not to be imputed to one who for a whole lifetime has fought a commercial war against England."[70]

The next day the Times, in an editorial, admonished Ballin about daring to call the war insane.

"For a German as eminent as Herr Ballin to bring criticism dangerously close to those at home who have been declaring Germany's part in it [the war] holy, because purely defensive, would seem inadvisable." To call the war insane "contradicts the assertions that each of the nations involved makes in its own behalf and depends on for the sympathy of the countries still remaining out of the struggle and officially neutral," the editorial added. The Times then said that some people were hailing the sacrifices being made by the Allies and others in America were hailing the stand of the Central Powers, but "we do not talk of this insane war unless we belong to the group that calls all war indefensible and would prefer to it any sort of peace."[71]

Apparently Ballin was really hopeful, despite German reversals, that peace was not too far away. In late October he reported to Hapag stockholders that the ravages of war would require European nations to put tight restrictions on emigration to America and elsewhere when peace came.[72] This was the last even halfway hopeful comment from Albert Ballin.

Last Gay Night

She was "ablaze with lights" on the night of November 4, 1916. A ball was in progress. The next day's headline would read:

WAR CHARITY FETE
ON VATERLAND

Great Liner Houses a Fancy Dress Festival to Aid
Central Powers. Supper, Concert, Cabaret and
Dancing Enjoyed by More than 650 Guests

The whole pier was decorated with colored lights, and Hapag employees were dressed in fancy costumes as they met the guests and drove them in electric trollies from the street entrance to the VATERLAND's brilliantly illuminated and decorated gangways. Tickets cost $10, an exorbitant fee then, and the more than 650 guests bought "all kinds of souvenirs." The dinner was in the Grand Dining Saloon, with a concert afterwards under the direction of Otto Goritz, of the Metropolitan Opera Company.

A part of the starboard promenade deck was fitted out with flags and flowers. Pictures of a tour through Palestine were shown by means of a slide projector, and there was orchestral music, featuring the playing of harps. The deck area was labeled "IN HEAVEN."

Opposite, on the port promenade deck, the decorations were intended to suggest the infernal regions (the *Times* account was too proper to say "hell"). It was "artistically constructed by the crew and filled with small tables where waiters dressed as imps staggered to and fro carrying trays laden with glasses of cheering beverages." Commodore Ruser sat at a table surrounded by a bevy of fair women and appeared for a time to have forgotten that a war was on. Among those present were William Randolph Hearst and Mrs. Hearst. About $7,000 was raised.[73]

At about this time Eberhardt Wulff left the VATERLAND. He went to Ellis Island to begin the process of becoming an American citizen, having been promised a job with an electrical contractor in New Jersey.[74]

As the new year came around, America was shocked by Germany's demand that all U.S. ships on the Atlantic should paint their hulls with vertical red and white stripes to insure safe conduct through the submarine blockade zone around the British Isles and the French coast.[75] This order was the beginning of the end for the last traces of American neutrality. It became apparent to everyone that a break between America and Germany was coming. One more offer by American interests to buy all the Hapag ships came at this time and, much to Ballin's disgust, was turned down by the German Admiralty.[76] On January 30, 1916, Customs Collector Malone ordered another search of all the "Teutonic ships" in New York, and the police were told to keep a day and night watch on the fleet. On February 1 Germany began its long-threatened "unrestricted" submarine warfare against ships trying to break their blockade of the Allied Nations. On February 2 the officers from all the tied-up German ships in Hoboken met aboard the VATERLAND to discuss action in the event of war between the United States and Germany.[77] On the same day the *Times* revealed what everyone in shipping had known for three years—namely that the VATERLAND's coal supply was inadequate for a "dash to sea."[78] Also on the same day Collector Malone made another inspection of the German liners. He reported that the captains of all the ships had been ordered to destroy their ships' papers and to remove key parts of their machinery. New precautions to guard the ships were instituted, but one expert said it would be easy for the crews to damage them because the neutrality squad inspectors were never permitted below decks. Apparently all the previous inspections had been largely social. The Hague Convention and how it applied to the confiscation of interned vessels and the status of their crews became a topic of great interest.[79]

The New York *American,* in a story typical of that newspaper's sensational style, made known on February 3 that the "machinery of the giant liner VATERLAND has been dismantled in the last 24 hours under the very eyes of the neutrality squad who have been patrolling the pier." The account added that what had not been destroyed was thrown overboard and "sank deep in the mud and cannot possibly be rescued."[80]

On the same day Commodore Ruser denied that his ship had been damaged; the truth of his denial would be confirmed in months to come. He reaffirmed his denial that she would make any effort to leave the port illegally.[81] About 150 German crewmen left their ships for shore leave despite warnings from company officials that they might be placing themselves in a difficult position. Also on the 3rd of February, the American Line's NEW YORK sailed, still painted black. Captain Roberts, her master, said he would not recognize any path laid out by the Germans nor would he have his ship painted like a "synthetic zebra."[82]

106

William B. Wilson, Secretary of Labor, got into the picture two days later by reminding all German crew members that they could not permanently leave their ships without passing through Ellis Island. The neutrality guard was doubled on February 5, and Collector Malone denied that he planned to seize the ships. On the following day the Collector again denied that the German liners had been damaged by their crews, and added that 18 crew members had been sent to Ellis Island after they had declared their desire to become Americans.[83] The next day another crew member "defected," a Miss Elsie Schwartz, matron on the VATERLAND. She created quite a stir and was most indignant at the atmosphere of confinement at Ellis Island.

"Germany is not at war with America," she declared when she saw the detention pens and guards. She "tramped the visitors' corridor and ate her evening meal under protest."[84]

Second Officer Christian Wilhelm Schultz, who had passed the winter months ice-skating and had come to know many Americans, also decided he would become a citizen. One of the Hapag officials from Germany had taken him aside and offered to get him back to Germany, implying that a decisive German victory was no longer a probability. He had told Schultz that Hapag wanted some good officer material on hand at the war's end to start things going again. But Schultz remained with the VATERLAND. He couldn't quite make the break.[85] Dr. Ecker, the Hapag director, who had been living aboard the VATERLAND with his family, moved ashore, taking up residence at the Hotel Majestic.[86]

For a few days the VATERLAND and her "Teutonic" sisters dropped out of the newspapers, but on other fronts the war continued to heat up for America. Newspapers were keenly interested in rumblings of trouble in Russia. Germany's new submarine offensive meant that any vessel bound for an allied port was in danger. The press hailed the successful completion of the NEW YORK's voyage:

"Here is a real American," the New York *Sun* said of Captain Roberts.[87]

The growing war fever was displayed by an intemperate *Times* editorial, which blurted out that "every day a new German plot comes to light." There had been a continuous series of "acts of war" planned "on American soil," the *Times* said.

"From the German Embassy, whose forced departure has not left Germany without more than sufficient agents of its will in America, to some poor devil in Hoboken; from interned officers and men violating their parole, from employees of steamships sheltered in our harbors taking advantage of the shelter to start bomb factories aboard, to college professors playing the part of informers, Germany has continually violated our neutrality, broken our laws, exerted an authority and dominion here as if she were in occupation of an conquered country."[88]

Some time in March a note came from Germany, possibly by secret courier, ordering all captains of German ships to cripple their ships' engines. International ship brokers, who somehow got wind of the order, made an offer shortly after this to buy all the Hapag ships in American waters, including the VATERLAND, at reduced prices. Albert Ballin still hoped that America would not enter the war and he did his best to push this sale, but it too was blocked by the German navy.[89]

On St. Patrick's Day, March 17, 1917, the ST. LOUIS steamed out of New York. Not only was she not painted zebralike, but she was well armed. Herbert Hartley was on the bridge as master; he had been elevated to the post shortly before that, when Captain Jensen had been forced to retire because of a stroke. Eight days later the American Line flagship arrived at Liverpool and was welcomed with great enthusiasm. Captain Hartley was honored at a performance of *Pygmalion and Galatea* given by a company brought down from London especially for the occasion.[90] This gallant little ship was to continue to cross the Atlantic throughout the war, surviving repeated encounters with submarines without a scratch.[91]

As if the ticking of the doomsday clock could be heard, Chief Steward C. Herrmann aboard the VATERLAND made an inventory of the liquors and other drinks aboard. He recorded that there were 4,825 quarts, 4,059 pints, and 150 splits in his wine storage room. He found 2,037 pints of soft drinks and 511 quarts.[92]

Others were also taking inventory. The U.S. Navy made a list of American passenger ships available for war purposes and announced on March 23 that there were 62 such craft sailing out of New York. With the exception of the six American Line ships and two Atlantic Transport Line vessels, these vessels ranged from 1,713 to under 8,000 tons.[93] The Navy also looked hard and long at its own tiny fleet of transports. The largest was of only 5,600 tons. Most were ancient vessels, such as the transport SUMNER, built in 1883 by, of all companys, Hapag, as their first RHEATIA.[94] Bernard N. Baker, an American shipping official, said that it was "a tribute to the genius of our quartermasters" that half of these ships were able to stay afloat.[95] The American Navy was not prepared either. Half of the 44 oil-burning destroyers and two thirds of all Navy ships were in need of repair when the nation was on the brink of entering the conflict. Instead of going into war service when the declaration came, they went into shipyards, staying an average of 57 days.[96]

It was recognized even before war came that the great task for the American Navy would be the job of ferrying American troops abroad. Rear Admiral Henry B. Wilson had been selected to go to England to begin planning for this mammoth job of transport. Instead, Admiral William S. Sims was named, and Admiral Wilson was kept at his post of organizing a western Atlantic patrol force. Both would have interesting connections with the VATERLAND/LEVIATHAN.[97]

As April came, America's active involvement was only a matter of days away. On April 4th the *Times* reported that the order to seize the VATERLAND and her German sisters was ready but would not be issued until after the expected declaration of war against Germany.[98] On the following day Collector Malone ordered 600 guards assigned to the duty of watching the interned liners spread out along the shoreline of Hoboken.[99] His order was a page-one story.

On Governors Island, Treasury officer John S. Baylis, a veteran of several voyages around Cape Horn under sail, waited and watched that evening. He waited for a telephone call. With him were Customs officials and 200 men on four harbor patrol boats.

"They were a fine group," said Baylis, who later, as Captain of the Port, would have to seize the French luxury liner NORMANDIE before World War II.

"It was raining like the devil.

"It was a vicious, bitchy night."[100]

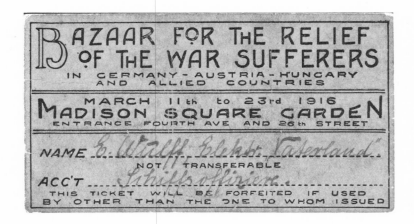

108

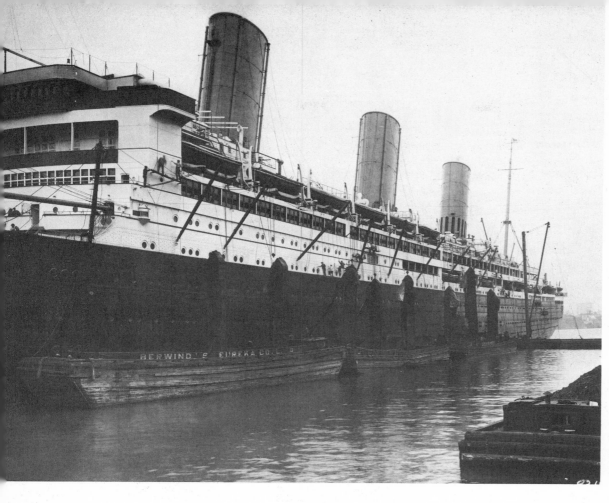

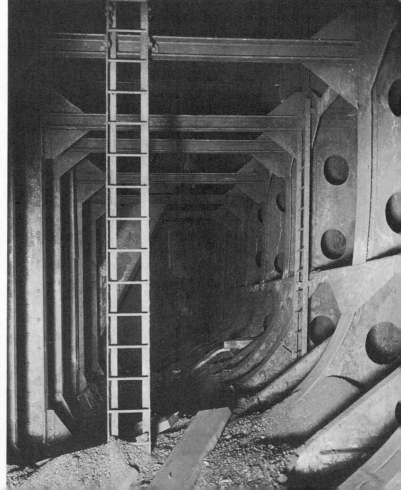

COALING was done by ultra-modern coal elevator devices at Hoboken. Working the port side (top) and between ship and pier (below). The #3 coal bunker (bottom right — Gibbs & Cox).

IDLE at Hoboken—VATERLAND's huge stacks rise above the other Hapag and N.G.L. liners (Bill Rau photo), and (below) stern view (Gibbs & Cox).

SEIZED—destroyer guarding VATERLAND and other ships (left), the VATERLAND flying U.S. flag (below left) and the Iron Cross hobnail fund raiser; with her new name (bottom right).

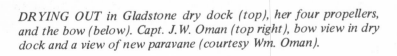

DRYING OUT in Gladstone dry dock (top), her four propellers, and the bow (below). Capt. J.W. Oman (top right), bow view in dry dock and a view of new paravane (courtesy Wm. Oman).

Chapter VII

AMERICAN

e embarked with 200 soldiers on four harbor patrol boats at 4 a.m. and sailed across the Upper Bay to Hoboken.

"We arrived at Pier 4 [Hapag's old Pier 2] and walked out on the pier.

"Every column seemed to have a Customs man behind it, for the pier had been under close Treasury Department surveillance for some time.

"The trip over had been a hard one because it was such a vicious night, and I was proud of our boys as they marched down Pier 4."

So said Commodore John S. Baylis, "Smiling Jack" of Coast Guard fame, the man who had been around the world under sail in 1903, the man who had been master of the New York Schoolship NEWPORT, and the man who seized the VATER-LAND.[1]

"There was a destroyer offshore supposedly watching the VATERLAND, and, hours after it was all over, at about 9 a.m. to be exact, they finally realized that something was happening on the pier and sent a junior officer ashore to see what was going on. I told them it was all over, long ago."

Commodore Baylis, who was then a lieutenant, remembers that on each of the other German ships he seized that wet and nasty morning the commanding officer had apparently been schooled to say, "I protest. . ." and to give a little formal speech. To a man, they all mispronounced the word "protest," making it sound like "I protect." All, that is, except the man on the VATERLAND's bridge, who came out loud and clear: "I protest."

Although war was not declared until 1:13 p.m. that day, Friday, April 6, the seizure of the German ships went on rapidly all morning under the direction of Collector Dudley Field Malone. The Collector, who admired Commodore Ruser very much, also had a particular affection for the VATERLAND. Years later he would say to Captain Hartley: "And I have always thought of her as my ship."[2] It was Good Friday, and President Wilson was surprised and shocked at the applause that greeted his war message to Congress. Back in the White House, he wept.[3]

About 300 men, all that remained of the VATERLAND's crew, were taken to Ellis Island, given health tests, asked questions, and offered the privilege of taking out first citizenship papers and entering the United States as immigrants. Second Officer Schultz and many others decided then and there to become Americans. The word was that the others would be sent to a camp in the South somewhere.[4] Commodore Ruser, not aboard at the time of the seizure, was allowed to remain at liberty under his own recognizance.[5]

Customs guards, along with a special group of 60 men from the Police Reserve, 37th Precinct, New York City, were assigned to protect the VATERLAND.[6] The official Navy history of the ship records that at this time there were several attempts to smuggle explosives aboard via the coal chutes from barges alongside. Although this report has all the earmarks of wartime rumor, it led to the rule that all unauthorized boats were to keep a distance of 100 yards away from the VATERLAND.[7]

Throughout the nation, 91 German and Austrian merchant ships were seized that day, valued at more than $100,000,000. The New York *Times* reported that the engines on all of them were found damaged "except the VATERLAND."[8] This exception, while basically true, would not stand unchallenged for long, so eager was the public to believe the worst. The VATERLAND was indeed a sorry sight, with her lower decks "filthy and unsanitary," and a general appearance of neglect everywhere. Her officers had managed to remove and probably destroy her operational manuals, machinery plans, and virtually all blueprints.

The few that were found when Hapag's 45 Broadway headquarters were raided were depreciated as "inaccurate."

There was confusion and indecision as to what to do with the VATERLAND and her German sisters. While the seizure had been accomplished by the Customs Service, which was under the Treasury Department, the Army, the Navy, and the Shipping Board, established in September, 1916, were all involved.[9] The Shipping Board took charge of the ships and named Captain Jamison to be the VATERLAND's master, although he was not in good health. Captain John L. Beebe, also of the American Line, was named navigating officer.[10] Captain Paul C. Grening, a Globe Line cargo ship master, was called on to help get the big ship in shape, and there was some talk that he might be her captain if Jamison was not fit.[11]

Almost every day stories were carried in the New York papers about the ship and her seamen. Two days after the seizure a coal passer named Tiedt, who had escaped the crew dragnet, gave himself up. On the same day the manager of the Ritz-Carlton Hotel's famous restaurant in New York was quoted as denying that any of his waiters had been among the VATERLAND's crew members who had been arrested and put on Ellis Island.[12]

On April 11 the *Times* published a letter from one R.B. Cooke suggesting that the interned German seamen should be used as ballast on unarmed merchant ships sent into the war zone, as nice a bit of hate-mongering as the war had yet produced.[13] Fortunately, some people still had a sense of humor, as both the *Times* and the *Tribune* showed three days later with another story:

"100 German Soldiers Hidden on the VATERLAND" was the *Tribune's* headline, but the subhead spilled the beans: "Tin Toys of Commodore's Son Found by Inspectors." Hans Ruser, Jr., was 10 years old and had moved off the ship with his mother to a room in Hoboken. By this time the Commodore had been ordered to join the others at Ellis Island. Collector Malone had the toy soldiers wrapped up and sent to young Hans. He also ordered the Fire Department to pump out what water had accumulated in the VATERLAND's bilges and set a team of mechanics to work to straighten out some of the confusion aboard the monster vessel.[14]

On the same day that the toy soldier story broke, Louis Hanz, another VATERLAND seaman who had escaped arrest, was found in Manhattan and locked up in the Greenwich Street Police Station.[15] Federal troops took charge of the German piers on April 19, relieving the Customs guards, and the installation became the government's major shipping base.[16] By the following day, cost estimates for repairing the nine largest German ships seized were in hand and a warning from Germany was published that if the United States tried to use any of the ships they would be torpedoed.[17]

From the beginning the VATERLAND posed a unique problem because of her great size. America had no experience in operating such a monster and no one was sure what should be done with her. Secretary of the Navy Josephus Daniels declared on April 21 that Navy recruits would be housed aboard her and other interned German ships in Hoboken.[18] From England Admiral Sims advised against the VATERLAND's use as a troop carrier because she would be such a big target. He had decided that German submarines were the war's biggest problem, and he insisted on a system of convoys for American troopships. There was some opposition to this from the British, in part because their own news censorship had been so complete that even some government officials did not know that U-boats were sinking Allied ships at the rate of 50 a week.[19] That others agreed with Admiral Sims is shown in a letter received by the Shipping Board May 4 from a hosiery and glove manufacturer named John H. Fedden. He suggested that the VATERLAND be used in the Pacific. With German submarines at their "maximum efficiency," she would be just too big a target in the Atlantic. If used in the Pacific, he added, she would release from that area an equal tonnage of smaller vessels, reducing "the danger of a sudden great loss."[20] This kind of talk would not die out for months.

One of the first Navy bluejackets aboard the VATERLAND was a lad named R. Lincoln Hedlander. From his first moments on the huge ship he made it his business to learn all about her from the inside out. He went everywhere. He found a mass of keys and, by experimenting, discovered where nearly all of them worked. This made him very much in demand. He found a VATERLAND breakfast menu for the maiden voyage tucked behind the printer's bench. He found a concert program. He found the ship's official document and took it out of its frame.[21] He was also busy recruiting his friends for duty on the big ship. The first man he signed up was Archie G. Holt, and in the next several days he got seven more stalwarts.[22] Another bluejacket among the first to board the VATERLAND was a lad who didn't know his real name. Brought up by foster parents he had always been listed as Percy, a foster, but when he joined the Navy he became Percy A. Frost. He was put to work ripping out lower deck staterooms and putting in bunks.[23] Ralph P. Cochran, another early arrival, wandered freely all over the huge ship on his first day aboard. Coming to the pilot house he scratched a mark in the brass band around the huge steering wheel. Years later it would be a choice decoration in his home in Vermont.[24]

Sabotage or No

ou will never run her. . . ."

These were the words that William H. Mackay, Navy engineer, heard the VATERLAND's chief engineer, Otto Wolf, say as he stepped ashore en route to Ellis Island. To Mackay they were a challenge, for it was he who was named chief engineer shortly after the seizure. He would serve under Captain Earl P. Jessop, engineering officer of the Brooklyn Navy Yard, who was put in charge of organizing the engine overhaul that everyone knew would be vital.[25]

One of the longest-lasting controversies involving this great ship is the question of how badly she was sabotaged by her German crew. It is known that an order to cripple her engines had been issued from the homeland the month before her seizure. The New York *Times* said the day after the seizure that the engines of all the German ships seized were found damaged "except the VATERLAND's." However, the public and the Navy were determined to believe that there had been major sabotage, and the whole question was so wrapped up in emotion that a dispassionate approach was impossible for a long time. Although the "very little sabotage" concensus was at first widely accepted, as war tempers rose the "total sabotage" theory crested and became so overpowering that any effort to deny it was looked upon as unpatriotic.

The whole question has been ably summarized by Captain Jessop:

"The VATERLAND, being the largest ship afloat and the most complicated, seems to have had inferior engineering talent operating her. Her engines are of the Parsons type of turbine, there being four ahead and four astern turbines on four shafts. All the ahead engines were found in excellent condition, and all the astern engines were found more or less damaged. The major part of this damage seems to have been due to faulty operation and not to any malicious intent.

"Cracks were found in the casing of the starboard high-pressure backing turbine. These were so extensive that it was palpable that the engines had not been used on the last run. This view has been corroborated since by the discovery of certain written matter on board showing that the vessel made the last trip on three propellers at reduced speed."[26]

Captain Jessop added that the ship's auxiliary engines were in fair condition, as were her boilers. The boilers, he added, showed evidence of poor handling. In summarizing his work,

Captain Jessop would later say that the lack of drawings had made the ship's restoration particularly hard and that "it has been only by the most patient and dogged following up of pipe lines and electric wiring that sufficient knowledge of this vessel has been acquired to render it safe to take her to sea."

The Navy was fortunate in having the services of Ernest H.B. Anderson, noted Scotch engineer of John Platt & Co., representing Parsons Marine Turbine Co. of Great Britain. The Parsons firm held a worldwide patent on the turbine, and the VATERLAND's machinery had been built by Blohm & Voss with their permission. Two or three days after the ship was seized Ernie Anderson went aboard to inspect the engine room with a junior naval officer. There was no heat or light. Clothing and shoes of the German crew were still hanging on hand rails and valve stems. In the pitch black of the main engine room their flashlights were like pin pricks. They saw the two inboard main ahead and astern turbines and then the navy man said: "Now you have seen the engine room."

Anderson reminded him that they had only seen two shafts, and that the ship was a quadruple shaft ship. Since the TITANIC disaster happened while the ship was being built she was better equipped with watertight compartments than almost any other vessel afloat. There were no doors between the main engine room bulkheads. It was necessary for Anderson and his companion to search around until they found a way to climb up and over the after bulkhead to enter the after engine areas. From there they were able to explore the after engine rooms, where they found the two low-pressure ahead and astern turbines. The only normal access from one engine room to another was by climbing ladders up several decks and over the bulkheads.[27]

Getting the engine repair effort under way was one of the most difficult problems facing those with responsibility aboard the VATERLAND in the first few days after the seizure. The ship was so cold and dank below decks that it took seven days just to ventilate her, once steam had been raised in two boilers and a turbo-generator had been put into commission. Every step had to be taken cautiously in the dark vastness of the firerooms and other machinery spaces, for no one ever felt quite sure that there were no booby traps.

"We were opening and closing doors and we did not know what minute, while groping in the dark with searchlights, something was going to happen to us," Chief Mackay remembered. He said that one day Ernie Anderson was missing for five hours.

"I searched for him an hour and finally found him at half-past six o'clock at night in the bilge of the ship searching for piping."

Mackay frequently made a point of saying that the VATERLAND chief engineer's remark as he left his ship was not said maliciously, but merely reflected his own inability to repair the damage done on her initial undocking at New York.[28]

The easiest to repair was the high-pressure ahead turbine in the main engine room forward, port side. It was found with its casing open and its rotor lifted out. The rest of the turbine was in perfect condition. The rotor was lowered back into place and the casing closed, and it was ready for use. The other ahead turbines were also found in surprisingly good shape, although certain cast-iron brackets had been fractured.

There was great damage in the blading of the astern turbines. The tips of the thousands of blades on each of those in the outer rows had apparently expanded when steam was admitted at one time, and had rubbed against the casing. The heat created had distorted the blades and put the turbines out of commission. In seeking to locate the trouble, the Germans had cut a 16-inch path through part of the turbine blading at several points. They had obviously tried to make the necessary repairs, possibly while the ship was still in service or maybe after her internment had begun. Brass pegs, for example, had been driven in at the end of some cracks in the casing of two of the astern turbines in an effort to limit the fracture. Had it been necessary to fabricate new casings, a six-month delay would have been

116

inevitable, but Captain Jessop recommended using the new and little-known technique of electric welding. His proposal and its acceptance and successful accomplishment must be recognized as a major achievement in the story of this ship.[29]

Restoring the damaged blades was another task of frightening proportions. The Coe Brass Works of New Britain, Conn., closed down its entire commercial production for two weeks to make the thousands upon thousands of new blades needed. Engineers from Westinghouse and General Electric came to New York to install them. All the tools needed, many of which simply did not exist in America, were hurriedly made to order by the Brooklyn Navy Yard.

The several instances of real sabotage were of minor importance, relatively easily detected and repaired. Some piston and connecting rods had been cut with hacksaws. The engine room telegraph systems were smashed. Certain machinery parts which the Germans thought could not be replaced were missing. Some steam pipes had been disjointed and plugged with solid pieces of brass and then joined again, to show no evidence of being tampered with. The threading of some bolts had been filed almost smooth so that the bolts, being put back on, were held by one or two remaining threads. They would have given way under any real pressure, but a thorough program of checking, testing, and double-checking cleared away these minor irritations. There was some evidence that a plan had been prepared to burn the VATERLAND, but no one could explain why it had not been carried out, and most authorities discounted the whole notion.

Over the next several decades there would be repeated statements that written instructions for the wholesale destruction of the VATERLAND and other German ships were found when 45 Broadway was seized. In 1923, when the sabotage controversy flared anew, newspapers tried in vain to locate these documents or copies of them.[30] They could not be found. They have never been located or documented to this writing. On May 5, 1917, the *Marine Journal* summed up the case for sabotage when it noted that many of the German ships were not so seriously damaged as was supposed and added that "German efficiency manifest in the wrecking of their machinery is being outmatched by American efficiency in the work of restoration." That the damage was not really as bad as first suspected was attributed to the fact that "the German officers and men, like good seamen, hated to damage and disable their own gallant ships or they underestimated Yankee mechanical ingenuity and resource."[31]

In addition to the sad evidence of grave damage to the astern turbines, it was discovered during the engine restoration that other difficulties had been experienced by the VATER-LAND's engineers on her seven 1914 crossings. A faulty ash-ejector device was found which must have created an almost continuous flow of seawater over the fireroom floor. This was not corrected until after the ship's first crossing as an American troopship. As many as 4,000 of the fire bricks in the boilers had to be replaced after each of her voyages as the VATERLAND. Her German engineers had had great trouble with leaky tubes at the back end of all her 46 boilers. Things had not been easy for the VATERLAND's black gang.[32]

Paul Revere Smith, later a leading American steamship executive, was assistant machinery superintendent on the Hoboken piers during the VATERLAND's restoration. He found a damaged turbine blade and had a souvenir paperweight made out of it.[33] Another man pressed into service to help with the mammoth restoration job was John V. Shelden, chief engineer of Long Island Sound's greatest paddle steamer, the Fall River Line flagship COMMONWEALTH. He took a leave of absence to do his bit.[34] Despite all this experienced talent, the pace of engine-room restoration flagged, and it was not until the Navy finally took over the job that any real zip and punch were added to the task.

Meanwhile, a variety of big and little things happened during May, the first full month of American ownership of the VATERLAND.

Her picture was shown in *International Marine Engineering*, the journal of the industry. It showed the German seal at her bow, golden and clean. She looked sleek and shining in the photo and she completely dwarfed the PRESIDENT LINCOLN next to her.[35] On May 6 Christian Wilhelm Schultz took out his first citizenship papers. He hoped to get a job in a bank on Wall Street. To his surprise, he was almost drafted into the U.S. Army, being rejected only because he was not a full-fledged citizen. He had made several unsuccessful efforts to get his trunk and personal possessions from the VATERLAND but they were all gone, stolen.[36] Eberhardt Wulff had moved to Dover, New Jersey, where he became an electrical engineer in a hosiery plant, working from 6 a.m. to 6 p.m. When he married the former Elsie Kusel, of Bremen, his name got into a newspaper and he was almost arrested. The authorities had confused him with Otto Wolf, the VATERLAND's chief engineer. The Army was looking for Wolf to charge him with sabotage.[37]

On May 12, Congress in a joint resolution put the official stamp of approval on the VATERLAND's seizure.[38] The resolution authorized the President to take possession and title to any vessel within our jurisdiction and owned by a citizen of a nation with which we were at war.

During May the nation sent only 1,718 men to Europe. The little 5,000-ton Morgan Line steamer MOMUS was the first ship to sail with troops, Captain John Maxim in command. Her chief officer was Harold Cunningham, who was shortly to be assigned to the VATERLAND and later would become her master.[39] As May ended, the Federal Government took over the Mountain Park Hotel in Hot Springs, North Carolina, to house Commodore Hans Ruser, 49 other German officers and seamen from the VATERLAND, and men from the other German ships who had decided not to become citizens.[40]

She Becomes a Troopship

It cost more than one million dollars to convert the sumptuous VATER-LAND into an American troopship.[41] After the seizure, and while a beginning was being made toward repairing her engines, divers were sent below to examine her underbody, check her four propellers and her rudder, and make sure there were no bombs attached anywhere. This had been one of the fears. Although it had been supposed by some that the VATER-LAND would fit into a new dry dock built in Halifax, it was soon realized that she was much too big. Aside from the dock that had handled her in Hamburg, there was only one place in the world where she could be examined out of water—a new dry dock in Liverpool.[42] It was necessary to list her over by pumping water into the ballast tanks on one side and emptying those on the other. In this way at least a part of her accumulated coating of barnacles and marine growth was removed. To get more of her hull out of water, piles of steel weights were stacked on one side while men worked on the other. At best it was a make-do job. Men swarmed on the high side, first scraping and then painting. Her entire outer body and waterline area were given a coat of gray paint, which transformed her into a ghostly shadow of the Hapag sea queen she had been.[43]

Among the earliest of the specialists sent aboard to assist in the conversion of the VATERLAND was Arthur F. Van Dyck. His duty was to get her wireless in operating condition. When he inspected the shack he was astonished to find, in addition to the usual Telefunken set, a lot of equipment hidden in drawers and behind bulkheads. It was so arranged that it could be put into operation in minutes, but the German operators had removed all instruction books and wiring diagrams. It took him three months to get the equipment into usable shape.[44]

Bertram Seaboldt, who headed a company bearing his name, was put in charge of restoring the navigational instruments and getting new equipment.[45] The stacks and masts were all painted, and great piles of life rafts were brought aboard and stacked on deck in all available open spaces. All the work done in the wireless shack, on the bridge, and on A, B, C, and D decks was nothing, however, compared to the transformation wrought from E Deck down. The VATERLAND had boasted 1,500 staterooms. All but the 300 first-class cabins, which were retained for officers, were ripped out and replaced with troop compartments. Tiered iron racks known as "standeez" were put in these areas, three high. By using every cubic inch of available space it was estimated that as many as 17,000 persons could be crammed aboard, including the crew.[46]

The destruction that took place in the process of making this space available can only be regarded as one of the sad stories of the war. It was frightening. Bathtubs were broken with sledgehammers to get them out of the way. Cushions and chairs were often just tossed overboard. Wall fixtures were ripped out of their sockets. Porcelain and rubber tiling were painted over and ruined. Leaded-glass windows were removed and packed away in boxes, but the work was done so carelessly that three fourths of them were broken in the process.[47] Instead of unscrewing mirrors, workers tore them from the wall and smashed them. Henry Dipple, one of the Navy bluejackets assigned to the ship right after she was seized, remembers with shocked disbelief how the workers from local shipyards went about their task.

"We called them wreckers," he said.[48]

"At the rate they were going, however, the war should have been over before the ship was ready to leave the United States," he added.

Mike Sullivan, then the editor of the Submarine Boat Corporation's house organ "Speed-Up," had a young cartoonist on his staff named Salmon. Salmon was moonlighting after his regular Navy work as an electrician on the VATERLAND, and his favorite topic of conversation was how sad it was to see the "gutting of the German whale," as he put it. He was seriously concerned about the brazen thievery that was stripping the once-great liner of her costly fittings, decorations, and furniture.[49]

"It was a pity to see what they did to that ship," remembered William Schwartz, who was shifted by the Navy from the battleship TEXAS to the VATERLAND to help work on the engine repair assignment. One of his pals on this detail was Herb Rowedder, later to become the ship's photographer and still later second officer.[50]

In some respects the thievery was even worse than the wanton destruction. It was like a giant anthill with everything in reverse. Instead of thousands of tiny ants each laboring to carry a grain of sand to the anthill, the VATERLAND was like an anthill with thousands of ants carting things off her, day and night.

"It was outrageous. Her officers and men simply looted her, taking anything and everything. It was so awful that I never forgot it, and when, in the Second World War, I was captain of the port and had to seize the NORMANDIE, I made darn sure it didn't happen again," said Commodore John Baylis.[51]

One sailor wrapped a lovely linen tablecloth around himself, put on an overcoat and got away with it. It remained a prized memento of the war in the home of Henry E. Whittle, pharmacist's mate aboard the VATERLAND.[52]

All the wines were taken off in June by Inspector Percy Reynolds of the Custom House. Assistant Paymaster Judkins, formerly of the Hotel Biltmore, checked them as they went aboard a Custom House lighter alongside the ship. Many paintings, including portraits of Bismarck, Lincoln, Washington, and Theodore Roosevelt, some of the best pieces of furniture, and a "gold table service" were also taken off under careful watch. Despite all efforts to make sure that the wine was guarded carefully, several Custom House guards and a dock patrolman were found drinking fine Moselle wine in a stateroom on F Deck near the swimming pool. About 20 empty bottles were found in the cabin when the raid took place.[53]

One reason that so much was stolen was the great number of people aboard the ship. There were scores of commercial shipyard workers, machinery specialists, Navy bluejackets, and Shipping Board officials and staff members, not to mention a great variety of watchmen. Several "home defense" guards were caught trying to get off with silk curtains, spreads, and bed linen. Shipyard workmen were found removing the taps from water faucets. Navy Yard electricians were apprehended with blankets stolen from the ship.[54]

Sometime before the Navy assumed full control of the VATERLAND a bitter letter of complaint was sent to the Treasury Department spelling out details of the "looting." The letter charged that the stolen goods were worth thousands and thousands of dollars, that "valuable pictures, paintings, and an immense quantity of furniture were taken out and given away or sold privately," and, finally, that $45,000 worth of wine was stolen and given to friends of the contractors around Hoboken. Although the letter was not signed and has apparently disappeared, the report it engendered—written by H.G. Stuart, Special Deputy Collector of Customs at New York, to Secretary of the Treasury McAdoo—has survived, and a letter from F.O. Rowe, Assistant Secretary of the Treasury, to Edward N. Hurley, Shipping Board Chairman, has also been retained in the National Archives.[55] The Treasury report goes into some detail about the wine situation, noting that the ship's wine room had a strong door and heavy lock. The inventory made by Lt. Judkins showed 777 fewer pints of wine than had been in the wine room two months earlier, and 1,104 more pints of soft drinks. The wine was sold at auction and bought by L.Gretsche & Sons for $10,092.80, or about 77 cents a bottle. The lost 777 pints would have been worth only $500, a far cry from the $45,000 charged in the anonymous letter.

As to the art objects, the Stuart report is less explicit. He noted that all of the VATERLAND's hangings, paintings, rugs, etc., were carefully inventoried, cleaned, and stored.[56] This report identifies a Mr. Bowman, who was in charge of the inventory of the VATERLAND's paintings, as being from the Hotel Biltmore. Lt. Judkins, who was serving aboard the VATERLAND and who supervised the transfer of much of the art work, the gold plate, and the wines from the liner to a Custom House launch, was also formerly with this New York hotel. Some months later a German newspaper clipping found on a dead German soldier charged that the only great painting to survive the mass looting of the VATERLAND was the one that had been above C Deck at No. 1 stairway. This was the picture of the mother and her two finely dressed sons in a garden. The news clip added that this painting "now hangs in the Hotel Baltimore in New York." Could it have meant Biltmore?

"The big ship was never built to carry troops and ammunition, and to make it fit for such uses the thieves tore out all of our beautiful art and all of the fine woodwork, without any feeling whatsoever. Twenty freight-carfuls of wood and furnishings were taken from the ship and loaded in Hoboken to be burned." The clipping ended by ridiculing the American effort to rebuild the VATERLAND to carry up to 15,000 troops, saying that all the German ships seized would only be able to carry up to 28,000 men and 5,500 officers, "so the Americans will have to change their hopes."[57]

The unsigned letter to the Treasury had noted that "the man who is now in command or in charge of the VATERLAND is familiar with what has happened and is horrified at some of the things that have been done." This must have referred to Captain Jamison, but the reply by Collector Stuart, written many months later, when Captain J.W. Oman was in command, noted with true bureaucratic cunning that "this would be most alarming, if true," adding that Captain Oman "had no knowledge of the subject and was naturally not horrified." The reply blamed such pilfering as was done on the large numbers of men "of unknown antecedents" who were working aboard. With tongue in cheek, Collector Stuart concluded his report by offering to make a full investigation if the name and address of the informant was furnished, as if nothing could possibly be done unless that information was known.

The whole question of supervision, repair, and guarding was made much more complicated by the VATERLAND's uncertain status. The looting complaint had gone first to the War Department, then to the Department of Justice, and finally to the Treasury, which turned it over to the Shipping Board. Both the War and the Navy departments had taken possession of some of her fittings and sent them to various storehouses. Most of the material eventually was put in warehouses in South Norwalk, Conn., according to the Shipping Board.[58]

Perhaps one of the saddest stories of this period involved the painting of old, peace-loving Ludwig, of Bavaria, the ship's godfather. Navy wireless operator Howard McKissick, assigned with Arthur Van Dyke to the VATERLAND, remembered that portrait, but did not know whom it depicted. Like all the other gobs aboard, he assumed it was of the Kaiser.

"Hi. Hi. But it did not take we sailors long to mutilate that pix," he recalled.

"I would have loved to have had that oil painting of the Black Forest, but I imagine some gold braid latched on to it. Hi. Hi."[59] The four Gerard de Lairesse paintings of Pandora were too big to steal. They were loaned to the Metropolitan Museum of Art for the war's duration.[60]

The Navy's history of the LEVIATHAN, ignoring the looting charge, reports simply that about $150,000 worth of silverware and the vast accumulation of the ship's stores and provisions as well as her magnificent table linens, china, and glassware were placed on the pier.[61] Several public auctions were held.

At one of these auctions the Kaiser's bust from the Social Hall was bought by a Westport, Conn., innkeeper named Dominic Vetromile. It took four men to move it.[62] Mr. Vetromile also bought a massive rubber floor from the ship. It came like a giant jigsaw puzzle, with several hundred three- and four-inch pieces that fitted together tongue and groove. He used it in his place, the Miramar Inn.[63]

Some heavy round wooden tables were bought by the Hanover Square Restaurant, New York. The screw holes in the flaired pawlike legs of these black wooden tables were used to bolt them to the deck. They are still in use in this downtown Manhattan restaurant at this writing, below New York's famed museum-restaurant India House, whose collection includes one of the large bells from the LEVIATHAN.[64] For many years the office of the Chairman of the Maritime Commission, successor to the Shipping Board, was decorated with a thick and beautiful rug from the VATERLAND. Countless other items have remained in offices and homes around New York, recalling the wealth that was aboard this flagship of Albert Ballin. There is a gold telephone in a home in Bayside, Long Island. It came from the Kaiser's suite.[65]

Bluejacket Fred Jones found two small silver platters from the Kaiser's suite. They had knife marks on them and 55 years later he donated them to the South Street Seaport Museum. He also acquired a surgical shears from the operating room.[66] A beautiful silver and glass inkstand, several saloon chairs, wine-storage kegs, solid brass ornamental lamp-lighthouses, stained-glass seals from the Smoking Room, dishes, knives, forks, metal serving plates, one of the large iron-cross ornaments made out of hobnails, and one of the lignum vitae VATERLAND paperweight ornaments were located during the writing of this book.[67]

While the upper decks were being cruelly torn apart and desecrated, below the liner was being slowly restored to working order. By the end of June, 38,000 new blades had been installed in her four astern turbines.[68]

Other June developments having a bearing on the ship's story were: On June 14 the authorities made public their decision to pay the interned crews the same wages as American seamen were getting.[69] On the following day Congress placed the management of any seized ships under the authority of the President.[70] A week later 470 more German sailors left Ellis Island for North Carolina.[71] Finally, on the last day of the month, President Wilson officially turned the VATERLAND over to the Shipping Board.[72] Troop movements from America rose sharply in June, with 15,000 leaving for the war in Europe. A feeling of disillusionment, however, began to spread in Britain, for more than just token forces were needed to tip the balance. Every effort was made to speed up the conversion work in Hoboken, as the troop-lift capacity of the seized German liners was many times that of all the existing American ships put together.[73]

Work to be done on the VATERLAND was of staggering proportions. There was a growing feeling that the Germans might have been right when they said she could not be put into operating condition by the Americans. There were literally miles of steamlines to be checked inch by inch. There were more miles of water lines, and miles and miles of electric wiring. The task would have been a gigantic one even if all the blueprints and specifications had been on hand, but the Americans had to work blind. Each small accomplishment was cause for celebration. On July 10, when the mid-pressure rotor was revolved in the ahead and astern directions and found to be in splendid working order, there was cheering throughout the forward engine room. The cast-iron brackets which had supported the turning gear had been fractured, but were relatively easy to repair. Ernie Anderson made a mental note of this; it was just one more illustration of the fact that the Germans had confined their sabotage to unimportant "support" parts of the machinery.[74]

July 10 was a significant day in the Washington story, for by resolution the Shipping Board directed its New York office to charter the VATERLAND to the Navy. The Navy was authorized to take over all repair contracts and make such modifications as it saw fit. The Navy would have complete control of the vessel's operation. At long last there would be one authority, one responsible driving force behind the restoration of the VATERLAND. And it was high time—it had taken more than three months to reach this decision.[75] President Wilson approved the Board's decision on the following day, adding that the VATERLAND and her ex-German sisters would "constitute the shuttles of a ferry" across the Atlantic.[76] Two days later Secretary of War Newton D. Baker and Secretary of the Navy Daniels jointly recommended that the VATERLAND and certain other vessels be commissioned in the Navy for transporting troops during the continuation of the war. On the same day this step was approved by the President.[77]

A Navy Ship

n advance party of thirteen Navy bluejackets came aboard the VATER-LAND on July 24, for on the following day she would become officially a Navy vessel. One of them was William Robert Blake Stevens, named after a 17th-century British admiral. Stevens would shortly become messenger to the new captain, J.W. Oman, an Annapolis man who had been assigned to take command of the world's largest ship.[78] The first entry in the official Navy log follows:

"8 a.m. to meridian. At 10 a.m., July 25, 1917, the U.S.S. VATER-LAND was placed in commission by Captain J.W. Oman, U.S.N.; Ensign A.H. Bateman, U.S.N.; Assistant Paymaster L.B. Foster, U.S.N.R.F.; Assistant Paymaster H.B. Judkins, U.S.N.R.F. Fifty-five workmen were on board, work going on in the engineering department and on deck under the direction of the Shipping Board and Customs officials. Divers cleaning bottom. Signed Fred K. Harper, Lt. j.g. U.S.N.R.F."[79]

Although there had been a few bluejackets aboard the VATERLAND since April, after July 25 she was all Navy. One of the new crew was J.J. Callahan, who came down with a group from the Newport Naval Training Center. On the question of German sabotage it was his feeling that they simply could not have put their hearts into it. Despite the destruction below E Deck and the frightful looting, he found that there was still much of beauty left.

"I recall the carved wood figures in the Smoking Room. We admired them and heard they were the work of a famous artist. I remember the big marble and tile swimming pool; saw it many times later filled to the brim with the brown canvas impedimenta of the soldiers. We felt the VATERLAND, to paraphrase one of Gershwin's songs, was 'a wondrous toy just made for us sailor boys.'

"We swarmed over her from crow's nest to double bottom, night and day until the arrival of some big contingents of sailors and some brass cramped our style. We inspected all the magnificent staterooms and public rooms. I remember one suite with heavy glass windows instead of port holes. We called it the Kaiser's suite."[80]

Among the officers assigned to the VATERLAND in those early days was Alton B. Sharp, a graduate of the University of Michigan, later to become president of the noted coastwise company known as the Eastern Steamship Lines.[81]

Her new Navy chief engineering officer was Lieutenant Vaughn Veazey Woodward, son of an Ohio River steamboat captain and another Annapolis graduate. His fame would be assured by this assignment, and he would earn not only the Navy Cross but a citation from President Wilson.[82]

On the matter of sabotage, Woodward was positive:

"Most of the vessels seized had been deliberately wrecked by the crews, but the commander of the VATERLAND evidently would not permit wanton destruction of his vessel."[83]

Chief Bill Mackay, who remained aboard through the completion of the engine restoration, stepped down a notch when Woodward was named Chief. His work would not be forgotten and he would receive the Congressional Medal of Honor for this assignment.[84] It was a good team below decks, and despite a one-day strike in August, the repair job continued with all reasonable speed.[85] It was realized from the start that the VATERLAND would be the last of the former German ships to be put into transport service. While the work aboard her went ahead with renewed vigor, others of her Hoboken sisters were restored and put into service. The day after the Navy took over the LEVIATHAN, the former North German Lloyd KRONPRINZESSIN CECILIE was commissioned as the U.S.S. MOUNT VERNON. Her sister, the KAISER WILHELM II, became the U.S.S. AGAMEMNON. Albert Ballin's historic AMERIKA, her name anglicized to AMERICA, would also be commissioned by the Navy in due course, along with the GEORGE WASHINGTON, which kept her name.[86]

Above deck there were many changes during this period. The Social Hall became a hospital and the gym an isolation ward. The doctor's office became the sick call station. The swimming pool was turned into a baggage room, and the after baggage compartment became a brig and powder magazine. The Main Dining Saloon was converted into a mess hall for troops.[87]

Frank Flowers, from Boston, had enlisted in the Navy in 1898 and had served in the Spanish American War and the Boxer Rebellion. He came aboard the VATERLAND as senior chief commissary steward and he would become so famous that in World War II a Liberty ship would be named in his honor.[88] His job was to convert the galley to serve up to 10,000 troops per trip, and he would do this so well that he would earn the Navy Cross.

"He inaugurated a system which was adopted as a standard for the entire transport service," Secretary of the Navy Daniels would say later. "His ability, zeal, devotion and experience helped build up an efficient commissary system, which was little changed during the entire war."[89]

Food

When Flowers first went to sea, a ship's crew was divided into different "messes" of twenty men. Each mess handled its own food. This had been changed at the turn of the century, and each ship was made the basic food-providing unit.[90]

Flowers found the five galleys on the VATERLAND in a bad state of deterioration. He consolidated them into two, one for the troops and crew and the other for the Army and Navy officers and so-called passengers. For the troops he used the old main galley, and for the officers he used the old Ritz restaurant galley. Twenty-seven 100-gallon steam kettles were installed, along with new bake ovens, dough-mixers, heavy-duty electric meat-grinders, and, joy to the sailor, three large electric potato-peelers. Frank's pride was a Grand Union potato-masher which he devised. It would mash about 2,000 pounds of potatoes or mix the same amount of hash in 60 minutes. Another of his pets was a large German steam box into which six barrels of peeled potatoes were dumped. It worked so well that three similar boxes were built, giving Flowers the means of boiling 24 barrels of potatoes at one time.

As for serving the food, Frank Flowers' imagination stood him in good stead. Twelve huge galvanized iron tanks were built and installed under the magnificent dome painting in the Main Dining Saloon. Eight held huge square food containers kept hot by jets of steam from beneath. Four others were for washing mess kits and rinsing them in clear salt water. Each soldier would clean his own kit before leaving. Special wooden mess tables were built, 3½ feet tall and without seats. The men had to eat standing. A similarly inventive approach to questions of food storage, refrigeration, and personnel training was taken. Although at first only three men were assigned to Flowers, in due course he had about 100 working with him. Most were inexperienced either as seamen or as cooks, but their "high standard of intelligence and eagerness" overcame the problems, Flowers said.

The food used aboard ship on a typical voyage was enough to serve the crews of ten battleships. For a typical quarter, the food bill was $750,000. Among the items bought each shopping day were 60,000 lbs of tinned meats, 25,000 lbs of salt meats, 120,000 lbs of smoked meats, and 260,000 lbs of fresh meats. In a summary of his work written some years after the war, Frank Flowers noted that at one time there was a plan to put 20,000 troops on his great ship. The commissary department reported it was able to meet the necessary requirements for such a staggering load.[91]

Albert Ballin had wanted to call her EUROPA, and she had been known as Hull #212 for many months, but now she was the U.S.S. VATERLAND and so her Navy bluejackets came to think of her in the summer of 1917. Caps and ribbons for all enlisted men bore the name "U.S.S. VATERLAND."

"I shall never forget the stunned silence of the group around the ship's bulletin board when the new name LEVIATHAN was posted," remembered J.J. Callahan.

"We were already proud of the old girl and felt that the name U.S.S. VATERLAND possessed considerable *chic.* We could neither pronounce nor spell LEVIATHAN. We never suspected its Biblical origin."[92]

By order of Navy Secretary Daniels and without any formality the name was officially changed on September 6, 1917.[93] Many years later, Mrs. Woodrow Wilson was a passenger on the ship and told Commodore Hartley how it had been chosen. She had been asked by the Shipping Board to suggest a good name for the great vessel. According to her story, she

had never been so perplexed by a problem before. She searched through books and pored over dictionaries. She asked many friends for help and pondered scores of suggested names. Finally, in desperation, she walked into the President's oval study in the White House and confessed her dilemma. The President, without even lifting his head from his papers, said:
"Why, that's easy, LEVIATHAN. . . .It's in the Bible, monster of the deep."[94]

A New Name

little did Mrs. Wilson or the President realize the almost prophetic vision of the choice, for the ship which would do so much to defeat Germany, hot-bed of anti-Semitism, was thereby given a name of true Hebraic origin. The Hebrew word is "liwyathan," and means long-jointed sea monster.[95] It is a word used colloquially in Israel.[96] The Bible has five references to a "leviathan," variously using the word to describe an aquatic animal, a crocodile, a dragon, and a whale. Webster's *New International Dictionary* gives us a second definition: "something huge and formidable of its kind."[97] John Milton's *Paradise Lost* uses the word to describe Satan lying chained on the burning lake in Hell.[98] Thomas Hobbes entitled his treatise on the state *Leviathan*. The word "leviathan" has been used in many other writings, including Rabelais' stories and Lord Bacon's version of the Psalms, and now appears in most dictionaries with the meaning "monster of the deep."[99]

Many ships have been named LEVIATHAN. There was an old Scottish railroad ferry built in 1849 with this name.[100] The world's largest vessel of her day, and perhaps the most ill-starred ship ever built, was christened LEVIATHAN on her launching date–November 3, 1857. She is better known as the GREAT EASTERN, a name she was given after her original owners went bankrupt.[101] A British suction dredge and a Port of London Authority floating crane are both sailing under the name LEVIATHAN at this writing.[102]

Getting back to the chronological story, there was a small fire on September 23. It was on F Deck aft and it happened early in the morning, but the flames were quickly put out. Two days later repair work on the pesky low-pressure astern turbine on the port side was finished and it was closed up, with some 13,500 new blades in place.[103] The next day, to go from the sublime to the ridiculous, a large amount of "imperial sausage" was received aboard.[104] Then a carrier pigeon dropped dead on deck and a fireman was court-martialed for using profanity.[105] The low-pressure astern turbine on the starboard side was closed October 4 and ready for testing. Three days later it was coupled up with the low-pressure ahead turning gear and everything went well. On October 11, the same day that turbine-specialist Marcus P. Iverson joined the LEVIATHAN, the high-pressure astern turbine casing was replaced, containing 6,500 new blades.[106] Iverson, who would end up as the LEVIATHAN's chief engineer on her final trip, had been called to Navy service by telegraph at 4:30 the morning war was declared. He had served on the U.S.S. CHICAGO until transferred to the LEVIATHAN, where he was assigned a turbine station as a chief machinist's mate. His cabin was on G Deck.[107]

The New York *Tribune* had two LEVIATHAN stories on October 20, one a human interest story about her conversion and the other a warning. The warning came from a Captain Hans Mortensen, master of the American bark PAOLINA, which had been sunk a month before by a German U-boat. The submarine captain's first question when he picked Mortensen out of the water was "When will the VATERLAND go?" Captain Mortensen warned that the Germans "have set a trap for her and are eagerly awaiting her first voyage as a troopship."[108]

The feature story was entitled "In the Shadow of the Big Ship," and was accompanied by two pen-and-ink drawings of the great LEVIATHAN surrounded by small ships.

"About her eddies a strange composite stream. Men, beans, barbed wire—harsh barbs an inch in length—shoes, shrapnel and sugar, jam, typewriters and bacon and more men and more men. . . ." The world around her appeared dwarfed from her porthole. The other transports, coming and going "seem like tugs which themselves have the agitated proportions of water bugs." The article added that in the transformation from liner to troopship the "magnificent gold service of the Kaiser's table, comprising 80 pieces of solid gold, disappeared." It had been last seen being checked off the ship by Lt. Judkins, formerly of the Hotel Biltmore, when he turned it over to that Customs launch in charge of Inspector Percy Reynolds, but who has it now "is the subject of much official speculation."[109]

Ship's Organization

nder the direction of the ship's three executive officers, Commanders William N. Jeffers, John H. Blackburn, and Adolphus Staton, the ship's complement of 68 officers and 2,240 men began to shape up. There were two main groupings, one for the deck and the other for the engine. The deck force was divided into nine divisions, four doing deck work proper, such as manning guns, lookout stations, and fire control spots, and five performing special services like carpentry, painting and plumbing, navigating, hospital work and guard duty. Deck divisions were divided into four sections, while engine divisions were made up of three sections each. Each man had a number comprising his division, section, and personal numbers.[110] William F. Engel, of the first division, third section, would have been #131, because he was first man in his section.[111] Engel wore a white band around his left arm at the shoulder on his blue uniform and a blue band on his white uniform. He was a coxswain. Engineers like M.P. Iverson wore red bands on blue and white uniforms.[112]

The ship's organization was described in a 23-page blue dittoed instruction sheet. It began by giving the basic dimensions of the LEVIATHAN, such as her 65,000 tons displacement and her 24-knot speed. There were pages on her cargo booms, derricks, and winches, and a note that she had four passenger elevators and six for provisions and freight. Her ground tackle was described, with a note that while she had a stern chain locker and hawse pipe, there was no stern chain or anchor, a deficiency she had had since her earliest days. Her machinery and firerooms were described briefly. A note pointed out that gun crews would mess at their guns in the danger zone. The ship's system of sea watches was reviewed. A section on lifeboats noted that boats numbered 31 and 32 were to be kept rigged out and ready for instant lowering at all times.

There was a lengthy part dealing with the ship's routine in port, with the duties of boatswain's mates, petty officers, messengers, buglers, side boys, electricians, signalmen, quartermasters, gun strikers, and the anchor watch spelled out. Rules about liberty, as shore leave is known in the Navy, were set down. In discussing uniforms, there was a note showing how extreme were the precautions against submarines. No one was permitted to wear white or light-colored clothing on deck at sea after sundown!

Payday was set for the 5th and the 20th of each month, and allotments could be made to relatives. Crew members could have friends aboard but they could not be shown around the ship. They were restricted to F Deck lobby. Officers could entertain in their cabins. Among the general regulations was one prohibiting the playing of musical instruments during working hours and another outlawing the possession of dice. Lending or borrowing money was forbidden, and it was a court-martial offense to lend money at interest. The crew were not permitted to visit the troops being carried, and the troops were not allowed in crew quarters.

"Leaning over the rail" was prohibited, and no spitting or throwing of remnants of food or rubbish over the side was allowed. It might be spotted by submarines. Smoking in the heads was strictly forbidden.

Lengthy rules about fire drills and how to behave in the event of a fire at sea were set down. The concluding admonition, in capital letters, was:

AT ALL TIMES: – MOVE QUICKLY; – KEEP ABSOLUTE SILENCE; – KEEP COOL; – DO NOT RUN.

Dock Trials

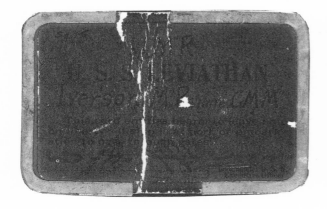

In late October large-caliber guns were placed aboard the LEVIATHAN and a depth-charge chute erected on her stern. Fire-control and range-finding apparatus were installed.[113] The last of the 8,000 new blades in the starboard inboard high-pressure astern turbine were installed, and on October 31 the turbine was closed. This was the last of the major engine repairs made necessary by the combination of that disastrous undocking in May, 1914, plus years of neglect and some superficial sabotage.

Early in November preliminary steam trials on all the turbines were held, with the turbines uncoupled from the propeller shafts. They were driven at up to full speed, 180 revolutions per minute. A slight hitch developed in the starboard high-pressure astern turbine when a regulator valve jammed open and the turbine gained momentum too rapidly. There was a loud bang and it was found that the piston valve was fractured. It had been fractured for a long time, it was concluded, and that may be the explanation of why this turbine was damaged more than the others.[114] Final dock trials were held on the morning of November 12. Everything went well, and Lt. Woodward reported that the ship was ready for sea duty.[115] There were many who kept their fingers crossed. In fact Admiral Sims was still actively pressing against the use of the LEVIATHAN. On November 2 he wrote:

"The ship is so big a target. I have previously reported against using the LEVIATHAN for the present. I am assuming, too, that all of the troops we have to transport for the next few months can be accommodated on other transports. Whenever the situation becomes more pressing I presume we shall have to use the LEVIATHAN and take the risk."[116]

The crusty Admiral's prejudice against the LEVIATHAN would take a twist few could have anticipated.

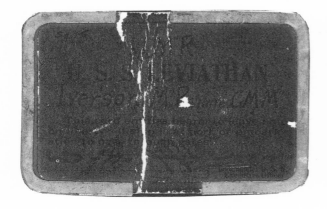

Chapter VIII

SHE SAILS AGAIN

n attractive green-covered telephone directory for the LEVIATHAN was issued on Saturday, November 10. Its thirteen pages were bound together by a white cord. The first name on the list was that of Rear Admiral Albert Gleaves, Commander of Convoy Operations in the North Atlantic, U.S. Navy, although he rarely even came aboard the ship. He had room C-154 and his telephone number was 195. This was also Captain Oman's room, although his phone number was 53. Commander W. N. Jeffers was listed as the executive officer. He had room C-151 with telephone number 35. Lt. Cmdr. J.H. Blackburn, shown as the navigating officer, had room B-2 and telephone number 4. Lt. Cmdr. Woodward had D-338 and his telephone was 98. Lt. Harold Cunningham was in B-4, and his roommate was Lt. A.E. Harding. Ensign Beebe had Cabin B-9.[1]

The telephone book was printed aboard the LEVIATHAN, as were a whole series of other booklets having to do with different phases of her routine. As the days passed and as all the last-minute details were being ironed out aboard ship and at the bustling Army base on the Hoboken piers, the same Helen Fleming who had known the VATERLAND so well before the war (because her girl friend's uncle was a steward) again found a way to keep up her love affair with the great ship. She had taken a Civil Service examination and won an appointment as a stenographer in the Army Quartermaster Corps on Pier 2, Hoboken. Wearing a regular Army uniform, she was in continuous contact with all the rebuilt ex-German vessels. She came to know the LEVIATHAN's crew as they passed on and off the big ship, including Thomas F. Zero, better known as Zip, and Mark Iverson, two chief machinist's mates.[2] Complete secrecy enveloped all the troopships and their movements, but everyone knew that the LEVIATHAN would be sailing soon. When the bluejackets stopped to take a drink of water at the scuttlebutt, they passed the word that everything was ready. "Scuttlebutt" is the shipboard term for drinking fountain, and the term has come to mean sailor's rumor. There were many rumors as to where the LEVIATHAN was going, but the wise ones were certain she would be headed straight for France. But there were also many who didn't bother with rumors and just lived from day to day in the new world of war and excitement. One such was Tom Lindquist, already a veteran of six months in the Navy. On Wednesday, November 14, he wrote home.

"Dear Mumma," he began, on the back of a postcard of the VATERLAND, still with its German caption. He would be home Monday or Tuesday and would get his pay before then and hoped to bring some money home.[3]

It was several weeks before Tom's mother got that money or saw her son again, for on November 17, three days after he posted the card in Hoboken, the LEVIATHAN finally sailed. Aboard were 241 Marines, and Captain Oman ordered them at sailing time to stand around the upper decks where they might all be seen, to give the impression that the ship was loaded with troops. There was considerable alarm about the trap that German subs were said to have set for the liner.[4] Everyone assumed that she was beginning her first voyage as a troopship, and the Army did everything it could to bolster this belief, even to the loading of several hundred bales of hay aboard. It was placed on deck where it could be seen, to suggest that a large cavalry unit was sailing. The crew joked about the hay and, when anyone asked what it was for, they would quip: "Well, maybe we have horse marines aboard."[5]

Crowds of well-wishers gathered quickly when it was seen that tugs were gathering to undock the LEVIATHAN. On the ship's bridge with Captain Oman was Captain Allan C. Howell, the undocking tug pilot. A former merchant ship master, he had joined the Dalzell

Towing Company in 1912 and was, in 1917, chief harbor pilot for the Shipping Board. He knew the undocking would not be an easy one, for the ship had lain in the same slip for well over three years. He remembered her precipitate departure on her maiden voyage. It was 9:30 a.m. when steam was admitted to the turbines and the four huge propellers began slowly to turn in the muddy Hoboken waters. There were those who doubted that the huge hull would even move, for when she had been seized it had been found that the silt was 27 feet high around her keel.

The ship throbbed ever so slightly from the motion of her wheels, and a sensation of life penetrated the most remote crevices of the huge city within a steel shell. Massive mud slicks appeared over a 100-foot area under her beautiful counter-stern as her slowly moving wheels (propellers) churned the bottom into black froth. The bubbly film darkened the waters around the tugs. Bluejacket Dipple counted 46 tugs. Slowly, and with great dignity, the giantess began moving backward, as a white bloom of steam burst—silently for a flash, and then with a roar—from her reverse whistle on Stack #3. It was a prolonged and thunderous blast, and it shook the red brick bar fronts up and down River Street. Someone in the pilothouse was literally hanging on the whistle cord. But it was largely show, for all harbor traffic had been stopped just for this sailing. Ernie Anderson and Chief Woodward held their breaths on the control platform deep below in the engine room, and Captain Howell watched tensely with Captain Oman eight decks above them on the bridge.

Then she was really moving, slipping past the pier as if the pier were moving backward, her freshly painted gray hull crowned by three gray stacks and framed in a mountainous mass of tumbling coal smoke. Majestically she cut her way through the water, now blue and fresh, as her hull slipped gracefully out into the currents bringing water down from the hinterland of New York State. The tugs shifted in response to shrill whistled signals and began pushing against the river's downward thrust. Slowly the full, overhanging stern, with its seal of Hamburg and German eagle decorations still intact, was forced around, and the tall bow, minus its decorative scroll work, was pointed down toward the Battery and the Narrows. She was poised and ready to begin the second and most hazardous era of her brave career. Everyone waved and cheered.[6]

The first day's voyage was a short one.

In line with the policy of extreme caution, the LEVIATHAN only went down to a point off massive old Fort Wadsworth, just beyond the Quarantine Station on the eastern edge of green, hilly Staten Island. She anchored there for the rest of the day and all of Saturday night. She rested while a thorough check of her engines was made. At high tide she hoisted anchor and slowly steamed out of the Narrows and off in an easterly direction toward Nantucket. Her engines were shifted to their high-pressure cruising combination and she was gradually worked up to a speed of 18 knots. Many ships saw her, and this helped to corroborate the rumor that would be spread along South Street and West Street that night—that she was indeed heading for France.

The LEVIATHAN had six-inch guns aboard, eight of them. There were two on the forward deckhouse, two on the well deck forward, and four at the stern.[7] They were tested with targets dropped over the side on Monday the 19th.

"We found a number of windows broken on the upper deck due to the concussion of the firing," W.F. Engel remembered.

"Our gun crews were very efficient."[8]

The day was exciting for another reason: it saw the ship's first real Abandon Ship drill at sea. A 12-page booklet entitled "Abandon Ship" had been prepared and was studied carefully by all on board before the exercise took place. It was explicit to the most minute detail, such as a caution to Army officers not to wear spurs when Abandon Ship was sounded. A sampling of the tersely worded paragraphs will give the flavor.

"When the call 'To quarters' is blown, at any other than the regular time 3 p.m., all officers and men will immediately repair to their quarters.

"This will be done expeditiously but without crowding or confusion on stairways or decks.

"All sentries will immediately see that all men in the vicinity of their posts proceed at once by the nearest route to the quarters occupied by them. Extreme measures are authorized in the enforcement of this provision.

"If it is decided to abandon the ship, the bugle call ABANDON SHIP will be sounded."

Abandon Ship

most careful detailing of clothing followed, with the order that life preservers were to be worn but not overcoats, and with the rule that a blanket was to be carried in winter months, made into a "tight roll around the shoulders." A canteen was always to be carried when the ship was in the war zone and "no water under any consideration will afterwards be used out of these canteens until the ship reaches port" unless the ship was abandoned. Gloves were to be worn by all individuals but no property of any description "will be carried by anyone," nor any arms or ammunition, except by officers in charge of troop compartments or mustering stations.

A center spread in the booklet laid out the troop compartments on one side and showed, on the other side, the different officers in charge. Lt. Cunningham, for example, was responsible for the troops in all the forward areas. He would lead them in an emergency to the boats atop the forward deckhouse.

Each route was spelled out in detail. As a kind of postscript it was noted that once the Abandon Ship routine had been mastered a variation would be tried. In that variation, under good conditions half the troops would be kept on deck in daylight hours; each group would be located in the vicinity of the boat or raft mustering station to which it had been assigned for the drill, and it would just stay there when the Abandon Ship call was sounded.

There were problems on the trial, and the wisdom of making the short voyage was amply proved. One serious situation developed the third day out, when a valve stem on the port steering engine broke. The starboard engine was cut in, but on the next day, the same thing happened with its valve stem. The ship could not be steered; she lay helpless—a sitting duck for submarines. New valve stems were found, put in place, and promptly broken. To make everything seem much worse, a box filled with broken valve stems was found in a storeroom, sickening evidence that the Germans had had similar difficulties. For a full 24 hours the LEVIATHAN moved ahead in brief spurts and starts. Chief Woodward haunted the steering engine compartment, grappled with blueprints, and thought. He grew haggard, and the ship's doctor ordered him to rest. During one of his brief spells of tossing on his couch, a solution came to him and he rushed to the machine shop. Using a new pattern and heavier workmanship, machinists made a new valve stem. It worked, and they made another for the other steering engine. Both valve stems worked, and they continued to work throughout the LEVIATHAN's entire troopship period.[9]

Ernie Anderson had some anxious moments when it came time to test the astern power units. It was found that when she was given full speed astern the engines could not be stopped. Fortunately there was enough space to maneuver and time to close the main steam stop valve in the boiler rooms. On dismantling the astern throttle valve it was found that the spindle was broken. The valve would open but could not be closed. It was now evident what had really happened with the Germans in congested New York harbor on her first return voyage. When the ship could not be stopped going astern the engineers had opened the ahead turbine throttle. The extreme overload on the astern turbine had stripped the blading and when the rotors continued to rotate both cases were smashed.

"It will take 90 days to repair this," Anderson quipped darkly, but, fortunately, he was overstating the case.[10] The ship had turned from her easterly course and was heading south. At night she practiced zigzagging as if she were in the war zone. Then when she was 1,000 miles along toward Cuban waters there was another crisis. It was a minor one, but one which could have had disastrous consequences. The ship was running blacked out, with all portholes closed and painted a deep black, to insure that not the slightest hint of light got out. The strictest rules were in force against smoking, and even the bridge lights were dark green and visible for only a few feet. Suddenly the ship's antenna, 200 feet up and stretching 700 feet between masts, caught fire. The ship was outlined from above, and there was great commotion on the bridge. It soon developed that Radio Operator Van Dyck had been experimenting with the German equipment and had gotten the power up to 20 amps in the antenna. He was delighted with his success until he got an abrupt order from the bridge to shut everything down. A seaman put out the fire on the antenna, but it was a long time before Captain Oman cooled off. No more high power tests, and the Captain wasn't the least bit interested in the radio man's explanation of the importance of proving out the secret German equipment.[11]

The LEVIATHAN steamed past Watling Island, or San Salvador, as it was first known, where Columbus landed; and then she headed for Cuba. Seven days out of New York she came to anchor off Guantanamo Bay, at the mouth of the harbor. Her Cuban-bound troops were taken ashore in tenders and a few Navy people came aboard. Whiling away the time at anchor, James V. Shand, chief butcher, and some others decided to try to catch a shark. They saw lots of them sweeping and turning in the clear water alongside. They used a double-pronged hook and a long piece of one-inch hemp. To attract their victim, Shand tied an entire cow's liver to the hook. Over the line went, and it could be seen clearly 30 feet below the surface. In no time a shark had taken the bait. The men had tied the end of the line to a stanchion, and as soon as the shark swallowed the hook about 40 men grabbed the line and raced back across the width of the ship. The thwacking monster was slowly, and with much sweat, hauled up the clifflike side of the LEVIATHAN and over the rail, where it lashed around and snapped until exhausted. The butcher finally killed it by driving a cleaver into its skull.[12] Four sharks were caught, averaging 10 feet in length. The sailors cut out their backbones and made fancy carvings out of the pieces.[13]

On the return voyage a short trial was made at full speed. The four propeller shafts were turned at 171 revolutions per minute for the equivalent of 22½ knots. An estimated 65,000 shaft horsepower was developed and the main turbines worked splendidly.[14]

The Black Gang

Although nearly all American vessels were coal-burners at this time, nothing like the LEVIATHAN had ever been worked by an American engine room crew before. There were 17 engineering officers and 950 men. Although the ship was filled with labor-saving devices and was far ahead of most other vessels of her day, the basic task of putting coal into her 46 boilers was still strictly hand work. Each boiler had three firing doors. They were numbered 1, 2, and 3. The doors on the opposite-facing boiler were numbered in an opposite way so that firemen would not bump together. The firing, or coal throwing, was regulated by bells, one ring for #1, two for #2, and three for #3 door. The bell system was controlled by an operator who watched a master steam gauge, and he would set the time interval between bells on the basis of speed required. It was a direct throwback to the tub-thumping cadence of the stroke leader in the Phoenician war galleys, where slaves rowed to the drumbeat. For standard speed there was a six-minute interval. For full speed the bells were speeded up to a three-minute interval. And the black gang jumped. Even after the ship was converted to an oil-burner, the men in the firerooms thought of themselves as the black gang. Originally a term of derision, it became a badge of honor.

A third-class fireman, or coal passer, would carry the coal from the bunker in a wheelbarrow and dump it in front of each boiler. Then a second-class fireman would do the actual firing into the furnace. Only three shovels of coal were allowed for each door at each bell, although Second-Class Fireman John W. Thomas in Boiler Room #4 used to throw in a fourth whenever the chief watertender was not looking. Such was the spirit of the hour. There was one chief watertender in each fireroom and one division officer in each propeller shaft over the four firerooms. Each watch had about 200 firemen.

After the second-class fireman fired his door, a first-class fireman raked the next firedoor and another second-class fireman sliced the next. The tools required were a shovel, a slice bar, and two hoes. One of the hoes was more like a rake and was used by the first-class fireman for leveling the next fire to be coaled and for removing clinkers. These tools were stored in what was called an ash pit. The slice bar was a steel bar about 10 feet long. It was run along the grate bars to raise the fire and turn up clinkers.[15]

Gulping 138 shovelfuls of coal every three minutes, the massive gray-hulled ship steamed at top speed through the warm Gulf Stream on her roundabout way back to New York. Five years and three months later she would make the same course at a rate never equaled before by an ocean passenger liner, to open her era as a sumptuous U.S. luxury liner; but now her troopship career was about to commence.

While she sailed for home a speech was being given in Dresden by Albert Ballin's old nemesis, Admiral von Tirpitz, an address that may have tipped the balance in America's decision as to how the LEVIATHAN was to be used. He said first that the entry of the United States into the war was "disadvantageous to us in morale and many other ways." He insisted, however, that from a military standpoint America's entry was of little significance "because it is the tonnage question that is decisive." He meant that America just did not have the ships to transport the needed men and equipment to Europe. Taking a slap at Albert Ballin, he said he regretted that the submarine had not been used more extensively earlier in the war, and called it Germany's "powerful economic weapon." He predicted that by employing it to the fullest, Germany would win the war.[16]

Back at Hoboken on Thursday, the 29th of November, the LEVIATHAN became the center of a high-level and stormy controversy. Admiral Sims was not alone in his opposition to the use of the liner as a transport. A report by Admiral David W. Taylor, Chief of the Navy's Bureau of Construction and Repair, noted that the ship's great size would make her an easier target than most vessels and would give the enemy a better chance of a successful torpedo hit. Admiral Taylor said also that a successful enemy attack on the LEVIATHAN would "in all probability result in greater loss with consequent increased moral effect."[17] Assistant Secretary of the Navy Franklin D. Roosevelt sent a copy of this report to *The Navy and Merchant Marine Magazine*, and showed a copy of it to one of his brilliant young Harvard friends, Ralph E. Cropley. Cropley made it the basis for a four-page, single-spaced diatribe to Secretary McAdoo.

Although Cropley had only a smattering of knowledge in the field of naval architecture, he wrote as if he were an authority. His letter began by quoting an unnamed British ship captain as saying it would be a crime to use the former VATERLAND (he never called her LEVIATHAN) as a troopship. The use of such a "damnable ship would not only be a waste of money but would end in the murdering of eight or ten thousand of our boys," Cropley wrote.

"The VATERLAND has been back here a week after being away 12 days," he added, and many of her sailors were saying that they had been frightfully seasick on the trial trip. Cropley knew because he had met them in the Hoboken YMCA "War Hut," he wrote.

"This is not surprising news to anybody knowing the peculiarities of the OLYMPIC, MAURETANIA and other top-heavy ships which are too long for the seas and can't get out of their own way," he added.

The strange character of the letter began to emerge when its writer indicated that he had promised Secretary Roosevelt not to publish any letters on the subject "if the VATERLAND is sunk and turns over on her side, drowning our boys like rats in a cage." But, after the war, they would be published "if she is sunk, but only if she turns turtle in sinking." The basis for his alarm, apparently, was the transverse (lengthwise) bulkheads that all large passenger ships had. Because of these, a big passenger ship that was torpedoed might fill up on only one side, list, and go over from the weight of her tall superstructure.

"If it can be assured that the VATERLAND, if she should be strafed, would sink on a level keel, I'd raise no objections," he wrote knowingly.

His grandiose generalizations and morbid predictions of disaster notwithstanding, Cropley did get around and did know important people. He implied that he was at a private dinner party with Captain Haddock of the OLYMPIC at which this noted British sea dog "stated that his private opinion was that it was wicked to use the VATERLAND as a transport for if she struck a mine or was torpedoed he believed she was top-heavy like the rest of the gigantic liners and in six minutes would flop over on her side." Cropley, a master at repetition, then said that "everybody in the shipping business" knew that the design of ships like the VATERLAND was "fundamentally wrong and in peace times a person takes his life in his hands whenever he travels on them."

He urged that more small ships be used and that the VATERLAND be made into a hospital ship "if she will be respected" as such by the Germans. Otherwise, he concluded, she should be a prison ship, anchored in the Hudson between Tarrytown and Yonkers.[18]

Ten days before the LEVIATHAN began her trials the Bolshevists had seized control in Russia and German arms were freed to renew the attack on the western front. The German 1918 offensive, which would push the battle line almost up to the point of extreme penetration of their 1914 attack, was about to begin. The trickle of American troops had remained a trickle. Few British ships had been pressed into the American troop run, and the pressure to put the great LEVIATHAN into transport service was continually mounting, despite outbursts like Cropley's. Her successful high-speed tests on her trials were used by the Navy as evidence that she could outrun the fastest U-boat, and the decision to put her on the run was made.[19]

Although there would be echoes of the controversy, preparations for the LEVIATHAN's first trip continued. Because she could not be dry-docked and because it had not been possible to have any inclining experiments or stability tests, it was decided to keep the number of troops carried down to 7,500 men, 500 naval officers, and a crew of 1,500.[20]

"IMPORTANT!! READ AT ONCE"

This is what was printed on the cover of a booklet entitled "Naval Transport Regulations – USS LEVIATHAN," put out at this point. Copies were to be given to every man aboard. Sixteen pages long, the little document spelled out rules for darkening ship, for the various drills to be held, for smoking, for washrooms, for showers and latrines, for the hospital, sick call, and messing – and even for the barber shop.

It concluded with a plea that sounds naive by the standards of a half century later:

"On the day of embarkation and during the day of sailing the officers of this ship have duties involving details far surpassing anything a shore going man can possibly know. In order that you may be transported over seas in safety and comfort and landed in good health, months of thought have been devoted to these details by them. So think twice before you make any requests. If it is necessary then write it down on a slip of paper as it will find its way to the proper person quicker in that way. Don't kick or offer any criticism until you have thought it over carefully, taking into full consideration the short time you have been acquainted with problems of this sort and the fact that this ship is carrying double the number of troops of any other ship in the world."[21]

Commander Adolphus Staton, who was self-conscious about his German first name and always used only the initial "A," issued a special one-sheet list of Embarkation Instructions. He was so alarmed about the danger of confusion on this first departure that he ordered all troops "to get into bunks as soon as found and remain in bunks until compartment is filled." Even then they were to remain in their compartment.[22]

The great day finally came. It was a Friday, December 14, and 6,839 troops from the 82nd Brigade, the 163rd and 164th Infantry were aboard, with 277 Army officers led by Brig. General Edward Vellruth. Also welcomed aboard were 138 nurses from base hospitals 31 and 34.[23]

First Voyage Again

or the second time the LEVIATHAN would have a maiden voyage, but how different from the one she had had when she was the VATERLAND! Snow was falling, had been falling heavily for the last three days. It was a raw, cold morning, but aboard ship, at least in the words of the cheerful Navy history, all was excitement and high spirits.

"Nothing could dampen the ardor of the troops and sailors on board. We were about to cross the ocean, most of us for the first time, and the hazard of the submarine, whose operations were more active at this period of the war than at any other time, and the excitement of the adventure, if nothing else, was sufficient reason for everyone to keep his spirits up."

The Navy's story of the first trip is all sweetness and light, but there were many problems. It was determined almost immediately that the LEVIATHAN's coal was too deficient in quality and quantity to enable the ship to maintain full speed throughout the voyage. A dispatch was sent to the Commander-in-Chief announcing a 24-hour delay in the LEVIATHAN's scheduled rendezvous with an escort of destroyers off the coast of Ireland. The new date set was 8 a.m., December 22. The LEVIATHAN traveled alone, with no convoy or escort, for none could have kept up with her, but seven destroyers were scheduled to meet her off Ireland. At 8 p.m. on December 18 they set out for Queenstown. Commander S.W. Bryant was in command of the flotilla of "tin cans," and, unfortunately, he had not learned of the LEVIATHAN's dispatch delaying the rendezvous for 24 hours. The weather was at its worst as he led his group of small craft out for what was to be a wait of four days.

The clocks were advanced 47 minutes each day as the LEVIATHAN maintained a steady 158 revolutions per minute, giving her an even 21 knots. Heavy swells caused many of the troops to suffer *mal de mer*, and the effectiveness of the first gun practice on December 19th was anybody's guess. There were drills aplenty and the troops were repeatedly reminded that a lighted match was visible half a mile at sea at night. As the ship was approaching the war zone, with everyone on edge, winds at 65 miles an hour and the blackest of dark nights, the emergency siren, a most horrifying, spine-chilling sound, went off. It was a false alarm. The freezing winds and spray had contracted the wire controlling the siren and set it to wailing. There was "quite some excitement," the Navy history says.[24]

The voyage was a nightmare for Commissary Chief Frank Flowers. The problem of disposing of garbage under war conditions was terrible. It could not be thrown overboard until one hour after nightfall. The rule that all wood food crates had to be broken up and carried far aft to the firerooms to be burned made almost as much work as was required by the actual messing.[25]

It was also a nightmare for Fireman J.W. Thomas because of the ash-ejector system. The discharge for burned ashes was below the waterline, and, because the ship was zigzagging, the outside pressure was too great for the pump pressure, and there was a flareback every few minutes. Water came in and over the floor plates and washed the coal against the bulkheads. It was so bad that the men had to fire from the wheelbarrows. The swirling water was hard to pump out because the pumps would become clogged with the fine coal down in the bilge wells. Thomas had to go down into the well in his area to clear the coal from around the suction pipe. He was often up to his mouth in coaly slurp. Later the discharges were raised 27 inches and new injectors installed.[26]

But to some the fireroom was a lark. A few of the troops volunteered to stoke coal and seemed to enjoy it. What they really relished was the privilege of eating three good meals a day at a sitdown table at the crew mess, as pay for their work. One of these volunteers, a bright and cheery lad, came back on the LEVIATHAN only a short while later, wounded and minus a leg.[27]

Shortly after midnight on December 22 direct radio contact was made with the destroyers. The LEVIATHAN reached her rendezvous point at 6 a.m. that Saturday morning and at 7:30 the first of the destroyers found her. It was a moment of great relief and elation aboard the LEVIATHAN, and aboard the destroyers as well. From the big vessel the tiny craft looked battered and weary. They were so covered with spray and green water that their masts seemed more like periscopes. Getting messages across to them was most difficult, despite the full page of special signals that had been issued for the LEVIATHAN. The final line of this instruction sheet added confusion to the situation when it said:

"The above is in addition to and not substituted for gun fire."[28]

The whole matter of convoys in wartime was a relatively new and unformulated business. Blinker signals were low-powered and primitive and signalmen were untrained. The LEVIATHAN had only one blinker on her bridge. Voice radio was unheard of then. To make matters worse the LEVIATHAN had orders from Washington that conflicted with those sent by Admiral Sims on such key points as the determination of the time of day, the establishment of zigzag patterns and the breaking of radio silence. The fact that the destroyers had been out for four days did not help in creating a spirit of understanding of these difficulties.[29]

For most of Saturday the escorting destroyers managed to maintain their screen around the LEVIATHAN. It was necessary for the troopship to reduce her speed to permit the smaller craft to keep up, and even with this slower speed one of the destroyers was forced to drop out of formation. The inability of the escorts to keep up with the LEVIATHAN must have been a matter of grave concern to Captain Oman, who was very conscious of the opposition by Admiral Sims to the use of the LEVIATHAN as a troopship and of the reasons for this opposition. Slowing down in the war zone was not his cup of tea, particularly as enemy submarines were known to be in the area. Heavy rains made it difficult to signal visually. Radio silence was maintained. Heavy weather and poor visibility produced a slight scattering of the escort during the night. The LEVIATHAN had been ordered to proceed through two route points. She had also been ordered to keep outside the 50 fathom curve, a curve which jutted out between the two route points. A minor course change had to be made. In attempting to inform the escorts of this change some confusion resulted from a communication failure. A signal was misunderstood. By dawn, however, the escorts were all in position and the convoy passed through the rest of the danger area with no problems. It was a day of great excitement, and of surprises. Early in the afternoon a submarine was sighted. She flashed the proper recognition signal. A Britisher! Then an aluminum-colored blimp, almost invisible in the fading light of the western sky, appeared. She was on scouting duty. A friend! Sunset that very short Sunday was at 3:30 p.m., and the LEVIATHAN headed up St. George's Channel toward the River Mersey. She and her escorts arrived off the Skerries at 7 p.m.

A pilot was on the lead destroyer and when dark had enveloped the LEVIATHAN he boarded her and directed her to an anchorage for the night. There was only a sliver of moon and all night the destroyers circled protectively. The voyage had been timed to take advantage of the dark of the moon on this last critical lap. The LEVIATHAN could only enter the Mersey at the peak high tide of the new moon, and at 6 a.m. she was again moving, stealthily, toward the bar. She passed close enough to the Bar Light Vessel to hear a cheerful "Merry Christmas" via a megaphone hail. She was safe.

The rise and fall of the Mersey tide is 21 feet and once having crossed the bar the LEVIATHAN was again trapped by the tide. Before she could attempt to get into the great new dry dock at the mouth of the river, she would have to wait for nearly three weeks for the full moon high tide, but she would get her troops off first and then move down toward the dry dock, a prime reason for making Liverpool on this first trip.

The Mersey was so shallow that as the ship moved upriver Captain Oman ordered some bluejackets to be let down on either bow to cling precariously to the huge anchor chains and drop the lead. He had to know the depth. These sailors shouted out their soundings and the message was relayed to the bridge by some young ensigns, a number of whom had just graduated from Pelham Bay or a similar training station. Admiral Cyrus Plunket was with Captain Oman on the bridge. He was shepherding a load of 16-inch naval guns being sent to France. As they listened tensely, one very green young ensign, misunderstanding the standard sounding chant of "by the deep nine," which meant at least 54 feet of water, relayed it as "Five feet nine." Captain Oman turned to Admiral Plunket with a wry smile, whereupon the Admiral uttered a line that was to become a wartime classic:

"What the hell — are we wading through dew?"[30]

Another conversation on the bridge that morning was less cheerful. It was that between Commander Bryant, destroyer escort officer, and Captain Oman. Just what was said has not been recorded, but the destroyer man had come aboard in a fit of temper. Seaman Bill Stevens, the lad named after the British admiral, was at his station as coxswain on #7 gun when Bryant came aboard and remembered hearing him speaking in a heated manner and threatening to break Captain Oman for having out-run the destroyer escort contrary to orders from Admiral Sims.[31]

Shortly after 10 a.m. the LEVIATHAN reached the Princess Landing Stage at Liverpool. She was greeted with the news that the pilot boat that had been circling her while she was at anchor the night before had struck a mine and sunk.[32]

Thousands of miles away, what turned out to be the last blast of an earlier controversy was fired by General Tasker H. Bliss, in a memo to Secretary of War Baker. Bliss proposed that the LEVIATHAN should be used as a station ship at Brest instead of as a troopship.[33] This was the final protest made by any top official over the service of the LEVIATHAN.

Herbert Fuchs, Navy engineer, had expected to be part of the first liberty party to land at Liverpool at 4:30 p.m. on that first day of the ship's visit to this British seaport. Not only did he not go ashore, but he stayed aboard in the brig. He had failed to salute one of the ship's officers.[34] Needless to say, the troops had all been disembarked before this minor tragedy took place. They had formed up in a large open square and marched away, greatly envied by some of the crew, who were eager to get in there and give the Huns hell.[35]

The next day was Christmas and it was a bleak, cold, unhappy one for most of those aboard the LEVIATHAN. The prospect was most unexciting. It would be three weeks before the ship could be moved on another high tide into the new Gladstone graving dock at Seaforth Sands at the mouth of the Mersey. Then she would be held there for at least another three weeks, because of all the work that had to be done on her bottom. So in all likelihood the voyage home would not even start for some fifty days. Fifty days in Liverpool in midwinter was not something to look forward to.

Liverpool

The presence of nearly 2,000 American sailors in the British port was bound to mean all sorts of problems for both crew and British citizens. The tendency of Americans to boast about their country and to flash their full pocketbooks, not to mention the jealousy of the local swains whose girls left them for the rich Americans—all these things had already dampened the original good spirits on both sides.

Henry Whittle, LEVIATHAN gob, had an uncle living near Liverpool, a rather crusty old gentleman who voiced what must have been a fairly common opinion when he said: "Am I to judge all Americans by the sailors I see in Liverpool?"

Henry, who had a quick wit, replied: "Am I to judge British women by the girls I've met here?"[36]

Another cause of complaint by the citizens of Liverpool was the way the Americans called their copper pennies "clackers." This slang term originated from the fact that most sailors had no place to put their change. Their only pockets were a small watch pocket and a tiny slit for cigarettes in their blouses. So they tucked these larger coppers in their socks, and eventually the coins would work their way down into their shoes, clicking and clacking as the sailors walked along. Most LEVIATHAN seamen had a tough time getting used to English money.[37]

Whittle's jibe about British girls notwithstanding, many LEVIATHAN seamen found them delightful. Axel Eddie Swallow married one, and his best man was Chief Machinist's Mate Marcus Iverson. The party was long and late, and Iverson walked back to the ship alone that night. Iverson's orange liberty pass, about 1 inch by 2½ and framed in a tin edging for longer life, has survived to this writing. It was signed by W.M. Jeffers and on the back was a note: "If found please attach stamp and return to USS LEVIATHAN, care of Postmaster, New York City." On this same side was written the name "Mary" and the phone number "Mon 1283."[38]

Perhaps this was the young lady that Marc Iverson got to know in those early days of the LEVIATHAN's first visit to Liverpool. He was leaving the ship one day to see her when he was stopped by Captain "Buggs" Oman. That was his nickname to the crew. A short, dapper man who looked more like a Methodist minister than anything else, Captain Oman called to the Chief Machinist's Mate:

"Hi there, you, Chief. . .what's the idea of going off ship out of uniform?" Iverson was wearing a handsome bow tie, similar to those worn by British naval officers. Four-in-hand ties were regulation on American vessels. Iverson saluted and stood awkwardly while the Captain turned to First Lt. James W. Ford, officer of the deck. No one noticed Iverson's queer stance. He was ordered back aboard ship to put on a proper tie. Later he passed inspection without comment and succeeded in delivering a heavy bag of sugar to his lady friend ashore. He had held it under his left armpit all the time.[39] This was one reason the girls of Liverpool quickly dubbed the LEVIATHAN their "Big Christmas Box."[40]

Many times LEVIATHAN seamen managed to get ashore without a pass. The standard way was for the seaman to turn his dress blues inside out to make them look like a working outfit. Then he would acquire a can of swill from a cooperative messman and carry it dutifully off one of the small after gangways. Once ashore he could easily get lost among the mountains of stores on the dock and be off. Careful shore patrols were established to keep on the lookout for trouble. A typical 7:30-to-midnight patrol was made up of 26 men from the LEVIATHAN. An ensign would be in charge, with a boatswain's mate 1st class as his petty officer. The patrol would be divided into five groups. In addition to their uniforms they would wear watch caps, overcoats, leggings, belts and night sticks. Four men with the boatswain's mate would be stationed at the Dale Street Police Station at the pier head. Four more would cover the area from Water Street to Dale. Four would patrol from London Road and Lime Street to Adelphia Street. Because it was always a trouble spot, eight men with a coxswain were assigned to the vicinity of the famed American Bar. One of these men was James J. Callahan on the night of Wednesday, January 2, 1918, and he saved his assignment sheet.

The LEVIATHAN's captain was liked and admired by his crew. All during the period of the ship's restoration in Hoboken his patience and thoroughness had earned him the respect of all hands. After the arrival at Liverpool he made his report to Admiral Sims and then proceeded to prepare for the difficult job of dry docking. Captain N.C. Twining, the Admiral's Chief of Staff, brought to Captain Oman's attention the report of Commander Bryant. The destroyer commander challenged the accuracy of the LEVIATHAN's navigation as an explanation of the confusion over the two route points. He cited instances where inadequate communications had produced complications. Realizing that Admiral Sims was an old destroyer man himself, Captain Oman spent most of January 2, 3 and 4 in the Admiral's office consulting with Captain Twining and others as to how to respond to Bryant's comments. He explained how the LEVIATHAN's navigation was based on all the latest and finest devices and should be relied upon far more than the finest efforts made on the deck of a bobbing destroyer. He had no intimation that his explanation was not fully understood. He completed his comments on the voyage and returned to the LEVIATHAN satisfied that the first voyage was regarded by Admiral Sims and his staff as completely successful.[41]

In Dry Dock

ocking the LEVIATHAN in the Gladstone graving dock was a major operation made doubly difficult because her exact hull lines and shape were not known to the Americans or British. Lt. A.W. Minuse, who had played a major part in her conversion into a troopship, did the job. To double-check the stresses, he stretched piano wires and placed sighting battens inside the ship so that even the slightest sagging or bending could be spotted immediately and checked. Knowing the weight distribution within the hull and having a pretty good idea of the underwater shape, he had massive wooden blocks placed in what would turn out to be just the right positions, with wedges and great tree trunks to shore up the ship along her sides. The tide was right on January 14 and the LEVIATHAN moved down the Mersey, but high winds prevented the docking and she had to return to the landing stage. The spring tides would last only one more day, so, despite none-too-perfect conditions and very swift currents, the ship moved out and downriver again on the 15th and with less than an hour's leeway made it into the great stone dry dock. The entrance was so tight for her great width that she could not use tugs to assist her, and the job done by her docking pilot was a brave one. He was a senior Cunard Line master. Two weeks later the LEVIATHAN's officers would be shocked to learn he had been lost on a torpedoed Channel steamer.

After the dry dock's mammoth door, or caisson, was closed, the water was pumped out, slowly and with frequent long pauses. As her great hull, the largest moving object in the world, slowly settled on the center-line blocks, divers worked frantically putting chocks in place along her keel. The whole process stretched over three full days. When it was all done the LEVIATHAN had embedded herself two inches into the surface of the blocks. The battens showed that her 950-foot hull had relaxed by only 1-3/8th inches. Work began at once on her underbody, now exposed for the first time to American eyes.[42] Butcher Jim Shand was among the many crew members who walked around the sludge-covered bottom of the dry dock to look up at the monster that was their home. He pocketed a large barnacle that he had managed, with great effort, to pry off the hull. He would keep it for the rest of his life.[43] J.J. Callahan was among the crowd, and years later he wrote:

"Looking between the props lengthwise along her bottom was like looking at New Jersey through one of the Hudson River tubes."[44]

The dry dock workmen, who had seen all the great liners, admitted they had never seen anything like the VATERLAND, as many gobs still called her. They marveled at the extra thickness of her side plates.

One inconvenience in particular made the 27-day stay in this dry dock memorable to her crew. After the dock was pumped out and the ship was high and dry, all heads (toilets) aboard were closed and sealed. Temporary wooden sheds had been built at the end of the dock and quite a walk from the ship. It was January, with typically cold, damp, foggy English weather. The wind always blew in from the sea.

"I remember well how you had to duck and sidestep sheets of used and stained toilet paper sailing in the wind on your way to a seat—where you did not linger."[45]

Osmond McFarlane, an enlisted man who was serving as an orderly, had an experience that he would remember and recount many times in years to come. He didn't like sleeping in the bowels of the ship. After a little experimenting here and there, he discovered a fine corner in the former Ritz-Carlton Restaurant where he could curl up for the night. Once after a big supper of salmon and breaded scallops he awoke with a pressing need to urinate. For this he had brought with him a large pot. As he relieved himself quietly in the dark, he felt nature calling along other lines and just could not hold back. At this point Ensign Lester F. Harris approached with a flashlight.

"Did you just take a crap?" he bellowed. Without waiting for an answer, Harris took his name and ordered him to report "before the mast" tomorrow. The next morning Osmond found himself and 51 others charged with "defecating" aboard ship.

"I don't know what you are talking about," Osmond said when called. "I just took a crap."

When they finished with him he was $16.80 poorer and one word richer.[46]

Seaman Second Class J.J. Callahan and several friends were more successful in their effort to get out of the stuffy crew quarters. They simply chose an empty officer's cabin, put a slide bolt high up on the door, high enough so it could be reached from the outside via the transom, and settled down to luxury living. Jim's confederates were two redheaded brothers named Willie and Harry, who had a pal in the galley who kept their suite well stocked with good things to eat. They enjoyed four or five nights of high living, eating jam and biscuits and drinking the best coffee to their hearts' content, and then disaster struck. Harry had gone to the galley and Willie and Jim were reading magazines when a loud rap came on the door. Knowing it wasn't Harry, they listened.

"Send for the carpenters," a voice barked outside.

Debating momentarily whether anything would be gained by making it easy for them to open the door, the pair decided to go for broke! They retreated into the suite's inner cabin, bolting the connecting door, and tried desperately to open one of the big portholes. The deadeyes had been dogged down by a conscientious shipmate, probably with a marlin spike. They couldn't budge them, and, as they spelled each other, they heard the outer door come crashing in. Then suddenly one of the dogged-down rings moved. It opened and they peered out and down to the stone floor of the dock, a drop of 80 feet. But, just to the left was a line running from above and secured below to one of the timber shores. The rest was child's play to a couple of wiry sailors. They backed out of the port, slid down the line to the timber and inched their way across its 18-foot length to the top of the dry dock. Then they hustled for the head on the dock, casually joining several others returning to the ship, where they crossed off two names in the guard's book and were safe. Hurrying back to the scene of the action, Willie eased up behind his brother's shoulders and casually whispered: "Anyone we know involved?"

Harry had iron control, but his eyes bulged and his ruddy complexion turned magenta. "Well, for cripes-sake," he undertoned.

Seaforth Sands was several miles from the center of Liverpool, and at this time was served by two trolley lines and the overhead railway, both of which stopped running at 11 p.m. There were few taxies, and many a LEVIATHAN sailor missing the last car had to walk the long road back to the dry dock. The street's gas lights were far apart and fog often obliterated them entirely, so the men often had to find their way by following the trolley tracks. Occasionally a policeman on his bicycle would pass. Most of the LEVIATHAN gobs went first class when they took the overhead railway back and forth, much to the annoyance of the locals, who grumbled about being invaded by a lot of bloody Yankee sailors.

Camouflage

amouflage—painting a ship to make her hard to see—had been a matter of growing interest to all navies for some years before the war. Theodore Roosevelt had contributed a 110-page paper on the subject. One imaginative American idea called for the painting of three destroyer silhouettes on the side of a large troopship in the hope that this would frighten a submarine captain. The ex-North German Lloyd liner KRONPRINZ WILHELM, renamed VON STEUBEN, made one voyage "protected" by such a painted escort.[47] In England the noted marine artist Norman Wilkinson developed the dazzle pattern camouflage, intended to confuse the enemy. When the Navy took over the LEVIATHAN, it asked William Andrew Mackay, New York artist and interior decorator, to develop the finest protective coloration for her. With a staff of 60 men, including a young artist named Frederick J. Waugh, he "worked night and day," a contemporary account says.

"We painted a false bow wave along the side of the ship, which, by foreshortening, made the vessel seem farther away than it was," Mackay said. "We broke down all vertical lines, destroying the ship's silhouette, and we painted on false bow lines which made her appear to be going in another direction."[48]

The camouflage was put on while the LEVIATHAN was in the Gladstone dry dock. It was so effective that when her war zone destroyer escort came out to convoy her, they were not sure in which direction she was going and are said to have had to circle her to make certain. One destroyer officer even said she was a menace to her convoy.[49] The false bow wave on her port looked like a dozen giant saw teeth, rising from the anchor to forward of her bridge. She had eight painted triangles rising from the waterline on her starboard. Both sides of her hull had wide swaths of dark rising in a long curve. This covered nine radial stripes aft on her starboard. It resembled a giant hockey stick on her port. No one seems to have noticed the irony of the situation: the camouflaging of the LEVIATHAN and other American ships was widely hailed as a patriotic achievement, whereas the idea of their being painted with red and white stripes to gain safe conduct from the German navy had been haughtily rejected.

Another change made in dry dock was the addition of a small steel triangle where the bow began to turn up from the keel. This was put there so that wide steel spreaders or paravanes could be attached to the bow to clear the way of mines.

On January 26 Admiral Sims sent a personal note to Admiral W.S. Benson, Chief of Naval Operations in Washington, asking that Captain Oman be replaced. Siding with the escort commander's views of the disputed route position he made three statements, all of which have since been found to have been incorrect. He said that the escort destroyers had recently left the coast, whereas they had been at sea for four days. He said that little attention was paid by the LEVIATHAN to the ability of the destroyers to keep up with the vessel after she got into the war zone. Actually the big troopship had been forced to slow down to let them keep up with her. Finally he said that the LEVIATHAN had passed with only one escort through the most dangerous area where two submarines were known to be operating. The escort commander's own report had stated that only one of the destroyers had dropped behind. Queried from Washington, Admiral Sims recommended action "in such a way as not to humiliate or discredit the officer concerned, who may be very able and capable, but is not suitable for his present duty."[50]

Far back across the Atlantic in a New York restaurant an unidentified German was heard to boast that "the VATERLAND is at the bottom of the sea, thank God, and will never carry another American soldier." The troopship's long stay at Liverpool had given rise to all sorts of alarmist stories. As one report put it, the Germans, "frustrated in their attempt to destroy her machinery, immediately began to sink her with rumor."[51] On January 30, 1918, in an effort to counter "recent German assertions," a story was released from the "American Army in France," making known that the LEVIATHAN was in service and had carried troops "to the Entente allied ports." The new and old names of 15 other former German ships now in troopship service were also given out. The New York *Times* carried, as a shirttail to this story from overseas, a quote from Secretary Daniels in Washington to the effect that the LEVIATHAN was capable of carrying 10,000 but that 8,000 was considered the largest number which she could comfortably accommodate. He added that in the conversion American engineers had increased her speed "by several knots."[52]

Home Again

hen the world officially knew that the famous VATERLAND, renamed the LEVIATHAN, was in transport service and was at Liverpool, it was possible for the Lord Mayor of that city, Major Utting, to have a reception and dance in honor of her officers. It was held February 5 at the Town Hall. Mrs. Utting, the Lord Mayor's wife, was listed on the program as "the Lady Mayoress." A pianoforte solo by Miss Gwen Hutchinson, and a sketch entitled "Maud's Bathing Experiences," by Mr. Richard Allen, were two of the eight features presented. Then there were refreshments and the "impromptu dance."[53]

The frightful job of coaling the LEVIATHAN began on this day. It took until the 10th to complete it. The first 1,400 tons were laboriously carried aboard while the ship was high and dry in the Gladstone dock. It must have been carried across planks from the dock's flat top in wheelbarrows, thousands and thousands of loads, and then laboriously wheeled this way and that to the coal bunkers deep within the hull. The remaining 6,400 tons needed for the return trip was brought alongside in barges after the dry dock had been partially flooded. The barges were let in when the tide was low, but even with up to 37 feet of water in the dock the LEVIATHAN did not float. Finally at 1:20 p.m. on February 10 the ship moved, seemed to quiver slightly, and then floated free. She was drawing 38 feet, 11 inches aft and 39½ feet forward, and she had a very slight list to starboard, less than half a degree.[54] On the next day she moved very slowly out of the dry dock and headed back upriver for a brief 24-hour visit to Liverpool proper.

It was again the dark of the moon when the LEVIATHAN left the cold and foggy port of Liverpool and headed for the Irish Sea. The crew was celebrating Lincoln's birthday when an explosion nearby shook the LEVIATHAN so that all hands rushed to the deck to see what had happened. One of the destroyers had spotted a suspicious-looking spar in the water and had dropped a 300-pound depth charge.[55]

The weather was terrible and the escorting small craft had great difficulty keeping up with the big troopship. They got farther and farther behind, and eventually lost sight of their dazzle-painted charge. For a time they satisfied themselves by saying they were "within radio call," and then the LEVIATHAN released them. She was ploughing through waves that threw spray over her flying bridge, normally 100 feet above water. Gun rails were torn apart, lifeboats were lifted from their fastenings and smashed, and much superficial damage was done. This continued for the whole voyage and only ended off Newfoundland. And then it was fog, fog so dense that the ship's fog whistle had to be kept blowing steadily. No fear of U-boats; just let them get in the way.

The night after the LEVIATHAN sailed from Liverpool some 145 bluejackets from a small American freighter arrived, eager for shore leave. They were hit by the backwash of anti-LEVIATHAN feeling that made them isolated and unhappy to say the least. Apparently the LEVIATHAN's 2,000-man crew had celebrated their last night on shore with a series of fights, capers and odd hi jinks that had left a bad taste in that cold, wintry British port.[56]

On the night of February 18 the LEVIATHAN passed Nantucket Lightship. The next morning she came up a fog-blanketed New York Bay. A Sandy Hook pilot, Captain William S. McLaughlin, guided her into Pier 4, Hoboken, with the help of a tug which Captain W.J. Bernard, of the Shipping Board, had stationed at the pier's end. The tug's whistle blew continuously, guiding the LEVIATHAN into her almost invisible slip. She was moored safely and her first voyage as a transport was completed.

Chapter IX

NEW PRIDE, NEW RULES, NEW CAPTAIN

"Seventy thousand tons of Steel,
Massive monster from Bridge to keel,
Raised to Wilhelm's glorious zeal,
Guns now Fire O'er Prussia's seal*,
Germany's Pride's - American!
The VATERLAND's, 'LEVIATHAN' —"

 his poem was written in ink beneath a colored reproduction of a fine water color of the LEVIATHAN, done by young marine artist Fred Hoertz.[1] The LEVIATHAN appealed to the public's imagination. She was accepted as a troopship and a sense of genuine pride in her greatness was emerging.

Many things had been learned on the first voyage, and during the two weeks she remained in Hoboken her printing press was kept very busy putting this knowledge into readable form. A dozen new pamphlets were put out, along with new editions of older ones. Many of the new rules illustrated the problems that had come up on the trip to Liverpool. There was much overlapping and duplication in the booklets, and some evidence of "collegiate language," but on the whole they were carefully thought out and most serious. A sampling of some of the regulations will give a good idea of just how complicated it was to run the world's largest troopship.

The new booklet about troop embarkation was filled with such minutiae as these:

"Troops will have their packs slung over one shoulder only on the dock."

"Life preservers must not be used as pillows or cushions or permitted to get wet. Compression lessens their efficiency."

Each step of the way was spelled out for the boarding troops, as in the following instructions for the 187 men entering Troop Compartment H-3 via Gangway No. 1, G Deck Forward:

"Gangway enters into G-9; break column into two lines, proceed forward on both sides, down ladders in and behind No. 1 hatch, through G-3 into compartment."

The booklet for troop compartment officers was equally detailed:

"Don't whistle or permit any soldier to do so."

"Insist on the men bathing and shaving, it improves their morale and makes them easier for you to handle."

"Singing is permitted during daylight hours."

"Every compartment has its spit kits for expectoration and in case of seasickness."

An 18-page pamphlet entitled "Navy Transport Regulations" was packed with new rules set in small type:

"Men vomiting on deck should be made to clean it up. Men should realize it is no disgrace to be seasick and that anyone can feel it coming. It is a mean trick to vomit in the home of others who are all around. Use the seasick cans and keep the deck clean."

"Every man should realize that it is practically impossible to sink this ship with its water-tight doors closed."

"The following articles are sold for cash in the two troop canteens: toilet articles,

---

(*The LEVIATHAN's stern was still decorated
  with the Seal of Prussia.)

shaving outfits, stationery, smokers' requisites, and candy and garters.''

Apparently some officers had stolen blankets and linen on the first trip, for now these items had to be signed out for and were to be "checked up on before disembarking." Again the question of spurs came up, and officers were ordered not to wear them on shipboard. Censorship was very much in force, and the troops were strictly limited as to what they might write:

"You are permitted to write postals to be placed in mailbags and taken ashore before ship sails and to state the following: 'Arrived safely abroad,' and your name, nothing more. Postals will be mailed after cable is received that ship has reached foreign port thus saving two or three weeks in relieving the natural anxiety of your relatives."

Still another book of regulations had two exclamation points after its title and was given a subtitle saying "Read at Once." It was filled with such tidbits as: "Do not leave toilet paper on the latrine seat or on the deck; place it in the trough. REMEMBER, Your Home, and not a Pig Pen."

Troops were urged to "be a man at the time of disaster."

They were reminded that drinking fountains were sterilized once daily.

They were told to study the deck plans of the ship on the bulletin boards, for "they have been prepared with care and hundreds of unnecessary questions can be saved by consulting them."

Different Colored Billets

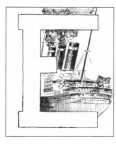
ach soldier had a ticket or "billet," which by its color spelled out not only what compartment he would be in but which deck he might go to for exercise. Yellow tickets used D Deck forward. White used B Deck starboard and port. Green were to go on A Deck amidships. Orange tickets were for C Deck around the mainmast. Red was for D Deck aft. Blue was for E Deck stern. Buff indicated C Deck stern. All troop compartments were to be inspected twice a day, at 9:30 a.m. and 1:30 p.m.

Seventy-six men on each watch were charged with policing the troop compartments, and they had an entire booklet to tell them what had to be done. One of the hundreds of rules was:

"Woodwork must be protected from abuse such as cutting of initials, scarring from shoes, etc."

The booklet about messing noted that any soldiers who had experience as bakers or butchers "are needed." They would get three meals a day and would eat with the crew, while the other soldiers had only two meals, the first at 7:30 a.m. and the other at 3 p.m. This would be changed later to 8 in the morning and 4 in the afternoon in a second booklet which had other refinements about moving through the corridors, orderly eating, cleaning mess kits, and returning to compartments.

This horror note was the first item in a booklet for Army medical officers aboard the LEVIATHAN:

"It is found that a greater morbidity rate exists among troops occupying lower bunks than among those in upper tiers. Much of this is due to dissemination of dust, dried sputum, etc., by the natural draughts through the compartments."

This pamphlet went on to say that not more than 25 venereal cases would be treated each day at the clinic. There would be two venereal and vermin inspections on each voyage.

Commander Blackburn, who had taken Jeffers' place as Executive Officer, contributed a booklet for the Army guard, a unit of 458 men who came aboard ahead of the other troops and did nothing but guard duty for the entire voyage. He outlined the 124 posts throughout the LEVIATHAN and spelled out 19 rules that every man had to memorize. One was "to stand my post in a military manner, keeping on my feet and constantly alert, observing all that takes place within sight or hearing."

The Navy also had a guard aboard the ship and their booklet went into great detail over care of prisoners in the brig. All such men were to be released at once if the ship was imperiled. The Chief Police Officer "shall be watchful over the prisoners, visit them at least once every four hours during the day," and, "when confining them he shall take care to have sufficient assistance at hand...must always be prepared to confine additional prisoners." The men in the brig were to bathe and shave on Tuesdays and Fridays. Those in solitary were to keep their own cells clean. They could have no reading matter, smoking materials, knives, or cards. The Navy guard for Post No. 11, located near the forward magazine where the ship's ammunition was stored, was instructed to "feel the deck frequently with the hand to detect any possible heat caused by fire in the bunker."

The Navy guard was to use the "utmost courtesy" when calling the attention of any Army officers to infractions of the rules.

The band was part of the Navy guard, and it was to be made up of 22 men plus the ship's four buglers. One bugler was to be on the bridge at all times at sea.

A booklet for Army lookouts noted that the commanding general aboard would designate a senior lookout officer and 50 lookouts as soon as practicable after embarkation. Ten were to be on duty during each watch.

A new Abandon Ship policy was outlined in that pamphlet. All lifesaving equipment was to be put in the water before any of the ship's people got into the boats or rafts. Survivors would come down life lines and ladders into the water and then get in the rafts. Boats and rafts would then move off to about 100 feet from the side of the ship.

"The primary purpose of the boats is to pick up the people in the water and deposit them in rafts," the pamphlet explained.

"When rafts are fully loaded, additional survivors may be taken as permanent passengers into the boats. All rafts on one side of the ship will lash together and after the ship sinks, these two groups, starboard and port will be further lashed together. Each boat is equipped with 10 Coston lights. Lead boat would fire one every 10 minutes. Then next boat etc., making it possible to have continuous flares appearing for 83 hours if 50 boats get away from the ship."

The booklet stressed that it would take many hours for "this ship to sink, and therefore there need be no excitement for there would be ample time to abandon the ship in an orderly manner."

In capital letters a final admonition read:

"MAKE CERTAIN THE PLUG IS IN PLACE BEFORE LOWERING THE BOAT."

The LEVIATHAN had 72 boats at this point in her career, and a different officer was assigned to each. Frank Flowers, for example, had Boat #9. His chief commissary steward, a dark-skinned, always joking chief petty officer named William J. Linn, had boat #12. He would become renowned in later years as the ship's chief steward. Lifeboats #17 and #18 were in the charge of Dr. Spencer G. Strauss and Dr. Max M. Braff. They were designed as invalid boats and were located immediately aft of the midship stairways on C Deck, where there was a sideport opening so stretcher cases could be carried aboard. The rafts were stacked in piles of seven along A, C and D decks. Each had a capacity of 15 men. Two separate procedures for abandoning ship were outlined, one for eastbound crossings with troops aboard and the other when she had only her crew to worry about.

A different kind of pamphlet listed 841 items under the general heading of "Machinery Index." Item 609X was a sailing launch engine, proof that there were sails aboard the LEVIATHAN. The index made an interesting distinction between the first two funnels and the last. Items 44A and 45A were shown as Smoke Stack No. 1 and Smoke Stack No. 2. The third funnel was listed several pages later as item 155A–"Stack No. 3." It was shown under the simple heading of "Stacks," for it was a dummy and not a real smokestack.

Another oddity in the index were the 16 telescopes. None were of the kind normally associated with navigating a ship. Eight were "coal telescopes" and eight were "soot telescopes." They were to show the engineers whether the smokestacks were smoking too much and whether they were sooting up. Among the countless steam auxiliaries were shown two steam sirens and two steam whistles.[2]

Telemotor Trouble

ne of the technical advances incorporated into the VATERLAND was a complicated hydraulic telemotor to control the ship's steering. While basically simple in design, it had been a continuous problem to both the Germans and Americans. It may even have had something to do with the near-disaster that happened to the liner on her first undocking from Hoboken in 1914. It had never been entirely satisfactory. After the first trip to Liverpool Navy electrician Charles A. Ward, assisted by Bill Gallagher and Bill Carpenter, were ordered to find out what was wrong. They decided they would have to trace the whole system from the bridge 800 feet aft to the steering engine. They made a detailed drawing of the fuse box on the bridge and traced the twin copper pipelines, port and starboard, back to the huge quadrant steering gear that meshed into the rudder head. Then they put everything on paper on a large drawing board they set up in the ozone room. Every link and every connection was drawn out and it became apparent that an utterly minor electrical weakness had caused the trouble. The German designers had put the bridge instrument night light on the same series with the telemotor. Under certain conditions the telemotor could not function properly. When Ward told the good news to Engineering Officer Wilhelm H.F. Schulter, the latter was so elated that he called the captain on the spot.[3]

No one knew for sure, as the end of February approached, just how soon the LEVIATHAN would sail again. Eager crews from the shore rushed to increase her capacity from 7,500 to 12,500 troops. New bunks, four deep, were installed on the enclosed promenade decks. They were simply rough bedsprings fastened to the bulkhead and made so they would fold out when in use. Paul Thompson, later to become a leading New York salvage specialist, took a photograph of the new bunk arrangements. This snapshot and others were later made into a souvenir album entitled "Aboard the U.S.S. LEVIATHAN" and sold to her soldier passengers. The Navy authorized the ship's crew to be increased from 2,000 to 2,500 to handle the additional soldier passengers.[4]

But the most important change was one that would cause wide repercussions and be a shock to many. The scuttlebut had it that Admiral Sims had been displeased with Captain Oman because he had refused to stand offshore in the war zone to await the destroyer convoy. But no one was prepared for the blow that struck the ship's company on February 28, when Captain Oman was ordered to assume duty as Commandant Second Naval District with headquarters at Newport. This would mean that he would be raised to Rear Admiral, but it was obvious that he was being kicked upstairs. The crew were very loyal to their Captain, and this whole affair cast a gloomy spell over the ship. On March 3 Captain Oman's replacement arrived. He was Captain Henry F. Bryan, a slightly younger man, square-jawed, slit-eyed and smiling.[5]

In preparation for the new load of troops that would shortly board the LEVIATHAN, Commander Blackburn, on the same day that Captain Bryan came aboard, issued a brief typewritten order to all division officers instructing them to detail men to clean out all trash barrels aboard the ship every two hours between sunrise and sunset "and to use every other effort in your judgment to keep the ship clean and in good order."[6] Captains might come and go, but Commander Blackburn would not relax his tight control over even the most seemingly unimportant phases of the ship's operation, and the LEVIATHAN was fortunate to have such a stickler for details as Executive Officer Blackburn.

Magnificent Sight

The LEVIATHAN was a magnificent sight standing at the pier in Hoboken. Great giant white lightning streaks were painted on her dark hull, some of the streaks several hundred feet long and looking like flashes from thunderbolts cast by some monstrous god of war." So wrote Jackson E. Towne, a doughboy in the 32nd Division about to board the huge ship. A lover of ships, he had crossed in 1912 on the OLYMPIC.[7]

To young Frank Rohr, private in the rear rank in the Field Artillery of that same division, the great nameless vessel that he and his pals were approaching had to be the VATERLAND. He had been all over America since enlisting in the Army, but having grown up in Hoboken, and played on the piers and bulkheads, he was not fooled even by the fantastic camouflaging. His fellow soldiers, mostly lumberjacks from Wisconsin and Michigan, wouldn't believe him when he insisted they were going to sail on the world's largest ship. But Frank's moment of glory was short-lived, for no sooner was he aboard than he was assigned to guard duty, and he so close to home. He had to stay aboard and see his friends gaily scampering down the gangplank on leave.[8]

The loading of troops took all day. There were men from the 120th and 121st Field Artillery, from the 2nd Motor Mechanics and from the 9th and 10th Brigades. Five civilians, 47 field clerks, 439 Army officers, and 7,751 troops made up the 8,242 total. It was a far cry from the 12,500 that could be accommodated, but it was more than ever before had been packed aboard one ship in the history of the world. The crew had not been expanded as authorized and numbered only 1,957, for a grand total of 10,199 souls aboard.[9] Boatswain's Mate W.F. Engel jotted in his diary that the ship sailed at 9 a.m. on the 4th of March. He was very conscientious about this diary of his, carefully noting the exact hour of each arrival and departure. He also listed by name every man in his division aboard ship, all 138 men.[10]

As the big ship sailed down the harbor, many thousands got their first good view of her dazzle paint job, since it had been foggy when she had arrived two weeks before. One who thrilled at "this majestic and dazzling sight" was J.A. McFadden, a 19-year-old recruit serving in Fort Jay on Governors Island.[11] At 12 noon port watches aboard ship were discontinued and sea watches begun, according to an order by First Lieutenant Otto L. Hankinson, directly below Commander Blackburn. While at sea, the 4 p.m. to 8 p.m. watch would be "dogged," the order said. This meant that two two-hour watches would be held during this period so that there would be a shift in the order of the eight officers assigned every 24 hours.[12]

One day out, with the ship making a steady 20 knots through smooth seas, Commander Blackburn reminded all the ship's officers of the procedure to follow in case the ship was mined or torpedoed at night so that the vessel would be lighted promptly.

"Call up #2 Primary Station, Ship's Phone 161, and use the words: 'Emergency - light ship.' "[13]

A moment of excitement occurred on March 7 when a trail of smoke was seen on the horizon. Fortunately it was a British cruiser. The two ships passed thirty minutes later about

15,000 yards apart. On the same day a soldier was put in solitary confinement for making seditious remarks.[14]

There were 18 radio operators aboard the LEVIATHAN, and one of them was Howard McKissick. At least two were on duty at all times. The men stood four-hour watches like regular deck officers. Years later McKissick, writing to another of the ship's radio men, Chet Underhill, had this memory to pass on:

"I always wanted to be on the after midnight watch as I had a very good friend who was a baker on the ship, a big colored guy from Meridan, Miss. Every night I would hear a knock on the booth, which was air sealed, and there would be that baker with a fresh pie he had baked for the officers and the marine guards and an additional one for me. Hi. Hi. I would share the pie with the other operator. I thought high heavens of that colored baker. Hi. Hi. He called me Mr. Sparko."[15]

There couldn't be many boys aboard like Jackson Towne, the lad who saw the camouflage as god-of-war thunderbolts. To start with, he remembered years later that the cots, made from a "great forest of pipes on which dark brown strips of cloth were stretched," were much better than the hammocks ordinary sailors had. Then he read Carlyle's *French Revolution* in the head, the only place where the lights were not shielded. Because of this fine light, the heads were a favorite hangout of crap players, and once Towne heard the following colloquy:

"Who the hell is that guy who is in here reading all the time?"

"I don't know," came the answer.

"It's some God-damned bookworm!"

Reading in the head wasn't very comfortable, since there were no chairs or even benches. Towne simply squatted on the floor.[16]

On the 8th of March, the ship's gunnery officer, Lt. C.G. Boucher, notified all gun captains that flat-nose or nonricocheting shells would be kept in all guns. He explained that they carried half as far as long-pointed projectiles, adding that "if you want to shoot at 800 yards the sights must be set at 1,600 yards." If this is done correctly "the shell will then dive below the surface and hit the submarine, explode and blow it up."[17]

Submarine hunting was very serious business, and another memo on the subject came out a couple of days later. If the enemy was spotted less than six points off the bow and not more than 2,000 yards distant, the LEVIATHAN was to head for her at "best speed" and ram her; otherwise she was to head "directly away from the sub at best speed." If only a submarine's wake was seen, a gun was to be fired to show escorting craft where the sub was. The memo, sent by Commodore Blackburn, added that if a torpedo was seen and was too close to be avoided by maneuvering, the ship should seek to escape "by going full speed ahead or backing." He noted that the LEVIATHAN's rudder effect was slow.

"While under escort do not use the guns except as a warning shot to indicate direction and not even then if it endangers one of the escorts," his memo warned.

Six short blasts on the siren would indicate a sub off the bow. If this was followed by one long blast, the enemy would be to the starboard. Two long blasts would mean to port. A square green flag with a broad white diagonal would be the flag signal for an enemy to starboard. A red flag with a broad white diagonal would mean the enemy was to port. The whistle signal for a U-boat astern would be 12 short blasts on the siren in pairs, followed by one or two long blasts to indicate starboard or port.[18]

Wireless contact was made on March 10 with the seven destroyers coming out to meet the LEVIATHAN. They were sighted the next day, early in the morning, a meeting that for the master of the lead destroyer was a never-to-be-forgotten experience. The officer was Lt. Cmdr. Oscar Badger, later one of America's most famous admirals. He was aboard the MANLEY. He had not known of the change in command aboard the LEVIATHAN, and when he learned that Captain Bryan was on the bridge his heart skipped several beats, for he realized he could get first-hand word of his bride Isabelle. They had been married only six weeks when he had sailed abroad for European duty. Captain Bryan was his new wife's brother-in-law, and as he approached the meeting with the LEVIATHAN his excitement rose. And then the sighting. And then the thrill of that faint roar of greeting carried by the wind and spray from the throats of the cheering troops aboard the LEVIATHAN. Oscar Badger had tears in his eyes and he was not ashamed of them.[19]

And there was a feeling of joy aboard the LEVIATHAN, and of sympathy for those aboard the escorting destroyers. Jackson Towne saw them pitching and rearing and heaving and rolling and rising in a sea that would have bothered any ship "but a great giant like the LEVIATHAN." He was feeling a little better, having been called up for guard duty, thus escaping the crowded lower troop compartments. He was stationed in a guard house improvised at one corner of the bandstand in the Social Hall, and slept on the promenade deck nearby. It was the last night of the voyage. Towne did not feel very happy when a loudspeaker advised all deck guards that in the event of a sub attack they should jump into the water with their life preservers and not worry about its being cold because they were in the Gulf Stream. The water didn't look warm to him, and he put more store in the "rumor" that the LEVIATHAN had many separate air-tight compartments and wouldn't sink like the TITANIC.[20]

And then in one icy moment all the fears of everyone aboard were galvanized by the sound of the destroyer MANLEY's forward battery. She was seen to swerve to port and start firing her 5-inch gun. As she swerved she dropped a depth charge.[21] The LEVIA-THAN, with equal abruptness, veered sharply to starboard and the radical right turn put her hard over, bringing from everywhere the sound of crashing china. Frank Rohr was sure that a torpedo passed silently across her bow.[22] Many thought the LEVIATHAN had struck a mine, but there was no further firing and the formation resumed its course through St. George's Channel in the Irish Sea.

Hissing at Liverpool

 ackson Towne was surprised to hear hissing from crowds at the Princess Landing Stage the next day at noon as a hasty debarkation began. The British had suffered so much and it had taken so long for the Americans to begin to arrive in any numbers that a cynical attitude had developed. It was not until after the American victory at Château-Thierry that many Britishers began to appreciate the Yankees. The troops lined up quickly and were marched away to a railroad station bound for Winchester. There was no cheering.[23]

The next morning, even before all the soldiers had been taken off, the LEVIATHAN went down the Mersey toward Seaforth Sands. As she went she met a ferry which unfortunately came too close and was drawn in by her tremendous bulk and its resulting suction. Considerable damage was done to the small craft, which had been warned to give the troopship the right of way. The LEVIATHAN was dry docked without further trouble and the rest of the doughboys landed there.

"It was fine to see regiments of American troops, with flags unfurled and bands playing popular Yankee airs, marching to war," the 1919 Navy history says.[24] No mention was made of the hissing.

Again the tidal problem at Liverpool required her to remain nearly a month in the dry dock. Vice Admiral Gleaves became convinced that he would not get the maximum use out of the LEVIATHAN unless he could find another port where she could debark her troops.

149

He ordered Captain Bryan to survey the situation at Brest, where the channels were ample for the ship's great depth at any stage of the tide, although she would not be able to come up to a pier or landing stage in the small inner harbor. She could anchor just outside and unload her troops into tenders. With the help of Captain of the Port Loizeau, Captain Bryan designed a monster mooring buoy. It had nine anchors and 300 fathoms of chain in three legs, weighing 180 tons in all. Now Brest was ready to receive the LEVIATHAN.[25]

The sale of "fish and chips" rose every time the LEVIATHAN came in to Liverpool; the Americans couldn't seem to get enough. They would bring bags back to the ship, eating even as they climbed the gangplank. The port had some pleasures. One of the most enigmatic was the "shawl women," as they were called in the LEVIATHAN's engineers' mess. These were the wives and widows of seamen, a whole community of women who wore black clothing and always had shawls over their heads. They were all the same, remembers Marc Iverson. They came out at night and went to the pubs. They didn't mind at all if someone bought them bitters and they chatted and lingered long at the bar, but that was it. No more.[26]

There was one pub where Americans were particularly welcome, and it was called Ma Edgerton's American Bar. It was on Lime Street. Men from the LEVIATHAN and other Yankee troopers did not like the warm, flat, thin English beer known as bitters. They much preferred Guiness stout, and Ma would save it for them, much to the disgust of her English patrons. How delicately Ma Edgerton managed to handle this problem was demonstrated to a group of American engineers one evening when a Tommy came in to the bar. He was loaded with knapsack, gun, and food kit and was a short, tired-looking Tommy. He dropped his gun, looked up at the row of tall Americans, swaggered a little and said in a loud voice: "Give me what they're having." Ma Edgerton, at her motherly best, hurried round to him, edged him away and gently persuaded him to accept bitters "like other good Englishmen always have." Later she refused his money and quietly encouraged his departure. In 1948 Marc Iverson, then a chief engineer on a United States Lines freighter, visited this same bar with another LEVIATHAN veteran, Jackie Wilson, an officer on the freighter. Ma Edgerton was still there, a very ancient, very feeble little lady sitting before the fireplace. A waitress brought her over and she took Marc's hand and said she remembered him.[27]

Ferry commuters from Birkenhead to Liverpool would see the three huge stacks of the LEVIATHAN. Crew members, particularly engineers, used to take pleasure in astounding them by looking down on them from the top of the third, dummy, stack.

"How they would gawk," J.J. Callahan remembers.[28]

John Burris, an electrician, nearly had a fit near the end of the stay at Liverpool because he couldn't have his afternoon tea. Upon investigation he concluded that his fellow crew members had pocketed every last bit to take ashore as gifts to tea-thirsty Britons.[29]

At home the war hysteria was growing apace. On March 18 the *Tribune* had a feature story denouncing German spies and listing among its "Rogues' Gallery" Count von Bernstorff, Karl Boy-ed, and Dr. Bunz. The Hapag headquarters was described as "the most dangerous sub-centre of conspiracy, of forgery and of perjury in the country." The piece was a superb example of how in just four years a country's attitude can do a complete about-face, and how the press, in reporting news, can be swamped by a wave of popular war frenzy.[30] Even the *Times*, so proud of its objective news coverage, was a victim. A week later it positively chortled with vindictive glee in describing how the large Hamburg-American Line sign on Pier 4, Hoboken, had been painted over or "obliterated," as it said.[31]

Another example of wartime hysteria was an ad in the April *Marine Engineering* paid for by the Kearfott Engineering Company. It showed a three-foot-long wooden club with a sharp steel end from which protruded four circles of five steel spikes each. The caption:

"An official photograph of the club which is used to finish off wounded Italian soldiers.

32,000 of these were recently captured by the Italians from the German army."

Kearfott, which was profiting immensely from the wartime shipbuilding boom, called upon the magazine's readers to "have your share in America's answer to German savagery" by buying Third Liberty Loan bonds. "Save Civilization, Save America, Your Own Family and Your Own Home. . ." the advertisement urged.[32]

While last-minute preparations were being made aboard the LEVIATHAN to start back home for another load of American boys, an 18-page blue ditto manual entitled "Organization for Submarine Defense" was issued. Copy 15 went to Chief Gunner's Mate W.S. Allen, who preserved it and passed it down through the years. It was marked "Confidential." Some of the language verged on the quaint, such as:

"It has been proven that the periscope can be seen before the submarine is near enough to have any sporting chance with a torpedo."

But it was not all a game, as some of the other language showed:

"Lookouts shall stand watches in pairs, relieving each other every half hour. One of the two men shall CONSTANTLY keep his eyes in his allotted arc. . .must not talk. Even if a sub is sighted, he must give his undivided attention to his own arc, as several submarines may be acting together. Upon sighting a suspicious object, the lookout shall at once sing out, attracting the attention of his relief, who shall spring to the voice tube. Report everything you see, for even barrels and driftwood may be attached to floating mines. Sea gulls often flock around a mine or a periscope moving slowly!"[33]

Again the coaling was a tremendous job. To save the crew, English contractors were hired and worked for three weeks while the LEVIATHAN was in dry dock. A few days before the time set for departure, it was found that the work was far from done and would not be done at the rate they were going. The crew had to pitch in. Knowing that each ton meant they were closer to getting home, they worked night and day and finished in good time.

In late March, 1918, Admiral Oman learned the full story of Sims' dissatisfaction and requested an immediate investigation. Because of war conditions his request was denied. In late 1920, following a year of study by the Navy Department, the matter was resolved entirely in favor of Admiral Oman. He was awarded the Navy Cross for his service on the LEVIATHAN, and he was given a complete exoneration in a letter from Secretary Daniels.

"I have carefully reviewed the papers on file in your case. I regret very much to learn that the action taken in relieving you of the command was so unjust to you and I am convinced that this action was not warranted by the facts. If all the facts had been before the Department at that time, the Department would not have taken this drastic action as it believes that there was nothing in the handling of the LEVIATHAN by you that would warrant such action being taken. Copies of this letter have been sent to Vice Admiral Sims and Rear Admiral Gleaves."[34]

Secretary Daniels went even farther. He told Admiral Oman in another letter that: "I took the matter up with the President and my fellow members of the Cabinet. I have told them that I found your judgement was excellent and they could trust to it. I congratulate you on the splendid services you have rendered."[35]

On April 9 a group of German prisoners were brought on board to be taken to prison camps in the States. They had been rescued from a sunken submarine, and to guard them properly, in accordance with the hysteria of the moment, a dozen British shotguns were purchased and sawed off by the ship's armorer "to make them more effective for this sort of work."[36] The enlisted men were put in the after brig and the German officers were given staterooms on C Deck. The Navy's history delightedly relates that when one of the latter complained that there was no hot water, his guard said:

"You people built the ship; why didn't you pipe it to suit yourselves?"[37]

151

On April 10, shortly before the ship's 9:45 a.m. departure, Lt. Boucher issued a four-point memo designed to protect the escorting destroyers from over-eager gunners on the LEVIATHAN.

"Attention is invited to the fact that some of the destroyers are camouflaged to look exactly like submarines at night. Do not fire at them by mistake."[38]

While the ship was in dry dock a new propeller was installed along with an electric log, or Pithometer. The latter was suspended from the ship's bottom and could measure the speed with great accuracy. After the ship was out at sea, it was found that the device wasn't working. Electrician Ward was asked to help engineer Bill Gallagher repair it. They had to take up several deck plates over the tank from which the Pithometer projected. They removed a gasket and lifted off the tank top, only to find the tank almost filled with water. The inner parts of the gadget were soaked. They were removed and allowed to dry, and then Ward climbed down into the tank and prepared to re-install the device. He intended to push it out into the ocean through a valve opening. When ready, he shouted up for the valve to be opened. It was, and within seconds Ward was standing up to his neck in ocean water. He had not counted on the pressure that was exerted that far below the ship's waterline. He couldn't possibly push the mechanical log out with the ship going at full speed, and was lucky to be hauled out alive. The water overflowed into other areas before the gang helping was able to close the valve. No further attempts were made to install the Pithometer, and Charlie Ward, in years to come, would tell and retell how he nearly scuttled the LEVIATHAN.[39]

The menu for the first dinner aboard en route home happened to be frankfurters and sauerkraut, and the German prisoners were delighted. Some were not so happy a few days later when they heard guns firing and thought that one of their own submarines might be attacking. It was only gunnery practice.

"The prisoners showed much interest as to what arrangements had been made for their abandoning ship, if occasion required, and did not seem pleased when they were informed that the same arrangements had been made for them as they had made for the lost souls on the LUSITANIA," it was recorded in the Navy's LEVIATHAN history, which added that, of course, this was not literally true.[40]

The ship docked at 4:30 p.m., April 17, and Isabelle Badger was waiting in the crowd on the pier. Captain Bryan had wirelessed an invitation to her to tour the vessel and have dinner with him. As she was being escorted around, she overheard the following quaint one-sided conversation:

"Now look what you went and done. . . .We gave you shore leave and this is how you repay us!"

Turning a corner, she came upon a sailor caressing his cat, who had just come aboard after missing the last voyage. She had brought with her a litter of kittens.

At dinner in the Ritz-Carlton mess, Captain Bryan told Mrs. Badger about how the MANLEY had been among the escorting destroyers and how her young Oscar had come aboard several times during the long stay at Liverpool.

"In fact, Isabelle, he was sitting in that very chair only seven days ago."

The story of the German prisoners came next, and then the Captain told her about his worries as master of the LEVIATHAN:

"You know, if we see a small boat in the ocean and if there are men in it and even if they are waving and crying for help—we can't stop. I must always think of the thousands aboard my ship. Who knows, that small boat may be a decoy to draw us to a mined area."[41]

The Navy's policy of secrecy had even prevented many from knowing that the VATERLAND's name had been changed. The April issue of *The Wireless Age* featured an illustrated feature article about the VATERLAND "now a soldier-carrier for Uncle Sam."

Fine photos and an amazing amount of detail on the ship made the article most unusual at that time; however, the thousands of crowded troops who had already sailed over on her would have had a good chuckle out of the following innocent passage:

"Troops transported by the VATERLAND should escape every hardship. They can not only be comfortably housed and fed, but have their every want anticipated. In the great Roman bath the soldiers can enjoy the pleasure and healthful stimulus of salt water bathing throughout the voyage. By utilizing the plunge throughout the 24 hours several thousand soldiers could thus be accommodated every day. On the whole the Hun appears to have made a valuable contribution toward the solution of the problem represented in the cry for America to get 'ship, ships, and more ships.' "[42]

"She's the Old DASHUND"

mong the 8909 men who boarded the LEVIATHAN on Wednesday, April 23, was a lad named John T. Carroll. Somehow he managed to find his way to the foredeck, where he spotted something that gave him a start. In plain sight was a large buoy marked "Brest" in large, red letters. Without saying why, he casually asked a sailor if the LEVIATHAN was going to Brest. The sailor said, "No, we're going to England, as usual."[43]

One of Carroll's fellow soldiers was Larry Foster, a big-league baseball player with a keen sense of humor and an observant eye. Assuming a Bronx accent, in imitation of the speech habits of many of his fellow doughboys, he set himself to writing a description of his experiences in a "country-cousin letter" which was published years later in his regiment's war history. As an expression of what many of the LEVIATHAN's soldier-passengers thought, it is priceless:

"To begin with we started for France from Campt Upton about 9 a.m. on the April 21. Soon we pulls into Long Island City and gets on a special ferry-boat resoived for us, and when we hears that we are making for Hoboken, and that we would have a few roll calls in that good old Irish town, the boys all feel pretty good. Also pretty dry, cause it was excrushiating hot. But I guess the gink who was running the excursion was one of them bone-dry guys and we lands flat on the deck.

"Well, Al, I wasn't much surprised to see that we was going to make the voyage on a boat with smokestacks. I had a tip on it from a guy who's pretty thick with the barber who shaves the major. And what do you think the name of her was? Yes Sir! the LEVIATHAN. Some giant, boy! She's the old DASHUND or something like that, made over, and listen Al, the guy who gave her the new name knew something, 'cause the foist part made a hit with the Irish and Algerians in the outfit. We get as far as the gang-plank and we have another long delay on the dock. But this was just military courtesy and we didn't mind. It seems the Commodore of the vessel was just dining at the time. And he takes about three hours to dine! So right here is where we gets our foist knockdown to corned beef. Our Cap. commands, (1) Eats, (2) Rations! Rations is the command of execution but before he says it we have 42 cans open, and when the Red Cross ladies hands us coffee and cake for dessert, which was delightful, we calls it a meal.

"It gets to be about 2:30 and at last we move. Yes Al, she's some boat! A whale! But I hear that an Irishman drawed the plans for her. I had a laugh, Al, when one guy sees the boat and says he don't get it as how such a boat made of steel can float. So I tells him as how the boat was made of iron, not steel. And she's made of wood inside, plenty of wood in proportion. That's where a guys education comes in Al."

Then Larry goes down to his "stateroom" and is surprised to find there aren't any rooms—"no doors or walls or curtains or anything, everything open!"

He asks someone about it and is told it is the "Iron Pipe Demountable System," but he says he would call it the "Sardine System."

"Well Al, once we gets under way there wasn't much excitement until Mess time, then all hands makes a dive for the Grand stairway what leads to the Ball-Room. That's where we dine, Al, in the Ball-Room. Can you amagin it Al, privates in the Ball-Room with hand paintins on the walls and ceilings! I don't know where the Officers feed. I guess they have to take care of themselves as best they can. As I was saying Al, the boys make the big rush for the lunch and every time I sees that rush it reminds me of the riots at the gates on the days that McGraw had me slated to pitch. Once we gets into the Ball-Room it's all big-league stuff Al, with Officers standing all around umpiring and any guy caught going to the plate more than three times in one inning is out. We only have two meals a day and that is enuf Al. Breakfast and dinner. For supper we have abandon-ship drill by the numbers in case the ship goes down."

A couple of paragraphs follow on how they are told to keep cool and take a blanket and jump into the water in case the ship starts to sink.

"I guess we would keep cool, eh, Al?

"Can you figure as how the — a guy's going to swim with a blanket on him? That may sound all right to a naval gazoop, but take it from me, Al I always have my belt filled with ammunish and my rifle handy. An if the boat goes down yours truly will take a Brodie off the stoin with his gun. . . .But believe me the 'subs' never had a chance. Our deck is decorated with guns all camoflowed and each of 'em run by the best Navals we got in West Point.

"Every night we close the portholes so as no sound can get out and hold an entertainment with movies which we enjoy, Al, but most of the nights we spend trying to shave ourselves with salt water. We always have our evenings to ourselves, Al, and I spent most of em on deck taking in most of the scenery which is always about the same,—one cloud follows us all the way over, I guess that's obsoiving things pretty close, eh, Al. Well that's my way."[44]

While Larry Foster was taking in the scenery, John Carroll was shocked to see a detail of seamen come out on the promenade deck with sledgehammers. They went at it with a will, smashing all the windows that had made the glass-enclosed prom such a comfortable feature of the VATERLAND. Apparently someone felt they reflected light at night, so out they all came, to be replaced with black-painted wood.[45] Another thing that Carroll didn't like was washing with salt water. As the voyage progressed he found in the bowels of the ship a tap that gave out wonderful fresh water. He never told anyone. His suspicions that France was their destination were substantiated by the fourth day out. He was impressed by the deck cargo of camouflaged artillery wagons, shell cases, and munitions. He was not impressed with the guys from the 11th Infantry, Southerners they were, who sat all night long playing poker in the latrines. He remembers that someone found a box of fountain pens, good ones, and was selling them all over the ship very cheap.[46]

Everyone became jumpy as the ship got closer to the war zone and the tension gradually rose till it fairly crackled. And that's how things were on the last day of April early in the afternoon when suddenly one of the starboard guns started firing. Other guns joined in and then they all stopped. The gunners had seen something suspicious, but it turned out to be only a spouting blackfish.[47]

That night, with the ship some 36 hours from the French coast, Jim Callahan and others of his 2nd Division deck force were rolled in blankets, off watch and sleeping at the head of the Grand Staircase with a petty officer standing watch to awaken those whose turn it was to man the various topside lookout stations. They were rolled up in the foyer between the Wintergarden and the huge doors opening into the Social Hall. Sleeping was not easy because music came from behind the black painted iron and glass doors. The Navy guard knew that some 200 Army nurses were dancing with a large group of officers. Finally Callahan dozed off.

"From a sound sleep we were awakened and jerked to our feet!

"The formerly dark landing was ablaze with light from the wide-open doors of the ballroom. Gold stripers were shouting instructions at us and a cluster of Army officers and nurses were in the doorway looking very serious. Loud in our ears was the rising and falling roar of the ship's two nine-foot sirens."

Callahan and the other guards were ordered to rouse the sleepers in the troop compartments in case the "abandon ship" order had to be given. Callahan's story continues:

"I rushed down about seven decks, wondering all the way if I would be able to beat the rush back up to topside. The compartment I was assigned to was a big one, brightly lighted with few sleepers. A lot were reading and many card games were going on. Way down there the noise of the sirens did not penetrate. The whole atmosphere was one of carefree ease. I tore around in a big circle through the groups, shouting my message, and then headed for the ladder to go back up. A big sergeant with a heavy Southern drawl barred my way. 'Look heah, you,' he said mildly, 'that isn't funny; you could cause a panic with a joke like that!' I felt like Angel Gabriel being told to go roll his hoop.

"By the time I got back the siren had stopped and the dance had been resumed, behind closed doors and minus the Navy officers. They had been summoned to an emergency meeting, for it seems the sirens had been tampered with and that there was probably an enemy agent aboard and, no doubt, a sub or subs somewhere nearby awaiting his message."[48]

"When we arose on the morning of May 1 we discovered we had a flotilla of destroyers guarding us," remembers nurse Anna L. Hawkins, going to France with 68 other nurses from Philadelphia.

"We had a very nice trip over on the LEVIATHAN, played cards and had dances; we were most always on deck at night, everything on the ship was very dark at nights. I have a black ribbon with U.S.S. LEVIATHAN printed on it."[49]

The war situation was getting more serious all the time, with German submarine successes at a high point. Back home the House military committee announced plans to send three million men to France.[50] The importance of the LEVIATHAN was now clear. She had 11,361 souls aboard as she approached the shores of France for the first time, and all but 2,052 were going over to fight.[51]

At Brest

The last few hours before reaching France were made under escort, but dense fog created a situation in which the escorting destroyers were as much of a hazard as a help. Once one of them hove to close alongside, having appeared mysteriously out of the fog. One of the LEVIATHAN's officers shouted over to him: "We don't know where we are. Do you?" The answer came back: "No." This was the area where enemy underseas craft had been most successful and were sinking ships every day.

And then a black and white buoy was sighted on the starboard beam, showing that they were on the right course and nearing the beautiful harbor of Brest, one of the finest in France, with a roadstead capable of sheltering 500 large vessels. While the approach was being made, gunnery officer Lt. A.H. Batemen dashed off a hand-written order to all watch officers:

"The harbor is being patrolled by French torpedo boats and submarines. Do not open fire on any such vessels."[5 2]

The LEVIATHAN entered Brest just as the fog lifted. She was far too large to go inside the old breakwater, and her troops had to debark into barges that came out to meet her. Captain Loizeau's gigantic mooring buoy was there to serve them, and debarkation began immediately. No sooner had the troops begun to leave through sideports on the ship's port, than coal barges came along the starboard side and the job of loading the coal began. Men from the several stevedoring regiments stationed at Brest helped, and the ship's crew, swarming down to the barges via Jacob's ladders, joined in the chore, eager to make a quick job of it and encouraged in their enthusiasm by two regimental bands playing the latest jazz music. After the troops had all got off, coaling was also done on the port side, the whole tremendous job being completed in a record 48 hours.[5 3]

John Carroll, Larry Foster, and the others, meanwhile, thinking themselves lucky to escape the coaling detail, were approaching Brest in tenders. The sun beat down on them and on a beautiful, hilly scene, with green fields, old farmhouses, and ancient fortifications. Once ashore, they were ordered to climb up the steep hills toward an ancient looking structure that towered over the harbor. Their packs got heavier and heavier as the LEVIATHAN diminished in size out in the roads. Their destination was the Pontenazian Barracks, built during the days of Napoleon. Carroll was sure they hadn't been cleaned since then, and the first task given the Americans was to clean them.[5 4]

No Paris

two-page mimeographed set of instructions for officers having liberty was issued by Commander Blackburn. It was all about Brest and listed certain areas that were barred to Navy personnel. It gave a schedule of boats to and from the ship and noted that all shops, including bars, closed at 9:30 p.m. The worst news, however, was that no leave was to be authorized for any officer to go to Paris or, for that matter, any place outside of Brest! Dashed were the dreams of half the crew.[5 5]

Admiral Henry B. Wilson, now Commander in Chief of all American Naval forces in French waters, had the U.S.S. PROMETHEUS as his flagship at Brest. His land office was in the Credit Lyonnaise building, Rue de Emile Zola. He is said to have been the only American who had his own bathtub brought over from the United States. A few years later, while Superintendent of the Naval Academy at Annapolis, he would use his influence to place his nephew aboard the LEVIATHAN as a junior officer. At Brest his assignment was to stop the frightful losses the Allies were suffering from U-boats off the coast of France. He still had doubts about the wisdom of putting so many men in one ship, and was most concerned with the safety of the LEVIATHAN while under his jurisdiction. He insisted that she take no more than three days to debark, coal and load.

"Get the big cow out of here," were his words, and it was his idea to have bands play while the coaling was under way.[5 6]

Inadvertently the Admiral had given the LEVIATHAN one of her first nicknames. She became known to many as the "Big Cow." There were also many who called her the "Big Train," and others with less imagination dubbed her "the big iron steamboat," or "the big three stacker." Because of her fancy war paint some came to know her as the "big chief."[5 7] The most famous nickname by which she is remembered today had not yet been born. To most soldiers who sailed over or back on her she is remembered as the "LEVI-NATHAN," or "LEVI," for short.[5 8]

Shortly before leaving Brest at 8 p.m. on May 5 her fog horn, sirens and boat whistles were tested, a Navy custom that always made her crew nervous. It sounded as if she was letting the enemy know that "ready or not, I'm coming."[59] There was plenty of work to be done on the way back and little time to relax—Commander Blackburn made sure of that. He issued a seven-page cleaning "bill" or order which outlined the responsibilities of every man aboard, spelled out every area that had to be painted or cleaned, from the moving picture house to the censor's room, and noted who had to do it.[60]

A bad fog forced the LEVIATHAN to drop anchor near Ambrose Lightship on the 12th of May in the afternoon, but it soon cleared and she was able to make fast at Hoboken at 9:28 that evening, safe and secure. The lucky few who had shore leave that night were greeted with shouts of joy and relief. Widely circulating rumors had convinced nearly everyone that the LEVIATHAN had been torpedoed and sunk with a "tremendous loss of life."[61]

S. S. Leviathan

Issued by the Jewish Welfare Board
to Soldiers and Sailors of the U.S Army & Navy

Chapter X

DANGER

Even before the LEVIATHAN reached Hoboken, wireless messages had alerted men like Dick Blauvelt, plant foreman at the Consolidated Iron Works on River Street, as to her needs. They knew what they had to do to speed her turnaround and were hard at it hours before she tied up.[1] The extraordinary three-day turnaround at Brest had given new point to the whole LEVIATHAN operation, and, although no one expected to be able to equal it at Hoboken, it was hoped she would be off again within a week.

A 700-man working party came aboard the evening of May 12, so they could get an early start the next morning. The ship's paymaster had 240 of them assigned to his office. Chief Engineer Woodward had 200 to clean out the boilers and install new fire brick. Others were assigned to help with the coaling, which began immediately. To let coal barges work on both sides, the LEVIATHAN was moved away from the pier a little, or "breasted out." Long timbers, or spur shores, were wedged between her hull and the pier to keep her out.[2] Things got moving fast, and it was well they did, for the LEVIATHAN's next crossing was to be her trial by fire, and she had to be ready.

The American troop movement really got going in May. In the first three months of the year it had averaged under 50,000 men per month, rising to more than 80,000 in March and double that in April. But in May a quarter of a million men went "over there." Over the next four months, the monthly total would rise to a peak of 306,350 in July and then drop to 180,320 in October, as if somehow, someone anticipated the war's end in November.[3]

On May 31, Major General A. Gronkhite, of the 80th Division, led 399 other Army officers and 9,944 enlisted men aboard. Including 99 Army nurses, 6 female civilian employees, 1 French and 2 English army officers, the total number of passengers to sail on this trip was 11,313. The crew brought this up to 13,341 souls.[4]

D.R. Stringham, a bugler in Company C of the 43rd Engineers, took pains to check his Abandon Ship Mustering Station on his Troop Billet card. It was No. 2, Location F-10. He was a bit taken aback at the seven orders on the back of the card:

"Keep quiet.
"Follow guide directly to your compartment.
"Find your bunk by number.
"Remain in your compartment until release sounds by bugle.
"Locate latrines and urinals.
"Read regulations and orders issued.
"Familiarize yourself with any plans on bulletin boards."

He knew they were for his own good.

He was a bit surprised to see so many German language signs still all about the ship, and the miles of new electrical cables strung along the endless corridors. Being of a precise turn of mind, he jotted down the exact time the LEVIATHAN cast off. It was 4:10 p.m.[5]

Up in officers' country, Lt. Joseph Ralston Hayden was delighted at his duty assignment for the voyage. He was going to have one of the ship's anti-submarine guns. Quite a contrast, he thought, for he was in command of one of the 14-inch batteries being shipped abroad on the LEVIATHAN to support the Allied ground attack.[6]

The voyage did not start out any too well. As the LEVIATHAN steamed slowly past the Staten Island ferry terminal at St. George, she was struck by a particularly heavy wind and blown slightly toward the side of the channel. To add insult to injury, the tide was unusually strong, and suddenly Captain Bryan and Sandy Hook Pilot William McLaughlin realized the ship was aground. Five long blasts were sounded with the whistle, and tugs hurried to the ship's aid. The ship remained stuck on the sand for about an hour and then slipped off into deep water and was away for Brest.[7]

As night fell and the LEVIATHAN was passing the south shore of Long Island, Henry Dipple, Navy guard, was horrified to spot a soldier lighting a cigar on deck.

"I threw the match out of his hand, and they put him in the guard house," Dipple said. "If a U-boat had seen that light, it could have been trouble."[8]

The next day, when the watertight doors were being tested, an Army officer became confused and his leg was caught. He was severely injured.[9]

Five days of beautiful skies and calm seas followed. The destroyer escorts appeared and took up their positions abeam and ahead. Everything seemed calm, and then came an S.O.S. The American Navy freighter CARLTON, 100 miles ahead and straight on the LEVIATHAN's course, had been torpedoed and was sinking. She was calling for help, but a quick exchange of signals among the speeding convoy ships determined that no help could be offered. The 20-knot express convoy changed course to the north and sped on toward France. It was a question of the fate of 14,000 on the troopship against the forty or so on the cargo vessel. By about 10:45 that evening, having passed the longitude where the CARLTON had gone down, the LEVIATHAN was brought back on a direct course toward Brest. Later her officers learned that the crew of the sunken vessel had been saved. All that night, with her lifeboat crews standing by at their stations, the LEVIATHAN surged on through the danger zone. A bright moon illuminated the convoy.

The Enemy Strikes

ord via wireless spelled out the spot and the hour that the French pilot would meet the LEVIATHAN, and, at that point, with the green hills of Brest off the ship's port bow and with the great troopship slowing in the water to permit the pilot to board her, Lt. Beebe, assistant navigator, saw a periscope!

It was on the port quarter. He called out, and Captain Bryan was at his side in a moment; but nothing could be seen. Moments later the sub periscope showed again, and Captain Bryan shouted out an order to hold course. Within 60 seconds, the LEVIATHAN, following her zigzag clock on the bridge, would have turned sharply to port, presenting a broadside to the enemy.

"Open fire on submarine, port quarter," was Bryan's second order, followed immediately by a call for the general alarm. The time was 12:29 p.m., the day May 30, 1918.

The enemy was 1,500 yards away, just outside the range of a torpedo, but had the zigzag pattern been followed and had the ship continued to slow for the pilot, she would have been torpedoed for certain. The submarine had obviously been aware of the LEVIATHAN's intention to pick up her Brest pilot and not only knew where this would be done but the exact hour. German intelligence had done its job well. In a flash Captain Bryan decided to investigate the idea of carrying a French pilot aboard permanently to avoid such moments of potential disaster. This was done.

As the LEVIATHAN headed for the French coast her speed was increased. Her four huge propellers bit into the choppy, blue French waters at 165 revolutions per minute. Guns 6 and 8 fired three 105-pound explosive shells, one just missing a small French fishing boat that happened to be in the area. Her master, who came aboard later, said he had seen the submarine. At 12:40 a change in course was made. More shots were fired and there was much cheering from the Army nurses who had left their lunch to have a "peek at the fun," according to the Navy history. Their enthusiasm and lack of fear in the "face of a deadly menace" were an inspiration to the sailors manning the big guns.[10] There was no indication that any of the guns hit anything.

At 12:59 another submarine appeared, also to port, evidence that a whole cordon of U-boats had been lying in wait. The same guns opened fire, blasting out nine snub-nosed projectiles to the lusty cheering of the brown masses of soldiers on deck. The enemy was left in the liner's wake and the convoy continued. Twenty minutes later a third periscope was spotted, also on the port side, and again there were blazing guns on the LEVIATHAN, and seven more shots. Her Navy gunners were trained not to waste their fire. Twenty-five minutes later she was in the harbor of Brest and her 2,028 crew members, particularly the sweating black gang, who had made a superhuman effort shoveling coal, were able to relax.

One of the LEVIATHAN's gunners was Lt. Hayden, and to his dying day he was sure his gun had made a hit. Lt. Hayden went on to fire the last shot in the war from the Allied side. It was timed to land on an enemy bridge precisely at 11 a.m. on November 11. It did, and, he remembers, the bridge was destroyed. Years later he gave the primer for that shot to the Smithsonian Institution.[11]

Despite strict censorship, the attack made news headlines around the world. Accounts that appeared in American papers were marvelous examples of what imagination can do. One report came from a Mrs. T. Parkin Scott, a socially prominent Baltimore lady, who had learned about the episode from one of the LEVIATHAN's officers. A good number of boys from Maryland had been aboard, and her story was published by the *Baltimore Sun* just two days after the troopship returned to Hoboken. It said the ship had been attacked by a fleet of 20 subs, and that two had been sunk and two others captured. Mrs. Scott noted that a school of torpedoes had been evaded, and added that the American onslaught "demoralized the enemy and the remaining undersea craft fled."[12]

The *Sun's* report was enlarged upon several days later by other newspapers. One headline made the spy idea the chief point:

SPIES PUT U-BOATS
ON LEVIATHAN TRAIL

Flotilla of Submarines Lay in
Wait for Her Near a
French Port
AS SHE TOOK ON PILOT
Cordon of Destroyers Gave No
Opening for Successful
Attack

Calling the LEVIATHAN the "major prize for which the whole German submarine fleet is fishing," this account said that she had been the target of three other attacks and that on every occasion "there has been an unprecedented concentration of submarines."[13] The destroyer FANNING was supposed to have sunk an attacking sub on one of the early attacks. The fact that none of the escorting destroyers broke ranks to attack any of the U-boats was credited in this report as having saved the LEVIATHAN, "for the other underseas craft were believed to be set to send their torpedoes through the opening that would have been made had any of the escorts left their charge."

Of the 3,000 "arrived safely" telegrams filed by troops in the wireless room of the LEVIATHAN on this perilous crossing none were sent.[14]

Again Lt. Cunningham, later to be master of the LEVIATHAN, had the toughest assignment of all during the very brief stay at Brest. He was in charge of the horrible job of

CAMOUFLAGE—what it looked like on starboard and port sides. Troops debarking at Liverpool (courtesy M.P. Iverson).

PEOPLE—a visitor outside printing office (LEVIATHAN Vet. Ass'n. photo); Chaplain E. McDonald (Dr. G. Schoelles photo) and Coxswain W.F. Engel with "Fritz" (Engel photo). Crew members cavort at Liverpool (J.W. Thomas photo). Stern view in dry dock (Iverson photo).

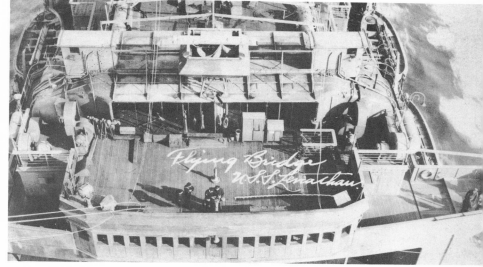

VIEWS FROM THE TOP—post card photographs sold to the crew and troops carried and taken from mast tops and funnels (Iverson and Thomas).

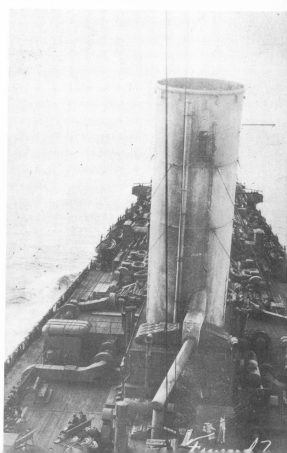

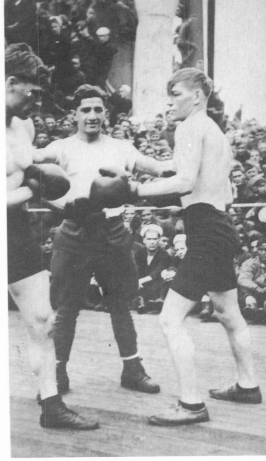

PIE EATING-RACE

SPORTS—more sailor postcards (3 at left courtesy A.B. Crummy). Charles Franklin Webber, C.P.O. sparring with Arthur Malc (courtesy Eileen Webber). Humphrey Bogar may be in the photo below (courtesy Felix A. Iwanicki).

THREE-LEGGED-RACE

MUSIC—the band performs (Ralph Cochran photo) and poses (J.W. Thomas and Vet. Ass'n. photos). Congressmen passengers also pose (Mary Robinson Godfrey photo).

UNDOCKING—the current has pushed LEVIATHAN across slip, up against next pier; her jack is still flying at the prow. Tugs pull to move her bulk into the stream. On facing page she is now out in the Hudson, her jack is down and the U.S. ensign has been raised from her main mast. At bottom right the LEVIATHAN is shown returning from France, puffing tugs heading her into the slip (Vet. Ass'n.).

COALING at Brest (J.W. Thomas photos above); LEVIATHAN nurses, with head nurse Mary Robinson 4th from left (M.R. Godfrey photo), and abandon ship drill (Iverson).

Sea breaking over Forecastle. U.S.S. Leviathan

SEA — LEVIATHAN as from GREAT NORTH- (J.W. Thomas). Sea king over forecastle e, J.W. Thomas). Bell VATERLAND name on it (C. Leonhardt). Looking aft from stle (Vet. Ass'n.).

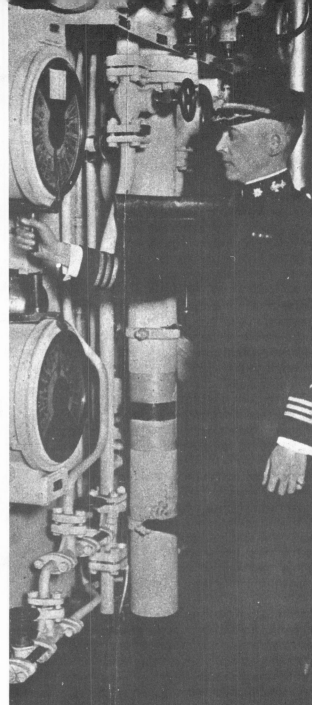

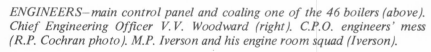

ENGINEERS—main control panel and coaling one of the 46 boilers (above). Chief Engineering Officer V.V. Woodward (right). C.P.O. engineers' mess (R.P. Cochran photo). M.P. Iverson and his engine room squad (Iverson).

coaling, and that he did it well is attested to by an all-time quick turnaround. The troopship arrived at 4 p.m. on May 30 and sailed at 6 p.m. on June 1, beating the three-day record of the last visit.[15] Part of the spirit shown in this coaling record was due to the thrill of their escape from the enemy submarine trap. Their will to work may also have been fired by the news, which came on May 31, that the PRESIDENT LINCOLN, Ballin's famous six-masted passenger-cargo liner, had been torpedoed and sunk. She was en route home and no troops were aboard, but her loss was a serious one because of her great troop capacity. She had carried 20,143 on five eastbound trips.[16] When torpedoed she was in the very center of a large convoy geared to make only 10 knots. Two of the LINCOLN's passengers who escaped together in the same lifeboat would meet again on the exact spot of the sinking 14 years later. One would be a passenger aboard the LEVIATHAN and the other would be her master.[17]

With a number of notable passengers aboard, the LEVIATHAN sailed for home late on June 1st and everyone expected more trouble. It came only an hour and sixteen minutes later. At 7:16 the wake of a periscope was seen to starboard. For some reason, the attacks always seemed to come from the northwest. Guns 5 and 7, the only ones that could bear upon the wake, began to fire. The U-boat commander knew his game, and was approaching in the glittering trail of a setting sun. The LEVIATHAN's green flag with its diagonal white stripe whipped in the breeze from the signal bridge of the troopship, telling escorting destroyers that the enemy was on the starboard side. One escort was on the scene so quickly that the LEVIATHAN's guns had to stop firing for fear of hitting her. Black smoke poured from the trooper's forward stacks as she was again driven at flank speed. Bluejacket J.J. Callahan was at the canteen with a bottle of ginger ale between his teeth. Suddenly he clamped down on the bottle so firmly that he thought his dental china had been shattered. The LEVIATHAN shook from stem to stern. A barrage of 16 depth charges had been laid down by the destroyer around the submerged U-boat and they rocked the LEVIATHAN from her keel plates to mast trucks, even though she was more than 10,000 feet away.[18] That evening as Chaplain Eugene E. McDonald, from Sea Cliff, New York, stood on the navigation bridge and read his evening prayer to everyone aboard, he said the words with an especial fervor and they were heard with more than usual appreciation. The morning came and the escorting destroyers were gone. The LEVIATHAN was alone, making 21 knots and glad to be alive.

The submarine attacks gave added reason for gunnery practice two days out, and the sinking of the PRESIDENT LINCOLN rammed home the lesson of preparedness. Captain Bryan personally named thirty officers as umpires to judge the target practice in all its phases. Each of the LEVIATHAN's eight guns had two umpires and others were picked to check sighting, spotting, range-finding, and the other steps along the way to accurate firing.[19] Gunnery Officer Bateman followed Captain Bryan's order with a page of instructions. Two targets were to be dropped June 6 about 2500 to 3000 yards apart, while the LEVIATHAN steamed between them. Each gun was to be given its chance, with salvo signals every eight seconds as the ship moved along the firing course. Each gun was to have five rounds. All shots that fell within 50 yards of the target were to be called hits.[20] A special drill would be held on June 5 to get ready for the practice session on the following day. Real ammunition would not be used in the drill, but everything else would be exactly the same as in the practice session. The drill went off well, and a high percentage of hits were scored in the actual target practice on the 6th. The LEVIATHAN's gunners were good.[21]

Meanwhile a continuous training program for lookouts was held, with the most rigid discipline possible. The failure of the lookouts on the PRESIDENT LINCOLN was hammered into the minds of the LEVIATHAN's lookouts as an object lesson. To make their areas of responsibility certain, each lookout station had a cast bronze disc nine inches in diameter, whose outer edge was marked off with the 360 degrees. It had a swinging pointer. Seaman First Class D.W. Hurley came to be so fond of his bronze disc that when he left the LEVIATHAN, after two years of service, he took it with him.[22] The disc's swinging pointer had upright sighting markers at either end, and when they were lined up with the object sighted, the accurate degree could be seen at a glance, to aid gun sighting.

The remainder of the voyage was made without incident, and on the morning of the 8th of June the LEVIATHAN docked at Hoboken. She had completed eight crossings as an American troopship, four round-trip voyages. And now it could be said that she had sailed longer under the American flag than under the German. But her fame as the troopship of World War I had only begun to be established.

Fifth Voyage

ail Lies Like These!" So the headlines read in a Liberty Bond ad published in the June *International Marine Engineering.* The lies they wanted nailed, they said, were: "That this is a rich man's war or a business man's war," and "that farmers are profiteering." The magazine had never had such prosperity; its pages were packed with giant ads from the thousands of companies supplying parts for new ships. The ocean would be spanned by a "bridge of ships" and America was building them. Shipbuilding, as in every war, was one of the industries that profited most. The money raised by Liberty Bonds paid for new ships. Nothing should interfere with its flow, so "nail lies like these."[23]

Nine days were required for the turnaround this time, and the usual bustle of activity filled each day at Hoboken. Ensign Herbert B. "Slim" Rowedder was busy taking pictures around the ship, for he had been named to the ship's history committee. Others were not allowed to have cameras. Slim's real passion was for flowers, but he would be a seafarer for many years to come, eventually becoming one of the ship's top peacetime officers before retiring to run a nursery.[24]

During the stay, many of the crew had a five-day leave. The nation's railroads had instituted a new one-third rate for military personnel, and many went home. Others sampled Hoboken's and New York's low life society. Under the heading *"Order Order Order Order,"* Commander Blackburn issued a stern command requiring any who had been exposed to venereal infection to drop their liberty passes in a box marked "Yes" upon returning. There was also a "No" box. Those dropping their passes in the "Yes" box must "immediately report at the G.U. Clinic, aft on E Deck for prophylactic treatment," the order said. Any man becoming infected and not taking treatment was guilty of a court-martial offense.[25]

The hospital attendant was shocked when several Army nurses, returning to the ship, dropped their passes in the "Yes" box. He was stumped as to how to treat the matter, especially as none of the nurses turned up at the clinic. He eventually assigned Seaman Joseph D. Keane to make delicate inquiries with the nurses. It was an embarrassing assignment, but Keane somehow bulled it through. The girls had never read the *"Order Order Order Order,"* had no idea what the "Yes" box was, and just dropped their cards in the first place they spotted.[26]

The tugs were ready, the 32nd Engineers, 145th and 146th Infantry, and several machine gun battalions were aboard, Major General S.C. Farnsworth was in command of the 10,423 troops, and the crew and ship's officers were all on hand. In all, 13,156 hearts beat within the vast iron shell as the LEVIATHAN sailed that June 15 at 10:30 a.m. A variety of passengers were with her, including two Y.M.C.A. men, five English and French officers, and one Army lieutenant who for some reason was listed as a Navy passenger.[27]

As the LEVIATHAN slowly emerged from the protective windbreak of her pier, her bulk was exposed to a gusty gale blowing from the upper bay. It and the turning tide soon took command, and the troopship slipped sideways upstream almost half a mile before the panting tugs regained control and turned her to face downstream.[28]

So brazen had the enemy become that it was now deemed necessary to escort the LEVIATHAN along the coast for several hours. One destroyer did this, and then she was off and on her own. Although the military now appreciated the importance of the LEVI-ATHAN, comparatively few of the public even knew she existed, let alone appreciated the part she was playing. One published story stated that 3,750 tons of food was needed to provide 210,000 meals on one trip on an unnamed ship. The reporter had to be thinking of the LEVIATHAN, although he evidently made the mistake of assuming there were three meals a day for every one of her 10,000 aboard. His account is so lifelike, however, that it must have been based on fact.

"The khaki line seems limitless. It must seem longer than that to those who remain in the rear, but the coffee in the big pots remains hot, the stew continues to steam and in less than seven seconds each man has an equipment replete with food. . . .

"One man takes gravy on his rice and jam on his bread. The next takes gravy on his bread and jam on his rice, using the combination to produce a crimson tinted mixture. The food needed to feed several thousand men at sea ranges beyond the glutton's dream. You get the answer in the ship down below the waterline, where 7,290 loaves of bread have been baked in one day and eaten."[29]

The summer heat and the close quarters everyone worked in, plus the tensions of the eastbound crossing, did things to the troops. There were many fights, lots of grumbling, and countless unpleasant incidents like the case of Isadore Louis Bierman. He and two chums were medics. All three were just 18. One of Bierman's chums, a lad named Laurence G. Hoes, thought his name was funny and got a kick out of shouting for him in a loud voice. He yelled "Isadore" all over the ship and Bierman was quickly tagged by everyone. Nothing wrong in that, but one boy from the West seemed to have a mean streak and took it out on poor Isadore. Every time he would pass, this fellow would whisper, "Christ-killer."

This began to get Bierman's goat, and finally, one hot hot day, he passed the offending character seated on his bunk and, sure enough, the Westerner whispered, "Christ-killer." Isadore blew his top, rushed him and kicked him in the groin. He had hobnail shoes on, and the kick drew blood and a big crowd. Isidore explained as best he could to an officer and the fracas blew over, but the other chap never forgot. He let Isadore know that he planned to get him. Thanks to Isadore's two fellow medics, the threat was never carried out.[30]

Charles Franklin Webber, Navy chief petty officer aboard the LEVIATHAN, helped cool things on this and many other voyages. He was a fine amateur boxer and enjoyed putting on boxing exhibitions on the open deck aft. He went along on every crossing the LEVIATHAN made as a troopship, and his battered ears were evidence of his love for boxing. Webber had begun his nautical career as an engineer on a tug, and went on later to serve aboard merchant ships. He never lost his passion for boxing.[31]

Well aware that they were soon going to be in the submarine zone, the crew and troops aboard became more and more tense. As if unconsciously responding to this, Commander Blackburn on June 18 put out a memorandum warning the Navy officers that, in the event of actual abandonment of the ship, they should keep all troops and personnel, except females, out of the boats until they were water borne. He pointed out that the boats might not be strong enough to sustain the weight if they were lowered fully loaded.[32]

On the same day the LEVIATHAN suddenly and without apparent cause began to sail in great circles, to the surprise and consternation of all those who did not know that her steering gear had broken down! It was fixed, but not until many anxious moments had passed.[33] Needless to say, this did not contribute to any feeling of relaxation on the big ship's bridge or in her engine room, for everyone was sure the U-boats were waiting to attack again in the Irish Sea or off Brest. Perhaps it was to calm things down a bit that Commander Blackburn issued a long, single-spaced memo on the morning of the 20th, telling all officers how to fill out the quarterly marking sheets on which each division officer was to put his recommendations for advancement in ratings for all those under him. The sheets were distributed throughout the ship. Blackburn, an old Navy man, stressed that a great effort should be made to restore the "old Navy standards", which had been lowered during the influx of men recruited early in 1917.[34] It may have helped to have such a massive and serious paper-work problem tossed in their laps. Virtually every crew member aboard was involved, and, whether the officers went right at it or not, they at least had a major routine task on hand in case they became jumpy. Picture the LEVIATHAN speeding through the danger zone that night with her 2,000-man crew mulling over forms as complicated as a modern income tax return.

No submarines attacked, and at 2:30 p.m. on the 22nd the LEVIATHAN reached the safe port of Brest, with four destroyers escorting her on the last lap. Dozens of coal barges were out in the roads waiting, and they eased alongside as the LEVIATHAN's great bow anchor chains clanked out of the huge hawse sockets and splashed into the harbor waters. Troop tenders came along on the other side and the soldiers started debarking, each carrying his next meal: two sandwiches, a large piece of cake or gingerbread, and two pieces of fruit. From a hundred portholes lines of all sorts were dropped to a flotilla of small craft. Each line had a basket or bag at its end with new American dollar bills inside. In a flash the money was gone and in its place were bottles of cognac. And up came the lines while those in charge looked the other way.[35]

Coaling

 he coaling assignment was such a tough one that the ship's officers continually tried to make sure than no one shirked or managed to avoid his share. Commander Blackburn spelled everything out in great detail in his coaling order for this visit:

"The only men to be excused from coaling will be mess men, Officers of the Deck, passengers, and men detailed handling cargo," he said, "and those handling the cargo will turn to coaling as soon as the cargo is over the side."[36] Coaling was done around the clock, in three eight-hour shifts. Lt. Cunningham, Lt. Ford, and Lt. E.E. Jones had charge of these three watches.[37] The job was a truly horrible one, with every chunk of coal having to be loaded into hand baskets and lifted from the antiquated lighters and barges onto the LEVIATHAN in a way that "would make the coal handling corporations about New York weep and tear their hair," according to one of the ship's officers.[38] In addition to the regimental bands, which blared on both sides of the ship all through the night, there was instituted on this visit to Brest a program of hearty singing. Megaphones carried the voices from the coal barges to the innermost passages of the ship while the soot-caked men labored. The work was done in two days and another three-day turnaround was in prospect.[39]

While the crew rested after the coaling was finished, another frightening thing happened. The PRESIDENT GRANT, sister to the ill-fated LINCOLN, broke loose from her moorings and drifted over toward the LEVIATHAN. To any other ship, the 18,000-ton GRANT would have been a monster, and it looked as if she would crush in the LEVI's side, causing major damage. The bigger ship lay helpless, at her mooring. Fortunately, the GRANT's thrust was softened by a covered barge alongside the big trooper. The barge was smashed into kindling and the LEVIATHAN escaped with nothing more than a scratch. Albert Engel, 16-year-old member of the black gang, remembered this close call as one of the high points of his time aboard the LEVIATHAN. Another occasion that sketched vivid lines in his memory was when he drank a glass of ice water while passing coal in the boiler room. He didn't know any better and went out like a light right on the coal pile. When he came to, they had the water hose on him and an old chief watertender roughly grabbed him and gave him a boot, saying he would get twice that if he ever got caught drinking down there again. Engel had signed on at 15 and had made one trip on deck but didn't like it. Once, during his first few days aboard, he had become so lost trying to find his way out of the engine room that he ended up at the top of the dummy stack before he had his bearings. It was a great view, he remembered.[40]

When the LEVIATHAN sailed, at 6:30 p.m. on June 24, her print shop wore an air of gloom. Art Lockwood, one of the printers, had come down with cerebro-spinal fever and was in a French hospital. He had been taken ill very suddenly just before the ship reached Brest.[41]

One day out, just after the four escorting destroyers had broken away and headed back to the French coast, a suspicious object was sighted on the starboard side, and Numbers 5 and 7 guns opened up. Nine shots were fired and the escorts turned and very quickly came back. A thorough search uncovered nothing, and the big vessel continued on her course alone.[42]

"No food, except to officers actually delayed by duty, will be served from the galley after the limit of time set forth above," Commodore Blackburn said in a memo to officers. The relief of escaping from the war zone without attack had apparently brought with it a letdown of discipline, and the Executive Officer was determined to tighten things up, and promptly.

"Officers will not linger over their meals. . . .

"The Smoking Room and not the mess room is the proper place to lounge.

"When ship's officer has reason to believe that he will be delayed by duty, he must notify the 'Ritz' by telephone at least fifteen (15) minutes before meal hour if practicable."[43]

The LEVIATHAN reached Hoboken at 11 a.m. on July 1, and one of the first visitors aboard brought the sad news that printer Arthur Loges Lockwood had died in Brest. The lieutenant in charge of the print shop wrote to his mother in Bloomfield, New Jersey:

"It was with greatest sorrow that I learned. . . .

"His duties in the printing shop brought him directly under my supervision, and so I was in closer touch with him than any of the other officers. Arthur was one of our best men. . . .Many times it was necessary to get out rush orders, at times when liberty was being granted, and Arthur was one of those on whom the hardest work fell and I could always depend upon him. Your son was to have been made a chief petty officer during our last westbound trip. . . .Though it was not his privilege to die in battle, his death was every bit as glorious, for it was in the service of his country in this titanic struggle of might against right."[44]

In port, more of the LEVIATHAN's lower deck areas were filled with bunks to accommodate more troops. The presence of so many shore workmen was a problem; and an order was issued to stop them from coming above E Deck. Workmen had not only been found wandering around the ship but even gambling and smoking and "soiling compartments where they have no business." So new posts in the alley ways were set up and nine men assigned to this guard duty. A separate toilet was set aside for civilian workmen.[45]

While maritime unions were only beginning to evolve at this time, there was one strong labor group in shipping—the Marine Engineers Beneficial Association. On July 2 this outfit reached an agreement pledging no strikes during the war. Many of the Navy engineers aboard the LEVIATHAN had been MEBA members, and this patriotic development made them happy.

A very real note of doom was struck on the same day. Word was received that the big troopship COVINGTON, formerly Albert Ballin's world-cruising liner CINCINNATI, had been torpedoed and sunk. The vessel was returning from France and had no soldiers aboard, but six of her crew were lost. Her sinking was a second major shock to the Navy, for, like the PRESIDENT LINCOLN, she had been in the choice, safest, centermost position of a large convoy. Seven other liners were in the convoy. They all scattered and none were harmed.[46] The convoy had been protected by seven destroyers, but somehow the torpedo had gotten through. Because the convoy speed could not exceed the best the slowest ship could do, it was likely that the ships were making not much above 10 knots. Here was another example of the great importance of the 22-knot LEVIATHAN, which, by going alone, could make twice the average convoy speed and carry nearly three times as many troops as her nearest American rival.

Commander Blackburn, still trying to tighten up discipline, put out another short memo advising officers that they would be charged for any meals they missed unless they advised the mess treasurer in advance.[47]

Some Famous Names

On July 7 a very special passenger boarded the ship, with suitable honors. He was the young, handsome, and socially prominent Assistant Secretary of the Navy, Franklin Delano Roosevelt.[48] He was going abroad to make a tour of the naval bases in Europe. Two of the LEVIATHAN's crew were men who were to become famous. A young ensign aboard, De Coursey Fales, later became one of America's most famous yachtsmen. A thin young sailor named Humphrey De Forest Bogart became a great film star. He was a quartermaster and a member of the 6th Division on the ship. He rose to helmsman, a spot of real responsibility.[49] There were just under 13,000 aboard when the LEVIATHAN sailed July 8 at 6:30 p.m., escorted by the destroyer WALKE. Brig. General Wm. J. Nicholson was the commanding general of the troops aboard.[50]

The general tendency to relax had even spread to the lookouts, and an effort was made at this time to make troops do lookout duty. Many sailors had been put on report for sleeping in the crow's nest, and it was thought that if a soldier was up there with him, the sailor would not let himself go. The idea was given up, however, after most of the soldiers froze halfway up when asked to do crow's nest lookout duty.[51]

The lookouts took things a bit more seriously after the morning of July 9, when a large mass of wreckage was passed. Obviously the remains of a sunken vessel, it put everyone in a depressed mood and may have been partially responsible for the most extraordinary memo ever issued by Commander Blackburn, a memo filled with sarcasm. It was addressed to all division officers and read as follows:

"Leroy Blackwood, seaman second class, a member of this ship's company, has distinguished himself in the art of stringing the newspaper reporters, and it is believed that he should be awarded some sort of a medal for his wonderful ability. It is suggested that there be engraved on the face of this medal, 'CHAMPION BULL THROWER.'

"The following is quoted from a Trenton, N.J., newspaper, and speaks for itself:

" 'Leroy Blackwood of 125 Kulp Place is again home on a furlough after another successful and thrilling trip across on the transport LEVIATHAN, on which he is a first class gun pointer. Blackwood was wounded in a fight with a submarine on the last trip, when pieces of shell splinters struck his arm. A short time ago on a trip back to this country, the LEVIATHAN had an 18-hour running fight with the U-boats, in which five of them were sent to the bottom. Blackwood now has credit for sinking three submarines and a torpedo.

" 'On their last trip over the members of the crew had a five-hour fight with submarines. Blackwood, who is a member of the stern crew of the ship, observed the wake of a torpedo just under where the gun stood. Firing at blind range he was lucky enough to strike the torpedo with a shell, exploding it. He received congratulations from his Captain for his feat. The Officers are now trying to get a medal for him for distinguished service.'

"All members of the crew are urged to congratulate Blackwood on his heroism and wonderful record. They may well feel proud in having such a shipmate."

Commander Blackburn ordered this memo to be posted on all bulletin boards and in the engineering department.[52] It is rather sad to note that Blackburn went so far as to have his name kept off the "roster of crew" in the Navy's history of the LEVIATHAN.

The Commander issued a very different kind of memo about another man aboard as the ship neared the end of her crossing. A blue-eyed, brown-haired, fair-complexioned man named Harry L. Smith, a private in the 314th Infantry, had disappeared. A search of the ship was ordered. Commander Blackburn noted that it was possible that Smith might be in a Navy uniform. His most distinguishing marks were the tattooed letters "H.S." on his left arm. A muster of all unlicensed crew members was ordered and each man's left arm was to be carefully examined. Whether he was found was not reported.[53]

A final Blackburn memo listed the daily schedule for "Sea Routine" and for "Port Routine." In port the day would begin at 3 a.m. and would end at 9:05 p.m. with taps, pipe down and "keep silence about decks." The liberty hours were listed. The sea day started at 3:45 a.m. and ended with an 8:10 p.m. muster of sea boat crews.[54] This memo was a refinement on several previous sea and port routine schedules. Commander Blackburn was honing and polishing his crew to perfection.

The LEVIATHAN reached Brest at 1 p.m. on July 15, the hottest day of the year. Each of her officers received a note about the new Naval Officers Mess in that port. Dues were a franc a day while the ship was in port. To join, an officer must be proposed and seconded by members. The entrance fee was 50 francs. The Mess was at 35 Place du Chateau, and guest cards were issued only to those awaiting membership.[55] To be so exclusive it must have been quite a desirable spot.

Apparently quite a number of disaffected soldiers had been separated from the fighting front and were being returned to the United States. Captain Bryan received an order from Admiral Wilson to make special note of returning troops who had been dishonorably discharged, so that the ship's authorities would "have cognizance of all undesirables placed on board for passage.[56] Apparently a number of the American soldiers were coming to agree with George Bernard Shaw who, as part of his one-man anti-war crusade, was urging soldiers on both sides to shoot their officers and return home.[57]

Captain Bryan must have been more pleased with a second dispatch from the Flagship U.S.S. PROMETHEUS. It was a copy of a note of high praise from Admiral Wilson to Admiral Sims. It said that the LEVIATHAN had taken 4,400 tons of coal and 1,500 tons of water aboard and that the cooperation of the captain, officers, and men was "excellent and the spirit shown by all hands most commendable." It had been found that keeping the speed to 21 knots and going directly to Brest and back made it unnecessary to load a capacity 8,000 tons of coal in the French port.

Another memo that has survived from this stay in Brest came from Commander Woodward. He was irritated because the ash-ejector on the port side of No. 1 Fireroom had been operated for 40 minutes, but had been shooting out ashes for only four. "Such careless operation and lack of supervision is to be depreciated under any circumstances, but particularly when ash-ejector pump or any other machinery subjected to hard service is involved."[58]

In addition to the dishonorably discharged soldiers, the ship's return passenger list had several other points of distinction. She had the captain of the lost COVINGTON and his officers; also the crew of the freighter BUFFALO, torpedoed a few days before. But most important, she brought home 116 sick and wounded, including some who had been victims of the first poison gas attacks. This particular passenger category would expand drastically as the war continued, until 2,134 wounded would be brought back on the ship's eleventh westbound crossing.[59] One of the wounded on this return passage had been brought over by the LEVIATHAN on her first trip, and, with several of his buddies, he had volunteered to pass coal in return for the right to eat at the crew mess. His name was McGonigle and he would pass no more coal, as he had only stumps where his two arms had been. During an entertainment given for the benefit of the wounded on the return trip, McGonigle stood up, waved his stumps, and said he was glad to be going home on the ship that had taken him over.[60]

Another passenger who didn't fit any category was Felix Iwaniki, a 16-year-old Navy veteran who had survived the sinking of the COVINGTON. His brother had just been killed in France, and he had asked to be sent home on the LEVIATHAN, expecting to be discharged in light of the situation. He was put aboard the LEVIATHAN, given a 22-day leave at New York, and ordered to return. He remained with the LEVIATHAN for 14 more crossings.[61]

The LEVIATHAN Is "Sunk"

The westbound crossing which began July 18 was a quiet one, with no shots being fired except at gunnery practice. But there were plenty of enemy underseas craft out there, eagerly looking for the LEVIATHAN. And they thought they got her! On July 23 readers of the morning edition of the *Hamburger Fremdenblatt* were first stunned and then overjoyed at a front-page story from the Chief of the German Admiralty. It was datelined Berlin, July 20, and it announced that the American troop transport steamer LEVIATHAN had been sunk off the north coast of Ireland!

The report was received "with deep sadness in all German lands, especially in Hamburg," the newspaper said.

"This fate for the proud ship was not anticipated in 1913 as Crown Prince Rupprecht christened it on that festive day.

"Who during its trial run a year later would have thought of its destruction? It was a feeling of relief for all to hear that after the outbreak of the war the giant steamers VATERLAND and IMPERATOR were safe, the IMPERATOR in Hamburg and the VATERLAND in New York.

"But later, as the clouds in the American skies darkened, everyone became very uneasy about the fate of the VATERLAND. And as the outbreak of war came, the greedy hands of the Americans quickly reached for the precious German property, the masterpiece of the German shipbuilding art."

The Hamburg story mentioned how the German crew had cleverly made the ship's machinery "as useless as possible," and how the Americans had had great trouble in mastering the "complicated steering gear," and how they had "expressed astonished admiration for the ship's 'monster-greatness' by giving her the Old Testament's name for sea monster: 'LEVIATHAN.' " The ship had made several voyages with troops, always surrounded by a swarm of warships, as seen in newspapers of neutral countries, but all these "security measures did not help. She fell victim to the formidable German weapons which had made the enemy's seafaring a dangerous enterprise."

The Germans' position was a difficult one. On the one hand they wanted to boast about the size and greatness of the VATERLAND, but on the other they did not wish to admit the importance of the work the LEVIATHAN had done. Now with the sinking this ambivalence was largely dissipated. The Hamburg report was able to say: "The sadness of the sinking was diminished by the knowledge that we destroyed one of the enemy's greatest means of war transportation. And already in our hearts stirs the hope that one day, after the happy ending of the war, a new ship VATERLAND will be built by our proud Hamburg-Line, and no enemy hands will grab it again."[62]

The evening edition of the same paper had another front-page story giving a summary of the Berlin reports about the sinking of the LEVIATHAN:

The *Vossiche Zeitung* compared the sinking to the loss of a battle, hailing it as evidence of "the skill of our U-boats."

The *Berliner Lokal-Anzeiger* claimed that Germany had accomplished through the VATERLAND a "remarkable double victory," because she was the largest ship in the world and a product of Germany and "was now sunk by Germans after being deceitfully seized by the enemy." This source said that the Americans should now see the truth in the old saying that "crime does not pay."

The *Taegliche Rundschau* commented on how hard it must have been for the U-boat commander to sink the "easily identifiable ship," but added that the dire war emergency made "this grave deed" necessary.[63]

Unaware of these newspaper stories, the LEVIATHAN continued on her sixth west-bound crossing. Before she docked, M.P. Iverson was given a flattering "to whom it may concern" note that helped him get his license as a first assistant engineer. He had earned favor with Chief Woodward because of his successful completion of a difficult assignment known as "bilge diving." He had been asked during the ship's conversion to a troopship to help put on paper the many different pipeline systems in the machinery spaces. His mechanical drawing training at New York Shipbuilding Company, Camden, New Jersey, had come in very handy.[64]

As the LEVIATHAN was preparing to dock, a swarm of 12 tugs gathered to help. With the excitement of a secret arrival and the other pressures of the moment, it was a bit of comic relief to hear one of the tug skippers shout out:

"Where in hell can I make a line fast to this hotel?"[65]

Preparations were rushed for a quick turnaround, and a major policy decision was made. For the first time the LEVIATHAN would not sail alone, but with two other very fast ships, the GREAT NORTHERN and the NORTHERN PACIFIC. Built by James J. Hill for his overnight luxury service between Seattle and San Francisco, these two so-called "Palaces of the Pacific" were 24-knot vessels. Tiny in comparison to the LEVI, they were nevertheless thought to be fine sea boats even though they had never been on anything but coastwise runs. It was decided to try them as companion troopers to the giant LEVIATHAN. There were even those who said they might outrace her if given the opportunity.[66]

Chapter XI

SAILING IN COMPANY

t finally came.

Grudgingly, out of Amsterdam.

An admission that the LEVIATHAN had not been torpedoed. A great three-stacker had gone down, all right, but she was the JUSTICIA, the 32,000-ton Holland-America Line flagship so proudly announced at the San Francisco Exposition, way back before America entered the war. Then she was named STATENDAM. Cunard had planned to name her NEURE-TANIA, but she had become JUSTICIA instead, and was being operated for the British government as a troopship by the White Star Line. She was westbound when the Germans caught her, and had no troops aboard.

The Amsterdam report noted that "implicit belief in the veracity of German Admiralty reports received a rude shaking in Germany."

The *Lokal-Anzeiger*, of Berlin, went even farther when it said it would be wrong to assume that all German U-boat commanders habitually overestimated the tonnage sunk. This paper said it hoped that the VATERLAND would be caught sooner or later.

One editor, who had gone so far as to claim that the United States would have to pay for the VATERLAND even after she had been sunk by a German submarine, refused to accept the report from Amsterdam. He refrained from comment until the U-boat commander himself returned and gave his report.[1]

Between July 25 and August 3, unmindful of the furor about her in Germany, the LEVIATHAN rested at Hoboken. A fresh detachment of 506 supernumeraries (non-commissioned men with ratings) came aboard. About half of them were detailed to the Engineering Department, and the rest spread through the various deck divisions.[2] Commander Blackburn tried to keep the crew turnover to the minimum, but with so many men involved a continual change could not be avoided. The Commander's passion for detail moved him to issue a brief memo on July 29 about flashlights and their use. All officers were instructed to have them in their possession for use "in case of actual abandoning ship, only."[3]

Commander Blackburn had found a man after his own heart in First Lieutenant O.J.W. Haltnorth. On August 2, this officer spelled out the duties of the ship's sanitation and embarkation officers. He divided the ship into two parts, putting Boatswain Johnson in charge of all matters affecting seamanship from the bow to midships, including cargo loading hatches 1, 2, and 3. Boatswain Waterson had the rest of the ship, from the swimming pool aft.[4] In a general memo to all officers, Lt. Haltnorth noted that a general laxity had developed "in the stowage of loose articles such as life jackets, bunk bottoms, lumber, etc." He added that he hoped the ship "can be run without any friction," pointing out that Commander Blackburn had shown his confidence in him by naming him First Lieutenant and saying: "I shall make every effort to retain this confidence."[5]

During this stay in Hoboken, Commander Woodward's wife came up from Norfolk to see him, bringing their nine-year-old son, Vaughn H. Woodward. The boy was fascinated with the ship and had a guided tour with a special Navy bluejacket assigned to take him around. He was allowed to ride down in the elevator from the top deck to the engine room, where the maze of machinery fascinated him. He and the sailor had a ragged game of ball on deck which ended when the ball went over the side. Young Woodward was sure it was lost, but it had fallen into a coal barge and some kind soul retrieved it for them. But by then they had lost interest in ball-playing.[6]

On August 2 the LEVIATHAN began to take on another record-breaking number of troops. She took aboard 10,305 enlisted men, 179 over her capacity, and a variety of English and French officers, bringing the total troop load to 10,893. She had the largest crew list of her Navy life, 2,143 men, and also one Y.M.C.A. man and 521 Navy and civilian passengers. In all, she would carry 13,558 persons. Col. W.O. Johnson was the commanding officer of the troops.[7]

She sailed the next day at 3 p.m., and as she passed out through the Narrows a sailor on the Navy collier ORION snapped a photo of her. A close look at this snapshot makes the LEVIATHAN seem to live again, so well does it convey a sense of motion. One tug is falling astern, her escort task finished. A second tug is just below the LEVIATHAN's forward stack, her white smoke leaving a puffy trail along the ship's gray hull. A thin trail of smoke is coming from the LEVIATHAN's forward stack, fragmenting into grayish blobs by the time it reaches the third or dummy funnel and more or less disappearing as it passes the raked main mast.[8]

Outside Sandy Hook the LEVIATHAN was joined by her two convoy sisters, the GREAT NORTHERN and the NORTHERN PACIFIC. These sleek ex-passenger liners had two raked stacks and looked the racers they were. They were of only 8,358 gross tons, however, mere toys compared to the 54,000-ton LEVIATHAN. The three racers were the only ships in the American transport fleet capable of 20 knots or more. A destroyer joined them and escorted them 24 hours on their way.[9]

For four days only the ordinary things happened. Blackburn issued a terse memo criticizing officers who signed permission slips for crew members to leave the ship at Hoboken, citing in particular a case in which a fireman had showed a pass signed by Lt. James P. Watson, of the Engineer's Division. "No one shall give authority for men to leave the ship except the Commanding Officer, the Executive Officer, and the head of department having the day's duty." The Commander also restated the order that forbade LEVIATHAN crew members to go to the Army canteen on the piers. "This is absolutely forbidden, because men of this ship, except when working on the pier, are to proceed direct to the gate on regular liberty or leave and not to loiter anywhere on Army grounds."[10]

There were several canteens aboard the LEVIATHAN, and they were very popular assembly points. On a typical day 10,000 sales were made, with receipts of as much as $6,498 recorded. Lemon drops, which seemed to have some value in preventing seasickness, were immensely popular. Three tons of them were consumed on a typical eastbound crossing.[11]

Seasickness was a real problem, but was universally treated as a joke except by those who had it. During a bit of heavy weather a LEVIATHAN wit rushed into a forlorn group of seasick soldiers, shouting: "Here comes a torpedo—straight for us." The only response came from a white-faced sufferer: "Thank God."[12]

On August 8, a dinner audience in New York heard Admiral Gleaves say that the LEVIATHAN was being sailed at greater speed by the United States Navy than she had ever been sailed by the Germans.[13] This statement certainly did not jibe with the facts, but it would be repeated time and again.

Never quite satisfied with even the smoothest routine, Commander Blackburn, on the same day, issued a five-page command detailing plans for debarking the largest load the ship had ever carried. He first noted that the order in which the various units would debark could not be stated until the landing officer boarded the ship at Brest. There would be two large troop lighters, the SMEATON, holding 2,200, and the KNICKERBOCKER, which could carry 1,500. Two gangways would be used, both on C Deck, one forward on the starboard side and the other aft on the port. Troops were to proceed from their compartments either to the Troop Mess Hall on F Deck (the old first-class Dining Saloon) or to B Deck aft. Their routes to the gangways were detailed to the last turn. The life preservers that they took off as they left the ship were to be stored in piles off the deck outside the "Ritz" dining room. Bunk bottoms would be rolled up lengthwise in bundles of 10 each and stowed. Bunk side bars would be unshipped and piled up. Seasick cans and cuspidors would be "emptied, cleaned and scrubbed," and other measures to insure clean and healthy conditions were spelled out. Officers' cabin trunks were to be placed outside their cabins by 8 a.m. the day of arrival.[14]

Man Overboard

The stress on cleanliness could not have been more appropriate but there is some doubt about how thoroughly these orders were carried out, for on the ninth voyage the LEVIATHAN was to be the victim of one of the most tragic epidemics ever suffered on shipboard. But Voyage 7 had its share of tragedy, too, and it came on August 8, 1918.

The day started badly. A storm had come up in the night and the LEVIATHAN was heaving and rolling in the great ocean waves. The two smaller troopships were in far worse trouble, lifting and crashing down in a desperate manner, when suddenly a flag hoist signal from Captain W.W. Phelps on the bridge of the NORTHERN PACIFIC brought the dread news:

"Man Overboard."

All three troopers immediately went into a previously determined maneuver, making great circles around the area. The man who had gone overboard was a soldier. He had left a note indicating that he planned to end his life, but those on the LEVIATHAN and the GREAT NORTHERN did not know this. William Rutherford, a member of the fire control gang on the LEVIATHAN, had an experience that, for him, seemed to compound the tragedy. When the man-overboard report was received, Bill was aft in the neighborhood of the four after guns. The LEVIATHAN's gunners were looking for the lost man through their gun telescopes, very clumsy instruments for this purpose since they could move sideways or vertically only as the gun itself was moved. About half an hour after the man-overboard message came in, it was announced over the fire-control that the search was being abandoned and that the three ships would resume their zigzag course. At this very moment a member of one of the after gun crews shouted that he had seen a man floating in the wake. He stepped aside so his gun captain could check. The captain also saw the man through the gun telescope. He reported this to his control officer, who asked for a bearing. But by this time the ship had begun to swing around to her original course. It was impossible to fix the point where the man had been seen, and the LEVIATHAN proceeded on her way. Her two smaller companions were told that a man had been seen, but were ordered to resume normal formation as no further delay could be permitted. Bill Rutherford remembered thinking in shocked helplessness that if the soldier was conscious he would see the three vessels turn and sail away just as rescue appeared possible.[15] Had the ships been in the war zone, even this brief search would have been ruled out.

This became a double tragedy, for while the NORTHERN PACIFIC was circling, a second man jumped or fell overboard. No one ever knew why, and he was never seen again. After the ships resumed formation, the continuing heavy weather forced the two smaller ships to request a reduction in the convoy speed, much to the disgust of those on the bridge of the LEVIATHAN.[16]

Despite the weather and the heaving of the ships, gunnery practice was continued. On the 9th it was announced aboard the LEVIATHAN that Chief Gunner's Mate Floyd I. Collup had scored a remarkable 71 percent hit average for the past week, to top the twelve best men in spotting. Everyone aboard was eager to try out the new "Y" guns installed July 27. The LEVIATHAN had two of them aft and each could toss depth charges loaded with 300 pounds of T.N.T. A test was finally made, using four large paint drums filled with wet sand. The cans arced out and landed in the ocean about 200 feet astern, rather too close for comfort. Had there been real T.N.T. in them, serious damage might have been done to the ship's rudder and propellers.[17] Fortunately, the LEVIATHAN never had to test her depth charges with live ammunition.

On August 10 Commander Blackburn issued two more memos, one on the procedure to be followed in placing enlisted men "on report before the mast," which meant bringing a man up on charges for some rule infraction, and the other a clarification on the matter of shore leave passes. In the latter memo it appeared that Lt. Watson had won a round against the ship's Executive Officer. Blackburn's memo corrected an earlier one by noting that Lt. Watson had only signed an application for a pier pass, "which action was perfectly proper." The engineer who had received the pass application had tried to use it as a pass, instead of going with it to the Log Room to get it approved.[18]

During the night of the 10th, while the LEVIATHAN and her two small consorts were racing with their destroyer escorts toward the coast of France, an amusing thing happened. The convoy was maintaining total radio silence for fear of the enemy, but an important message had to be delivered to one of the destroyers. Even a flashing Morse code signal might alert submarines to their presence, and so the officer of the deck decided he would try to find someone aboard with a particularly powerful set of lungs to shout the message across the waves. The helmsman recommended a sailor named Thomas J. Bolger, known among the crew as a fine singer. He was called, and, with the aid of a megaphone, he did the job. The next morning, young Bolger received an order to come to the bridge. It was from Captain Bryan himself. Tom, an inveterate chewer of tobacco, was sure he was going to get a dressing down for spitting on deck. Instead of a reprimand, he won hearty congratulations for his "heroic" voice.[19]

As the convoy approached Brest on the 11th of August, a submarine was seen on the LEVIATHAN's starboard. The three speeding troopships altered course to port and another submarine was sighted on that side. The gunners on all three ships opened up as all three turned sharply and headed for the open sea. The escorting destroyers veered and cut this way and that across the suspected areas, dropping depth charges with great enthusiasm, as the troopships sped toward the western horizon. The sounds and excitement of the skirmish brought more war craft out from Brest to insure the safety of the three troopers, and when they finally returned to the scene they became the center of a veritable flotilla of Allied naval vessels. To the nurses in particular, this whole episode was an event never to be forgotten. When the first submarine was sighted, they were ordered into the lifeboats, and they remained there during the final progress of the armada into the safety of the harbor.[20]

By now the crew had the coaling operation down to a fine system. The deck crew, plus any helpers they could get from among German prisoners or Americans at Brest, handled the coal on the barges, passing it up through 20 ports on either side to the engineer force, who took it and delivered it to the bunkers. As a rule, at least 200 engineers had to trim, level, and properly fill the cavernous bunkers in the outer shell of the ship. Shovels, chutes, and wheelbarrows were used, but most of the work still had to be manual. The men came out of each coaling session dog-tired, sweaty, and black all over.[21]

Only a 48-hour stay at Brest was necessary this time, and on the 13th of August the LEVIATHAN was away again, with eight Congressmen, 152 wounded, another 700-odd passengers, and her crew of 2,144.[22] Again the GREAT NORTHERN and the NORTHERN PACIFIC were along, with an escort of destroyers. The LEVIATHAN's crew watched with keen interest as several depth charges were dropped near some suspicious wreckage. They could always tell when a destroyer was about to fire one, because she would speed up. Her bow would rise and her tail dip and moments later a great cloud of water and spray would rise from amid her foaming wake.[23] Night came, and the speeding ships left the French coast in darkness. Several hours after the early summer sunrise a submarine appeared between the LEVIATHAN and the NORTHERN PACIFIC, to the consternation of the troops on deck. To everyone's relief, it was an Allied craft.

Gunnery Practice

The Germans' claim that they had sunk the LEVIATHAN had by this time become common knowledge, and the ship's gun crews, now more than ever, were constantly on the alert. The westbound passages were much preferred for gunnery drills because the ship was virtually empty and the sound of firing would not excite 10,000 warbound soldiers. Gunnery Officer Lt. Bateman set forth a daily routine for drill to begin Thursday, August 15. From 8 a.m. to 2 p.m. daily he scheduled a series of sightsetting, checksighting, loading, and spotting drills for all personnel.

"This is essential in view of the fact that we have only the few days at sea in which to train," he said.[24] In addition to her eight 6-inch, 50-caliber guns, the LEVIATHAN had a variety of other weapons. She had two 1-pounders, two Colt machine guns and one Lewis, 150 Springfield rifles, and 75 Colt automatic pistols. She also had four range-finders.[25]

On Saturday, August 17, following a whole day of battle practice, the crew were once again given real targets to shoot at. Two were dropped about 2,000 yards apart, with the ship steaming in between. With the ship on "the firing course," a General Quarters was sounded and all gun crews and observers took their stations. When the targets bore about 30 degrees, range 3,000 yards, the gunnery officer sent out signals for the salvo to start, giving the initial range, deflection and order to commence firing. Five rounds per gun were allowed. All shots falling within 50 yards short of or beyond the target and 20 yards to right or left were called hits.[26] Whenever they were sighted, whales were used as targets for machine gun crews, who were permitted to fire about 30 rounds of ammunition.[27]

Meanwhile, on the less exciting side of things, Commander Blackburn decided that a new booklet should be issued on rules for Naval Supernumeraries. He called for suggestions from his fellow officers on Wednesday the 14th, giving them until 6 p.m. on the following day to get their ideas in, so the booklet could be written and sent to the printer by the following Thursday and be ready for Voyage 8, to start August 31. Not only was the LEVIATHAN self-sufficient in many ways, but no one dawdled. Not too much imagination was shown in the rules that came in. Most were such standard bits of advice as "bathe daily," "always wear life preservers," "throw nothing overboard," etc. One officer suggested a caution against talking to soldier passengers of "possible dangers of the trip or of sea experiences which would disquiet a landlubber." Doing so, he added, might lead them to panic in an emergency, which "might endanger your life."[28]

With the new rule book well under way and three good days of gunnery drill behind them, the crew put on the first of a series of musical satires that were to become an important morale-builder for the ship's company. It was entitled "The Darktown Telephone Exchange," and a handsome program was printed to give it style. Directed by Lt. W.H.F. Schluter, the one-act skit was attributed to "The LEVIATHAN Boys." It was set in a "Gilded Cafe" at 135th Street and Lenox Avenue, New York City, and the time was "just before the draft." Tom Bolger, of the loud voice, played Madam Butterfly and had one of the eight musical numbers. A piano, a violin, and a banjo livened things up. Ed Kennedy was in charge of the show's properties, C.C.M. McNally did the scenery, and Chef Travise furnished the eggs "used in this production."[29]

At 9:45 p.m. on Monday the LEVI reached Hoboken. There was a tug strike and she had to come in to her slip without benefit of docking pilot or tugs. And it was night. Navigator Harold Cunningham was in charge, and gained no little distinction. His feat was to be remembered years later when he was named master of the LEVIATHAN.[30] The arrival was also notable for the fact that the LEVIATHAN was beaten by one hour by the GREAT NORTHERN, a victory that the smaller ship's crew would crow about for the rest of their lives. But, as the Navy's history of the LEVIATHAN explains, "she had traveled 100 miles less to do so."[31]

Instead of staying only a week this time, the LEVIATHAN was at Hoboken for 11 days. The tempo of activities aboard the huge ship was greatly reduced during these port stays. Most of the deck officers were away on liberty, with only four teams of four men each standing watch on the bridge. The typical tour of duty began at noon and ran 24 hours, with two men standing four hours on and four off. This worked out so that each of the 16 watch officers had one day on and three off.[32] The chief assignment these men had was supervising the coaling. Even at Hoboken this was a major operation requiring a stream of memos from Commander Blackburn and Lt. Haltnorth.

The Commander never let up on the smallest detail, as witness his memo of August 22 reminding all officers that they must be back aboard ship at 9 a.m. after having a night off.

"Although this information has been given to officers at various times," his memo added testily, "it is repeated that when an officer goes ashore he must return to the ship by 9 a.m. the following morning unless otherwise excused by special permission."[33]

Apparently something was brewing on the highest level in connection with the distinction that existed between regular Navy officers and Naval Reserve men, for on August 30 a mimeographed list was prepared of all 68 LEVIATHAN deck officers. Presumably a similar list was prepared for the engineering officers. The deck list showed 30 regular Navy men. All the others were reserve officers except Jean Metayer, the French pilot.[34] A couple of days later, after the LEVIATHAN had sailed, the point of all this listing became apparent when Commander Blackburn quoted an order from Secretary of the Navy Daniels. It called for an elimination of any and all differences in the uniforms of regulars and reservists.

"Every officer in the Navy," the order went, "shall be designated and addressed by the title of his rank without any discrimination whatever."[35]

Voyage 8

oading for Voyage 8 began on August 30. A total of 13,362 souls were taken aboard. The Army was represented by 10,541 bodies, including 99 nurses, 78 non-commissioned officers, and 4 clerks. A Japanese naval officer, a Y.M.C.A. man, and 597 enlisted bluejackets were listed as part of the crew.[36] Colonel William G. Ownbey was the commanding officer for the Army personnel aboard.[37]

The tug pilots had gotten her undocking down to a fine system. The F Deck gangway was hauled ashore at 1:19 on August 31. Seven minutes later all lines were let go, and only 14 minutes after that the ship slowly began moving astern and out of the slip. It took the 950-foot hull just seven minutes to back clear of the slip, and only 19 minutes later she was past the Statue of Liberty.[38] She drew an amazing 42 feet forward, considerably more than she had ever drawn as the VATERLAND, and the difference was in the weight of the mass of human flesh aboard, as well as in the mountains of stores, deck cargo, and coal.

At 4:38 the ship stopped briefly to drop Pilot McLoughlin and to put the paravanes overboard. By this time nearly 4,000 British ships and several hundred American vessels had these P.V.s, or "otters," to protect them from floating mines.[39] Then the GREAT NORTHERN took up her position to the starboard and the NORTHERN PACIFIC started off to port and all three set off on their zigzag course at 20 knots. The LEVIATHAN ran things, with her zigzag pennant dipping to show each course change as it came up.

The first two days were calm sailing. On September 2, spotters identified the wake of a submarine about two miles astern. It disappeared and no shots were fired.[40] The skies clouded over and a heavy swell started the three speeding troopships rolling. Remsen B. Sickles, a 17-year-old seaman, was shocked at the way the ship seemed to be leaking, although what he assumed were leaks were actually torrents of water taken aboard from the waves cascading over bow and stern. A new face in the crew, young Sickles was also somewhat shocked at the notices posted in crew quarters stating that if the ship had to be abandoned no sailor would leave until all the troops were off.[41]

As the weather worsened, the GREAT NORTHERN and NORTHERN PACIFIC were unable to keep up the pace and asked that the convoy speed be dropped to 13 knots. For 14 hours the ships smashed through heavy seas, with waves and spray flying everywhere, even reaching the LEVIATHAN's forward smokestack. A photo taken of the LEVI by someone on the GREAT NORTHERN showed a wave hiding all but the tops of her masts and stacks and part of the stern. The picture was later used as part of a LEVIATHAN souvenir photo album sold to troops aboard.[42]

Life continued on the storm-wracked vessels, and Lt. Haltnorth found it necessary to send a memo asking all his officers "not to take part in dancing during working hours." Since their working hours were from 8:15 to 11:30 a.m. and from 1 to 4 p.m., it appears that dancing was not confined to the evening hours.

"The above memorandum is sent out for the best interest of all concerned," the Lieutenant felt called upon to explain.[43]

MOUNT VERNON Torpedoed

ne of those who were not stopped from dancing was a young congressman named F.H. La Guardia. Also aboard was a British passenger, the famous artist Norman Wilkinson who had had a part in designing the dazzle camouflage which had been painted on the LEVIATHAN in the Gladstone dry dock six months earlier. Her camouflage had worn off and no one had the time or energy to restore it. She was a mottled, dirty, rusty gray now.[44]

The great four-stacked former luxury liner KRONPRINZESSIN CECILIE, renamed MOUNT VERNON, may have saved the LEVIATHAN on September 5. She was returning from France in company with her near sister, the AGAMEMNON, formerly the KAISER WILHELM II, and six destroyers. They were on virtually the same course as the LEVIATHAN and would have passed within sight of the eastbound high-speed convoy a day's sail off France. The MOUNT VERNON's lookout sighted a periscope barely 600 yards off her bow, and only moments later the sleek former German flyer was struck by a torpedo. The ship was saved, thanks to quick action by all hands, including Adolphus Staton, her executive officer, who had formerly been with the LEVIATHAN. She was saved because her watertight doors held and her quick change of course prevented any other torpedoes from reaching her. But when her watertight doors slammed shut, 37 men were trapped in an amidships compartment and drowned as the water poured in from the hole made by the torpedo explosion. One of the war's most miraculous escapes saved a 38th life. The seaman had been trapped in the punctured compartment too, but with superhuman determination he had managed to wedge and force his way up and out onto an upper deck through an air funnel that ventilated the flooded section.[45]

Only a few of the LEVIATHAN's officers knew of this tragedy when she passed the scene of the torpedoing the next day, but another bit of news blinked across the air waves to them from the GREAT NORTHERN. Captain Phelps of that ship had just been notified that he would take the LEVIATHAN on the next voyage. This was Captain Bryan's seventh and last round trip as master.[46]

The crossing had one more shocker, literally. As the three troopships and their four destroyers were approaching Brest, the waters were shaken by an "extremely heavy explosion." Chief Engineering Officer Woodward hastened to call the bridge and assure them that there was nothing amiss below. To make matters worse, it was night and by this time most of the LEVI's crew had learned about the MOUNT VERNON. And then the explanation came, via blinker flash from the destroyer MCDOUGAL, directly abeam. She had accidentally dropped a depth charge from her stern. If the explosion had shaken the LEVIATHAN, imagine its effect on the little escort craft.

Arriving at Brest late on the afternoon of the 7th, the LEVIATHAN's crew were happy to spot the MOUNT VERNON safely in dry dock. At 8:33 p.m. the LEVIATHAN was safely tied up to her mooring buoy. Instead of drawing 42 feet forward, as she had done when leaving Hoboken, she now drew only 36 feet, 7 inches.[47]

The arrival was watched by thousands from the shore each time the LEVIATHAN came into Brest. A seaman aboard the AGAMEMNON who had been through the MOUNT VERNON torpedoing saw her come in this time, and the experience left a vivid picture in his memory:

"I will always remember the awe-inspiring sight she made as she passed through the high cliffs that formed the entrance to the harbor. Behind her the sun was setting and she was pictured on a grand scale in silhouette."[48]

Coaling began at 1:15 a.m. on the starboard side and fifteen minutes later on the port. A slightly longer stay than usual was necessary because of the sad formality of receiving all but one of the dead MOUNT VERNON seamen. They were brought aboard on the 8th at 3 p.m., with proper ceremony. In instructing Ensign Allen how to observe the ritual, Commander Blackburn noted:

"The Ensign will be half-masted when the tug bearing the bodies is seen nearing the ship and will remain until the word has been received that the bodies have been deposited in their resting places on board, and will again be run up to to the masthead."[49]

In another related memo stamped "URGENT" in large letters, the Commander reminded all officers that the MOUNT VERNON was able to make 15 knots with two firerooms "punctured" and that the loss of life was confined to the men in the punctured firerooms "BECAUSE ALL WATERTIGHT DOORS IN THE SHIP WERE KEPT CLOSED AND DOGGED." The capital letters were his. He called on every man aboard "to constitute himself a strict observer to see that the ship's regulations in regard to watertight doors and air ports are carried out to the letter."[50]

Captain Bryan was pleasantly surprised to receive a "communication" from Colonel Ownbey when the troops left the LEVI at Brest. On September 9 Commander Blackburn ordered that it be published for all to read.

"Before leaving the ship I desire to express the sincere appreciation of myself and the entire staff for the valuable assistance you and your crew have given us on our voyage across the sea," the Colonel began.

"Our relations with you and your officers have been cordial and pleasant; our voyage under the circumstances was delightful. I desire to especially mention the co-operative work of Commander Blackburn. . . .Trusting that you may continue to be successful in the stupendous task of moving thousands of our troops over the seas, I beg to remain, etc."[51]

The strict disciplinarian in Commander Blackburn came to the surface again on September 10 when he issued a memo lecturing LEVIATHAN officers on behavior. The uniform does not, he said, bestow on its wearer special license. This is a "false and fatal idea." The uniform should only be seen "amid worthy associations and in places where no dispute can stain it." The officers were warned to set a good example:

"Let your men see you always a master of yourself; clean, temperate and discreet. . . avoiding always the very appearance of evil, by habit, bearing and language. . . .Though we are outside the bounds of our own land its laws and customs have not changed. In France you are making the reputation of America."[52]

The LEVIATHAN sailed for home on September 12 at 5 p.m. The return crossing was quiet except for one periscope spotting by the GREAT NORTHERN. Again the enemy was seen two miles away and far astern of the racing convoy. Again no shots were fired.[53] Among the important passengers were five congressmen and Secretary Roosevelt, with two secretaries. The survivors of two sunken ships, the LAKE LASANG and the LAKE PEWAUKEE, were also aboard, along with Red Cross, Y.M.C.A., and other civilians. Sick or wounded passengers numbered 270. Including the crew, the ship had 2,821 persons on board.[54]

It was decided to drop the alternate Abandon Ship drill planned for use on westbound crossings, and always conduct the drill under full load conditions. Commander Blackburn stressed in a note to all officers that this critical drill should be repeated and repeated until it was second nature to everyone aboard.[55]

Through the efficient line handling of the longshoremen under the direction of Captain Walter J. Bernard, the arrival at Hoboken on September 19 established something of a record. Six minutes after the first line was thrown from the ship, she was securely docked.[56]

No one attached any significance to it, but the dashing young Assistant Secretary of the Navy had not been feeling at all well the day before the ship landed. When she docked he was so weak that he had to be carried off and rushed in an ambulance to his mother's home at 47 East 65th Street, New York. He had fallen victim to what was then known as the Spanish influenza. It had been brought to America on transatlantic liners from the Mediterranean and seemed to be spreading with alarming rapidity. Before the year was out, 12,562 would die from it in New York City alone. In the entire world it would claim an astonishing toll of 21,000,000 dead.[57]

Several Blackburn memos kept things from becoming dull during the Hoboken turnaround. On the 20th he transmitted a "blue law" memo from Secretary Daniels insisting that no Navy officer should use an automobile or motorboat on a Sunday. The only exceptions would be cases of "strictly official business and this official business must be of a military character and such as cannot be transacted on any other day."[58]

Another memo noted that Rear Admiral T.J. Cowie would act as the Liberty Loan Officer. All men were asked to give the "same enthusiastic support which made possible our overwhelming subscription of the last loan."[59] Another long memo a few days later described the different Treasury certificates that were available. They ranged from $500 to $100,000 and drew 4 percent interest.[60] Cameras were now to be permitted on board the LEVIATHAN and other troopers, following a directive from Secretary Daniels to prepare a history of the Navy's Cruiser and Transport Force. No view of foreign ships, of Allied submarines or aircraft, of Allied harbors, shores, or ports were to be made, and all photos taken were to be turned over to the censors. As many "interesting and descriptive photographs as possible" were to be made and turned in to the commanding officer.[61] Another Blackburn memo informed the officers that a 50 per cent reduction on hotel rooms was available for men in uniform registered through the Officer's Service Department, although there would be no hotel rate "lower than one dollar per night."[62]

Epidemic

arly in 1918 Richard D. Zucker enlisted in the Regular Army. He was attached to the 14th Cavalry and sent to the Texas-Mexican border. Learning that most of the cavalry units were being dismounted and turned into so-called machine gun troops for France, he decided to make a transfer. He had learned how to operate a wireless set and decided to shift to the signal corps, which had originally been horse-drawn. The unit he wished to join still had a horse-shoer on its rolls, and that gentleman was eager for a change. Dick Zucker took his place, and he and his 323rd Field Signal Battalion were shipped to Camp Upton at Yaphank on Long Island. Many of the men were new recruits and had no sense of discipline. Some ate their emergency rations. They were at Yaphank for only four days. No leaves were allowed because the flu epidemic was at its height. And then they were ordered to Hoboken to board the LEVIATHAN.[63]

Others to board the LEVI on the 28th of September, or to attempt to board her, were groups of replacements from various Eastern camps under Major General Leroy S. Lyon.[64]

Captain William W. Phelps, who had assumed command on September 21, certainly had a difficult indoctrination period. He was well aware of the flu epidemic and had taken steps to make sure that his crew would be as safe from it as possible. Many soldiers had dropped limp and dying on the march from their camps to the trains that were to bring them to Hoboken. Others fell while lined up on the pier. Still others were stricken aboard ship and had to be removed to hospitals before she sailed. Only 11,809 were put aboard the LEVIATHAN for this crossing, which shows how many had already contracted the often fatal illness. To make matters worse, no one seemed to have a comprehensive view of the situation. The Army groups whose men were infected were not isolated, but were scattered aboard the LEVIATHAN according to the regular embarkation plan, spreading the infection to many different compartments.

"I well remember that departure day," J.J. Callahan wrote. "The troops were walking up our forward gangways and a steady stream of them were being carried down our after gangways on stretchers. We finally pulled out. All crew members were ordered to wear white cotton nose and mouth protectors and to take throat sprays three times a day. These were administered by male hospital apprentices."[65] One apprentice caught flu and became very weak on sailing day. He told Chaplain McDonald that he did not want to die because of the great need for his help back home, but he was the first to go. Only two other Navy men died, however, during the frightful crossing, and both were passengers. Before the French shore was reached, there were 96 dead Army men aboard, and many hundreds of others from the ship died later in hospitals in Brest.

The LEVIATHAN sailed on schedule at 1:45 p.m. on September 29, dropping Pilot McLaughlin and picking up her two smaller consorts off Ambrose Light Vessel. The German submarine campaign had been stepped up and everyone aboard knew that the LEVIATHAN was still target number 1. On her first several crossings she had left New York without escort; then one destroyer was thought necessary; and now, on Voyage 9, she was met beyond Sandy Hook by two destroyers, a "dirigible balloon" and two "big aeroplanes," as Corporal Zucker wrote home to his mother. How his letter got past the censors is hard to understand, but it did, and his mother promptly gave it to a local newspaper, where it was published in full.[66] A tugboat and several Allied ships had been attacked off the Atlantic coast by enemy U-boats. Every precaution had to be taken with the LEVIATHAN. To confuse the U-boats, it was decided to head south instead of east. Her new course confused a number of others as well, among them young Navy Ensign Ken Harder on Sub Chaser 119, running along the Jersey coast on the night of September 30, experimenting with a new ultra-secret sounding device to detect submarines. Suddenly a monstrous form appeared out of nowhere, heading right for them.

"She damn near hit us," he recalled.

She was the LEVIATHAN and she steamed almost to Florida before making her turn eastward. Captain Phelps wanted to keep out of normal sea lanes at all costs.[6] [7]

It was horrible aboard the LEVIATHAN.

Troop space H-8 was so poorly ventilated that the men who had been sent there first were moved to other compartments. Many were sick and not only did they add to an already crowded situation, but they spread the illness. Sick bay was packed, and a nearby section had to be emptied and assigned to those with flu. Its 200 bunks were filled in minutes with men who had collapsed on deck. Another section with 415 bunks was vacated and its former occupants ordered down to the poorly ventilated H-8 area. Still another sick ward was established and as promptly filled. The chief Army surgeon aboard, a Colonel Decker, and two of his assistants came down with the disease, leaving only 11 Army doctors to care for the 878 men who were now crammed into three sick wards. Thirty nurses and 20 other Army officers were ill in their cabins. The other nurses, joined by the Navy medical officers, all pitched in, working in relays to the limit of their physical endurance. Countless others in the crew stepped forward to help, men from Paymaster Farwell's department and others from Frank Flowers' commissary particularly distinguishing themselves. The latter not only prepared the meals but helped feed the sick. Special diets were necessary in hundreds of cases. Some 15,000 pounds of oranges were issued, for example, to make orange juice.[6] [8]

There was not only influenza aboard, but mumps and measles too. With flu, a victim is first affected with a kind of lassitude that makes him lose interest in everything. Hundreds just lay in their bunks, not even complaining, until they became so weak they developed pneumonia. Most of the deaths were from pneumonia.

Life Went On

On October 1, a Tuesday, with his 1,000-foot ship a miserable, fetid world of fear and fever, the new captain took time out to issue the following command:

U.S.S. LEVIATHAN

M E M O R A N D U M

1Oct18.

Subject: Paper work.

1.   To follow a standard practice:

        (1). In all cases do not express the date like-
              12/27/18. Express the date 27Dec18, without
              spacing or any other intervening characters.
              Put the day of the month first. Also it is

advantageous when dates have to be columnized-
it takes less space. Thus 27Dec18 requires
seven type spaces. 12/27/18 requires eight
type spaces.

(2). Put all <u>file numbers</u> in right upper corner.
Although Naval Instructions say left upper
corner, the right is more reasonable because
all paper clips naturally are put on the upper
left corner and that makes it difficult to pick
up the file numbers.

2. All Heads Depts. give necessary orders to all officers.

With the ghastly sights of a rampant epidemic all around them, this memo must have struck those under Captain Phelps as a sign of hard times to come. What kind of man was their new commander? What a contrast to the smiling, jolly bluntness of old Captain Bryan, who had left just about everything to his executive, Commander Blackburn. Fortunately for the LEVIATHAN, this paper work memo was a rare display of a personal obsession. The real Phelps soon emerged as a brave, broadminded, and able officer.[69]

Two other memos came out that day, neither of which had the date in the prescribed manner. One was a new set of battle practice rules and the other a list of umpires and gunnery exercise officials. Such things as this, however, were given relatively little attention on the plague-ridden ship.[70]

Another memo, which was undated but which must have appeared at about this time, begins: "ATTENTION: SALUTE: TWO:" It set the hours at which "subscription for the LEVIATHAN NAVAL BALL will be taken at the Keyroom "D" Deck, 'midships." The sale was to begin Saturday 5Oct18. This time the date was given correctly. The price of a ticket, admitting the buyer and one guest, was $5, while additional guests could be brought at $1 each.

"Receipts issued for subscriptions taken will be exchanged for tickets upon arrival in New York or very soon thereafter. It is suggested that those receipts be carefully preserved."[71]

A tersely worded and very serious memo from Commander Blackburn was issued "1Oct18." The memo reminded lookouts that death could be the punishment for anyone who slept upon his watch or left his station before being regularly relieved. The lookout duty was one of the most important duties assigned to anyone, it said, adding that "the Captain wishes every officer or man standing lookout to realize this fully. . . .if the enemy is permitted to approach without detection through laxity of the lookouts, it may well mean the destruction of the ship."[72]

Meanwhile, although all of the healthy 9,000-plus aboard were undoubtedly tense and fearful, life did go on. Corporal Zucker's 323rd Company was fortunate. They had a six-piece band, a banjo, mandolins, guitar, and violins. They played every night in the mess hall: shades of the VATERLAND's magnificent German orchestra. They did much to cheer those who were well enough to eat. Zucker himself was given a pass designating him as a "sign painter." It gave him access to all parts of the ship and may have saved his life, because with it he could go up to the outside decks and breathe the fresh, pure sea air.

"I always carried paint brushes and paint but never had to paint a sign," he said. It was evidence of the sad state of discipline and routine on the disease-racked ship.[73]

While the danger of allowing the sick men to remain in their bunks was known, the crowded conditions in the greatly enlarged sick bay made this unavoidable. There was a continuous stream of men going to sick bay, being turned away for lack of space, and dropping on deck or in the passageways. Many forgot where they belonged. Others got lost trying to return. Any number lost their blankets, clothing, food kits, and other possessions. There were so many men sick that all types of policing duties normally carried on by Army personnel for their own benefit went undone. It became necessary for the relatively healthy Navy crew to fill in on the most urgent cleaning details. The administrative direction of Colonel Decker was sorely missed.

As the Epidemic Spread

The first pneumonia death took place on October 2. The body was embalmed and encased in a Navy casket. On the next day another radical enlargement of the hospital area was made, and, from this point on there were enough bunks to handle the worst cases. Three more deaths were recorded. It was estimated that there were about 900 influenza cases aboard.

To make matters worse, a rough spell set the LEVIATHAN to rolling and heaving. Hundreds of men became seasick, and many of these assumed, quite naturally, that they had flu. The situation was made much worse by the inexperience of the Army doctors in recognizing simple seasickness. As a result, many otherwise well men were put with the infected soldiers in the various isolation wards.

"Big as the LEVIATHAN was, she rolled and pitched like a lifeboat," Dick Zucker wrote home to his mother. "She rolled as much as 25 degrees one night. Dad will explain how much that is to you. It seemed almost like upside down. Many of the boys were seasick, but I guess my seafaring blood came to the top and I enjoyed it."[74]

Colonel Ernest W. Gibson, of the 57th Pioneer Infantry, was given a four-hour tour of the engine room by young Ralph F. Cochran, a refrigeration engineer in the crew. Both were from Vermont, but neither realized that this chance coming together would end up with Cochran owning the choice souvenir from the LEVIATHAN many years later.[75]

Grover Cleveland Hollings, a pharmacist's mate, had an experience which did not add to his enjoyment of the crossing. He couldn't sleep in the crew's quarters because it was so crowded, and he put up a cot in the pharmacy. One night when he was settling down for a few minutes' sleep he saw a big rat crawling up on his blanket. Waiting as long as he dared, he lurched forward, threw a sheet over the animal, wrapped it up and heaved the whole thing over the side. On other crossings—happier ones, when there was no epidemic—Grover had some real parties with the medicinal alcohol in the pharmacy.[76]

Father Mac had the most difficult crossing of his career. As if to add to his almost overwhelming burdens, one of the Army chaplains who were helping him with the dying was threatened with court-martial when he opened a porthole slightly at night to satisfy a dying doughboy's plea for air.[77]

By now the whole crew—sailors, cooks, stewards, everyone who could walk—was battling the epidemic. There was no difference between day and night. Ten died on October 5. Twenty-four more went on the 6th. Adequate record-keeping was becoming impossible. Many half-dead soldiers would drag themselves to a ward, find an empty bunk, and lie down, without applying to a medical officer at all. Many had been given tags to put around their necks, but the tags had never been filled in. Some of those who died were delirious and didn't know their names. Their papers and identification had long before been lost. As the voyage drew to a close, it was estimated that there were 2,000 active cases of influenza, with another 1,000 who had recovered.

Most of the dead were emaciated, just skin and bones. Many were lanky mountaineers from Tennessee and Kentucky who had never been more than a few miles from their homes. It was a Navy rule that an autopsy must be performed on anyone who died on shipboard, and so there were rows of tables set up on B Deck (where gay Sarah Haas and her White Rats had posed for their photograph not so very long before) and all the way across the Atlantic these tables carried a succession of skeletonlike soldiers, laid out naked, entrails piled on their chests, big toes tied together with string and another piece of string around the penis.[78]

After the first 40 died, there were no more caskets. Then the ship ran out of embalming fluid. The bodies had to be put in the ship's refrigerators, for, according to Navy records, none were buried at sea until the living troops had debarked at Brest.[79] J.J. Callahan disputes this, saying that when there were no more coffins, 25 or 30 bodies were sewed up in canvas with fire grates at their feet and slid over the side with a eulogy and a prayer. Then, he says, they ran out of fire grates and tied small canvas sacks of coal at the feet, "and so it went day after day with the final prayers becoming briefer each day."[80] Seaman Sickles also remembers when they ran out of caskets. He says there were burials at sea on two or three occasions.[81]

The day the LEVIATHAN reached Brest, 31 more deaths occurred. Debarkation of the sick into an Army ambulance boat began at noon and by nightfall all but 200 had been taken ashore. Fourteen of these died before they could be removed the following day. In all, 966 patients were removed by the Army hospital authorities.[82] Fifty-eight of the dead aboard on arrival were buried in France, 33 were brought back to America, and the rest were buried at sea in the war zone the morning after the LEVIATHAN began her westbound crossing. The burial took place at sunrise "after an imposing prayer by the chaplain," and with the flag at half-mast, taps sounding, and three volleys fired, according to the ship's Navy history. The LEVIATHAN was speeding at 21½ knots as the coffins were lowered into the sea.[83]

For the first two days out of Brest, all hands aboard were going through the motions almost mechanically, their senses dulled by the fearful experiences of the epidemic. They were happy that they had survived, glad to be heading home again, but their cargo of wounded veterans prevented them from any outward display of the joy of living. One of the wounded men died on October 9, the day the LEVIATHAN sailed.[84] Captain Phelps tells how he was struck by the spirit of the casualties aboard:

"One of the lasting impressions comes from these wounded boys. Instances will never be forgotten, how the hopelessly maimed and paralyzed lay for forty-eight hours in clothing and life belt patiently, cheerfully, smilingly enduring a discomfort we well and sound people chafed under. In inspecting the ship one would always meet smiles from these men and see their faces radiating some holy sublime light. There seemed to be the glory and pride of sacrifice permeating the sick bay. One felt small and futile in the midst of such an elevating atmosphere."[85]

The LEVIATHAN Ball

n eight-page issue of "The Red Watch Mark," issued by the engineers, came out October 9. The lead article in this tabloid-style newspaper plumped for the projected LEVIATHAN Ball. It was to be held in the Grand Central Palace "or some other place that will accommodate 4,500 people," it "will be gorgeously decorated. . . .you will feel like a million dollars the minute you step in. . . .two orchestras will stand watch and watch." Those who don't dance "will enjoy the grand march and cabaret. . . .priceless supper

no regular salt should miss." The event was "in no way connected with the Y.M.C.A. . . . bring any number of guests, but only two of these can be men." The ship's black gang was chided for not buying as many tickets as the deck force.

An editorial in the same publication warned against feeling overconfident about the war. "It is madness to consider the Germans losers while their armies are fighting everywhere on Allied soil. The German army has not been broken. It still holds immense areas of conquered territory. Therefore Germany remains victorious. . . .This war cannot be won until the Pan-German idea is crushed. This is the conceit that makes a Prussian an offensive animal everywhere; that makes him believe that he is so much better than any other man that he should dominate the world. . . .The Huns must be crushed and humiliated to the dust. They must be made to realize that they are beaten and beaten to a pulp. . . ."

A page entitled "Society Jottings" began:

"REWARD!!!! — The Society editor will resign in favor of anybody who can get anything on Lt. Andrews. Compared with the Dean, a sly fox is a frank and earnest boy."

Another item noted: "Now that the Mess Hall has its Victrola, why not send the Apollo-formed Riker over to recruit the Dolly Sisters to dance during dinner?"

And another, marked "Joke(?)" had this to add:

"What's 'matter? Oh! Someone opened the door and In-flu-enza."[8 6]

On October 16 at 8 a.m. the LEVIATHAN tied up safely at Hoboken. "It was a nerve-racking voyage and we were all greatly relieved that the trip was over."[8 7]

Alongside the LEVIATHAN was the troopship AMERICA, Ballin's pride of 1905. She was a sad sight, having sunk mysteriously at her pier the day before. She had been completing her coaling and had 5,000 troops aboard. It is supposed that her bilge keels held her in the mud as the tide rose. Her coal ports were only four feet above the waterline and they were all open. When the water first began trickling in, she might have been saved had the order been given to close all her ports, but this was not done and soon the sea poured in until she filled and sank into the mud.[8 8]

THE RED WATCH MARK
U. S. S. LEVIATHAN

Vol. 1   Jan. 29, 1919   No. 19

PUBLISHED every week by the Engineering Department for the dissemination of general and professional information among the officers and men of the Department, and as an endeavor to further promote our pride and interest in our shipmates and in our Department.

Chapter XII

THE WAR ENDS

his points to a fine sense of duty and will help to win the war."

So said Captain Phelps in a message to the LEVIATHAN's engineers, praising them for not having an absence or a single tardiness the 16,048 times that engineers went on watch during the last crossing. The Captain also hailed the black gang because less than three fifths of one per cent of those on the sick list during the epidemic had been engineers. His comments were preserved for posterity as the page-one item in the October 16 issue of "The Red Watch Mark."[1]

On October 17 Lt. Haltnorth called on everyone in the crew to prevent influenza by covering all coughs or sneezes with a handkerchief, by frequently washing hands, by spitting only in spit kits, and by turning any violators over to the nearest Army officer.[2]

Jim Callahan, who was transferred to other duty on October 18, took with him not only many LEVIATHAN memories but a nickel-plated and glass Hapag inkwell as a souvenir of the VATERLAND's glory days.[3]

A particularly malevolent anti-German editorial was carried in the October 23 issue of the engineers' newspaper. It stressed how important it was to have more than a military victory over the enemy. This was the only way to bring the lessons of the war home to the Germans, the editorial said.

"When the logical deductions of their spectacled Hun apostles of rapine and slaughter are read in the light of their own blazing cities, in the crash of their own dynamited historical monuments, in the ruthless waste and ruin of their own countryside, then, and not until then, will they know in a way they will not speedily forget just what the war they so exultantly plotted and launched upon a peaceful world really means. . . . They have no conscience. . . . no honor. They must see with their own eyes and suffer in their own persons."

Quoting the British Foreign Secretary, Mr. Balfour, the editorial concluded: "Brutes they were when they brought on the war and brutes they remain."[4]

What irony that the ship's printing press, designed by the peace-loving Albert Ballin for colorful musical programs and handsome menus on his "ship of peace," should be used to print such strident examples of war hysteria at its worst. And it was doubly ironic for those who lived to see Germany, embittered by the harsh terms of her unconditional surrender in World War I, turn for leadership to Adolf Hitler.

The LEVIATHAN ball had to be cancelled because of the danger of spreading flu.

"We saw the soldiers stretched out on the well deck, and we knew what laid them low," a ball notice in the engineers' newspaper pointed out. "None but a fool would risk himself, and those he cares for more than himself, to the horrors of the same epidemic."[5]

"The handsome and devilish electrician, Peter Knowles, has returned to the Ark. Nothing else was big enough to hold him." So went one of the "Society Jottings" in "The Red Watch Mark." Under the same heading, a poem by James Montague compared the VATERLAND with the LEVIATHAN. Its last three verses ran like this:

"But now the stars and stripes float out above the Titan craft,
"And Husky lads in olive drab are swarming fore and aft.

"A Navy Captain on the bridge, below a Navy crew,
"Have taught a haughty Vaterland what 'YANKEELAND' can do;

". . .thousand men on every trip, and when they strike their blow,
"The Kaiser's mightiest ship may prove the Kaiser's mightiest foe!"

Daylight Saving Time came into effect for the first time throughout America on October 27, 1918, sailing day, and Commander Blackburn on the 24th notified all officers that the ship's clocks would be set back half an hour at 2 a.m. and again at 4:40. The ship's bells would not be sounded until daylight.[6]

The LEVIATHAN sailed with only 8,123 troops aboard, her smallest load since her first voyage back in December 1917. No one aboard dreamed that this was to be the last voyage under wartime conditions, but the steady decline in the number of troops carried—10,893 on her 7th trip, 10,541 on the 8th, and 9,366 on the 9th—suggests that the pressure was easing.[7] The ship's crew of 2,327 included Maurice Safford, her regular Y.M.C.A. man, who had a particularly frustrating experience. He had been with the LEVI almost from the start, and was always trying to think of ways of cheering the troops up on their way to war. Remembering the wonderful morale booster that the banjo group had been on the last hectic eastbound crossing, he brought with him this time a hand organ. He had barely had a chance to show it around after the ship had made her 11 a.m. departure from Hoboken when it was commandeered in a friendly way by two soldiers of Italian heritage. One was a very tall lad and the other small and agile. The little one played the part of a monkey, with a long rope and acrobatic tricks. The tall soldier pretended to be the organ grinder, and actually collected considerable change from the delighted soldiers. None of the money ever got to the Y.M.C.A. however, and the organ itself disappeared. It was never found, despite Safford's persistent efforts. Safford's counterparts aboard from the Knights of Columbus and the Young Men's Hebrew Association did their best to help him track it down, but it had been so adroitly hidden it was never spotted. It doubtless ended up in the trenches.[8]

When the LEVIATHAN sailed, Pilot McLaughlin was cornered quietly by Ensign Allen and told that he had violated the ship's censorship rules by talking too much. No action beyond a verbal warning was taken against him because his contribution to the safety of the ship each time she came in or sailed was highly respected.[9]

Captain Phelps was learning to admire not only the spirit of his men, but the remarkable degree of efficiency that they had developed. His respect for Chief Engineer Woodward was high. The Captain put some of his thoughts down on paper:

"Every motion by each man in the engine room is controlled by a series of signals. The boilers are fired, and draughts and feed are controlled by the engineer on the operating platform setting automatic signals. The firing, particularly, is so uniform that on the bridge one is sensible of the regular intervals at which the outpouring volume of smoke indicates that charges of coal are being thrown on the grate bars."[10]

This efficiency saw dividends in coal consumption. It dropped from a high of 1,157 tons per day on one of the VATERLAND voyages to an 816-ton average at 20 knots eastbound and only 720 tons a day westbound. Thus it was possible to load her full 8,300-ton capacity at Hoboken and only 5,000 tons at Brest.[11]

The ship had undergone a most thorough cleaning during her stay at Hoboken, and Voyage #10 was begun in high confidence. The crew knew they were good. They had been through enemy attacks and had survived. Their experience on the last voyage had given them an *esprit de corps*, and they had an immense pride in their ship. On every trip new devices and engineering refinements were being tested. It was rumored that a new super-secret communicating invention was now available to the bridge. With it Captain

Phelps was able to talk to the escorting destroyers and not just send Morse code messages to them. It was called wireless telephone.[12] This facility was tested when the LEVIATHAN passed the AGAMEMNON en route home. Two of the crew of the four-stacker were friends of Chaplain McDonald's, and he asked the AGAMEMNON's master to look after them. The boys involved were, like the Chaplain, from Sea Cliff, a little Methodist camp meeting town on a bluff overlooking Long Island Sound.[13]

As the LEVIATHAN raced across the Atlantic, the wireless messages brought more and more news that hinted peace was near. The German army was definitely retreating after the Battle of Meuse-Argonne. On October 30 Turkey dropped out of the war. On November 1 Austria and Hungary became separate republics and the threat from that area became a thing of the past. There were serious stirrings of revolt in Germany. A new ship's publication for everyone, called "The LEVIATHAN Press," noted that heavy and continuous air fighting "resulted greatly to our advantage," adding that "nearly 22 tons of bombs were dropped by our squadrons."[14]

As the voyage neared its end it became apparent to the crew that Brest was not their destination. The scuttlebutt was that they were going to cold, dreary Liverpool. This bad news was confirmed when familiar Irish Sea land sightings were made. But good news awaited them! On November 2, with terrible weather, "the troops will never forget the feelings that uplifted us when we made out the destroyers' smokes at about the appointed time and place." Captain Phelps is talking. "And in an incredibly short time they clustered about us, each in her appointed position, as if from out of the sea. The conditions on board the destroyers were uncomfortable. The little boats would rear and plunge, would pound and flood themselves until it appeared that everyone on the bridge was drenched. It was often necessary to slow down the convoy, for it has been known that destroyers in such conditions have pounded their seams open and sprung leaks."[15]

The good news came from the destroyers. It was that all German submarines had been recalled on October 21! The talk of mutiny among German submarine crews apparently had something behind it.[16]

Aground!

 o one took any chances, however, and the strictest watch and guard were maintained. The arrival at Liverpool was made in dense fog and climaxed by a grounding that frightened many of the troops aboard because of a startling list the LEVIATHAN took as the tide went out. The Mersey has a 27-foot tidal drop and some of the boys were sure the troopship was going to turn over. Anselmo F. Dappert's story shows how they felt. He had been placed in command of a heavy tank company at Camp Colt, Gettysburg, by a young Army captain named D.D. Eisenhower. All but 40 of his 271-man company had arrived in civilian clothes, and Dappert had had only five days to process them for the LEVIATHAN crossing. Once aboard he had looked forward to a little rest, but instead was never busier in his life. He had the responsibility of garbage disposal for the whole crossing. It was rough, but in the process he got to know many of the men in the galley, and before they debarked at Liverpool he was presented with three barrels of sandwiches for his company.

"As we pulled into Liverpool the fog was closing in and the weather was dank and disagreeable," he remembered.

"I watched the British pilot come aboard to get the ship properly berthed. He was dressed in a smart uniform wearing a Sam Browne belt, an eye monocle and swinging a swagger stick. He missed the dock by a thousand feet or more and the ship nosed into the sand and began to list. In an hour or so the ship's starboard railing was in the water and the troops were taken off in lighters after walking down the ship's side.

"My recollection is that the ship's starboard railing was actually in the water but recollections after the passage of 52 years may be a little fuzzy.

"However, certain recollections are still very distinct. Ladders perhaps 20 feet or more long were extended from the decks of the lighters and laid against the side of the ship. The angle of these ladders was such that the troops after walking erect down the port side to the top of the ladders walked also erect down the ladders. The ladders were in the nature of gang-planks and were equipped with rope hand rails."[17]

Dappert's men were taken to the pier and formed up to await a train to Winchester. He put them at ease, and, checking on his three barrels of sandwiches, spotted some strange soldier digging into one and stuffing his overcoat.

"I wheeled him around and much to my surprise he was Dutch Teaney, with whom I had been in high school back in Taylorville, Illinois. Of course he got the sandwiches."[18]

Pressed about the degree of the list, Mr. Dappert repeated his memories and added:

"That she did not wind up like the NORMANDIE in New York buried in the sand for years has always been a mystery to me."

The LEVIATHAN certainly did ground, and did list, and most of her troops were taken ashore in lighters. She grounded because the fog had slowed her progress so much that the tide changed and was running out before she reached the landing stage. She did list and her troops did climb down into the lighters, but the list was not enough for her rail to be in or even near the water. Chief Machinist's Mate Marc Iverson remembered that the troops were all off in about three hours.[19] Boatswain Second Class Bill Engel remembered that the ship was held fast until the tide rose and tugs could release her.[20] The Navy's official history says she "stuck in the mud for about seven hours," during which time she unloaded most of her troops. She was able to come up to the landing stage itself at about midnight.[21]

While all this was happening, those aboard who were interested could read the latest war news in the LEVIATHAN's newspaper. "Our low flying aeroplanes operating over the battle front" found many excellent targets, and "full advantage was taken of these with bombs and machine gun fire, great confusion and many casualties being caused among the enemy."[22]

The next day a two-page, single-spaced "ORDER" outlined procedures for dry docking. After 4 p.m. on the 4th, no toilet or latrine aboard was to be used. The dry dock door, or caisson, would be opened at 11:40 p.m. At 6 a.m. on November 5 all hands would take station "for centering the ship over the blocks, as the water was slowly pumped out of the dock." A thorough clean-up job was outlined aboard ship, with a careful separation of paper, wood, and tin cans being ordered.

"Liberty parties will be marched to the gate by one of the Junior Officers of the Deck detailed by the Officer of the Deck."[23]

Meanwhile, as the peace rumors flew and the Houses of Hohenzollern and of Hapsburg were shaking, the engineers' newspaper on the LEVIATHAN saw fit to editorialize on "just what constitutes a good book." "Why not extract from life all the pleasure there is in it? A man who does not realize the possibilities of finding pleasure in books is as bad off as a man who does not know there is such a thing as a play or a baseball game."[24] Under "News," the same source reported that Austria-Hungary was definitely out of the war, that Berlin itself could now be bombed since by air it was only 80 minutes from the Allied lines, and that Admiral Sims had prohibited all travel by American servicemen in England because of the influenza epidemic still raging. Under "Society Jottings," it was pointed out that a telephone was to be installed between the LEVIATHAN and Cattle's Coffee Pot on Lime Street. "This is for the purpose of notifying the electrical gang when the ship is going to sail.

Why do the electricians hang out there? Ask Adams, the electrical Beau Brummel."[25]

Ballin's Last Stand

n the day the LEVIATHAN came to grief on the Mersey mud, German headquarters asked permission to send representatives through the Allied lines to get Marshal Foch's terms. Foch was commander-in-chief of the Allied ground forces. On the 8th he met with the German mission in his railroad car. The next day Kaiser Wilhelm abdicated. At 5 a.m. on the 11th of November the Armistice was signed, but for six more excruciating hours the guns roared. And then at 11 a.m. the Armistice took effect and around the world there was rejoicing. Everyone on the LEVIATHAN went wild. Liberty was announced for 1 p.m. and even drab, cold Liverpool looked good.

No longer would LEVIATHAN men gape at the piles of horse meat in Liverpool butcher shops after each great battle on the Continent. Never again would Jim Callahan grind his teeth into the glass neck of a ginger ale bottle as a depth charge shook the ship. No more would a gunner see a drowning soldier through his gun sight while the LEVIATHAN turned away in mid-Atlantic. The full debt of 8,538,315 lives was paid and the murder of that little-known Austrian archduke was avenged. Of the 2,000,000 Americans carried across the Atlantic, one out of every 20 had gone on the VATERLAND, renamed LEVIATHAN.

Of all the men associated to date with the story of this noble ship, this ship of peace, the one most profoundly involved did not live to see the end of the war that had broken him. Albert Ballin died on November 9, 1918, just as much a victim of the horrors of that tragic and pointless conflict as any soldier who had been blown to bits in the trenches. For years he had been aware of the fate that war would bring not only to his company but to his country. His efforts to prevent the war have been reviewed.

"It is no exaggeration to say that the one failure of his life was his inability to do so," writes British marine historian Noel Bonsor.[26]

One of the great problems in Berlin had been the way the Kaiser had been kept uninformed about how the war was going. On August 8, the day which Marshal Hindenburg called Germany's darkest day, Hindenburg and Ludendorff agreed Germany must seek peace. Ballin was chosen to tell the Kaiser that defeat was inevitable, and a meeting was arranged for him at the royal palace at Wilhelmshohe on September 4. When he got there, the Kaiserin, realizing what was afoot, begged Ballin not to endanger the Kaiser's health with bad news. The Emperor was in the middle of another nervous breakdown. The interview took place and, as had happened so often before, Wilhelm's childlike high spirits and groundless confidence played so on Ballin's pity that he could say nothing. He left the palace convinced that the Kaiser would remain hopelessly deceived until the final day. Ballin could foresee the revolution that was coming in Germany, but he remained hopeful that President Wilson could bring about some kind of compromise peace settlement. The American President's scholarly and magnanimous pronouncements had made him a major international figure.

When German seamen mutinied at Kiel on November 3 the spirit of revolt quickly spread to Hamburg. On the 8th a Soldier and Workers' Council actually seized a part of the Hapag headquarters. Albert Ballin was there and was personally threatened. Walking home, he was met outside his house by his distraught wife, who had been waiting to tell him of several anonymous telephone threats that he would be seized for his anti-labor attitudes. To the socialistic-communistic underground he was a leading example of the hated right. All these things were too much for him, and a hemorrhaged ulcer, plus too many sleeping pills, took his life that night. Authorities differ as to whether his death can properly be called a suicide.[27]

The remainder of the LEVIATHAN's stay at Liverpool was a totally different experience for her crew. With peace, so many things were different. Naturally the LEVIATHAN sailors did not cease from their perpetual search for girls, nor did the disgruntled English males alter their negative attitude toward this quite-normal sailors' passion. LEVIATHAN stragglers wandering back to their ship late at night were not always safe.[28] But on many other fronts, the Yankees, or "Yanks," as most Britishers called them, relished their new role as tourists and took in the sights with gusto. To them the great draft horses in teams of four pulling their heavy loads were wondrous things. And the steam trucks called "lorries," with their firemen sitting up next to the drivers and their boilers on their wide running boards—they had to be seen to be believed. But the thing that brought the loudest guffaws was the employment of "knock her up men." These were older men who were paid to wake people up in the morning. They had their regular schedule, some starting as early as 5 a.m. Each carried a long stick and would tap on his patron's window until he came out and waved him on.[29]

Back Home

The LEVIATHAN's accomplishments began to be publicly recognized in the United States. Congressman George M. Moring, of North Dakota, who had been one of her wartime passengers, inserted in the *Congressional Record* on November 7 an address hailing her part in the war effort.

"To my mind it is nothing short of a miracle what has been done on the LEVIATHAN with a green crew. I mean green in point of experience. They were a splendid lot of young men, who enlisted to help Uncle Sam win this war. Commander Blackburn said they just had to make a crew out of the material they had. And how they worked at it. The men were continually being assembled in groups and schooled in their duties. . . .The great service of this branch of the Navy is seldom thought of. Considering the constant danger of submarine attack, their service, though less spectacular than that on the battlefields, calls for no less courage and valor."[30]

A more scientific tribute to the LEVIATHAN came in the form of a paper read on November 14 in New York. It was given by Professor William Havgaard before the Society of Naval Architects and Marine Engineers, and it explained that the LEVIATHAN was a comfortable ship to sail on because she was a slow rolling vessel. It took her eleven seconds to roll at a draft of 40 feet, 11 inches. He compared her in this respect with the GREAT NORTHERN, which took 7.4 seconds to make a complete roll. The professor hailed the efficiency of the ship's design, adding that she needed only 820 tons of fixed ballast, less than that carried on the GEORGE WASHINGTON, only half her size. He confirmed one of the points brought out in 1917 by those who warned against using the LEVIATHAN as a troopship. Her centerline bulkheads would make her assume a 19-degree list automatically if two engine rooms were flooded on one side, while the GEORGE WASHINGTON, with no centerline bulkheads, would merely settle 2½ feet.[31]

The first act in what was to be one of the most heated controversies in the LEVIATHAN's career took place at this time. Early in November the International Mercantile Marine's Board of Directors accepted a British offer to buy all the British-flag ships being operated under the control of the giant Morgan-dominated shipping combine. This would have ended the awkward situation that I.M.M. found itself in—being American-owned but operating British-flag ships. It made the I.M.M. the most likely purchaser of the entire lot of ex-German liners being used as troopships, and this is doubtless what was behind the decision. What other company was better suited to operate the LEVIATHAN in peacetime?

Then I.M.M. president, P.A.S. Franklin, received a personally written letter from President Wilson asking him not to sell the British-flag ships. Franklin immediately acquiesced, replying with a personal letter to the President. A few days later the acting chairman of the Shipping Board, Bainbridge Colby, told the I.M.M. president that the Board would buy all the ships in question. The fleet included such great liners as the OLYMPIC. It numbered 85 vessels aggregating 730,000 gross tons. Perhaps the government planned to use them to bring the troops home, or possibly the Shipping Board had visions of a great new American merchant marine. Certainly it was guided to some degree by the tremendous wartime demand for ships. It was a day of heady dreams for people involved in shipping and shipbuilding. But whatever the reasoning, the I.M.M. was blocked from selling its British liners. The consequences of this development for both the big shipping combine and the LEVIATHAN could not possibly be imagined at that time.[32]

Summarizing the LEVIATHAN's war record to date, the New York *World* in late November said that she "had been worked harder than any vessel was ever worked before." In the 236 days she had served up to November 5, she had landed 399 men daily on French soil, on the average, or a little more than a 12,000-man division a month.[33]

Football

he object of this war has been to correct the German people so that other people can exist in the same world with them," said a surprisingly moderate editorial in the November 13 issue of the LEVIATHAN's engineers' newspaper. "Therefore we do not want any general extermination or any general hanging. We want cold justice done and nothing more, because that is the only way that our object can be accomplished."[34]

The same issue had a grand little poem entitled "The LEVIATHAN Over There," describing how a LEVI bluejacket tells a hometown girl friend all about France, the French girls, bursting bombs, and the war. The poem ends:

> *"But there's one point I didn't tell —*
> *It might have made her sore —*
> *I'd been to France a dozen times,*
> *But never'd been ashore."*

While the LEVIATHAN was in her dry dock, a call came for football players. About 125 responded and they practiced on a cinder field at the bow of the ship. A game was arranged with some Army Engineers stationed in Liverpool and feelings ran high. Three full teams were chosen, with substitutes, trainers, equipment men—the works. Another group of crew members organized their own "U Boat Squad," and, to loud cheering from the sidelines, upset the first team of the regulars, with a resulting reshuffle of favored players.[35]

The big game took place on Thanksgiving Day at Everton Field. The players from the LEVIATHAN were a bit self-conscious because their uniforms had been made by a woman dressmaker in Liverpool, but they played with great spirit nonetheless. So did the Army Engineers and the game ended in a tie. It was a moral victory for the LEVIATHAN, for the other team had had much longer to practice. It was a LEVIATHAN victory as far as statistics were concerned, also, for although they did not score they gained twice the ground the Army did. Nearly all the crew and officers, including Captain Phelps, attended, and Eugene Deschamps led the LEVIATHAN cheering.[36] An English newspaper described the game as "a demonstration of the nearest approach to actual warfare we have ever seen," adding that "we were greatly surprised that there were not more casualties than there were, for the opposing teams went at each other as though they were deadly enemies about to destroy each other by brute force." After the game the players and others of the crew had a happy variety of dances and receptions to attend, thanks to some hospitable English friends.[37]

The November 27 issue of "The Red Watch Mark" is filled with references to Liverpool girls, who were called "Duckies" by the LEVIATHAN seamen.

"W.T. Door and J. Howden Blower had made quite a hit with the Liverpool duckies," one note said.

"As a lady-killer, Mackintosh of Squad 4 takes belts, medals and cups. If you don't believe it, ask him. He says he gets the duckies all jazzed up before they can get their second wind.

" 'Limey' Adams, the handsomest electrician aboard ship, must think a lot of his duckies, because he gets red from the neck up, also cold feet, when any one of the gang comes near. He believes in that motto: 'Never introduce your girl to your best friend.' "[38]

The ship's stay was longer, much longer, than her typical turnaround at Brest, because the tidal situation controlled the dry dock and because it was decided to do a lot of work on her hull. She had endured nearly a year of the most intense, steady use and was very much in need of a scraping and bottom survey. It was a month and a day before she was ready to sail, but now everything was changed. Instead of racing back for more fresh troops, she was to be sent to France to begin the mammoth job of returning the American Expeditionary Force. It had taken a year and a half to get them over there, and they would all be home, except the dead, in ten months. The great fleet of seized German liners had made the eastward movement possible, and these ships would be assisted in the westward duty by more seized German ships, notably the VATERLAND's sister ship IMPERATOR. Found in excellent condition at Cuxhaven, the 52,000-ton vessel would soon be converted to carry 1,400 passengers in first class and 9,000 troops.[39]

"Better Than the Sun"

ith the war's guns silenced, other guns began to fire. There were revolts and riots throughout Germany, Russia, and the Central Powers. The Kaiser, who was finally told, fled to Holland, and a strong move was under way to have him extradited and dealt with by a tribunal of the victorious governments. Although during the fighting the Allies had been able to rally behind Foch, they were now confused and divided. Partly because of his lofty manner and partly because of his idealism, all eyes were turning to President Wilson. A Reuter's news agency dispatch published in the LEVIATHAN's newspaper reflected this almost worshipful attitude:

"There is reason to believe that views exchanged during the conferences in London during the last two days have been fully communicated to President Wilson in order to reach him before his departure for Europe. There is reason to believe that the President's advisors are of the opinion that the views of the conference regarding the position of the ex-Kaiser are likely to coincide with those of Mr. Wilson himself."[40]

Wilson's plan to come to Paris for peace talks added to his stature. He would be the first American President "to set foot on European soil." He was sailing on the GEORGE WASHINGTON, accompanied by a staff of 1,200 and escorted by the battleship PENNSYL-VANIA, flagship of the United States' Atlantic fleet. Among his retinue would be a Marine guard and a Naval band. The departure date was set for December 4, the same day the LEVIATHAN was scheduled to leave Liverpool for Brest.

While the ship's staff was preparing for the largest load of sick and wounded she had ever carried, plus a vanguard of returning sailors and doughboys, the "Red Watch Mark's" society editor picked up several items that reflected what was happening better than a straight recounting of facts:

"To hear the fellows arguing along G-Deck about where the ship is going you would think the Skipper sent his orderly down to one of the G-Deck wash rooms before each trip to find out where the coal passers had decided to take the ship."

No one was sure where they would get their load of homeward-bound passengers, but things were looking up and big changes in the ship had been made while she was in dry dock:

"Sutton of Squad 8 says he is so glad that they took the paint off the ports. Now he can flirt with the mermaids on the way back to the States, so as to keep in practice."

Under the heading "Due for a Long Wait" was written:

"Phoebe is waiting for Skee at the Landing stage."

Another note mentioned that regular passenger airplane service had been established between London and Paris.

"Passengers are taken over by airplane at the rate of 100 miles per hour, while their baggage is sent by the ordinary freight routes. A charge of $75 is made for passage."[41]

Before leaving Liverpool a contingent of American sailors from the base at Eastleigh were taken aboard. Chaplain Norris L. Tibbetts described high points of their railroad trip to Liverpool:

"The first draft left at 6:30 p.m. For once, anyway, no one missed muster and in the rain and mud they marched away. I heard them going down the road beyond the railroad tracks. . . .A group in front was howling that famous Eastleigh war song, 'Hail, hail, the gang's all here!' A little farther down the line they were singing the 'Long Trail.' The band went up to meet them at the station and started them on their way. . . .Everyone was happy, and as the sailors piled into the compartments, the doors had to spread their hinges to let the smiles through.

"U.S.S. LEVIATHAN looked better than the sun the next morning!"[42]

This was Tuesday, December 3—and it was a cold, dark day without any sun as the boys from Eastleigh marched aboard.

"It required the better part of the day to settle down in the compartments. Some were forward, but most of them were aft where the gentle vibrations of the four propellers could rock them to sleep," Tibbetts added.

Commander Blackburn was not silent as it came time to depart. He notified all officers that they would proceed to the same lifeboats during Abandon Ship drill that they always had gone to, despite the fact that the boats had all been renumbered. A revised Abandon Ship drill order would be printed soon. Troops were still to be put through the same drill, despite the fact that there were no more submarines to fear.[43]

The short voyage across the English Channel to Brest brought one of the most scary happenings of the LEVIATHAN's career. The gobs from Eastleigh and other passengers had boarded her in dry dock, and she sailed directly from there, not bothering to go back up to the landing stage. As she steamed down the Mersey she passed the H.M.S. COCHRAN, a British cruiser that had run aground and was two-thirds under water. Her bow, foremast, the tops of four smokestacks, and the very top of her main mast showed forlornly above the waves. It was late afternoon as the LEVIATHAN headed out into the Channel. The sky was clear and the weather lovely for the first few hours, and then she ran into a violent Channel storm. It was late afternoon and already dark. The ship's bow plunged and rose with a shudder and a heave, pouring tons of water every which way over her foredeck and out through her scuppers. The forecastle was under water more than out of it. The hours passed and the ship labored on. At the storm's height an unbelievable report came up from the engine room. Something was striking the ship's keel. Not once, not two or three times, but continuously and most alarmingly—and the ship was making an unflagging 20 knots! They were heavy thuds and they came without apparent order or regularity. The ship, moreover, was in deep water, much too deep for any sunken ship to reach up and touch her. The thudding, nevertheless, was coming from something deep down in the water, deeper than the forty feet the ship was drawing. The engineers were at their wits' end and those on the bridge could offer no answer to the frightening puzzle.

To the brave souls who went down into the lower holds and the bilges to listen for the crunching wham, the thing took on an eerie quality. There would be long pauses, with the ship rolling terrifically and lifting and plunging, and then another dull and ominous thumping slam. The LEVIATHAN's nickel-steel, double-thick keel was strong, but could it stand such a succession of underwater blows? Many worried. Several investigations were begun, but the watch officers hardly knew what to look for. Although it was worth a man's life to be on the foredeck at all, it was here, eventually, that the trouble was found. The stem anchor capstan had released a number of fathoms of anchor chain, allowing the many-ton bow anchor to dangle down along the stem into the water and to drag along the bottom, where it slapped up at the under keel from time to time. Only those who were actually aboard on this occasion can imagine how it could happen and the sensations of terror it caused. The LEVIATHAN was immediately slowed down and the electric windlass put into motion to slowly drag the monstrous links and ponderous anchor up from the smashing waves and back into its huge stem socket. A close watch was kept on the capstan for the rest of the night. As the ship entered Brest the next dawn, a number of large fish were found on the foredeck.[44]

Chaplain Tibbetts summarized the port of Brest in one word: "Coal!" Many of his gang were pressed into service to load the 7,500 tons that had to come aboard. "We could have put on a good minstrel show, for the make-up was all there and there wasn't much to take it off. Salt water plus no soap is no match for coal dust and King Coal always wins."[45]

Captain Phelps decided it was high time that the old Navy rule against assigning nurses to sea duty was scrapped. He cabled home that he would not sail the LEVIATHAN again without regular nurses as a part of the crew.[46]

Now that the war was over, the LEVIATHAN story began to be recorded in newspapers. The New York *Globe* reported on December 5 that she would reach the port on December 15 with 9,000 soldiers, the "first large number of unwounded men to return to this country."[47] The *Mail* said she would bring 10,000, many ill and wounded.[48] A big buildup of enthusiasm could be foretold and the hero of the day was the LEVIATHAN.

One man aboard, Robert Morris Armistead, an Army wireless operator who had been invalided out of France to England, was apparently not bothered either by the coaling at Brest or the terrible storm on the way over from Liverpool. He was deeply immersed in a game of craps. It had started in a corner of his E Deck compartment on Tuesday, December 3, and was still going strong on Sunday, December 8, at 2 p.m. when the LEVI sailed for home.[49]

On the 8th Lt. E.E. Jones distributed a mimeographed list showing who was aboard. There were 11,218, including the crew. Among these were 1,421 wounded, 252 survivors of sunken merchant ships, and 15 Army nurses.[50] For the first time the LEVIATHAN sailed without destroyer escort. She sailed alone. The Navy crew grumbled about having to stand gun watch.[51]

Commander W.D. Puleston, who had been relieved of the command of the U.S. destroyer flotilla in Europe now that peace was come, was a passenger. Commander Frank Tompkins, who was in command of the soldiers aboard, had been a victim of mustard gas at Fismes. All the other officers with him at the time had died and he had been temporarily blinded, but now was recovering. Six veterans of the American victory at Château-Thierry were aboard.

"Many of our friends of the Army wear decorations, and on some of those brave breasts, the *Croix de Guerre* with the palm is conspicuous and indicative of unusual valor," wrote one of the Eastleigh sailors, a machinist named T. Franklin Bludworth.[52] His account was a strange mixture of war propaganda and fact. He said, "There is every evidence that the vessel was designed by the Germans and built primarily for transporting troops," but he followed that statement with the admission that "the capacity of the fresh water tanks is only sufficient to sustain 4,500 passengers for about seven days, or the time required to make the run from Cuxhaven, the seaport of Hamburg, to New York."

Both Bludworth and Tibbetts were seasick going home.

"It would indeed be a stretch of the imagination to call this a pleasant trip," Tibbetts remembered. "No one can find much pleasure in life when he's seasick, and here we draw the curtain or step to the rail. Let each man forget or recall as he pleases, but don't tell too big a story to the home folks. It sure was rough stuff for two or three days. They say it is sometimes much worse. If so, let's watch it from the shore, or wait for the Trans-Atlantic bridge!"[53]

Those who felt a little better on the third day out, well enough to read the ship's newspaper, saw a report from Wales recommending that passengers and mail be carried by air between London and major British cities. To make such a service pay, a fee of a shilling a letter might be required, the news item said. Another headline reported that British troops had reached the Rhine. It was nearly a month after the Armistice, but the Allies were making a leisurely approach to defeated Germany.[54]

The next day was one of anticipation. All eyes watched the western horizon, and then there she was, first a speck and then an ever larger outline—the GEORGE WASHINGTON bearing President Wilson. There was much flag-flying and gun-saluting as the two ex-German Atlantic liners passed each other, each performing a service so completely alien to their original purpose.[55]

A third former German liner made the news a day later when the America, successfully raised from the mud, was towed to the Brooklyn Navy Yard for repairs. She had been up to her engine tops in muck and the clean-up job was one of the dirtiest ever, according to Lester Hammond, a Navy gob who helped do it. He later would serve on the LEVI.[56]

President Wilson arrived in France on the 14th, his ship receiving a tremendous welcome as she rounded the outer capes off Brest. He went to Paris to begin the peace talks, which were expected to be lengthy. It was reported further that the Allies would probably not occupy Berlin. All this was in the December 14 issue of "The LEVIATHAN Press," printed and read as the ship passed the Grand Banks and headed toward Nantucket and a great welcome in New York.[57]

The welcome posed a problem for Commander Blackburn and others. They were concerned about how the ship would behave if all 10,000 troops aboard rushed to one side to see the Statue of Liberty, for example. With her coal bunkers and her fresh water tanks empty, she rode higher than at any other time and was more sensitive to shifting weight on topside. With a ship like the LEVIATHAN, there was really no danger, but the authorities went to great lengths to prepare for the worst. Some of the rules they put forth were extreme to the point of absurdity.

On entering New York the troops were to take Abandon Ship stations and were to be given a lecture on the dangers of a "light ship." Then, "if in the opinion of the Captain the ship takes an alarming list he will have the buglers sound attention in which case all persons should stand fast and maintain silence. In case it becomes necessary to send troops below all buglers will sound recall at which all the troops should be returned slowly and orderly to their compartments."

Once this procedure has been followed "there is no objection to the troops taking more favorable positions in the immediate vicinity on rafts and boats." Then came an admonition that sounded perfectly insane: "It is further requested that absolute silence be maintained after the ship gets within 100 yards of the dock." To this was added: "The bands will play on the upper decks."

What they were trying to do was to keep the officers in "absolute control of their men." This, it was said, was necessary to "avoid disaster" should a critical moment arise.[58]

Wives, Sweethearts, Mothers

unday, December 15, came and the morning papers were filled with LEVIATHAN! She is due at 5:30 a.m., one report said, although her docking depended upon the lifting of a heavy fog which hung over the area. "More public interest has centered upon the LEVIATHAN than upon any other transport that has come into this port since the American troops started homeward," the same paper added.

"Even in war time, because of her size, the big liner has been an unusual attraction whenever she arrived or departed. She is the biggest passenger vessel afloat, and on her trip which will end today she carries the largest passenger complement of soldiers and civilians that has been brought to New York since the United States entered the war."[59]

Despite the fog and early morning mist, crowds of people flocked to the New York and New Jersey waterfronts. For a stretch of a quarter of a mile, River Street in Hoboken was one solid mass of wives, sweethearts, mothers, fathers, brothers, sisters, and friends eager for a first glimpse of their returning heroes. It started to rain and yet "all waited hopefully for the eruption of noise and perhaps a glimpse above the pier roofs of funnel tops that would tell the ship had come home."[60]

The police cutter PATROL was sent out by Mayor John F. Hylan's secretary, Grover Whalen, to welcome the LEVIATHAN. Representing the Mayor aboard was Rodman Wanamaker, of the famous department store bearing his name, the Sanitation Department Band, the Police Glee Club, and some 200 members of the welcoming committee. She set out from Pier A off the Battery at 7 a.m. All morning she moved about the Upper Bay, hoping the fog would lift. During the greater part of the day, crowds were ten deep along the Battery Sea Wall and at other vantage points.

"The fog was solid enough to crack nuts on," said *The Sun.*

All that while, the monster troopship was almost within whistle sound of Sandy Hook. She was first reported by the Sandy Hook Pilot Boat at 7:30 a.m., and at that point made one attempt to come up Ambrose Channel and through the Narrows into the Upper Bay, but she soon gave up and swung around, returning to a safe anchorage at one side of the fairway. She anchored for the night 26 miles from the Battery. At this point she was finally found by the PATROL, which had crisscrossed the Ambrose-Sandy Hook area in search of her for hours through the densest of fogs. Aboard the police boat the Sanitation Band immediately struck up a lively "Home, Sweet Home," and the committee cheered. From the crowded decks of the LEVIATHAN came "a thin ghost of a cheer," and the big ship's siren "whooped with delight."[61] The waves made it dangerous to approach too close, but the small craft persisted in her efforts at least to get within throwing distance so that a token gift of cigarettes could be tossed aboard. The *Tribune* reporter saw it this way:

"The task was hopeless, and after Davy Jones had been supplied with smokes and reading matter for many a day to come, and it seemed as though the next comber might dash the PATROL against the precipitous side of the LEVIATHAN, the smaller craft backed off and started for home."[62] The Rev. Dr. William George Ivle, of Brooklyn, the police chaplain, took advantage of the moment and held services of thanksgiving in the PATROL's saloon. He recited prayers and the Police Glee Club sang hymns as she made her way back through the fog. For the thousands who had waited all day in Hoboken it was a severe disappointment, but, as the *Tribune* pointed out, "even in clear weather the job of piloting and docking the LEVIATHAN is no child's play, and the navigators of the Navy, despite their anxiety to get to the dock, were taking no chances with the lives of some 9,000 aboard." Also disappointed that afternoon was the immigration cutter IMMIGRANT, packed with more reporters, photographers, and immigration men. She started out from the Barge Office at the Battery for Quarantine, but got no farther than the Statue of Liberty. Then, when word was received that the LEVIATHAN would not stop at Quarantine and that the examination of baggage of her civilian passengers would have to be made at Hoboken, the cutter returned. This striking break in the red tape curtain was made out of courtesy to the returning wounded. But still no LEVIATHAN, and everyone waited. To make things more complicated, word was received that the French Line's LA LORRAINE was coming in, fog or not, and so the IMMIGRANT again nosed out into the Bay. It turned out that the ship involved was the CHICAGO, another French liner, which had sailed Saturday from her pier up the Hudson and had run aground south of Swinburn Island just outside the Narrows because of the fog. As evening came, 50 Red Cross canteen women gave up their Hoboken vigil and their leader announced that they would be on hand again with hot coffee and sandwiches the next morning.[63]

"The Magnificent Noise"

The excitement of the LEVIATHAN's arrival had become a national matter. As the *Post* put it:

"The farthest corners of the country have been thrilled with stories, some true, some wild and fantastic, of the achievements of this vessel."[64]

The suspense built up after the first announcement of her sailing from Brest was heightened by the delay off Sandy Hook. When she finally did make her triumphal entry into the harbor it was an occasion long to be remembered. The *Times* said:

"There was almost as much tumult down the bay when the LEVIATHAN came up from her anchorage as there was in this city on the day the armistice was signed. The noise continued until the ship was made fast at her pier, and for nearly an hour afterward."[65]

A stiff northwest wind had lifted the fog early in the morning and the monster troopship weighed anchor at 6:45, about the time the Mayor's reception boat set out again to meet her. This time she had no trouble finding the LEVIATHAN and proudly escorted her from the Narrows up to the Statue of Liberty, where they were joined by several saluting tugs and the fireboats GEORGE B. MCCLELLAN and NEW YORKER. The latter let go with all nozzles and the two high curtains of white water shrouded part of the majestically approaching troopship.

"The soldiers went wild with joy at the sight," the *Evening World* said.[66]

As the LEVIATHAN approached the Battery the din increased and the Hudson became "alive with joyous sounds." Dense crowds, many of whom had waited since 6 a.m., packed Battery Park, cheering and waving handkerchiefs. Although it was only about 7:30 there was a snowstorm of paper from the windows of the Whitehall Building. Aboard the LEVIATHAN the returning heroes were everywhere, waving flags, towels, linens and their garments, sitting in the lifeboats, standing atop air funnels, on cargo booms, halfway up the masts on the ratlines. Their heads, thousands of them, were sticking out of port holes, their khaki and blue uniforms peppering the superstructure from bow to stern, their waving arms and high-flung hats making a tapestry of joyful motion.

All the way up the harbor the PATROL's band played vigorously and the Police Glee Club kept up a continuous vocal salute. More tugs joined the procession, each saluting, each being saluted. And over all rose the wail of the huge air raid warning siren that "was to warn New York of the airy argosy that Fritz was going to send here—but didn't," the *Evening Mail* noted.[6][7]

For the second time in only five years the LEVIATHAN was the center of a welcome of historic proportions. She would have many more as the years went by, but none with such an outpouring of emotion.

A strong tide was running and this was blamed for the awkward experience that the PATROL went through. As the big trooper was slowly being eased into Pier 4, the tide pushed her toward the adjoining pier and the poor PATROL was caught in between. The beamy police craft lost her heavy wooden fenders in the resulting crunch, but was saved from what would surely have been a disaster when the docking tugs managed to push the huge hull back toward Pier 4. It was more than an hour, however, before the first gangplank was lowered. On the pier at least three bands played. There was the Camp Merritt band, and another one from the 71st Regiment and one from the transport WILHELMINA, trained by John Philip Sousa.

"The musicians blew and drummed for all they were worth, but above the music of their instruments, the cheering of the crowds still prevailed, a great paean of joy rising from the full heart of humanity," the *Evening Mail's* man wrote.[6][8]

"Four bluejackets had got hold of four brass instruments," the New York *Sun* noted, "and were umpahing to the delight of every one afloat and ashore who could hear them above the magnificent noise."[6][9]

When the first gangplank was made fast the first person at the other end was the beautiful Gibson-girl wife of Chief Engineer Woodward. Lelia Woodward was overjoyed to see the smiling face of her husband at the upper end of the gangplank, and he beckoned her to come up. She was the first person aboard.[7][0]

Most relatives had to be content with seeing the tops of the LEVIATHAN's perfectly-proportioned smokestacks rising over the pier itself. But those who did rate a place on Pier 4, the officials, the Red Cross workers, the Y.M.C.A. and Knights of Columbus welcoming committees, and the press, were waving flags, jumping, shouting, clapping each other on the back, and screaming into each other's ears. A minor disturbance took place when Navy guards tried to keep the reporters off the LEVIATHAN, despite properly executed passes, press cards, etc. *The Sun's* reporter, irked mightily by this stuffiness, devoted nearly a third of his story to how the second lieutenants got their comeuppance, and credited none other than Captain Phelps with seeing that the press got aboard.[7][1]

Every major paper had columns of type about the heroic return, and more columns devoted to the war experiences of those the LEVIATHAN brought back.[7][2] Stories of heroism were mixed with rumors and exaggerations of all sorts. An Army lieutenant told *The Sun's* correspondent that there had been three suicides and 34 "natural deaths" on the voyage home and that 100 shell-shock patients were aboard as well as 100 bodies. In fact, the reporter found, there were only 15 corpses and two cases of shell-shock aboard, and there had been only two deaths on the trip from Brest. In addition, one sailor had died of pneumonia while the ship lay at anchor the day before off Ambrose.

A young doughboy from Brooklyn, his face completely shot away, welled with joy at the homecoming.

"I'm gonna take Ty Cobb up," he said—doubtless with a mental grin, for he had no grinning muscles left. "We had a swell party on this boat last Saturday night and Ty Cobb made a speech. Ty is a captain in the chemical part of the service now. I guess you know, and he came back with us aboard the ship.

" 'If I'm stealing second,' says Ty, 'and it flashes on any one of you who I am just as I'm sliding to the base, I want you to stand right up in the bleachers and yell out, "Hey, Ty, I'm a guy that was on the Lee-vy!" And I'll run right off the baseline and over to wherever you are in the bleachers and shake hands and sit down and have a talk about this trip. T'ell with whether we win or lose,' Ty says."[73]

Ty Cobb, famous Detroit slugger of the day, had been a little blasphemous, according to Y.M.C.A. representative Safford, but the troops loved his rip-snorting stories.[74]

Captain McDonald, 17 years a Navy chaplain, was hailed as the Father Duffy of the Navy, and his tenderness to the wounded and his gentleness to the others were the topic of many press paragraphs. His evening prayer was quoted again and again, and the story of how he used to say it every single sunset at sea.

"Agnostic, Protestant, Jew, Catholic, and atheist all stood rigid until the end of the prayer," the *Sun's* story said, "even though they were so many decks below the navigating bridge that they could lend a part to the prayer merely to the extent of facing toward the spot where they knew the bridge must be."

And all the while "the undersea Hun harpies, hugging the greatest ship as close as they dared, perhaps were stretching lacy strips on the surface of summer or winter seas just fore or aft of the speeding transport as their torpedoes slid harmlessly by and beyond their own masterpiece of shipbuilding. Nevertheless the bareheaded chaplain said the prayer each evening amid a silence broken only the swish of the wind and sea and, far below, the throb of the giant engines."[75]

Remson Sickles found many an interested ear for his stories about how badly the ship leaked. He blamed it on German sabotage, adding that "we never managed to fully restore her."[76]

Ferdinand Dornier, a 14-year-old French orphan, gained fame as a stowaway on this historic crossing. He boasted a soldier's blouse and attracted sympathetic help from all hands. A soldier took him ashore and to Jersey City, where it was hoped some family would adopt him. His father had been killed at Chateau-Thierry and his mother and 2½-year-old brother had been killed by Germans.[77]

T.A. Jones, private, made himself famous when he caught the eye of a Western Newspaper Union photographer. The next day's newspapers all showed him leaning far out of a promenade deck window sporting a captured German helmet and holding a German gun. In another photo he was shown standing on the Belgian block pavement outside the pier with his German helmet on his head.[78] The newspapers were filled with other photogrpahs showing the troops clustered all over the arriving ship, the wounded soldiers on deck, and the waving Red Cross flags on the pier. In most views the LEVIATHAN's huge American flag stands out.

Perhaps the happiest among all the happy soldiers returning on that December 16, 1918, was Robert Armistead, whose crap game did not end until the ship reached Hoboken. He walked ashore with $250 in cash and the same amount in I.O.U.s.

"I never saw either sky or water during the entire crossing," he said, but if he had missed the grand welcoming ceremony and all the arrival festivities, he had a second chance to experience it a few days later when he saw the whole thing in the newsreels.

"And a Leviathan she was indeed, filling the screen completely with her vast hulk barnacled with tiny heads from stem to stern resembling nothing so much as an old piece of Chinese 1000-head porcelain."[79]

The 96,380 passengers that the LEVIATHAN had carried for the Army and the 4,404 she had taken overseas for the Navy represented one-twentieth of the entire American Expeditionary Force. If only the combatant forces of the A.E.F. are considered, the LEVIATHAN carried one out of every ten.[80]

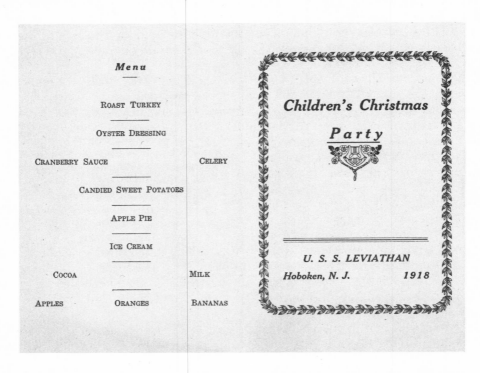

Menu

ROAST TURKEY

OYSTER DRESSING

CRANBERRY SAUCE   CELERY

CANDIED SWEET POTATOES

APPLE PIE

ICE CREAM

COCOA   MILK

APPLES   ORANGES   BANANAS

Children's Christmas Party

U. S. S. LEVIATHAN

Hoboken, N. J.   1918

Washington's Birthday Celebration

Programme
OF
ATHLETIC EVENTS
ON BOARD THE
U. S. S. Leviathan

MUSIC FURNISHED BY SHIP'S BAND

FRIDAY, 21 FEBRUARY 1919
SATURDAY, 22 FEBRUARY 1919

U. S. S. LEVIATHAN

4th June 1918

Order Order Order Order

For the protection of the personnel of this ship against contagious diseases every man returning from liberty or leave shall immediately upon return to the ship drop his liberty pass in one of the two boxes provided for that purpose under the headings of "Yes" and "No" respectively, thus indicating whether or not he has been exposed to the possibility of venereal infection.

The box marked "Yes" is for the passes of those men who have been exposed to venereal infection, and the box marked "No" is for the passes of those who have not been exposed. If a pass is dropped in the "Yes" box the person shall immediately report at the G. U. Clinic, aft on "E" deck for prophylactic treatment. When he has received such treatment, he shall enter his name in the record book kept there for that purpose. By so doing, he may avoid venereal infection.

Should a man incur a venereal disease, not having undergone prophylactic treatment, he will be guilty of disobedience of orders, a court-martial offense.

This order supercedes Ship's Order of 14 Feb. 1918.

J. H. BLACKBURN
Commander, U. S. Navy
Executive Officer
By Direction.

Chapter XIII

THE RUSH TO GET HOME

ow that the war was over and the LEVIATHAN had made her first triumphal return, the flood gates of publicity were opened and the LEVIATHAN story began to be told in earnest. On December 18, 1918, veteran ship news reporter Jack Lawrence went abroad for a tour.[1]

"It was the first time that such permission had been given since the ship was taken over," he wrote the next day in *The Evening World*. He had a full-page story with pictures of Chief Engineering Officer Woodward and Executive Officer Blackburn, of a troop berthing section, the mess hall, the swimming pool, and a bow-to-stern cut-away showing "how troops were accommodated."

He described Blackburn's office:

"Up in the big oval room that was once the luxurious library sits the man who acts in the capacity of business manager of the ship. To say that he is the busiest person on the North River would be stating the case conservatively. He is. Commander Blackburn has been executive officer of the LEVIATHAN ever since she was taken over by the Government. Through his efficient hands passes the great and intricate mass of details that necessarily arise in conducting the affairs of a floating city. Ranged about him in his office are his staff of assistants, mostly petty officers, and a corps of stenographers. Nearby is a telephone switchboard which connects him with nearly a thousand extensions on the ship and with the outside world. In the course of a five minutes' conversation Commander Blackburn found time to issue 27 orders, sign a dozen papers, talk to Washington and decline two dinner invitations," Lawrence wrote. It had been Blackburn who had permitted his inspection and he was grateful.

He went on to repeat the old story of how the Germans were sure the Americans could not operate the VATERLAND and how, when she was seized, they "indulged in a sly smirk." Reaching back into his own memory as a reporter, Lawrence quoted an unidentified German:

"They wouldn't be able to run her even if we had left her in perfect condition, but with all directions for operating the ship destroyed and a few German monkey wrenches dropped carefully into her vitals, the great VATERLAND will stand these Americans on their heads."

Lawrence was writing what people wanted to read. His story continued with its share of superlatives about the ship's wartime role:

"The feats she has performed will live in history long after the famous LEVIATHAN has found her way to the scrap heap or to Davy Jones' locker. They will probably never be equaled.

"The LEVIATHAN was the most hunted ship on the North Atlantic. . .was the prize de luxe for which every sub commander strove. . . .The Kaiser himself offered a purse of $10,000 to the U-boat crew that could deliver her deathblow."

He mentioned the troubles the IMPERATOR and the VATERLAND had experienced during their maiden voyages as evidence that the Germans could not handle them, contrasting this with "the smoothness with which the mammoth LEVIATHAN has been handled by her U.S. navigators." After a bow to her three Navy captains, he said the "actual navigating of the big transport has been directed by Lt. Cmdr. Harold Cunningham. . . . Those who have watched him at his work declare that he could tell Commodore Ruser and his five Captains a great deal about navigating the LEVIATHAN."

Reporter Lawrence had known Ruser, but some of the quotes he attributed to him do not ring true. He claimed, for example, that Ruser had told him the VATERLAND had been designed for a sustained speed of 21 knots and that she could not do better than 22 knots on her trials. On the matter of speed, Lawrence opined that now, with the proper coal used in sufficient quantities, the LEVIATHAN could lower the MAURETANIA's record for a transatlantic crossing. Young designing genius William Francis Gibbs, head of the construction department of the International Mercantile Marine, who even then had his eyes on the LEVIATHAN, saved this clipping and put it in his scrapbook.[2]

The Lawrence account praised the LEVIATHAN's surgeon, Dr. George Vaughn, as one of her most popular officers, adding a choice tidbit that only Vaughn could have known, to the effect that in 1908 he had performed an operation on the throat of the Kaiser. Vaughn had often wished for a chance to do the operation again, Lawrence quoted the surgeon as saying, and added: "It would have been one of those successful operations in which the patient dies."

Lawrence remembered the ship's VATERLAND days well, and his tour produced good contrasts between then and now:

"No one could recognize the interior today. . . .What was once the grand saloon and ballroom is now the hospital, with 145 beds, two operating rooms and a bacteriological laboratory. The former ladies lounge is a rest room for officers. The Ritz-Carlton is now the mess hall for officers and any first class civilian passengers, and is used for showing moving pictures. The smoking room, with its priceless wood carvings, is now an assembly room for officers. Chaplain McDonald holds religious services there. The main hall and stairway has been decked over and is an isolation ward. The huge entrance hall is a diet kitchen and sleeping quarters for sentries. The famous Pompeian bath is for baggage and mails."

Countless other papers had massive LEVIATHAN coverage, and a deluge of pictures added a new dimension to the columns of type describing her achievements. The *World* seemed to be trying to outdo all others, giving an entire rotogravure page to the LEVI the following Sunday. An eight-column picture of her was spread across the top, with four other views taken of her in dry dock at Liverpool and a picture of Captain W.W. Phelps, "who gets 24 knots out of her," as the caption proudly noted.[3] The very extensive *World* attention to the LEVIATHAN may have been partly due to the fact that their former editor, Frank I. Cobb, had been a passenger on her last crossing. He contributed an editorial used in the engineers' newspaper, "The Red Watch Mark," on December 18. It hailed the heroic transatlantic troop movement and American sea power and proclaimed that "the LEVIATHAN, the greatest ship in the world, will always remain the very sign and symbol of that gigantic achievement." His editorial noted that she carried more soldiers to Europe than Meade had had at Gettysburg, more than there had been in the whole U.S. Army at the beginning of the war. It went on:

"The men of the LEVIATHAN who did this work, who took their lives in their hands day after day and night after night, must rank forever with the heroes of Château-Thierry."[4]

This same newspaper reported that President Wilson was going to demand the punishment of German war criminals so as "to rebuke such acts of terror and spoliation" and "make men everywhere aware that they cannot be ventured upon without the certainty of just punishment."

On December 19, the next day, the International Mercantile Marine, in a step that would be of importance to the LEVIATHAN's future, agreed to sell its entire British-flag fleet to the U.S. Shipping Board. This was done in line with the government policy that this fleet was a valuable national asset and should remain under American control. The I.M.M. had planned to sell all this tonnage to a British shipping company, but had been asked not to by President Wilson, as mentioned above.[5]

Despite the publicity given the LEVIATHAN, the New York *Times* on December 23 published an editorial by one who felt that her story was not being told properly.

"Secretary Daniels still hangs the veil of secrecy over men who have deserved to be known to their countrymen, and known while the honor of their gallantry is still fresh. No sailor of the United States should be permitted to feel for a moment that he and his arm of the service are being unfairly treated; there should not be a sore heart under any sailor's shirt."

This matter was brought to light by a letter from one of the LEVIATHAN's crew, written December 17 and published on the same page as the above editorial in the *Times*. "I feel that it is my duty in behalf of my shipmates, not only on this ship, but on all the ships in the service, to make a protest. Everything we read in the papers is always praising the army...."[6]

On the same day that this letter writer was saying that he and his shipmates were feeling "pretty sore over the raw deal they have been getting," others in the LEVIATHAN were getting ready to make a lot of poor children happy. They decided to hold a giant Christmas party for orphans.

Orphans' Party

imey the baker, known as George Griffiths on the crew list, was thrown into a tizzy when told that Captain Phelps wanted a 100-pound Christmas fruit cake for the party. He had to have it by December 26 and there was no proper cake mixer aboard, and no nuts either. But Limey was not one to be cowed by problems like these. He found plenty of fruit and other good things and he chopped everything up with a flourish and out came a mammoth cake that tasted better than anything he had ever done before. It was ready on time, and his wife and mother were on hand to help at the party and to have their share of the cake afterwards.[7]

A nicely printed menu for the party was the contribution of the ship's print shop. It showed the "Program" as beginning at 12:30 p.m. with a sightseeing tour around the ship. Dinner was at 1:30, with music by the ship's band, piano, and singers. The smell of roast turkey (with oyster dressing) went all over the ship, and the 1,500 orphans made the most of it. They had all the trimmings too, from celery to cranberry sauce, from candied sweet potatoes to apple pie and ice cream. At 3 p.m. came the grand climax: Santa Claus in the Mess Hall. There followed a general distribution of presents that had been piled under a huge Christmas tree placed before an even huger American flag hung from the balcony under the painted dome. There were games and toys of all kinds. Many of the girls got little dolls in little doll highchairs. At 3:30 the happy throng was eased up to the Wintergarden on B Deck for moving pictures, games, and a puppet show. By 4:30 they started to depart.[8]

Lots of photographs were taken, and from the looks of the crew who helped and who stood around in the background smiling, the event was a grand success. Even Captain Phelps was on hand, looking a little stiff and uncomfortable holding movie star Baby Marie Osborn in his arms for the cameramen. She appeared a little older than a "baby" but was mugging admirably as her picture was taken.[9]

Not everything went as smoothly as might have been hoped. Some of the children escaped and explored the ship, a few coming out of ventilators dirty and a bit worse for wear. Two were found deep in the engine area, being regaled with stories by the men on watch. When they were all gone, every sailor got his present—a bag of goodies from the Red Cross.[10] One who never forgot the party was Jean Shand, son of the chief butcher, who helped his father in the galley.[11]

Captain Phelps was happy to learn December 28 that the Navy was going to allow Navy nurses to join the LEVIATHAN as part of her crew. Bunav (Bureau of Navigation) telegraphed the Naval Hospital at League Island, Philadelphia, and ordered them to detach Mary M. Robinson, Chief Nurse, and Mary Agnes O'Neill, reserve nurse, and have them report to Captain Phelps before midnight December 30 "for duty with the medical department of the ship."

"We were the first nurses assigned to sea duty with the Navy," Nurse Robinson remembered. "We were told that whether other nurses were sent would depend on how well we were accepted."[12]

"Crippled Temporarily"

or more than a year the LEVIATHAN's power plant had worked perfectly, except for minor problems such as boiler fire bricks that needed replacing and the faulty ash-ejector. A summary of the Engineering Department's wartime period written by Commander Woodward stated that up to Nov. 11, 1918, "the LEVIATHAN has never had an engineering casualty of any description, nor has the ship been delayed due to any cause in the engineering department."[13] Long before this proud record was transferred to a printed page, there was a major engine breakdown that forced a delay in the ship's next departure. She had been scheduled to sail December 31, and her passenger list included Bernard M. Baruch, then Chairman of the War Industries Board; Charles M. Schwab, steel magnate; and young Assistant Navy Secretary Roosevelt, recovered from his bout with flu and pneumonia.

The night before the ship's departure, with most of her passengers already aboard, it was found that the port low-pressure astern turbine was inoperative or "crippled temporarily." as the New York *Times* put it. The damage was said to be not serious, just "a few broken studs." The departure was postponed until January 7 and the passengers were offered space on the GEORGE WASHINGTON, just returned after taking Wilson to France.[14]

Woodward was not a man to weep over spilt milk. On January 2 he issued "Operating Order No. 33" spelling out round-the-clock repair details. He put four of his lieutenants in charge and selected five men to assist each of them. The officers were instructed to "supervise the job at all times both day and night," and were excused from all other duties. The enlisted personnel were also freed from all other duties. They were given special liberty as a reward for the intensive work required of them. Chief Machinist's Mate Iverson headed the enlisted personnel for the 3rd watch.[15] Unfortunately, the work was much more time-consuming than had been expected, and it was more than three weeks before Commander Woodward could report that the ship was ready to sail.

The power of the press became evident the day after the Woodward repair order. None other than Captain Phelps announced a message from Secretary Daniels. Ripping aside the "veil of secrecy" that the *Times* had accused him of hanging, the Navy Secretary let it be known that commanding officers of ships "are permitted to give interviews to members of the press and to relate their experiences during the war at their discretion, care being taken not to divulge important military information." Captain Phelps put this message in memo form, adding that "no officer will give interview except first applying to the Commanding Officer for authority."[16]

The matter of liberty was of keen interest to all hands during this prolonged stay at Hoboken, and Commander Blackburn on January 4 issued a memorandum to all officers on the subject. He spelled out that when an officer left the ship he must count the day he left as the first day of his liberty. As always he was most specific:

"Many officers have asked if they could not go ashore and remain on shore, their leave to begin the following day. This is always answered in the negative because an officer must actually be on board at some time of the day on which his leave begins."[17]

Another evidence that the engine breakdown was having a negative effect on morale may be seen in a testy memo to all officers in First Lieutenant O.J.W. Haltnorth's department:

"It is noticed that a lack of initiative on the part of Officers and men is very lax," the memo began in a sentence not distinguished for its clarity. "The First Lieutenant is constantly being bothered with minor details which are directly under the supervision of various officers of this department. The First Lieutenant has troubles of his own without having to look out for the work of some other Officer. It is noticed that too much time is spent by Officers in their rooms. I am personally responsible to the Commanding Officer in regards to the various duties, upkeep of the ship and I will not be the goat for anyone concerned in the future."[18] This cheerful missive went to one lieutenant, three ensigns, three bos'ns, and Carpenter Hudgins.

On January 6 Commander Blackburn was heard from again, but on a more congenial subject. He repeated Admiral Gleaves' proposal that a War Service Society be created to commemorate the valor of the Cruiser and Transport Force during the war, and asked the officers to send in their opinions. Here was something constructive to help his men while away the hours of waiting at Hoboken while officers in all other branches of the service were being discharged with the greatest possible speed. But the next day the Executive Officer was back on his old hard line. The Armed Services have always been famous for stilted phraseology, and this January 7 memo is a classic example:

"There have been several fires and near fires occasioned by doors impinging on the electric heaters installed in rooms," he began. "Officers occupying rooms where such conditions are possible will at once inform the First Lieutenant in order that that Officer may have a guard installed on the heater or door."

Imagine First Lieutenant Haltnorth's reaction when he read this and thought of having to post a guard to watch the door to every room in which there might be an electric heater. But the memo went even further. The First Lieutenant was ordered to make a report on all passenger rooms where "the possibility of a fire starting from doors impinging on heaters exists." And all officers were ordered not only to turn off any electric heaters when leaving their cabins, but to turn off all electric lights and to lock their doors "to prevent any chance of loss of property through theft." No one could say that Commander Blackburn had not thought of everything.[19]

The thrust just before the war's end had been to close the gap between regular Navy officers and reservists, but the Armistice changed all this. On January 9 Captain Phelps called for maintenance of the "standard of the regular service" in all future examinations. Any reserve officer wishing to remain in the Navy permanently was ordered to make immediate application "in his own handwriting."[20]

Keeping Up Morale

ew York's *Tribune* had a strange story on January 12, one with a LEVIATHAN twist. Federal authorities had been trying for a long time to find a Dutch sailor with an anchor and a star and the letters "P.Z." tattooed on his left arm and hand. They finally found him as he was trying to slip out of the United States for Holland. He turned over a secret code, but insisted that he had not sent any messages with it. He said he had been a secret agent for Germany, had been instructed to write any sort of simple communication in iodine, and had particularly been ordered to watch troop movements and sailings of the LEVIATHAN.[21]

The engineers' newspaper helped keep up morale. On the 15th "The Red Watch Mark" editorial was devoted to Theodore Roosevelt, who had died a week before.

"This man was so active, so vital, so aggressive, so much the very incarnation of life, that death for him seems grossly incongruous. His last words were: 'There can be no divided allegiance here. Any man who says he is an American, but something else also, isn't an American at all. We have room for but one flag, the American flag. We have room for but one language here and that is the English language. And we have room for but one soul loyalty, and that is loyalty to the American people.'"[22] He was an opponent of Wilson's League of Nations.

Other items in this interesting newspaper included one quoting a British air expert as predicting a transatlantic flight in May, adding that the time was coming when airplanes would be owned and driven "as automobiles are today." He was right on both counts.

Under "Society Jottings" a paragraph invited anyone wishing to see "new acrobatic stunts to drop in to G-103 any time after knock off. There they will see the notorious man ape. He can hang by his toes, in fact he is just as clever with his toes as he is with his fingers and sometimes he has a notion that he can fly. Anyone looking for signs of spring call on A.S. Robbins." Also there was an announcement inviting everyone to a Grand Concert where Pop Dougherty would play his famous little bagpipes and Ham and Spinney would give an exhibition of wood chopping and if "victims can be furnished will pull off a couple of murders." Lessons in how to save fuel by eating raw food were promised. Also, "Cabbage and Turnips Mullen will destroy a few Bulls, while Bob will furnish music and No. 4 Fireroom Chambers will sit on top of an Italian Symphony while DeCamillo turns the handle."[23]

Not all the news in this paper was cheery. In the January 22 issue an item estimated that 40,000 Allied soldiers had lost an eye in the war and that 7,000 had been totally blinded. At the bottom of one page a pun credited to the *Wall Street Journal* was slipped in to provoke a grin:

"The Kaiser's backers are quitting him von by von."[24]

First Peacetime Passage

n January 24, 1919, the LEVIATHAN had a new kind of sailing. It was quite a contrast to her ten wartime departures. For one thing, Commander Blackburn was among the missing. He had been given one trip off. Gone also was the tremendous tension; gone was the frightening sense of urgency; gone, above all, was the sense of impending danger. The ship was still a gray troopship run by bluejackets, but she was now more like a passenger ship and, instead of 12,000 nervous and worried troops, she had a list of 1,073 assorted voyagers, including 112 French navy enlisted men, 858 Polish soldiers, and some 37 United States Army field clerks. Her crew was as big as ever: 75 officers, 8 nurses, and 2,157 men.[25]

She still had to sail with the tide, and Captain Phelps has left a description of the undocking. It was low water slack at 11 a.m. This meant that on the New Jersey side the water was dead slack, with the incoming tide just beginning on the New York side. Tugs moved the LEVIATHAN away from her dock just before the incoming tide could begin to press her up against the pier. She reached midstream just as the beginning of the flood on the New York side could help turn her stern upstream to position her for departure. Leaving the port, she always sailed downstream on the New York side, where it was the deepest. Her draft of 41 feet, 10 inches made channel depths a major consideration. She got help from nature, for by sailing at dead slack she would arrive at Ambrose Channel floating on the next incoming high water, a necessity for her safe departure at this last barrier. Captain Phelps also pointed out that her arrival at Brest had to be timed by the tides as well, for if she had any headway on when making the buoy there, it would be impossible for the mooring party to work with the heavy links of her four-inch bow chain. She always had to approach the Brest buoy at slack water with her momentum "entirely gone."[26]

The voyage over was a placid one, and the chief form of entertainment was "The Transport Ace," the ship's newspaper. On January 28 passengers aboard read that American, British, and White Russian forces were being pushed back near Archangel in the face of shelling by the attacking "Bolsheviki" troops. The Navy was quoted as being concerned over a shortage of seamen, because, as it was explained, it was thought that many would leave the service to man the former German ships like the LEVIATHAN which the United States would take over under the terms of the Armistice.[27] The next day's paper predicted that the new Lloyd George coalition government in Britain was not expected to have a long life. Its most important step so far was its order that more good quality beer should be brewed. "But that will not go far. More serious is the matter of bread. The bakers claim that they are losing money and ask permission to charge more per loaf or else the Government sell wheat at lower prices. The situation is difficult."[28]

Headlines in the January 29 engineers' newspaper, often more lively than the regular paper, stated that the Kaiser was expected to return to Germany, that the Allies continued to fight in Russia, and that 203 German submarines had been sunk in the war. A small story, but one of great interest aboard, reported that the Hamburg-American Line's third monster liner, named the BISMARCK, was still in such an unfinished condition that she would not be able to steam in less than six months. The IMPERATOR, however, was going to be operated as an American troopship in return for food. It was said that she would increase the flow of returning troops by 70,000 a month, and would hasten the day when the LEVIATHAN crew could be disbanded, her troopship days done.[29]

In the gossip column the editor mentioned a slugging bee between Chief Weber and Master-at-Arms Michael J. Hylas in the mess hall Saturday night.

"We sure would like to see them in a real bout."

Another note spoke about Si Middleton's disappointment. He had heard so much about "those sea-girls before he went to sea." He was overheard the other day asking Miller, of Squad 39, where they lived, as he had always looked for them every trip and never seen any. Miller had difficulty convincing him it must have been sea gulls he had heard about.[30]

The day before the LEVIATHAN reached Brest those aboard learned from "The Transport Ace" that the 18th Amendment, banning the sale of alcoholic liquor in the United States, would take full effect one year from January 16th. Certain provisions of this new law would be enforced even sooner. There were few on the LEVIATHAN who had any idea of what an influence the Prohibition Amendment would be in the ship's future life.[31]

Fritz Crosses the Atlantic

 veryone wanted to get home, and the LEVIATHAN had 11,795 aboard, including the crew, when she sailed on her eleventh westbound crossing February 3, 1919. She had five Army prisoners and 2,122 wounded among the 9,470 Army total. She brought 2,325 Navy passengers. Among the civilians returning home were Mr. and Mrs. Hurley and Mr. S.S. McClure. Edward Hurley was Chairman of the Shipping Board, and McClure was a noted newspaperman.[32]

One who was not counted among the passengers was a dog named Fritz. Navy Coxswain W.F. Engel saw him being walked on deck by an Army captain and petted him the day before sailing. The dog obviously liked Engel, and the officer asked him if he would care for him during the crossing. After a few days of walking him about on a leash, Engel found that Fritz didn't need any such control but would cheerfully follow him all over the ship. Fritz ate all the time, his food being whatever Engel could swipe from the galley. Dogs were not allowed on the LEVIATHAN, but at that point no one bothered.

The engineers' newspaper of February 5 hailed the new American Merchant Marine. A large fleet of new troopships and fine steel cargo vessels was nearing completion and everyone at sea looked forward to full employment. "With every ship that slides down the ways, the demand for capable operating marine engineers will become greater and the reward for ambitious men will become richer. The merchant marine situation is like the California boom in the days of '49—it is a golden opportunity for men strong enough to seize it."[33] Or so it seemed.

Also reported in this issue of the engineers' newspaper was a new air cargo service between England and Belgium. Up to 4,000 pounds could be carried. Foodstuffs, clothing, and other necessities were the chief items being transported. The opening of a Navy dry dock big enough to handle the LEVIATHAN was also mentioned. It was at Portsmouth, Va., and had a length of 1,022 feet.[34] Under "Society Jottings" was this note:

"This coming payday J.G. Shaffer, of Squad 17, will attempt to extract half a dollar from Dearbanne, of Squad 14, on a bet which the former won. Shaffer is the only one ever known to beat the French Jinx in a bet, and it is as easy to collect the money from him as it is to hand clothes in the engine room when Mr. Miller is on watch."[35]

Poland and "Czechoslovak forces signed an Armistice finally and have stopped their private war," readers of "The LEVIATHAN Press" of February 7 learned. The ship was only 200 miles less than halfway home at 8 a.m. that day, the newspaper's masthead noted. Harold Costain, later to serve as president of the LEVIATHAN Veterans Association, took a picture of the band the next day on the top deck beside Funnel No. 3. Everyone looked cold.[36] After being photographed for posterity, the band went below to practice for their performance upon arrival at Hoboken. One number that they were instructed never to play at an arrival was "Hail, Hail, the Gang's All Here." They had played it the last time the LEVIATHAN had reached Hoboken, but many of the returning veterans had objected, remembering their dead buddies left on the battlefields of France.[37]

On February 10, the last day at sea for Voyage 11, "The LEVIATHAN Press" carried details of a proposed transatlantic airplane flight by three Navy seaplanes. They would take off from the Rockaways, on Long Island, and hoped to reach Plymouth, England, after four stops along the way.[38]

Nurse Robinson wrote home as soon as the ship docked:

"There is so much pent up emotion that one simply lives in a frenzy of excitement and fatigue. I had 28 nurses coming back, 20 for discharge. We had so much to do. The nurses are just like the men coming back. They think they should be out the minute they arrive, but red tape is slow. I wish you could see the 'boys' coming back from over there, cripples of all description but all with a smile and proudly displaying trophies of the battle, trying to get by with them so they wouldn't be confiscated. Six asked to stay on the ship as they were so much better and thought the doctor could cure them if they could stay. Poor things!

"The pathetic thing was the breaking out of flu among the colored troops. We had 8,000 colored troops aboard. They were frightened and confused men, and their officers had retired to their cabins. We had about 50 flu cases, a very small percentage, but about six died, it seemed so sad as they were so anxious to get home and they had to be pitied."[39]

The relatively few troops aboard and the Navy crew wouldn't soon forget the arrival on February 15 of two large groups of female passengers for Voyage 12. There were 100 Y.M.C.A., Y.W.C.A., and Jewish Welfare Board workers, all women, not to mention 246 girls going to work for the American Commission for Relief in the Near East. And the gals themselves would remember for many years the lusty cheers, whistles, and sounds of good cheer that their arrival provoked when they trooped up the gangplank. Also aboard was $5,000,000 in currency and 7,496 sacks of mail.[40] The ship sailed at noon, and it was a voyage whose return to Hoboken would be publicized even more widely, if possible, than her December 16 arrival, for she was slated to return the famous 27th Division.[41]

Whistles for "Y" Girls

The Near East Relief ladies were bound for Turkey as part of an American mission of mercy paid for by Cleveland and Clarence Dodge. The party would cross France and take a steamer from Marseilles for Salonika and then another vessel on to Constantinople.[42] Years later the group would have a reunion dinner aboard the LEVIATHAN. They were a cheerful lot and the first morning out many were enjoying the sea breezes on the upper decks when the ship's fire alarm siren dinned into their ears. Smoke began billowing up from below in the midships area near the purser's office. There was so much smoke that Elizabeth Favor and Florence Goodell didn't dare go down to their cabins on J Deck for their life jackets.

"I decided I would risk drowning (I float and swim easily) rather than choking to death on the smoke, and so I went to my station without the life preserver," Miss Favor said later. "I was reproved by the officer in charge of our life raft, but was not sent below."[43]

Someone had dropped a cigarette in a pile of dungarees stored in the swimming pool. It had smoldered for hours, only to burst into flame when fresh air reached it as someone removed the top layers of stored clothing. The fire was put out in a few minutes and things returned to normal.

Perhaps the luckiest and undoubtedly one of the prettiest of the Near East Relief girls, Miss Grace L. Reilly was invited to take her meals at Captain Phelps' table. Menus were printed on unused menu cards from the VATERLAND period. Printed inside, along with the food listings, was a poem about the LEVIATHAN by James J. Montague.[44]

Jessie Macdonald Scott, one of the Y.M.C.A. girls, remembered the crossing because it was so rough. Fewer and fewer of the passengers answered the mess call, and on one occasion "the ship listed 42 degrees, the greatest list in its history," she recalled. One night her mattress, with her on it, fell out of an upper bunk, but she was not hurt. She had a cabin with three roommates. A good many were sick, and she spent much of her time taking care of them and entertaining in the sick bay on the way over.

"I was grateful to be the Y girl for the 3rd Battalion of the 58th Infantry, 46th Division, Army of Occupation," she said.

There were six in Elizabeth Favor's stateroom. Besides the fire, she had a variety of memorable experiences, perhaps the most exciting being the time she and a fellow Y girl were smuggled into the engine room and given the grand tour.

"I recall being much impressed by the fact that when the bulkhead doors were closed in the event of an accident, men in the engine room would climb up ladders through the false stack and thus escape as the ship went down. I am glad that such a contingency never occurred during the life of the ship. We were invited by the sailors on duty in the furnace room to throw on a shovelful of coal. The other girl stood close to the furnace and when the door was opened she dribbled in the coal while the men urged her to hurry lest the steam pressure drop. Then came my turn. My dad had shown me how to stoke a furnace, to stand well back and throw hard so the coal would carry across the fire and hit the back wall, Well, it did not carry that far, of course, in that huge firebox, but at least it raised a cheer from the sailor-firemen which pleased me so much I remember it to this day, fifty years later," she wrote.[45]

Bishop Brent, Chaplain-in-Chief of the A.E.F. and the Episcopal Bishop of Alaska, was aboard and conducted religious services on Sunday mornings. Also aboard was a French Red Cross worker who had come to America to help the American Red Cross plan its campaign of service in France. He encouraged the Y girls to use whatever little French they had picked up, saying again and again: "You will not speak it correctly, but you will be understood."

Elizabeth Favor was fearful that her smallpox vaccination had not "taken" and went up to sick bay to ask for another one. With a kindly smile, the doctor obliged. Miss Favor was vaccinated in the presence of a handsome young pharmacist's mate, a fact that "embarrassed me very much." She went ashore with a wire protector over her arm, feeling very much a veteran already.[46]

During the eastbound crossing, the ship's newspapers continued to give reports about the American and British forces in Siberia, who were trying to assist the White Russian Army in their battle against the Red Russians. A "very substantial number of American forces" were in Russia on this impossible mission, it was reported from Washington on February 19.[47] An odd note from Weimar, Germany, reported that the German cabinet had voted "to repulse the Allied military advance being ordered," adding that "after a consultation the decision was changed and orders were given to sign the Armistice."[48]

On the same day the LEVIATHAN passed the GEORGE WASHINGTON with Wilson aboard; he was returning to try to convince Congress of the need to support the League of Nations. Nurse Mary Robinson remembers that "we all sent a prayer across the waves for his safe arrival." The President planned to leave for Washington immediately upon landing at Boston, forgoing all ceremonies. "He wishes to waste no time in going back to the Capital, in order to get a right line on business before the closing hours of the Congress," the ship's paper noted. "He will address Congress and make some expression of appreciation for the support the war Congress has given him. The continued rest seems to be doing the President good, as he is not as tired as when he left the port."[49]

Nurse Robinson chatted happily in a letter to her mother that she found time to write on February 20:

"We are in the Gulf Stream now and it is delightful.

"The climate is like Honolulu, but we start northward toward Brest soon; then it gets chilly. We have had a much more choppy trip this time, but the weather has been more enjoyable. I am an admirable sailor, feel like an old salt.

"We have the Armenian Relief Committee aboard. . .and Bishop Brent. He was in Manila during my time and is a truly great man. The Relief Committee are busy having school everyday, learning Arabic, Greek, French. . .They say that we will not bring any wounded but rumors are never correct. We expect to bring the 27th Division (N.Y.) home. Won't that be thrilling. It really is terribly exciting, everybody is so excited to get home and everybody talks to everybody else and the Army band and the ship's orchestra tries to outdo themselves in entertaining.

"My room is small but I boast three chairs and keep my afghan on my bed making it look like a couch so with my electric tea kettle and my new French teacups I invite some of the girls in to tea nearly every afternoon. Compared to other ships that I have been on my room is quite large, in reality it is just about the size of your bathroom, but I have a little entry way that makes my room sort of private, and a nice big window (for a ship) that looks out on deck and the beautiful ocean. I have had so much attention this trip, basket of fruit, so much candy that I do not know what to do with it and many books. It gives a nice warm feeling of friendliness to have people appreciate our being aboard. We were sort of isolated our first trip, but it was partly our own fault. In a way we cannot mix too much, so it took some time for us to get acclimated."[50]

A two-day program of athletic events was held on Friday and Saturday, February 21 and 22, as the LEVIATHAN neared France. Friday was devoted to wrestling and boxing matches, with the judges being the top three officers aboard: Captain Phelps, Commander Staton, who had replaced Blackburn, and Commander Woodward. First prize in wrestling was $5, second prize $2. First prizes of $3 each were given in the four preliminary boxing bouts, with the main event first prize being $9. Chaplain McDonald was the timekeeper. On Saturday there were a variety of contests in the morning, with a grand prize of $25 for the winning team in the tug-of-war, and prizes ranging from $5 to a box of chocolates in the other events. Most energetic of the afternoon events was the relay race around B Deck. Three times around was a mile and each man ran one lap, with the first prize being $6. There was a fat man's race, with participants weighing over 190 pounds. Among the events for the women was a 100-yard dash.

Saturday evening saw a variety show in the mess hall; anyone who wished to was encouraged to get up and sing. There were prizes for those who won the loudest applause. After the show there was a Mack Sennett comedy, a newsreel, and Elsie Ferguson in *Rose of the World*. In the officers' mess the evening movies were *Bell Boy*, with Fatty Arbuckle, and *Sunshine Nan*, with Ann Pennington.[51] The next day the LEVIATHAN was at Brest, her passengers were fanning out all over Europe, and a new group of returning troops were impatiently awaiting their turn to board her for home.

New York's Own

It had been like a private garden in which the Hun wandered throughout the night — No-Man's Land."

Or this is how it was until New York's Own, the 27th Division, arrived at the Dickerbusch Sector of the Flanders front. They replaced battle-weary British forces. Many of them had come over on the LEVIATHAN, and their enemy, of all people, was Prince Rupprecht of Bavaria, the man who had christened the VATERLAND and called her a ship of peace. As reported in the LEVIATHAN's newspaper, Rupprecht's armies had expected to come "sweeping down from the heights to crush those who stood between the Channel and the imperial plans and desires of Germany." The 27th Division had helped change history. Their victory had meant the salvation of the Channel ports, and England had breathed more freely. And now on February 25 they were boarding the LEVIATHAN for home.[52]

There were 1,177 wounded aboard along with the veterans of the 27th, plus 60 Navy passengers, 39 Y.M.C.A. people, two correspondents, and a Rumanian army officer—a total of 12,435 souls, including crew.[53]

The ship's newspaper for February 27 noted that at 8 a.m. the ship was 323 miles out of Brest, that Fatty Arbuckle's *Good Night Nurse* would be the comedy for the officers' mess that night, and that the troops would see the same actor in *The Bell Boy*. Among the news items was a story about how Germans interned in America were being returned at the rate of a thousand a week, and a report that the Poles and Ukrainians had finally stopped fighting.[54]

By eight the next morning the ship was 750 miles from Brest, and those who lived for the evening moving picture was eagerly awaiting Vivian Martin in *Molly Untangled*, if they were officers, or *We Can't Have Everything*, with Dexter, if they were ordinary soldiers. A top item on the single page of wireless news dispatches was a call by Secretary of the Navy Daniels for support by Americans of the League of Nations, for "there is no halfway

221

house." He argued that the United States must either support a vast naval expansion or "assume our share of responsibility for a world justice of peace in cooperation with other free nations."[55]

With the voyage nearly half over, the ship's March 2 newspaper had a story about a huge Italian "triplane" designed to transport 100 passengers. It was to have ten engines with a total horsepower of 5,000, and an average speed of 80 miles an hour. Captain Ugo D'Annunzio said it could carry 60,000 pounds across the Atlantic. It would be seaworthy as well as airworthy, and would have three decks.[56]

The same issue of the paper contained a report from Senator Knox, former Secretary of State, assailing the League of Nations as being contrary to the Constitution. He called for a different type of organization "which would preserve the Monroe Doctrine and save America from the results of European intrigue."[57]

On the same day Commander Woodward cracked down on discipline at the ship's "throttle board." Operating Order No. 46 noted that on "several occasions it has taken as long as five minutes to get in communication with the officer on duty." Woodward ordered that the officer at the board should remain there and never leave unless relieved by the other officer on duty, adding that "for reasons that are obvious this order will be strictly carried out to the letter."[58]

In "The LEVIATHAN Press" for March 3 there was a note saying that a black leather billfold had been lost. The loser "has sick wife to get home and all his money was in the billfold." A liberal reward for its recovery was offered.[59]

On March 4 the ship's paper carried a long history of the famous 27th Division. It also noted that more than 100,000 persons had tried to get tickets for the 4,000 seats in the Metropolitan Opera House to hear Wilson and former President Taft speak about the League. That evening, it announced, the LEVIATHAN movie for officers was Ambassador Gerard's *My Four Years in Germany*, while the crew had a much more amusing show: *A Dog's Life*, with Charlie Chaplin.[60]

New Newspaper

new and short-lived newspaper saw the light of day on the LEVIATHAN during this homeward passage. Called "Near Over," it was edited by Doughboy Bob Waddell and run off on the LEVIATHAN press by "Glenny," the ship's printer. Much less formal than either the engineers' paper or "The LEVIATHAN Press," it contained such items as:

"Speaking of Jerry souvenirs—the LEVIATHAN must hit pretty near the top of the list."

Another one was:

"Soldier of 27th Div. (upon boarding the Lighter which was to convey him out to where the LEVIATHAN lay at anchor): 'Gosh—why they told me we was goin' home on a Big boat, and this ain't nothing but a tub!!!'"

Damon Runyon, columnist for the New York *American*, was aboard. He contributed a half column of poetry about the 27th which was used in "Near Over."

With New York only hours away, "The LEVIATHAN Press" ran a supplement to its history of the 27th, noting among other high points that the division's rifle strength had been down to under 850 men when it was taken out of the front line, that it had advanced its front line from twelve to thirteen miles, and that in doing so it had captured 520 machine guns.[61]

The excitement was high in New York port on Thursday morning, March 6. The morning papers noted that 1,500,000 were expected to wave greetings to the returning troops aboard the MAURETANIA and the LEVIATHAN.

222

"BESIDES RECEPTION FLEET
GREAT CROWDS WILL LINE THE SHORE
WHILE BELLS AND WHISTLES SOUND A PAEAN"

So ran the headline in the *Tribune*.[62] This story added sourly: "Until the returning troops have passed through the lengthy and complicated sanitary ordeal that is Uncle Sam's first welcome to his homebound sons, there will be no opportunity for mothers and wives to take back into their arms the men they gave the country."[63]

A model 40 Aeromarine flying boat set out from Keyport, New Jersey, with C.J. Zimmerman as pilot. He planned to greet the LEVIATHAN by dropping two canvas bags of welcoming letters on her top deck. Mayor Hyland headed a welcoming committee aboard a small steam vessel that led a procession of other craft down the Bay to meet the LEVIATHAN at the Narrows. The flotilla was joined by a huge warplane which swooped over the big transport and appeared in all the pictures the next day. As the procession passed the Statue of Liberty, the shrill steam whistle from a humble dredge just inside of Bedloe's Island joined the chorus of salutes. The rising sun shone brightly, lighting up the starboard side of the great vessel, and with her bridge structure in dark shadows the LEVIATHAN moved past the jam-packed Battery. She looked worn, unkempt, and tired.

From one of the countless small boats the wife and the mother of Bluejacket W.F. Engel waved. He could not see them, but as he regretfully returned Fritz to his master, he knew they were there somewhere. Among the thousands who lined the shores was John Carrothers, the lad who had kept his mother waiting so long on the elevated train station platform in Brooklyn so he could see the VATERLAND make her maiden departure from New York five years before. Already this ship was a big thing in his life. She would be much bigger in the years to come.[64]

On deck, eleven of the top officers of the 27th posed for photographer Paul Thompson. They clustered around Major General John F. O'Ryan, their chief, who was allowed to stand a little forward of the others and who was the only one with a walking stick. The second man on his left was a young colonel later to become famous in World War II, Jonathan Wainwright.[65]

Soon she was tied up in Hoboken and all the whistles and the shouting had died down. Hours later she lay there almost deserted. Steam rose softly from her forward two stacks, water continued to discharge from countless hull outlets, her ensign rippled in the breeze from her overhanging counter stern, which still bore its original German decorations, and her vast inner catacombs were relatively empty and quiet. She had only five more round trips to go as a troopship, and after that who know what would be her fate?

Nurse Robinson mailed another letter home:

"Just arrived, at noon, and such excitement. New York gave the boys a Royal Welcome...We had a flu epidemic, of course, we will always have that, but it keeps us on duty today and tonight, then we get a 48-hour off. We didn't get ashore at Brest this time, but I am hoping to get ashore the next time and perhaps get a permit to go to Paris for a 48 or 72."[66]

The Transport Ace

Printed Every Day at Sea   On Board U. S. S. Leviathan

THURSDAY, MAY 8, 1919.

At noon to-day we are 2304 miles from Brest. The distance from New York is 796 miles. Lat., 40 deg., 22 min. No.; Long., 56 deg., 35 min. W. This ship is due in Brest Harbor on the afternoon of the 13th.

VICTORY LOAN GOES OVER   We all owe our thanks to the "Y" girls whose en-
          THE TOP IN GREAT RALLY!   thusiasm and interest formed the main spring of the

Chapter XIV

14,416 – A RECORD

orn, bedraggled as she was, the LEVIATHAN still had her greatest carrying feat before her as she waited that cold March, 1919, for her thirteenth voyage to start. Up to that point she had carried 132,140 eastward across the Atlantic and 31,862 westward. There had been 114 deaths aboard, most, of course, from the epidemic on her ninth trip.[1]

Commander Blackburn did not return, and Executive Officer Staton, who remained aboard, decided to do something about cleanliness. On March 11 he issued a six-page, single-spaced "ORDER" on the subject. He began by reminding everyone that no leaves at Hoboken would be granted until the quarters under each officer's control were cleaned and inspected. In preparation for the next big load of returning soldiers, he restated the rule that each Army unit was supposed to clean its own quarters before final permission could be given to debark, and added that the ship's officers were responsible for checking that this had been done. As soon as the troops were clear of the ship, Navy division officers were instructed to rope off water closets, latrines and washrooms to keep shore workers from soiling them. All spit kits were to be taken up, washed, and stowed away ready for admiral's inspection. Every inch of the ship was to be gone over, from the bow to the name on the stern, from top of superstructure to waterline. If Blackburn had been a hard taskmaster as to discipline, Staton was going to be equally demanding about cleanliness. His six-page order gives a fine walk-through inventory of the uses to which the interior areas were put.[2] That the ship was made reasonably clean and that many gobs did get ashore goes without saying.

Osmond McFarlane, he who had learned the meaning of the word "defecate" the hard way, had a chance to come to the aid of one fellow bluejacket who had overstayed his leave. This chap needed an excuse and, after thinking for a while, Osmond came up with the following:

"Tell them you were visiting your girl in Brooklyn and were a little longer with her than you should have been. Say you were on a trolley returning across the Brooklyn Bridge when you lost more time because the bridge had to be opened to let a battleship through."

The unknowing pal, being from out of town and not knowing that the world-famous Brooklyn Bridge was of the suspension type, offered the story with a perfectly straight face the next morning. Captain Phelps was so dumbfounded that he let the man go free, or so Osmond said years later.[3]

Others left the ship without passes. Getting off was easy, but the trick was to get back aboard. They would do this by getting hoisted up and over with a sling load of cargo, with the winchman knowing full well what was going on. On one occasion this hoisting procedure was observed by Lieutenant Commander Harold Cunningham, who simply smiled and walked away.[4]

Over 7,000 sacks of Army and Navy mail plus a small list of distinguished passengers sailed at 5 p.m. on Saturday, March 15, as the LEVIATHAN began her thirteenth voyage as an American troopship. Among the 104 passengers who rattled around in her long passageways and great public rooms was one Army enlisted man described as a "prisoner". Why he was going back to Europe the record does not show.[5] Secretary and Mrs. Daniels were aboard, as was the Hon. Henry Morgenthau, ex-Ambassador to Turkey. There were also ten congressmen, including Tom Connolly, of Texas. They were going abroad to study complaints made by many soldiers about the care they were getting while awaiting transportation home. Rep. John E. Raker, from California, came to be thought of as a great friend of all the LEVIATHAN nurses, remembers Mary Robinson.

"That in itself is a big story," she wrote years later.

Voyage Thirteen

Secretary Daniels made his presence aboard known early on the trip. On Sunday he addressed the Engineering Department in their mess hall. After being introduced by Captain Phelps, he gave a "stirring address," according to "The Red Watch Mark." He said the Germans deserved thanks for building such a ship as the LEVIATHAN, and, perhaps remembering how at first he had opposed her use as a troopship, told of how anxiously he had awaited news of her safe arrival on the other side during each wartime trip.

He urged the Navy crew to be patient while awaiting their discharge, saying it was up to the Navy to bring the Army home "because we could not abandon them in France." The ship's band played the national anthem.[6]

The next day the Secretary, the Captain, Commander Staton, and others went down to the troop mess hall on F Deck to hear Mr. Morgenthau speak to the crew. He declared that the feat of the American Navy in transporting more than two million soldiers to Europe had "terminated our isolation as a nation," adding that henceforth "we must maintain a bigger Navy to represent us in all parts of the world."

Accompanied by all the ship's top brass, Secretary Daniels further ingratiated himself with the engineers by making an inspection of the engine rooms. The engineers' newspaper said:

"The greetings exchanged between the Secretary and the men as Mr. Daniels passed through the machinery spaces were cordial and sincere and reflected the democratic attitude of Mr. Daniels toward the enlisted personnel."

In Fireroom No. 3 he "seized a regulation coal scoop and charged No. 3 Fire, No. 2 Boiler." So pleased with this egalitarian display were the engineers that they determined on the spot to place a brass plaque above the furnace door to commemorate the four shovels of coal "fired on the bell" on the 12 to 4 p.m. watch by the Secretary. The shovel was set aside by Commander Woodward to be kept as a "treasured souvenir of the Engineering Department," and it was decided to put it in a glass case in the mess hall.

On the third day out, the cooks and bakers presented Mrs. Daniels with a "very beautiful combination angelfood and fruit cake as a token of regard." The cake was designed by Chief Commissary Steward William J. Linn, who was only beginning his notable career on the LEVIATHAN but was already a well-known personality. The cake was baked under the supervision of Henry G. Heligensten, Ship's Cook, First Class, who had formerly been with the Hotel Vanderbilt.

"We extend to you, my dear Mrs. Daniels, as the First Lady of the Navy, the wish that you and your guests find as much pleasure in eating this cake as the men have had in designing and making it for you," Billy Linn said at the presentation.

Mrs. Daniels expressed her appreciation for the cake and thanked the men for their thoughtfulness, "The LEVIATHAN Press" for March 20 reported. On top of the cake was the inscription "To Our Lady of the Navy," and this prompted Mrs. Daniels to make some rather grandiloquent comments. She noted that she had made many cakes herself, among them some for the President of the United States, but "none of them equaled this cake in taste as well as appearance." She was "sure that the President had never appreciated any cake she had presented him more than she appreciated this one." She said the Navy had for a long time held her heart's best love because she had two brothers in the service. She added that she would treasure "this cake so highly that even the Secretary would have to be very good to get a part of it."[7]

Also in the ship's newspaper for that day were some of the dullest examples of wireless news dispatches it had ever carried, such as the report from Schenectady that a Benjamin Ripton had resigned after serving as dean of Union College for 25 years but that he would continue as professor of history. There was one news item, however, that must have caught every eye:

"A nationwide effort is being made to stay the putting into effect of the absolute prohibition law. Petitions are being circulated throughout the nation and already the number of signatures has reached well over five million and is growing by leaps and bounds. It is hoped to so affect the legislature that light beers and wines of a low percentage of alcohol may be manufactured and sold."

The next day Commander Staton passed on a memo to all officers requesting that copies of "every photograph and motion picture of Naval activities, ships, bases, personnel and incidents taken during the war" be forwarded to the Navy's historical section. As if this were not a big enough order, the memo asked for three prints of each photo and a full description.[8] He also had posted at all messes, a copy of a memo he had written to Navy headquarters at Brest, requesting transportation for 500 liberty men for Monday, Tuesday, and Wednesday, and giving other coaling, guard, and troop embarkation proposals. He requested that no returning passengers board the LEVIATHAN before Wednesday and that sailing be at 12:30 p.m. on Thursday, March 27.[9] Another memo issued on the same day spelled out to the most minute detail the way liberty would be divided up among the nine divisions. The concluding paragraph follows:

"Sections entitled to liberty will fall in on the deck (to be assigned later) by units as designated in the foregoing schedule when the word is passed for 'all the Liberty Party.' Liberty passes will be distributed by Junior Division Officers. Passes will be shown to the Junior Officer of the Deck when leaving the ship and deposited in the Liberty Pass Boxes (in the usual manner) upon returning." No man "undergoing punishment or in debt to the Government" could get liberty. The crew was cautioned against restricted areas in Brest and the memo warned that offenses in foreign ports are more serious than if committed in an American port.[10]

A two-page coaling order was issued over Captain Phelps' signature the same day. The time schedule shows what a tough detail this duty was:

    5:00 a.m. All Hands
    5:30 a.m. Breakfast coaling detail
    6:00 a.m. Turn to (all coaling detail in coal lighters promptly)
    9:00 a.m. Coffee and sandwiches served in the coal lighters—to be done by Supply
              Officer—must not interfere with coaling
    11:45 a.m. Mess gear, knock off coaling
    12:00 noon Pipe dinner
    12:45 p.m. Turn to (all coaling detail in lighters promptly)
    4:00 p.m. Coffee and sandwiches in coal lighters
    6:00 p.m. Mess gear, knock off coaling
    6:15 p.m. Pipe to supper
    6:45 p.m. Turn to sweep down all decks

Although the work was not around the clock, as it had been during the war, in all other respects it was a most unpleasant and difficult job. The Phelps order called for nine messmen, one boatswain's mate, one messenger, and one man on fire patrol from each

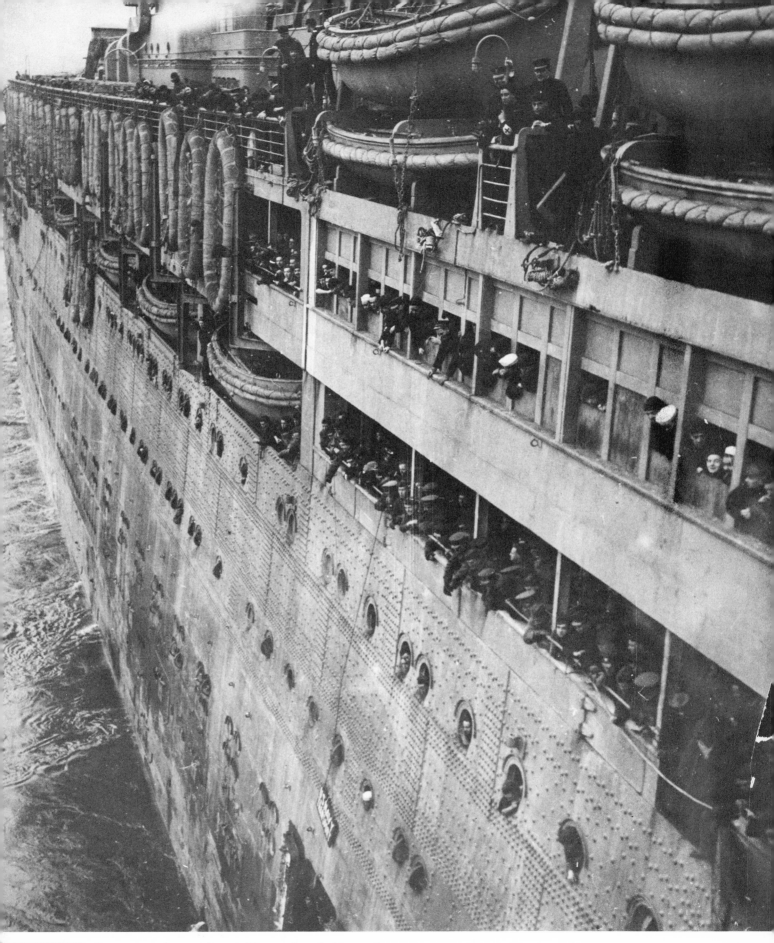

HOMECOMING–first return after war's end. The starboard sideport is already open, see bottom of picture, for the official party (Vet. Ass'n.).

WELCOMING the boys home, this ladder climber (top) does not seem to have any place to go. The soldier displaying his German souvenirs is private T.A. Jones. A close up at the right (Vet. Ass'n.).

*MOTOR CORPS women and their happy relatives (above) and a view of
the LEVIATHAN's Navy crew in the well deck forward (Vet. Ass'n.).*

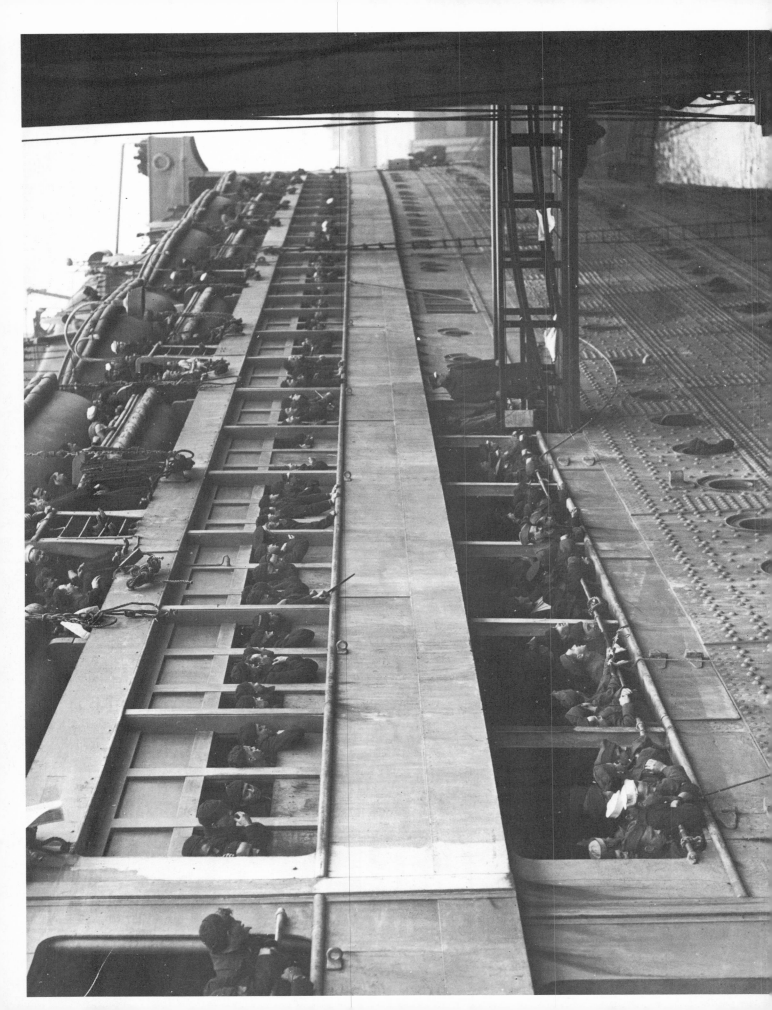

CHRISTMAS PARTY, 1918, Capt. W.W. Phelps holds Baby Marie Osborne; happy orphans (below) point to Santa Claus coming down smokestack, and receive presents in the main dining saloon (Vet. Ass'n.).

27TH DIVISION returns, crowds on deck were joyous, harbor welcome tremendous (Vet. Ass'n.).

MAYOR'S COMMITTEE OF WELCOME

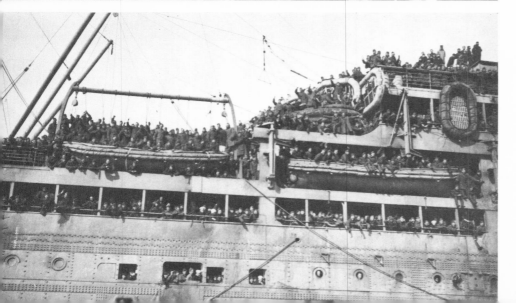

PROUD ARRIVAL—her camouflage worn off the gray monster returns home again (Herald Tribune photos).

Wonderful View of the Largest Ships in the World

The Imperator (on the left) and the Leviathan, being "man-handled" by a bevy of fussy little tugs on their re-

TWIN BEAUTIES—the USS IMPERATOR and USS LEVI-ATHAN in the stream together (above) and side by side in Hoboken, the latter's 3rd stack obscuring the former's first. See facing page for a view of the IMPERATOR docking as the LEVIATHAN sails.

U.S.S. IMPERATOR

OFFICERS return on *LEVIATHAN (top left)*
L. to R., Gen. E.A. Taufflieb, Adm. Griffin,
Adm. Taylor, Adm. Earl and Cm'dr. Wood-
ward. On bridge, L. to R., Capt. Phelps, Adm.
Taylor, Sect. Daniels, Adm. Earl, Adm. Griffin
(Iverson photos). The LEVIATHAN (below)
returning, as seen from the Singer Tower.

HOMECOMING, another voyage over, two fine bow views of the LEVIATHAN (Vet. Ass'n.), and a rotogravure view of her last homecoming as a troopship—her second career is over—three more to go.

MONSTER STEAMSHIP LEVIATHAN, FORMERLY THE GERMAN LINER VATERLAND, BEARING AS ITS MOST DISTINGUISHED PASSENGER THE COMMANDER OF AMERICAN EXPEDITIONARY FORCES, RECEIVING TUMULTUOUS WELCOME AT NEW YORK.

(© *Graphic News Bureau.*)

PERSHING—shown on A Deck en route home (C. Leonhardt), and saluting after ceremonies on the after end of A Deck with his officers (below). General MacArthur, just beginning his salute, is following Pershing out of the formation (Iverson).

division, and the very few others who were not required to work in the lighters. The ship's two motor lifeboats were in the water all the while, in case someone passed out and fell into the harbor. The band played all day. A shore coaling force helped, but they had to be watched carefully as this sentence will verify:

"The Supply Officer will also furnish two officers to watch coaling ports on the starboard side and report to Executive Officer any baskets negligently dropped into coal bunkers by shore coaling force."[11]

Nothing could better describe the hated coaling than a short poem written by someone aboard the LEVIATHAN:

> *When your eyes are full of coal dust,*
> *And your muscles creak and groan,*
> *And your weary bones are threatening to cash in,*
> *When the ringing of the banjos*
> *And the clinking baskets' moan*
> *Seem to shatter both your eardrums with their din,*
> *Just forget the pain of coal dust*
> *Or the lamp black and the loam,*
> *And don't forget your tired body has a soul.*
> *But think of the homeward journey,*
> *Of our gliding through the foam*
> *All because we filled those bunkers full of coal.*[12]

Although there were plans for carrying even as many as 20,000 persons in one trip on the LEVIATHAN, her largest number of troops up to this point had been 11,414. Now it was determined to pack even more aboard, and on March 22 a new evaluation of troop compartment capacity was published, according to which the ship could hold 11,955. It was decided that the nine forward compartments could accommodate 2,144. Amidships, 5,402 could be packed into eleven compartments, with the largest compartment holding 1,539 men. The sixteen after spaces could take 4,373, and 36 more could go in the non-commissioned officers' space. This grand total did not count the space for officers and first-class passengers high up in the ship's lofty superstructure, where she still retained 300 cabins from her days as the VATERLAND.[13]

"Pitching Like an Elevator"

n March 25 and 26 the largest number of persons ever to sail on one ship came aboard the LEVIATHAN—14,416. Of these, 1,152 were wounded or sick, including 22 Army nurses.[14] Every available space was utilized for man storage, even the swimming pool area. Returning doughboy Chester C. Nash remembers sleeping right under the wall instrument showing the ship's roll. The voyage was a very rough one and his diary records that it was the worst "the ship had ever taken with winds so severe that she was blown 100 miles off course." On deck "it was like a floating city block being first shot like an elevator almost vertical up to the sky and then plunged down into what threatened to be a deep dive." Nash was a good sailor and his diary commented on the excellent food and fine treatment, "considering the crowding."[15]

The largest group of men aboard were from the 338th Infantry of the 85th Division. Although they had been stationed behind the front lines, they had managed to capture a German. He was a non-commissioned aviator who had ventured across the lines in a German scout plane. He had shot his officer and brought the plane down without accident, wanting to surrender.

Among the news items in the ship's newspaper for March 28, the day after the ship left Brest, was a dispatch from Paris saying that Americans at the peace conference were beginning to feel that unless the "Bolschevist government of Russia" was recognized, no complete peace agreements would be forthcoming. Among the routine items was a note stating that French money would be changed every day from 1 to 3 p.m. at the Pay Office on B Deck. Commercial radiograms were being accepted at the Post Office on E Deck.[16]

A wireless report from Washington on the following day gave word that Charles E. Hughes had called the League of Nations "vague and ambiguous." There was concern for the President's health and a paragraph from New York said that "the enormous amount of work he has undertaken has forced him to reduce the time prescribed for relaxation." But he still took a walk each day with his wife or his doctor. There was talk he would run for a third term.[17]

A good summary of the voyage was penned by Nurse Robinson on Sunday, March 30. Going over was "too nice to be true, lovely time, hardly any work to do, just lived on deck and enjoyed it." At Brest she went ashore with Dr. Bunker "at a French Restaurant." The Doctor also took Miss Henderson, Chief Nurse at Brest; "he had known her before too." Nurse Robinson was careful to note that the Doctor's wife is living at Norwalk, so he wants me to go to see her when I get into New York. . . he is crazy to get home. . . I am going to write Mrs. Bunker, then if she wants to invite me alright. . . I am really very fond of her and she has always been very nice to me."

Nurse Robinson was most hopeful that "the ban on our travelling will be lifted. . . wouldn't it be terrible if we do not get a chance to go to Paris." She wrote that at Brest the crew were allowed ashore for the first time and 75% came back "stewed to the gills" so it isn't any wonder they aren't allowed ashore. "It is wide open and our fool-men think it sport to get drunk." She wrote that there were 12,000 aboard and "yet there is not the confusion we had the last time. . . troops are very well disciplined. . . sick bay filled as usual. . . chicken pox, measles and mumps." There were 150 shell-shocked men, 150 TB cases, two very bad. They have a party every afternoon on deck with ice cream, "huge plates" of it.

"Mr. Becker, the Red Cross man, a former Mayor of Milwaukee, gives out fruit every morning, and cigars and cigarettes in the afternoon, so all we do is clean up. He is the nicest thing, a graduate of Harvard, and his heart is the size of this ship. He keeps us supplied with good things too. The K. of C., the Y.M.C.A. and the J.W.B. men are not allowed in the sick bay—only the R.C. They are supposed to work with well troops. They don't like it very well, but one is enough for us. It is Christmas every day returning, and while the troops get only two big meals a day, they look like they were ready to burst. We have two bands aboard and they are very good, but the ship's band is the best. Our leader has real ability and the boys adore him. I get a big basket of fruit each evening from the chief in the Ritz. . . am so fed up with fruit I am going to ask for onions instead."[18]

On Sunday, March 30, the LEVIATHAN was 1,391 miles from New York. Those interested in such things could read in the ship's paper that the Hungarian "Soviet government" was ready to discuss peace with the Allies but would continue to fight if necessary. This was the first time that "The LEVIATHAN Press" had used the term "Soviet." Divine services were held in the A Deck lounge at 7, 7:30, 8, 9, and 10 a.m. Chaplains White, Hovorka, Johnson, and McQuarrie officiated. Chaplain McDonald was no longer aboard.

A Detroit news item in the Sunday paper said:

"It is a known fact that tobacco has established strong affections with four-fifths of the male population of America and that men will cling to it as a Brahmin to his religion. They decline to accept it as a bad habit and refuse to apologize for liking it."[19]

The next morning, with only 990 miles to go, passengers were warned to watch the ship's clocks for the correct time, since they would all be set ahead one hour in accordance with the new Daylight Saving system. The time change would be made "on the arrival off the coast," the ship's newspaper explained. Another news item was an editorial from an Omaha paper suggesting that when the German naval ships were scuttled Admiral Von Tirpitz should have been aboard one of them.[20] As the weather turned calm and pleasant, everyone felt more like eating. Frank Flowers and his staff established their all-time record of feeding 11,000 troops in one hour and 12 minutes.[21]

A copy of the ship's "Bill of Fare for the General Mess" was tucked away as a souvenir on March 31 by Butcher James Valentine Shand. It showed on legal size paper the meals for first class passengers for the next week. For breakfast that day there was pork sausage, rolled oats, boiled potatoes, fresh fruit, bread, butter, and coffee. For "dinner" at noon the main dish was pot roast, with parsnips and boiled peeled potatoes. For supper they had hamburger steak, fried potatoes, and kidney beans.[22] This was to be Butcher Shand's last trip and it also was Captain Phelps' last. The Captain took time to say goodby to the Butcher and asked him if there was anything special he would like to take home from the ship. For reasons unknown to history, Butcher Shand said he would like the lock and key from the ship's brig.

"They're yours; go get them," the Captain replied, and he did. Years later they were put on a plaque and presented to William Francis Gibbs, whose work with the LEVIATHAN will be the principal story of Volume Two. Captain Phelps also gave Shand the first American flag ever to fly on the LEVIATHAN. It had been hoisted on that cold and wet April morning back in 1917 when the ship was seized.[23]

The day before the LEVIATHAN reached Hoboken there was a straw in the wind which would have a hefty impact later. It was a letter from R.B. Stevens, Vice Chairman of the Shipping Board, to P.A.S. Franklin, saying that "national reasons no longer make it compatible with the interests of the United States to consider further the possible acquisition of the ownership of your British tonnage."[24]

To review the situation: The I.M.M. had tried to sell its White Star and other British ships, had received and accepted a good offer from Britain for them, and then had been asked by the President himself not to sell them. Now I.M.M. was told they were not wanted after all. It would take two more years for the final pieces of the complicated international puzzle to fall into place, and a principal victim of the tangle would be the LEVIATHAN.

On April 2 at 11 a.m. the LEVIATHAN was nudged into Hoboken.[25] Although this arrival lacked the fanfare and the shouting of the previous homecoming, when the 27th Division was aboard, it did not pass without notice.

"One Ship Brings City Full" read the headline of a New York *Times* editorial. The text began: "New realization and for a good many people, the first, of what a large ship the LEVIATHAN is, follows reading the statistical report made on her last voyage. . . . She carried, it seems, 14,426 human beings. . . ."

The editorial went on to note that if it had not been for a "misunderstanding on the part of somebody in Washington who did not know of all her possibilities" she could have carried 600 more "by the erection of 'standee berths,' whatever they may be."[26]

Among those who had liberty during this stay in port was Bluejacket George Cogswell. He wasn't as happy as he might have been, because of a particularly unpleasant facial problem. It wasn't a rash and it wasn't a boil, but his skin bothered him terribly. On the ship Dr. Vaughn had said to forget it, but, home in Hingham, Mass., his local doctor found two large facial tumors. He cut them out, working from the inside so as not to leave scars. The doctor's theory was that the tumors had started when George was hit in the face by a wet coal basket at Brest. The baskets were always falling into the water when they were tossed back onto the coal lighters, and the motor lifeboat crew would pick them up and toss them back to be filled again. One had hit George and cut deeply into his face, taking with it a liberal quantity of dirt, and sweat, and coal dust—and so the tumors.[27]

Nurse Robinson's next letter home has some big news:

"The next trip may bring forth developments that will relieve us of our job on board ship," she wrote. "This life is so full of complex problems that the sooner that it is over the better for my nervous system. It is very attractive in many ways but very difficult. It is very quiet in port this time. We have a new Captain!

"I am glad in some ways and sorry in others. It was the old captain who got us here, and now the new captain may not want us. Everyone hopes he will lift the ban on trips to Paris.

"The more I learn about men, the more perplexed I am. Talk about men not ever understanding women. I think the other way around would be better."

The nurse went on to remark about how difficult it was to understand the returning troops, about how they will need six months to get their bearings.

"Every one returning, officers, nurses and men, all act like they are a little wild, and, as they have lived such an abnormal life, I guess they are bound to be queer. Their main object seems to be getting out of the service and having a good time."[28]

Captain Durell

dward H. Durell was the new master of the LEVIATHAN. A member of the class of 1887 at Annapolis, his first tour had been aboard the PENSACOLA in European waters under Captain George Dewey. He was navigator of the NEW JERSEY on the "Great White Fleet's" cruise around the world. He left the command of the San Francisco Naval Training Station to relieve Captain Phelps.[29] A high forehead and small mustache made his face quite different from the hard-lined countenance of Phelps. He arrived on the scene just in time to be included in the Navy's history of the LEVIATHAN, which was nearing completion.

Another small but distinguished group of passengers boarded the LEVIATHAN to sail on April 7 on Voyage 14. "Side-boys, ruffles and flourishes have almost become a part of the ship's routine," is how "The LEVIATHAN Press" put it when describing the bigwigs who came aboard. They were headed by Newton D. Baker, Secretary of War, going over to settle war claims between the U.S.A. and the Allied governments. Also there was the new ambassador to France, Hugh C. Wallace, with his wife, his niece, and a private secretary. Among the seventeen congressmen was Fiorello La Guardia, making his second trip on the LEVI. Fifteen of the lawmakers were going abroad "to study the military situation and conditions," as the press was told.

A little boy of nine, however, got more attention than most of the dignitaries. He was Francis Warren Pershing. Secretary Baker, in all seriousness, asked the press not to let General Pershing know that his son was coming. It was supposed to be a surprise, for the General had not seen his son in two years, but the story went out on all the wires and was actually one of the items picked up and used by "The LEVIATHAN Press" when the ship was one day out. The same issue of the paper, apparently desperate for news, included several filler items about the LEVIATHAN herself, one of which mentioned the famous old story about the ship's rivets weighing five pounds. Also described in some detail were the three expansion joints, which "may be observed forward of Sick Bay, amidships and near the troop canteen." On B Deck, the item added, the joints could be seen in the form of "two brass plates running across the deck which move upon each other as much as 1½ inches when the ship is pitching sharply."[30]

By the second day out, Pershing's son was described in the ship's paper as being the best-informed passenger on the ship's inner secrets and "infinite mechanism." He had been given the royal tour, in fact, half a dozen royal tours. He was accompanied by a trusted Army sergeant who felt his responsibility so much that by the time he reached the LEVIATHAN he was exhausted. Young Warren spent much of the voyage in the restricted deck area reserved for nurses. The same issue of the newspaper reported that a speech about the public's acceptance of the League of Nations given in New York by the President had brought "some awful howls from league opponents." But, the news report added, Wilson's confidence was supported by a straw vote taken by the weekly news magazine *Literary Digest*.[31]

A tribute by Secretary Baker to "this great ship" was carried in the April 10 "The LEVIATHAN Press." He described her as "the glory of your transport service," adding that her story "is a romance. . . . Where shall we find such a tale of cooperation, efficiency and daring? It is a great career, worthy of the greatest ship in the world!"[32] These last six words, in the years to come, would be used repeatedly to describe the LEVIATHAN.

Secretary Baker was featured again two days later in the newspaper after he had toured the engineering department.

"My chief interest was in the boys who live out of sight but upon whose fidelity and work the whole welfare and propulsion of the ship depend. They seem to have an inconspicuous place of service but in the tragedy of the sea their opportunity for heroism comes first," he was quoted as having said.

"My next point of interest was the splendid efficiency with which Mr. Woodward has repaired the damage done to the ship. . . . The mechanical equipment of the LEVIATHAN was of course one of the wonders of our industrial age."[33]

Under "Topics in Brief" the April 13 ship's paper had this smile-maker: "Bullshevik navy is out of commission. Some beezark swiped the oars."

On April 14, the day the LEVI reached Brest, the ship's newspaper quoted a glowing tribute to the LEVIATHAN by Congressman D.R. Anthony, Jr., of Kansas. While admitting he was a landlubber, he said, "I know a good ship when I see one," and added that the LEVIATHAN was the first ship he had ever been on where "the proverbial ship smell is entirely absent."

Two items of aviation news were also published that day. A British seaplane left St. Johns, New Brunswick, for Ireland on the first transatlantic flight ever attempted. Three U.S. Navy hydroplanes were reported to be ready to take off on April 15 for Newfoundland for the same purpose.[34] The British plane would fail, and so would two out of the three American craft—but one of them would succeed.

The LEVIATHAN's brief stay in Brest was uneventful, and on the 18th of April she sailed for home again with well over 14,000 souls aboard. She had 12,080 passengers and her crew numbered 2,177.[35] Virtually all of the troops were from the famous Rainbow Division, so named because it was made up of National Guard units from all parts of the nation. They had gone over in October, 1917, and had been in the front lines from the following February until the Armistice. Heading one of their brigades, the 84th, was a young general named Douglas MacArthur.[36]

The ship's two newspapers, "The LEVIATHAN Press" and "The Red Watch Mark," were at this point combined into one called "The Transport Ace." Written "for the benefit and entertainment of all hands," it started out with much more news of what was going on aboard and with only a smattering of items from the rest of the world. The first issue came out on Saturday, April 19.[37] W.H. Stephenson, the editor, and F.I. Collup, the managing editor, regretted that only a small number of copies could be issued daily, but were proud to announce that once a week a four-page paper would be put out and 3,000 copies printed so that at least each crew member could have a copy and there would be a few for the passengers.

"We Bow"

e believe that through 'The Transport Ace' we can unite the whole ship's company in a closer bond and promote more shows, athletic meets, and parties," they editorialized.

Crew members were invited up to Room C-194 to help out.

"You will be welcome. You will always find the makings and a place to sit down and somebody to argue with. If you cannot write you can give the scribes the benefit of your opinion. . . . Your presence will help because it will show that you have the spirit of a happy ship."

Somewhat wistfully, the new paper noted that as the VATERLAND their ship had carried 2,370 kegs with a capacity of 80,000 gallons of Pilsner and Munchner beer.

"Think of the party we could have if we had this aboard now and we were allowed to 'rush the can.' "

Religious services for the next day, which was Easter, were listed, and the evening's moving picture schedule given. A brief news section included a report that Geneva had been chosen as the permanent headquarters of the League of Nations, and a "palace of nations" was to be erected there. Under "Society News" was the following:

"WANTED: A widow with six starving, sick children. Intention matrimony, in order to obtain my release from the Navy. Apply Box 4, Transport Ace. — Adv."

The following Monday, fitted in amid news items about the Bolsheviks, Prohibition, and the Victory Loan, was an item about the LEVIATHAN. Entitled the "Welfare Midway," it compared the alley forward of the Key Room on D Deck to the midway at the 1893 Chicago Fair.

"Here, on both sides are the dens of the various welfare organizations represented on board with all their denizens reported as good performers. The latest is the American Library Association, represented by Edward H. Virgin. The A.L.A. has camp libraries from California to Coblenz, and, in addition, is placing collections of books and magazines on all transports."

The editors apologized for being able to put out only 500 copies daily of the new paper. They listed all the things going on that day (April 21) to entertain the troops aboard, and there were many:

    10 a.m. — Band concert — 168th Inf. Band
    11 to 12 noon — Athletics
    3 p.m. — Band concert — 150th F.A. Band
    3 p.m. — Crack Squad, 168th Inf.
    6 p.m. — Band concert — 149th F.A. Band
    7 p.m. — Quartette

And all this was just what was happening on D Deck, aft. On the same deck forward there were similar events, climaxed by a 7 p.m. vaudeville show. From noon to 2 p.m. the Men's Mess Division Show was given for the F Deck men. Another vaudeville performance was scheduled for the officers' mess at 8:30 p.m. Also for officers and first-class passengers, the 166th Infantry Orchestra was scheduled to play for a dance at 8 p.m. in the C Deck lobby. It was the crew's turn to see the movies in F Deck mess hall and the comedy there was Charlie Chaplin's *The Adventurer*, with *The Serpent* as the feature, plus a Pathe war film.[38]

A new device designed to reproduce baseball games, play by play, was described in this issue. It was to be installed on the next trip through the courtesy of Leo C. Baum, representing the Jewish Welfare Board aboard. It was called "A Star Baseball Player Board."

The first four-page issue of "The Transport Ace" came out Wednesday, April 23. It was lively and readable.

"The Chief Printer is some salty and no mistake," one item began. "When the Secretary of War, wishing to get a better view of a passing ship, asked him if he had a glass, he said, 'No, Sir, but I have a cup you may use.'"

A beauty of a poem set in Brest was next to the editorial. It was entitled "A Salty Drama (in three reels)" and here's how it went:

Scene 1	Scene 2	Scene 3
Montgomery Nobb—	*'Rum chauds'—*	*Next morn—*
A 'gob'—	*Cognac flows—*	*Head forlorn—*
Seaman first—	*Spirits high—*	*Up for shoot—*
Great thirst—	*Hat awry—*	*Hard boiled 'Lieut'—*
Beaucoup sous—	*Heavy sea—*	*Thirty days—*
Liberty blues—	*Meets S.P.*	*Mend his ways.*

Under sporting news the editors had a line about Hank Gowdy, a former Boston Braves baseball great now with the 166th Infantry and aboard the LEVIATHAN. Gowdy, they said, was "rounding third base on the longest home run he ever made—Brest to New York."

Chief Quartermaster Whitaker was credited with having shown "bravery and great presence of mind" the previous Saturday when he had captured a large sea hawk which had followed the ship out of Brest for 24 hours.

"At first it was thought that the night marauder was a species of the Yankta-Zebra bird, which has that peculiar habit of flying backwards into the wind, and which has been made famous by the thrilling narratives of Chief Yeoman Brock, who has spent many nights hunting this bird in the dense forests of Hoboken."[39]

Considerable space was given to the Victory Loan, a fund-raising drive by the federal government. The mess boys in the officers' galley turned in 65 subscriptions totalling $5,250. One passenger, ex-Postmaster General Frank H. Hitchcock, on hearing this, made out a subscription for $1,000 and said he wanted it credited to the LEVIATHAN's account.

On the 25th, a Friday, the LEVIATHAN passed Sandy Hook at 3:44 p.m., reached Quarantine at 4:21, and docked at 5:25. Her arrivals and dockings on these post-war voyages were done with remarkable dispatch, averaging under two hours from Sandy Hook to pierside. The LEVIATHAN always used the south side of Pier 4, and a white paint indicator on the pier roof showed the pilot exactly where the forward corner of her starboard bridge should come to. Her slip had to be continuously dredged out, to keep the silt which poured down from the upper Hudson from filling in around her even during her brief periods in port. After this trip, and despite the pressure to get all the boys home, the LEVIATHAN stayed idle in Hoboken for nearly two weeks.

Chief Electrician Armstrong, circulation manager of the ship's newspaper, did not sail with the LEVIATHAN when she began her fifteenth voyage. His wife had given birth to an 8½-pound baby and he was granted leave for the round trip. His fellow workers on the newspaper staff, with an enthusiasm that would only have been possible at that period, added the following line to the little squib they ran about the baby boy's birth:

"This is a good start for another Army."

Commander Staton, who had now permanently replaced Commander Blackburn, was himself relieved for one trip by Commander C.C. Moses. Among the civilians who boarded the LEVI for her eastward crossing were 33 Y.M.C.A. workers and seven Jewish Welfare men. There were also a few French and Italian army officers. The American ambassador to "Czecho Slavia" was also aboard, one Richard Crane.

There had been so much favorable comment about the little three-stanza poem published on the last trip under the title "A Salty Drama" that "The Transport Ace's" editors asked its author, who had signed himself as "W.D.H.," to come forward and identify himself.

"You are good, we admit it, and we will appreciate future contributions," they said.[40]

The paper itself appeared with a new masthead, featuring an unbelievably poor sketch of the LEVIATHAN, whose only recognizable distinguishing feature was a huge bow anchor. But it dressed up the paper and remained in use for the rest of the publication's short life.

On May 7 Lt. Stuart A. Bishop, shocked because the Victory Loan collection aboard the LEVIATHAN was only up to $40,000 and was well below that of the GEORGE WASHINGTON, decided to do something about it. The LEVIATHAN seemed certain not to win a "President's Flag," offered to the transport that could raise the most in the final war financing drive. Bishop sent out a call for action:

"Should we, the largest ship, the largest crew, fail? Why not have a rally? Surely such a loyal crew as ours could not refuse an appeal if it were put straight before them all."

And so a rally was held. Movies were shown to get the crew to attend and the men were asked to sit with their own divisions at the F Deck mess hall tables. Y.M.C.A. girls were assigned to canvass them table by table, and a series of speeches began. Commander Moses started things off with a speech "that will never be forgotten." Red Cross representative Becker followed, and then came a rather dull address by Ambassador Crane.

"There seemed to be a little pause after Mr. Crane's speech had ended, so Linn, Chief Commissary Steward, known to us all, took matters in hand and started to get a little pep into the crowd. We are much indebted to his clear and snappy voice, it being always heard above the noise of the crowd. . . . He pleaded for subscriptions. A ship's cook spoke up and offered $500, which was promptly covered by Mr. Becker. So started the drive. Every large offer being covered by Mr. Becker or others. A bulletin board had been erected on the stage and Lt. Bishop was kept constantly on the go, changing the divisions' totals. The Engineers' force fairly outdid themselves, they seemed frantic and they cheered continually as their total was increased by thousands and thousands. Comdr. Woodward wore a golden smile and no one needed to ask him whether he was proud of his boys.

"Everyone was in the race. All divisions did their utmost and should this loan fail it certainly will not be the fault of the LEVIATHAN. The ship's nurses alone subscribed $1,500. Comdr. Woodward, Lt. Schluter, Phar. Redman, Bos'n Johnson, Lt. Estes, Pete Mellet, Frank Flowers were among the large subscribers of over $500. Three Engineers subscribed $1,500. Is there any other crew that can beat this? The LEVIATHAN Victory ship traveled across the ocean in a jump and is now practically in Hoboken. 'Bandy' and his famous Jazz Band kept things going. The night was a huge success, over $92,200 being subscribed, making a grand total of $172,250."[41]

A special word of thanks was offered by the ship newspaper to the "Y" girls "whose enthusiasm formed the mainspring of the drive, and especially to those who went through the firerooms in search of subscriptions," for the drive was ship-wide and by no means limited to the party in the mess hall.

"Box after box of smokes were consumed. Prizes will be awarded to Division and 'Y' girls when the count is confirmed. The slogan 'the largest ship, the largest subscription' was never meant to die," concluded the enthusiastic news report about the drive.

The Engineering Department was far ahead of all the others, with a $32,350 total, later increased to $48,100. The Fifth Division turned in $8,350, the best of the nine deck divisions. Mr. Becker personally pledged $8,800. In all, 1,271 men subscribed, 61.7 per cent of those aboard. Miss Carpenter, one of the "Y" girls, won a German helmet. It had been she who had led the girls into the ship's firerooms, where the temperature was around 128° and where water was swirling over flooded floor plates. Perspiring faces smiled at the quintet as they added more than $2,000 to the drive.

"Show me the man mean enough to refuse those girls and I'll show him the bilges," one fireman remarked.

"No Coney Island for me this summer," grinned another as he bought his $100 bond. Number 4 fireroom was temporarily flooded because of the failure to obtain suction on the bilges.

Race With the U.S.S. IMPERATOR

n May 8 the Navy Department announced in Washington that the IMPERATOR had been commissioned U.S.S. IMPERATOR at Brest at 1 p.m. on May 5. The dispatch was carried in the LEVIATHAN's paper of the 9th and it was also reported that Lt. John L. Beebe would head a list of LEVIATHAN officers to be transferred to the famous ex-Hapag liner, second largest ship in the world, to operate her as an American transport.[42] The IMPERATOR had survived the war in good condition and had been brought to Brest from Cuxhaven for the formal transfer after weeks of dredging had pulled her loose from the Elbe River's mud.[43]

Also on the 8th, as reported the following day aboard the LEVIATHAN, word came from Halifax that two out of three of the naval seaplanes had arrived safely, finishing the first leg of what it was hoped would be the first successful transatlantic flight. They had averaged 69 miles an hour on the 540-mile flight from Rockaway, N.Y. From Halifax they would go to Newfoundland and then across the 1,200 nautical miles to the Azores. They hoped eventually to reach Plymouth, England. There was no word of the third seaplane, which had taken off from New York at the same time.

On Friday morning, the 9th, the LEVIATHAN received a radio report from the French steamship EALE, 20 miles to the north, that she had spotted a floating mine.[44] More German helmets were given out to Victory Loan subscribers. The editor of the ship's newspaper decided to get a new Kelly press that could turn out 3,600 copies in an hour.[45]

On Sunday the LEVIATHAN steamed past the MOUNT VERNON, but they were in radio contact only, because the smaller craft was just over the horizon, about 40 miles distant. Secretary and Mrs. Daniels were aboard, and they radioed their best wishes:

"We never spent a happier week in our lives than that spent on the LEVIATHAN en route to France," their message said.

On the same day, interest in the Navy's attempt to fly the Atlantic increased with the arrival at Trepassy Bay, Newfoundland, of the NC-1 and NC-3, U.S. Navy seaplanes. The NC-4 had not been heard from.[46]

The arrival at Brest on Tuesday, the 13th, was an exciting one and there was an air of anticipation—for anchored near the LEVIATHAN was her distinguished sister ship. The U.S.S. IMPERATOR was under the command of Captain J.H. Robinson and had 2,000 in her crew. Many wondered why her old German name, with its imperialistic associations, had been kept, but it was obviously a case where the Navy bureaucracy could not make up its mind. This same kind of indecision was also probably responsible for the fact that no work to speak of had been done on her. She had just been cleaned up a bit. Although she had a huge peacetime passenger capacity, her full potential as a troopship would never be achieved. Only 2,000 troops were put aboard her for her first voyage under the American flag. She also carried 841 French wives of American soldiers and sailors.[47] Although somewhat worn after four years of minimum care, she still looked much fresher and more trim in her pre-war peacetime colors than did the VATERLAND, whose superstructure was crowded with liferafts and boats and whose whole appearance was one of shabbiness and hard use. Nevertheless the two liners, together again after so long, looked magnificent. There were many who wondered whether they might sail in peace under the American Line houseflag after all the troops were home. But uppermost in everyone's mind was the possibility of a race between the two three-stacked queens of the sea.

While coaling the LEVIATHAN, her crew demonstrated a bit of the enthusiasm with which they viewed the possibility of a test of speed between the two sisters. The job was begun on the starboard side by stevedores at 8:30 Tuesday evening, the very day the ship arrived. The crew started on the port side the next morning at 6:30. Despite the pumping aboard of water ballast, the 525 tons of coal loaded by the shoreside workers in their 10-hour headstart had given the huge hull a 2.5-degree list to starboard. Working with a zeal far surpassing the stevedores', the crew brought the ship back to an even keel by 10 a.m., and, despite the starboard water ballasting, made her begin to list to port. The stevedores, who continued to work after the crew had stopped at 9 p.m., carried bags of coal aboard all night long and brought the ship over to a 4-degree list to starboard. On Thursday, as the IMPERATOR was preparing to sail, the LEVIATHAN's crew returned to their labors. In no time they finished the job. In the 22 hours they had worked, they had stowed 2,050 tons of coal, compared to the 2,400 brought aboard by the stevedores in 32 hours.

The IMPERATOR sailed at 10:30 a.m. and was saluted by the LEVIATHAN as she passed out to sea. Although those on the LEVIATHAN were impatient to be off and after her, they were not scheduled to depart until the following day. Moreover, their most important passenger, Vice-Admiral Albert Gleaves, had not arrived as yet, and they could not possibly leave without him. He was completing a tour of evacuation ports in Belgium, England, and France. Leisurely he motored into Brest from Saint-Nazaire and boarded the LEVIATHAN. It was 7:05 when his flag was hoisted to her foremost top, where it was promptly saluted by the American and French warships in port.

Almost as promptly, the LEVIATHAN slipped her moorings and got under way. For the first time in their lives the "two fiery swords," as the old Hamburg-American house organ had dubbed them, were racing each other, and everyone aboard each ship could think of nothing else.

"We will probably arrive in New York a day ahead of her," a reporter for "The Transport Ace" wrote at his desk for the next day's paper. He added in a confident manner that although the IMPERATOR's machinery was in good condition, the inexperience of her firemen would make it impossible for her to make more than 17 knots.[48] The eleven-hour headstart was nothing, everyone thought.

Henry P. Davidson, Chairman of the American Red Cross War Council, was aboard with his wounded soldier son, who remained under the care of a nurse the whole crossing. There was another capacity load made up largely of men from the 89th and 33rd divisions. Several congressmen were also returning.

On the 16th of May, one day out, one of the LEVIATHAN's crew wrote a card to his father to be mailed when the ship reached New York. The card he used, by an odd coincidence, was an old Hapag picture of the IMPERATOR, horribly retouched, with the name U.S.S. LEVIATHAN on the bow and with masses of black smoke coming from all three stacks and impossible plumes of white steam also rising from each funnel. Three superimposed American flags flew bravely, and crude bow wave ripples were touched in to make the ocean look "real".[49] Of course the real IMPERATOR was off somewhere ahead, and no doubt her stacks were streaming black coal smoke eastward over miles of open ocean, for her picked Navy crew, many trained on the LEVIATHAN, knew that the LEVIATHAN was racing to catch up.

The LEVIATHAN was 323 miles from Brest at noon, and this was the last item that went into "The Transport Ace" for that day. The paper was rushed off the press and available to all on board by late afternoon. The story of the race with the IMPERATOR was a lead item. Another news item reported that the NC-4, the missing Navy flying boat, had been found, repaired, and flown safely to Halifax, where she set off for Newfoundland to join her two sister planes for their jump-off to the Azores.[50]

Sometime on the 17th the LEVIATHAN overtook the IMPERATOR. It had taken the second "fiery sword" three days to catch the first. Perhaps out of courtesy on the part of the LEVIATHAN, or possibly because of a fantastic effort on the part of the IMPERA-TOR's firemen, the two ships remained in sight of each other for the rest of the crossing. There were no further slighting references to the IMPERATOR and her 17-knot speed in the LEVIATHAN's newspaper. Instead the Saturday issue was almost entirely filled with straight wireless news items: "Belief Prevails in Paris That Germans Will Sign Treaty"; "Germany Remains Unrepentant and Refuses to Admit Guilt"; "New German Propaganda Started in Neutral Countries"; etc. A list of the 33 American divisions that had fought in France was given, showing how many prisoners each had captured. A call for a "LEVI-ATHAN Ball" was repeated, with the note that the ship would soon be out of commission.[51]

The next day LEVIATHAN passengers read about the remarkable achievement of the NC-4, the plane that had lagged behind her two sisters all along the way on the attempt to fly the Atlantic. She had reached the Azores after a 15-hour flight of 1,200 miles, much to the delight of Lt. Commander A.C. Read and the chagrin of the two other seaplanes. They had both been forced down at sea not too far from their goal. The story noted that the transatlantic capability of these planes had been designed into them as one way of fighting the German submarine menace. This comment was attributed to Assistant Secretary of the Navy Roosevelt.[52]

A crew member broke into print in the same issue of the ship's newspaper with a poem entitled "Our LEVI—." and it was not so bad:

> *There's a ferry boat a runnin',*
> *An' it's runnin' steady, too,*
> *Runnin' from Brest harbor,*
> *Manned by the boys in blue.*
>
> *She's ferry boatin' soldiers,*
> *From their 'Watch upon the Rhine,'*
> *And bringin' 'em all safely back,*
> *To 'Dear Old Mother Mine.'*
>
> *'Tis the U.S.S. LEVIATHAN,*
> *Who took a deadly sea,*
> *To safely transport soldiers,*
> *For the cause of Liberty.*
>
> *'Tis the old U.S.S. LEVI,*
> *Who dared the submarine,*

An' changed the tune of 'Wacht am Rhein'
To, 'The Wearin' o' the Green.'

The author was simply identified as "R.E.W."[53]

At 11:05 a.m. on Monday, May 19, Admiral Gleaves followed the lead of Secretary Daniels and Secretary Baker and shoveled coal into one of the ship's furnaces.

"As the bell rang, 39 firemen sprang to their positions and charged the No. 2 fires of 39 other steaming boilers," the ship's paper stated. It can be seen from this unexpected clue that she was not making her best speed, for had she been trying her utmost all 46 boilers would have been in service.

Admiral Gleaves' shovel, it was said, would be added to the shovels used by the two Secretaries and put on display in a glass case.

An oblique reference to the race with the IMPERATOR was made in the ship's paper on Monday when it was noted that Mrs. Phiester had been placed in charge of the American Red Cross work aboard because Mr. Becker, the man who had contributed so much to the Victory Loan drive on the previous crossing, had missed the boat, "due to the ship leaving on Thursday instead of Friday as originally announced."[54]

On Tuesday a "Smoker" for patients in D-20 was held, with entertainment by members of the 353rd Kansas Infantry. They had been on a three-month tour of the American area in Germany, giving shows to the troops. Among their most popular acts was one by Clifford Brown, billed as "the famous one-legged dancer." There was also a number by Jasbo Brooks, "The Cullud Jasbo Clog Dancer."

The Ninth Division issued an open challenge to any other division on the ship to compete in a sleepwalking contest, claiming that one of their petty officers was the champion sleepwalker of the ship "if not the entire Navy." The challenge must be accepted, it was stated, "on terms that the opposing contestants must not eat more than two pounds of head cheese on the night of the contest." Those wishing further particulars were asked to apply at the Guard Room.[55]

On Wednesday the LEVIATHAN slowly forged ahead of the IMPERATOR so that by noon of the next day she was about two hours in the lead. She reached Sandy Hook at 12:45 p.m. and passed Quarantine at 1:22, according to Lt. Commander Cunningham, her navigator. Another gala arrival welcome awaited her and again the harbor was filled with whistled salutes and plumes of steam. General Leonard Wood, the senior major general in the United States Army, and the man who had organized the 89th Division, was aboard the welcoming boat. So were the governors of Kansas and Nebraska, the homes of many of the 89th Division's troops. Thousands of others from these states were on hand at Hoboken and, as the *Tribune* described it, "These patient and intensely patriotic Westerners waited to give vent to their appreciation of an all star fighting force from 'back hum.' "

Only minutes after the LEVIATHAN docked, the IMPERATOR arrived and was helped into the northern side of the same pier. Never during their brief German period had the two giant vessels been at Hoboken at the same time. It was a big day for the port with a total of 27,256 soldiers landing from the LEVIATHAN, IMPERATOR, KAISERIN AUGUSTE VICTORIA, and four smaller troopships. Ballin might have taken pleasure in the fact that the three largest of these seven had been his ships. While he was not around to enjoy this little bit of irony, twenty German merchant marine officers aboard the IMPERATOR may have done so behind their beards. They were acting in an advisory capacity to the American officers. Among them were Hapag's Commodore Thomas Kier and Captain Fritz Kruse, both of whom had been aboard her under the Hapag houseflag.[56]

Chapter XV

"BIG CHIEF" COMES HOME

luejacket Thomas Lindquist mailed two LEVIATHAN souvenir booklets to his home in Glen Cove, Long Island, on May 22, the day that Voyage 15 ended. Thousands of others aboard did the same, and the LEVIATHAN story began to have new meaning in the hinterland. The cover of one of the booklets had the VATERLAND painting done so long ago by Bishop, with her old name erased. On the back cover was a fine water color by Fred Hoertz, a young marine artist. This painting was credited to the New York *Tribune*.[1] Most of the 10 photos in the album were taken by Paul Thompson. Another, with her camouflage fresh, identified her as the "Big Chief" in war paint. For the first time many people got to see what she looked like, how her troops slept four deep in iron pipe bunks on deck, how they ate, and how the great ship ran. The other album had ten different photos. The bridge was shown with the steering wheel up near the forward face of windows. In the VATERLAND days, her wheel had been inside the inner wheelhouse. Also shown was a scene in a galley, with 17 cooks lounging about.[2]

Voyage 16 began May 27 after only five days in Hoboken. At 5:30 p.m. the LEVIATHAN steamed past Quarantine and by 6:40 she had left Sandy Hook behind. The editors of "The Transport Ace" were busy looking over items for the next day's paper—it was only published while the ship was at sea. The pickings were poor. They had a letter from Admiral Gleaves hailing Commander Woodward and his engineering staff. There was a letter from Captain R.D. White, master of the NORTHERN PACIFIC, offering to match his baseball team against that of any other ship in the Cruiser Force. They had the moving picture schedule, but that was about all, until an exciting wire story came in over the airwaves. The NC-4 had landed at Lisbon, completing the first airplane crossing of the Atlantic. Most of the front page of the May 28 issue was devoted to this story. Commander John H. Towers, ranking officer of the original three-plane squadron, had been deprived of the glory of flying into the Portuguese port aboard the NC-4. He had been on one of the two others that had gone down off the Azores. The question of whether to let him go in with the surviving plane had gone all the way up to Secretary Daniels, who had ruled in favor of Commander Albert C. Read of the "unlucky" NC-4.[3]

Sampson's Place

ne of the favorite sports of seamen is playing crap. With the tension gone, the LEVIATHAN seamen had more time to themselves, and this pastime, while still strictly prohibited, came to be more than ever a passion of the devil-may-care fringe of the crew. Seaman First Class Dave W. Hurley found a way to add to his small Navy pay. He knew the "Benny Southstreet" of the LEVIATHAN, a sailor named William B. Sampson.[4] Dave knew his way around the ship, and one day Sampson asked him to find a "place," a spot where the dice could be thrown without interruption. Dave found the perfect spot. He had noticed that there was an unused elevator shaft running through his area, and so he made a key in the machine shop to open the outside door, and, once inside, managed to find out how to reactivate the electric motor and get the elevator to go. Sampson filled the elevator floor with blankets and invited those with money to come and enjoy themselves. Snugly out of hearing at the bottom of the shaft, the game attracted a never-ending stream of players, with Hurley standing guard and acting as elevator man to take up those who had lost all their green stuff. No one was interested in the bullion room only a short distance away from the bottom of the shaft. For Hurley this meant $200 a crossing, five times his Navy pay. Never one to miss an opportunity to make money, he invested his new income in the postcard business. A set of a dozen cost him 18 cents in lots of 5,000 and he sold them for a dollar.[5]

The LEVIATHAN reached Brest June 3 and headed for home again June 5. It was a very quick turnaround, partly because only 3,810 tons of coal was taken aboard. During the coaling the crew again easily outdid the shore stevedoring force. Actually, she was in French waters for only 49½ hours, four and a half hours less than her last record short stay. For this achievement she received on June 6 a message of congratulations from Commander Halstead, U.S. Naval Commander in France.[6]

A glimpse into the future was offered in one item carried by the ship's newspaper on the voyage home. Edward N. Hurley, Shipping Board Chairman, announced that three former German liners-turned-transports would be placed on the South American passenger run under the Stars and Stripes. They were the MOUNT VERNON, the VON STEUBEN, and the AGAMEMNON. Everyone aboard naturally wondered what would be done with the great LEVIATHAN. In New York on June 8, while the LEVI was in mid-Atlantic, the International Mercantile Marine turned down a second British offer to buy all their British liners. An unfavorable exchange rate killed this proposal.[7]

The Shipping Board was at this time in the midst of a debate on what to do with the tremendous war-built fleet of ships. Mr. Hurley submitted a plan on June 10 calling for government operation until the new fleet could be turned over to private operators. He proposed a development fund to encourage a strong merchant marine and called for larger mail payments to encourage an American passenger ship fleet.[8] How to handle the fleet of ex-German liners was becoming a major topic of conversation along shipping row in downtown Manhattan.

The Hurley plan was attacked by Vice Chairman R.B. Stevens of the Shipping Board, who opposed any kind of subsidy. He noted that before the war barely 2,000,000 tons of shipping was operated in overseas trade under the American flag, adding that by the end of 1920 the American fleet would have increased to 16,000,000 tons, of which 13,000,000 would be government-owned.

"American shipping organizations are not yet sufficiently developed," he said. "The ability of American ships to compete in the world's market is not yet demonstrated. American capital is not yet accustomed to shipping investments. For all these reasons I believe that the absorption of this great [war-built] tonnage by purchase will be slow."[9]

These two positions and the basic problems so well summarized by Stevens would be crucial issues in the future of the LEVIATHAN. It will be interesting to observe how the magnet of responsibility first drew Chairman Hurley, a member of a Democratic administration, to favor government ownership and operation of shipping, and then made the Republicans do a complete about-face and support a similar position under Harding. And the greatest lure in each instance was the LEVIATHAN.

The LEVIATHAN's sixteenth voyage ended at 9:55 a.m. on June 12. She had made the round trip in an amazing 15 days, 8 hours, and 4 minutes, beating her previous record by 7 hours and 1 minute.[10]

Eugene DeSchamps, a chief machinist's mate, left the LEVI at this point, after having served on her continuously since the day war was declared. He had been in the first group of men who had been rushed over from the Navy yard to help the Treasury men seize her. His most interesting memory was of the time a woman, on a $20 bet, had managed to board the outward-bound LEVIATHAN from a tug. It was on one of the wartime trips, and the gal was taken into custody immediately and incarcerated for the round trip. Another witness to the arrival of this unexpected and glamorous passenger was Gene's buddy, the man with the shortest surname in the U.S. Navy, John Peter Ix. Both DeSchamps and Ix would relish this memory and would even, perhaps, expand it to hint that they had heard that the girl in question was none other than socialite Wallis Warfield.[11]

Coaling at Hoboken was nothing like the job it was in Brest. The steam hoists devised for use by the IMPERATOR and the VATERLAND were employed, with civilian labor on hand to transfer the coal from barges into the hoists.[12]

Among the new men who joined the LEVIATHAN at this Hoboken turnaround was John S. Bowen. He had begun his career as a deck cadet on the ST. LOUIS when Herbert Hartley was first officer and Captain Jamison master. He was 27 and would serve on various American liners for the rest of a long life at sea, doing many stints on the LEVIATHAN.[13]

Captain Phelps Speaking

The LEVIATHAN began her seventeenth voyage at 11:05 a.m. on June 20th, and as she was approaching the great circle turning point off the Grand Banks, the New York *World* came out with an article written by her recent master, Captain Phelps, who had been assigned to the Navy War College, Newport, R.I. The piece contained several items of new and intimate information about the ship. During his five voyages Captain Phelps had learned much from Commander Woodward and others about the German period of his ship's life. Her original-design coal capacity had been only 6,500 tons, just enough to get her from Cuxhaven to New York. Captain Phelps knew also that this had been enlarged to 8,750 tons before her completion. In his article he mentioned this and surmised that the change was made to permit her use as a troopship in an expedition to South America or, perhaps, the Panama Canal.

"That these alternative expeditions were very plausible we have abundant proof in the writings, sayings and threats of the late Hohenzollern crowd," his article continued.

As to sabotage, Phelps was definite.

"The Navy found that no malicious damage had been attempted."

This position is mentioned because a few years later the matter became a front-page controversy, with Secretary Daniels on one side and Frederic Gibbs, brother of William Francis Gibbs, on the other. In this connection, Captain Phelps had a delightful note to add to the lore growing up around Commodore Ruser's name. He said it had come to him "first hand." Ruser was very proud of the VATERLAND; he had been the resident inspector at Blohm & Voss while she was being built, and he loved her. When he learned of German orders to damage her machinery and boilers, he forbade his engineers to do so, warning that he held himself responsible to the owners for her condition and adding that he would recognize only their orders on such a matter. Later he showed a surprising willingness to tell the U.S. Navy everything he knew about her plant and operation.

The Germans had always had trouble with the boilers, Phelps wrote, adding that an "army of boilermakers" would meet her at each arrival to patch leaking tubes. Woodward's engineering knowledge led him to conclude that there was unequal expansion in the boiler piping. He changed it, and up to the Armistice there was never a leaky tube in any of the 46 boilers. During all those months no outside labor was required in the maintenance of the boilers, except for the renewal of furnace doors.

Captain Phelps concluded by suggesting that if the United States kept the LEVIATHAN and the IMPERATOR and continued them under the American flag, it would be vital to increase the channel depths leading to our Navy dry docks. Although there were dry docks capable of holding these monster ships, he wrote, the channel approaches were all too shallow, and neither ship could be repaired on this side of the Atlantic.[14]

Nurse Robinson approached France with enthusiasm, for she had secured permission to make a visit to Paris. She could go all over France, for she had a whole trip off. Her next letter to her mother was much shorter than her earlier letters:

"Dearest Mother:

"Just a note. . .I am having so many thrills but I am not going to write about them just now. . .I would love to stay a year in Paris. I commence to believe that I was born under a lucky star."[15]

On June 27, when the LEVIATHAN reached Brest, an embarkation order was issued calling for the ship to carry mostly first-class passengers home.

"A sufficient number of troops will be placed on board to care for the necessary guard and fatigue duties," the order stated. It said that there were not enough cabins to accommodate the 5,000 passengers that had to be transported, and that only half of each troop compartment's capacity would be used to house those who could not be given staterooms. Troop galleys would also have to be employed and "the best that can be accomplished will be a cafeteria system."[16]

By first-class passengers, the memo, of course, meant officers. There were many detached Army officers at Brest, and they were all drawing officer's pay. The War Department had decided to send all below the rank of major "down in the hole" as an economy move. This meant taking them home in the troop compartments on the LEVI.

"Towering Like a Cliff"

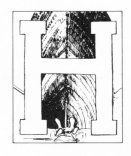

enry H. Amsden, a Medical Corps officer, didn't mind:

"We went by truck through Brest to Pontanezen Barracks, of unsavory memory during embarkation days," he wrote in his diary. "It is a huge camp, capable of accommodating about 100,000 troops and is a model camp in many ways. . . .Grub was very good and very cheap, all you could eat for a quarter or two francs. We spent most of the time in being inspected, getting all sorts of clearances, etc., and, after several hair-raising rumors, finally actually embarked on the LEVIATHAN Saturday noon, June 28.

"I made a couple of trips into Brest but hardly anyone was in a sightseeing mood. The chateau on the waterfront is an interesting medieval looking structure. The harbor is a rather poor one. The LEVIATHAN was lying at anchor a couple of miles out from shore, and we were taken out by lighter. She sure looked good, towering up in the air like a cliff. Some 3,000 casual officers were sent aboard, with about an equal number of troops, welfare workers, etc. Each officer below the rank of major was supposed to occupy quarters on the troop decks, and all the medical corps men did so, I guess, though about all the line officers of any grade had staterooms. We were given two compartments, consisting of canvas bunks, one for sleeping and the other for hand luggage. It was announced that owing to the exigencies of the situation a cafeteria system for chow would be adopted, which was soon found to be camouflage for mess with kits and chow line. The grub was fierce for the first three days; then I got a ticket to the first class mess, and fared better. We had perfect weather; the first day the boat pitched just a little, but after that there was no more motion than there would have been in a house. Sitting in one of the saloons and looking out on the water seemed like being in a summer hotel at the seashore. It was pretty hot below decks, especially in the latter half of the voyage."

After reaching Hoboken, Captain Amsden and two buddies made a beeline for a hotel and bath and then filled up on broiled lobster and ice cream.[17]

Another passenger on this crossing was 19-year-old Joseph G. McCue, who had served as warrant officer to Major General Joseph Dickman in Germany. His principal complaint was a lack of water to wash or shave with. "We all looked like a bunch of Bolsheviks upon landing," he remembered.[18]

Twenty-one-year-old Frank Tooker, a Naval Reserve cadet, had a glorious time on the trip. It was his first trip and although he spent the entire run home trying to get the coal dust out of his hair from the coaling at Brest, there were compensations.

"Officers' Mess was in a large and beautiful room. The menu for breakfast included steaks and chops; before midnight bridge watch we had coffee with cream and sugar, hot buttered toast and preserves." At night he danced with Red Cross girls. He had a stateroom with real beds whose linen was changed daily. He had his own private bathroom with an "insert electric wall heater." It was some experience. Tooker was particularly interested in the Sandy Hook pilot, Captain William McLaughlin.

"I was on the bridge at the time we picked up our pilot off Ambrose Lightship, and was impressed by his fine lightweight summer suit and Panama hat and quietly assured manner. He was greeted by the Captain, and he spoke softly when giving instructions to the man at the wheel. When tugs tied on to us he gave them hand signals from the wings of the bridge. A real pro."[19]

The Navy crew on the LEVIATHAN knew that housing Army brass in troop compartments would cause trouble, so a notice was printed and posted everywhere, explaining the War Department's "urgent request" that the LEVIATHAN bring home as many officers as possible, and warning that "some crowding is unavoidable." At the bottom of a copy of this notice preserved by the LEVIATHAN Veterans Association is the scrawled message "Thank You. Please Call Again."

But no matter what care was taken to soothe ruffled feelings and Army pride, there were some who could not be mollified. A story in the *Tribune* for July 6, 1919, the day after the LEVIATHAN reached Hoboken, reported numerous complaints. Officers had been forced to sleep in bunks, and to line up, mess kit in hand, and wait their turn at mess call! After they had gulped down their food they had to wash their own kits. Although some said that the speed of the homeward passage made up for everything, others were not so tolerant, and several asserted that they were entitled to first-class passage. Some even talked of sending in bills for $300 apiece—the difference between first and steerage fares. They said the quarters assigned to them were "unbecoming officers and gentlemen."[20] The next day Brigadier General F.T. Hines felt it necessary to deny from Washington that there had been any complaints about service or quarters by officers returning on the LEVIATHAN.[21]

"LEVIATHAN Special"

he LEVIATHAN's next-to-last voyage did not begin until July 13. Two new cast-brass propellers, each weighing 41,000 pounds, had been made for her at the famous Cramp shipyard in Philadelphia. One was to be shipped abroad for installation, if necessary, at the Gladstone dry dock in Liverpool. The other was to be kept at Hoboken.[22]

Edna Ferber came aboard while the LEVIATHAN was in New York. She was allowed to interview a few of the patients in the sick bay, but they were uncommunicative and the article she later wrote for the *Ladies' Home Journal* was not very interesting.[23]

In "The Transport Ace" for July 14, the ship's bandmaster called upon all violin players to report to C-708 for practice with the jazz orchestra. The front page was given over to two long articles, one about Wilson running for a third term on the issue of joining the League of

Nations, and the other about the return ocean crossing of Britain's dirigible R-34.[24] In Paris Bastille Day was observed, with many American soldiers marching in the great parade, most of whom would come home on the LEVIATHAN on one of her two final westbound crossings. The tempo of the times was slowing down and it could be seen in the ship's paper. Instead of stories about boxing matches on the LEVIATHAN or even Victory Loan drives, there were articles about the wets' prediction of victory in Congress and about the paralysis of Russian industry.[25] On the 18th of July Admiral Gleaves commended his transports for having brought home 1,246,789 troops between November 11 and June 30. A list of the different troopers and their troop totals was carried in "The Transport Ace," and, naturally, the LEVIATHAN led all the others, having carried more than twice as many as any other ship. Her total returned was 76,422. Her closest rival was the old AMERICA, which brought back 35,397.[26]

As the ship approached Brest, Commander Staton, back aboard, issued a letter to crew members on "how to do Paris and not be done," as it was headlined. With tensions relaxed, it had come to be Navy policy to conduct tours to the French capital for those on leave from the ship during her time at Brest. Special walking tours, bus trips, and boat rides were described. With six francs equaling a dollar, the nightly hotel rates of from five to ten francs were most modest. Dinner would come to ten francs and up, Staton's memo said. It was suggested that every man have at least $25 in addition to his transportation. There were "LEVIATHAN Specials" between Brest and Paris, leaving at 8 p.m. and arriving at 8 the next morning.[27]

On Sunday, July 20, the LEVIATHAN reached Brest, and this time there was no horrendous rush to load coal and make a record turnaround. It had been made known in Washington that General Pershing would return to the United States in August, and everyone aboard the LEVIATHAN speculated that her schedule was being readjusted to fit his plans. Her 18th westbound crossing would not begin until July 30th.[28] Many crew members were given seven-day passes to Paris. The time passed all too quickly, as always, and they were back on the ship and she was getting ready to go. She sailed on schedule, and the ship's paper for July 31, a Thursday, was devoted entirely to several official messages relating to transfer from the Reserve to the Regular Navy. Back home on that same day a report in the New York *Tribune* stated that the LEVIATHAN was to be continued under government operation. There had been widespread rumors that she would be turned over to the American Line, under the management of the International Mercantile Marine.[29] The Army was also hoping to regain the title to her and all the other ex-German liners that it had held briefly before.[30]

There were 8,739 aboard the LEVIATHAN as she headed for home, a comparatively small payload. The bulk were Army enlisted men. The spirit seemed to have gone out of the ship's newspaper, although now and then there appeared a quaint radio news item like:

"New York, Aug. 4 — Frederick Underlord, president of the Erie railroad, was arrested today because he tried to make a round trip on a Staten Island ferry without landing in Staten Island. Underlord will make a test case in behalf of the poor who use the ferry for outings." It was also reported from Dayton, Ohio, that a Major N.W. Schroeder had broken all airplane speed records when he flew at the rate of 137 miles an hour at an altitude of 18,500 feet.[31]

"We sail tomorrow," Nurse Robinson wrote her mother. "It is getting to seem the natural thing to be always going. It will be quite a come down when I can't go to France every month. You haven't told me where Charles is buried? If I were Aunt Sophie I would rather have him in France. . .there he lies among his comrades, a neat little grave, plainly but simply marked in a beautiful spot near where he died. All the cemeteries are alike. I tried so hard, and gave up going through Belleau Woods to look for it, but the elements were against us, and besides I did not know where he fought."[32]

At 7 a.m. on August 14 the LEVIATHAN, with only 31 passengers, sailed on her final voyage as a troopship. It was understood at the time that she would bring back units of the First Division, General Pershing, his son, and his staff. After returning she was expected to be sent to dry dock for refitting and then would be placed in transatlantic service between New York and French and British ports, the press reported. Her sister ship, the IMPERATOR, was scheduled to sail from Hoboken August 17 on her last trooping voyage, after which she would be returned to the Germans. England was pressing a claim for her as a replacement for the LUSITANIA. There was considerable controversy over what to do with her.[33] What would happen to the third of the Ballin trio, the unfinished BISMARCK, no one knew. German shipbuilding was at a low ebb, as an editorial in the *Marine Journal* took pleasure in pointing out. Riveters at the Vulcan plant, which had built the IMPERATOR, were said to be driving only 24 rivets in a given time, whereas before the war they had driven 75. As long as this continued, the German flag would be "a negligible factor on the oceans."[34]

The LEVIATHAN reached Brest on the 20th of August, and again her crew enjoyed a longer-than-usual shore leave. Among those who got 12-day passes to go up to Paris was Albert Engel, the youngster who had passed out after drinking ice water while coal passing.[35]

Bringing Pershing Home

General Pershing came aboard the LEVIATHAN. He needed rest but got little, for General Foch, Marshal of the French armies, came aboard to say farewell. As Nurse Robinson remembered: "That was a big day for us. To us General Pershing and General Foch were magnificent heroes. They were the beautiful people of our time."[36]

An indication of how much everyone had relaxed aboard the LEVIATHAN is the fact that many of the ship's lifeboats had rusted into position and could not be moved. It had been thought wise to have a thorough check of all boat falls to make sure that all the lifeboats could be lowered into the sea with ease. Deterioration is very rapid at sea, and the lack of wartime necessity had led to carelessness in upkeep. Once discovered, however, the situation was quickly remedied.[37]

Pershing's honor guard consisted of 100 tall Marines. They had been selected back in May, had trained in Germany, and had proceeded to Paris to be on hand when a new stadium named in the General's honor was inaugurated. They boarded the LEVIATHAN on August 30 and set up headquarters in Room 245, near Staircase #6, aft on the port side on D Deck. Their telephone was 96. First Lieutenant M.H. Silverthorn was in charge. Among the honor guard was a young six-foot sergeant named W.W. Weston, who carefully saved a handwritten list of the men in his group and a faint carbon of an August 30 memo describing guard duties. He remembered the weather was good on the trip. He remembered, also, how good the food was and how fine it was to have American cooking.[38]

The voyage across was all Pershing.

Halfway over, there was what radio men call a priority break in all overseas messages. A radiogram was coming in from the White House. President Wilson wired the LEVIATHAN to notify General Pershing that he had just been appointed a full general. This was the cue for a round of activities aboard. Pershing had had advance word of this promotion, and was prepared with a 7,000-word speech, which he read to the officers of the Rainbow Division from the after end of the promenade deck.

The Knights of Columbus had promised every soldier aboard a free radiogram home from the ship, and during the crossing 6,000 messages were sent. Another 1,000 still remained to be transmitted when the radio office was finally closed down after the ship docked on September 8. They had to be taken ashore and dispatched through Western Union at Newark.[39]

"The gray blanket of the seas was just emerging from the dullness of the night," as the New York *Herald* saw it, when the first boat load of welcomers slid up to within a city block of the LEVIATHAN, five miles out from Ambrose Lightship. The little craft was the yacht NATALIE MAE, owned by prominent shipbuilder William H. Todd. It was her privilege to be the first to salute the returning hero Pershing. The LEVIATHAN was slipping through the waters at a bare seven knots, awaiting the arrival of Sandy Hook pilot William McLaughlin.

"She was lined at her rails with Khaki-colored uniforms, and in silhouette could be seen on the upper decks and the hurricane deck the forms of men racing from place to place, tugging here at bundles, there at ropes and it was apparent that the soldiers, fifteen hundred or more of them, were preparing for disembarking," wrote the *Herald's* Quinn L. Martin.[40] He continued:

"From the west came the purr of aircraft. And then a big flying machine, carrying hundreds of copies of newspapers to be placed aboard the LEVIATHAN by means of a 500-foot cord that swung along beneath, came into view. The soldiers on board yelled their delight at the first sight of Americans come to greet them. A small motor craft darted here and there, in front and behind and at the sides of the ocean greyhound, its siren screeching and throwing spray high against the sides of the mammoth steamship. With more speed the LEVIATHAN was now nearing Gravesend Bay and presently came to the Narrows."

Then four destroyers came into the picture, their sirens blasting, and then another destroyer with the staff of Secretary of War Baker aboard. He would meet Pershing at the pier. Seventeen deep salvo "thumps" sounded from Fort Wadsworth and "with the dying of the last, one's ears could scarcely hold the tumult. It seemed, far out in the water, where one could scarcely see land even as yet, that the very air was filled with sirens and one thought of New Year's Eve or Armistice Day," the *Herald* rhapsodized.

"The pygmylike launches snorted and raced and seemed to skip after the great hulk that lumbered smoothly along. At each fresh spurt of noise the seamen and soldiers on board screamed and dared the followers to come closer. A heavily laden ferryboat next came into view, heading directly toward the big steamship. Around its sides was pasted a huge sign bearing the words 'Missouri Welcomes You.' Then came others bearing the insignia of the Knights of Columbus, from which candy and cigarettes were thrown, and the New York War Camp Community Service, each loaded to its very topmost peak with men and women and little children. They added their screams to the already deafening uproar, and then the Statue of Liberty, standing there as if the young woman were molded for that very moment, seemed to bend over a little farther, one imagined, as if she would like the best in the world to just place one hand on the shoulder of the nattily uniformed soldier wearing the four shiny stars on his sleeve, somewhere upon the passing craft, and say to him that she was downright proud of him and was glad to see him back."

Then four Navy airplanes joined the din, their fleeting shadows racing across the swarm of vessels following the "Big Train" as she made her last and most glorious entrance into New York harbor.

"If the water surrounding the Battery ever was really choked before with traffic it was more so choked now. Scarcely could the tugboats and the ferryboats and the pleasure excursions make their way. It was one solid mass of color and as one listened more closely he could detect the rollicking music of many bands—one band to every vessel that was large enough to carry it. The airplanes buzzed and dipped and slid along the water's surface only to rise again. There was life—the very deepest and sincerest and most demonstrative sort of life—everywhere."

Seldom before, even at the Armistice or when the LEVI had brought the 27th Division home, had reporters been so carried away, and the *Herald's* man was not to be outdone.

"Along the banks of the Hudson, both on the Manhattan and the New Jersey shore, from down to the very water's edge to the highest peaks, cramped into window sills and hanging to piers and floats, were persons waving their hands. Workers in grimy clothing were atop boxcars around the piers. Little girls wearing snow white dresses and with flags in their hands waved, and, through glasses, one could see their tiny mouths in motion, shouting out their own little welcome to their hero."

And along the downtown skyline:

"From the top of every one of the towering structures floated the flag of the nation. In the windows of every one of those buildings were hurrahing masses of persons attempting, but of course, in vain, to make their tiny shouts of welcome heard by him as he rode smoothly onward toward his pier."

The LEVIATHAN approached Pier 4, coming to a stop across the river along the Manhattan side, before making her turn.

"Motor cars gathered in every alleyway for blocks each way and the small vessels that had been chartered for the occasion now crowded closely around the big steamship, hemming her in on all sides, with hands and flags swaying from their sides and tops like corn tassels swaying in the summer breeze. There was rhythm in their motions.

"Presently there was a fresh outburst of screams as the LEVIATHAN turned slowly toward the pier and began nosing her way into the dock, which was literally imbedded in flowers and the colors of Old Glory. Hardly had the vessel slid in and stopped when the gangplank was placed and, while policemen and army officers fought with the crowds to keep them from entering and greeting the General in their own fashion, the General was buttoning up his coat and preparing his return to the soil on which stood the thousands to grasp his hand and give him a smile of welcome. . . ."

And the cheering, and the speeches, and the parades continued for days, and the echoes of the LEVIATHAN's last arrival as a troopship sounded on and on, passing into the subconscious of a whole generation of Americans. The LEVIATHAN had become a part of the heartbeat of America. She was the old LEVI, the Big Train, the biggest ship by far the Navy ever had, the most famous ship ever to fly the American flag.

Published Daily   # THE LEVIATHAN PRESS   *Navy Press News*

JANUARY 29, 1919.

ROME, ITALY (United Press).—About two hundred prominent Montenegro exiles forwarded to President Wilson an appeal requesting in the name of humanity, the evacuation of Montenegro by ex-Serbian troops and replace them with Allied troops to ensure the reconstruction of Montenegro.

Ninety transports established weekly freight service between Genoa, Venice and Trieste.

HORSEA WALES. Monsieur Tardieu at press luncheon in Paris, said that foreign journalist

NOTES

NOTES — Chapter I

1. McAllister, Capt. C.A., "The Repair of the LEVIATHAN–A Difficult Job Well Done," published in "The UNIDOCK," house organ of the United Dry Docks, Inc., 11 Bdwy., N.Y., June 1930, Vol. I, No. 8; illustrated, 2 pages. Also, 2-page mimeographed career summary put out in 1970 by Blohm & Voss (hereafter referred to as Blohm & Voss career summary). Also, interview with Gibbs & Cox electrician/designer Norman Zippler, 11,26,69; and letter from German historian A. Kludas, 1,17,70, which gives Nov. 4, 1911, as the date of the keel laying.

2. The VATERLAND had a sister ship which was to be bigger but which did not go into service until 1922 because of the war. She was christened BISMARCK but turned over to the British and renamed MAJESTIC.

3. These six are: MAJESTIC, NORMANDIE, QUEEN MARY, QUEEN ELIZABETH, FRANCE, QUEEN ELIZABETH 2–in order of their completion.

4. Passenger ships are almost always described in gross tonnage. One gross ton is 100 cubic feet of permanently enclosed earning space, with certain exceptions. British and American gross tonnage measurement systems are quite different.

5. My two chief authorities on the life of Ballin are his business associate Bernhard Huldermann's biography entitled Albert Ballin, translated by W.J. Eggers, pub. by Cassel & Co., Ltd. (London, 1922); and Professor Lamar Cecil's Albert Ballin, Business and Politics in Imperial Germany, 1888-1918. Princeton Univ. Press. (Princeton, N.J., 1967).

6. A good history of the North German Lloyd is the one by Von Georg Bessell. It is entitled 1857-1957 Norddeutscher Lloyd, Geschichte einer bremischen Reederei (Bremen, 1957). For an up-to-date history of Hapag, see Short History of the Hamburg-Amerika Line 1847-1967 (Hamburg, 1967).

7. Little has been written in English about this line. Their HELENE SLOMAN is known in America because she brought Henry E. Steinway here. See People and Pianos, A Century of Service to Music, by T.E. Steinway (N.Y., 1953). (The author has an autographed copy, for he contributed the picture of the HELENE SLOMAN when the book was in preparation.)

8. Huldermann, op. cit., 16.

9. Hamburg, Port of, "Ship Via Hamburg," p. 2, Sept., 1957.

10. Bonsor, N.R.P., North Atlantic Seaway, T. Stephenson & Sons, Ltd. (Prescot, Lancashire, 1955), 373.

11. The political and diplomatic side of Ballin's life is well told in Professor Cecil's 1967 biography. Huldermann's writings on Ballin's efforts to keep the peace are also most worthwhile, as he was actually an actor on the scene and one of Ballin's trusted younger associates.

12. Biographical references for all these men will be given as they are introduced in the book.

13. Cecil op. cit., 21 (quoting 1883 Lloyds).

14. Huldermann, op. cit. 24; Bonsor, op. cit., 129.

15. The French Line rebuilt their 1864 WASHINGTON in 1868 as a twin-screw vessel, and her success in the next two decades must have been keenly followed by Ballin. See Bonsor, op. cit., pp. 217, 597.

16. Vernon Gibbs, Commander C.R., Passenger Liners of the Western Ocean, John de Graff, Inc., (N.Y., 1957, 2nd ed.). Referred to hereafter as Vernon Gibbs: Liners. Also see Frank C. Bowen's A Century of Atlantic Travel, Little, Brown & Co., (Boston, 1930), and Bonsor, op. cit.

17. Vernon Gibbs, Liners, 159.

18. How delicate this matter really was can never be determined. It is interesting that it is not even mentioned in the Huldermann biography. He refers to the ship throughout with the proper spelling.

19. *"Across the Atlantic," 42-page brochure printed by Hapag, 37 Bdwy, N.Y., in early 1890s; author's collection. Referred to hereafter as Hapag 42-p. brochure.*
20. *The best study of speed records on the Atlantic is by Commander W. Mack Angus. It is entitled Rivalry on the Atlantic and was published by Lee Furman, Inc. (N.Y., 1939).*
21. *Bonsor, op. cit., 116.*
22. *Huldermann, op. cit., 133.*
23. *Hapag 42-p. brochure.*
24. *Hamburg, Port of, "Ship Via Hamburg," p. 3, Sept., 1957.*
25. *Huldermann, op. cit., 123.*
26. *Ibid.*
27. *Vernon Gibbs, Liners, 161, 183, and Angus, op. cit., xii,xiii.*
28. *Vernon Gibbs, Liners, 162.*
29. *Cecil, op. cit., 25. A story the author has heard, probably apocryphal, has it that Ballin used to count the silver when his express steamers reached port after each voyage.*
30. *Cecil, op. cit., 30. Prof. Cecil's excellent work is the basis for much of this summary of Ballin the man.*
31. *Bonsor, op. cit., 119; N.Y. Herald, 11,9,1903; N.Y. Herald, 11,17,1903. Both Huldermann and Cecil give long chapters on the Hapag-I.M.M. negotiations.*
32. *Cecil, op. cit., 109.*
33. *My thoughts here are a composite of information from John Maxtone-Graham, who has studied the works of Mewes and visited his buildings in Paris and London, and from Norman Morse, whose deck plan collection is one of the most complete in the world.*
34. *New Steamship Consultants, op. cit., 11; Huldermann, op. cit., 121-122.*
35. *Bonsor, op. cit., 120.*
36. *Vernon Gibbs, Liners, 165; Bowen, op. cit., 281; Fletcher, R.A., Travelling Palaces, Sir Isaac Pitman & Sons (London, 1913).*
37. *Cecil, op. cit., 108.*
38. *U.S. Maritime Administration, Dept. of Comm., "Fact Sheet" released about 45 Broadway, which had been its N.Y. headquarters, when it moved to 26 Federal Plaza in 1968.*
39. *This building was seized by the U.S. when America entered World War I and has remained a government property. It is being torn down at this writing.*
40. *Roper, W.H., The Atlantic Conference, 1921-1939, printed for private circulation only (Folkestone, England, 1940). There are no page numbers in this rare volume.*
41. *Oldham, Wilton J., "The Ismay Line," The (Liv.) Journal of Commerce (Liverpool, 1961), 167-168; and Anderson, Roy, White Star, T. Stephenson & Sons, Ltd. (Prescot, Lancashire, England, 1964), 106-110. Oldham infers that the third ship was always to have been called BRITANNIC. Anderson writes that she was provisionally named GIGANTIC and hastily renamed as a direct result of the TITANIC loss. Huldermann, in his Ballin biography written in 1921, speaks of the third White Star liner as the GIGANTIC (op. cit. 113).*
42. *Huldermann, op. cit., 132-133; Buell, Raymond Leslie, Europe: A History of Ten Years, The Chautauqua Press (N.Y., 1928), 4.*
43. *Cecil, op. cit., 198.*
44. *This friend was Siegfried Heckscher, and his article on Ballin was published Jan. 3, 1922, in Roter Tag, and is quoted by Cecil on page 165 of his biography.*
45. *Cecil, op. cit., 199.*

NOTES — Chapter II

1. *Marine Review, monthly nautical magazine published in Cleveland, Ohio, May, 1910.*
2. *Marine Review, June, 1910.*
3. *Isherwood, J.H., "BERENGARIA Ex-IMPERATOR," Sea Breezes, May, 1959, 326-332.*
4. *Scientific American, Dec. 17, 1910, 481.*
5. *Isherwood, noted British authority on passenger liners, defends the eagle as neither out of place nor out of proportion. Isherwood, op. cit., 326. That the eagle was an afterthought is shown in a painting of the new Hapag liner by Fred Pansing, American artist. As published in the 1910 Scientific American article, it carries the name EUROPA, but no eagle. The same painting, distributed to American newspapers in 1911 and still labeled EUROPA, has the eagle. A similar change was made in a painting by F. Bishop, of Bridgeport, Conn., copies of which the author has both with and without the figurehead.*
6. *Talbot, Frederick A., Steamship Conquest of the World, William Heinemann (London, 1912), 15 and 336.*
7. *Comparisons of the major ships building in 1911 are:*

	IMPERATOR	VATERLAND	OLYMPIC	BRITANNIC	AQUITANIA
Overall length	909	950	882' 9"	900	901½
Breadth	98	100	92½	94	97
Depth	63	63	64' 3"	64' 3"	64' 6"
Tonnage (gross)	52,117	58,000	45,000	50,000	46,150
Horsepower	62,000	65,000	46,000	50,000	56,000
Passengers					
First Class	908	780	735	790	618
Second Class	606	560	674	836	614
Third Class and					
Steerage	2,734	2,860	1,026	953	1,998
Crew	1,180	1,234	860	950	972
Total Aboard	5,428	5,434	3,295	3,529	4,202

These are the comparisons published by the Shipbuilder magazine, a British periodical, in June, 1914. The article is entitled "The Quadruple Screw Atlantic Line VATERLAND" and is carried on pages 347-359, with many plans and illustrations.

8. *The newest Atlantic liner at this writing is the 65,000-ton QUEEN ELIZABETH 2, whose stack has caused much adverse comment but is highly functional. Other big liners with radical stack designs are the ROTTERDAM, with two "king posts" serving as stacks, and the OCEANIC, with one large funnel far aft.*

9. *Walker, J. Bernard, "Maiden Voyage of the IMPERATOR," Scientific American, June 28, 1913.*

10. *Huldermann, op. cit., 121.*

11. *Anderson, A.O., published letter from him in Sea Breezes (May, 1964), 387; and Scientific American, Dec. 17, 1910, 481.*

12. *Siepmann, Ricardo, published letter from him in Sea Breezes (July, 1964), 75.*

13. *The Matson liner MALOLO, designed in 1927 by William Francis Gibbs, had lifeboats below her main promenade deck, as did the Dutch liner WILLEM RUYS, built during World War II. In the post-war era the ORIANA and CANBERRA have had similar lifeboat arrangements.*

14. *Walker, op. cit. A beautiful four-color brochure issued by the Hamburg-American Line before the IMPERATOR was completed has a full-page photograph showing the brand-new inner bottom contrasting with the slightly older-looking outer hull. See "Turbinen-Schnelldampfer IMPERATOR," Hamburg-Amerika Linie, 54 pages, 1912 (rough off-white cardboard and blue silk cover stamped in gold). Author's collection.*

15. *Grattidge, Capt. Harry, Captain of the Queens, E.P. Dutton & Co., (N.Y., 1956), 127; also Kurt F. Innecken, whose father worked in Blohm & Voss, and who attended the launching. His letters and translations have been most helpful in the preparation of this work.*

16. *Interview with E. Wulff at his home in New Jersey, Apr. 9, 1970.*

17. *The BISMARCK, later MAJESTIC, Hull #214, had split uptakes, as did the 20,000-ton twin liners RESOLUTE and RELIANCE, United American Line, laid down originally before World War I for Hapag and later bought back for German-flag service.*

18. *Dipl. Ing. Peter Klein's doctoral thesis entitled "Die Architektur Der Nordatlantik-Passagierdampfer - 1837-1914" goes into detail on this cruiser stern and other novel features of the VATERLAND. Copies of this two-volume work, privately published, are in the author's library. Translation by Mrs. Richard Shepard.*

19. *Blohm & Voss plan (positive), central superstructure, boat deck, boat arrangements, from bridge to after end of superstructure, plus foward elevation of bridge, with stack. Plan No. 408. About 10' x 2". Hereafter cited as Blohm & Voss Plan No. 408.*

20. *Blohm & Voss plan (positive) of forecastle deck, with side elevation from stem to bridge, and deck plan; also three separate plans of Deck I, Deck II, and Deck III from Frame 282 to Frame 316. Plan No. 409. About 3' x 2'. Hereafter cited as Blohm & Voss Plan No. 409.*

21. *Huldermann, op. cit., 127, and J.H. Isherwood, "The VATERLAND," Sea Breezes (June, 1964), 410-416; hereafter referred to as Isherwood, VATERLAND article.*

22. *Foerster, Dr.-Ing. E., and G. Sutterlin, Vierschrauben-Turbinedampher VATERLAND der Hamburg-Amerika-Linie (Berlin, 1918), 2.*

23. *The author has four of these five books. The fifth, dealing with first-class arrangements, is known to exist. Three of the four, given to the author by A. Kludas, Hamburg, may be described as follows:*
(1) BAUVORSCHRIFT fur den 4-SCHRAUBEN-TURBINEN-PASSAGIER und FRACHT-DAMPFER DER HAMBURG-AMERIKA LINIE-Schiff 212-Abteilung: "MASCHINENBAU," H.O. Persiehl, Hamburg; 242 pages of specs, 22 pages of index. Hard cover.
(2) BAUVORSCHRIFT fue den VIERSCHRAUBEN-TURBINEN-PASSAGIER-UNT FRANCHT-DAMPFER DER HAMBURG-AMERIKA LINIE: 212; Abteilung Schiffbau, H.O. Persiehl, Hamburg. 76

pages. (*Translation made available by Prof. Henry Benford, Chairman, Naval Architecture and Marine Engineering. University of Michigan.*) Hereafter referred to as Hapag specifications Book #2. Adams translation.

(3) *BAUVORSCHRIFT FUE DEN VIERSCHRAUBEN-TURBINEN-PASSAGIER-FRACHTDAMPFER DER HAMBURG-AMERIKA LINIE, Schiff 212, Einrichtung der II, III und IV. Klasse. H.O. Persiehl, Hamburg. 42 pages.*

The fourth was loaned to the author by M.P. Iverson, who served aboard the LEVIATHAN from 1917 to 1938. It may be described as follows: *TAFELN AU DEN BETRIEBSVORSCHRIFTEN FUR DIE DAMPF-TURBINENANLAGE DES SCHNELLDAMPFERS "VATERLAND"* – Blohm & Voss, Hamburg. 30 pages, 12 x 14 inches, detailed engine drawings done in india ink and printed; gone over by hand in red and blue crayon.

24. Henry Carter Adams II, who worked with W.F. Gibbs when the LEVIATHAN was converted in 1922-23, secured a translation of this volume, later made available to the author, as mentioned above, by Dr. Benford.

25. There is some slight variation between the printed specs and the Adams translation, undoubtedly due to the fact that there were probably different editions of this key volume during the preliminary stages of the ship's planning.

26. *Hapag Specifications Book #2, Adams translation, 3.*

27. *New Steamship Consultants, op. cit., 20.*

28. *Hapag Specifications Book #2, Adams translation, 12.*

29. These square windows were never installed, and the wing of the bridge was left unprotected. The 'midships bridge, such as the IMPERATOR had, was also never built on Hull #212. *Hapag Specifications Book #2, Adams translation, 17.*

30. *Ibid.*

31. These are the author's italics. See *Hapag Specifications Book #2, Adams translation, 19.*

32. Hamburg-Amerika Linie, "Summer Number 1914," house organ (English ed.) Hamburg, Germany, 1919, 235. (Hereafter referred to as Hapag, house organ, 1914.) A study of ocean liner mast heights prepared in 1939 by the Port of N.Y. Authority shows that the REX was the leader in this category at this time with a mast that rose 232' 3½" from the waterline. The QUEEN MARY's mast height was only 204'.

33. *Hapag Specifications Book #2, Adams translation, 24.*

34. *Ibid.*

35. *Hapag Specifications Book #2, Adams translation, 32-34.*

36. *Ibid.*

37. *Hapag Specifications Book #2, Adams translation, 3.*

38. A copy of this was sent to the author by Blohm & Voss; bow to stern elevation, keel to truck and deck plans of upper 5 decks. Item 13 list of drawings; B&V. designation: A NR 901-000-1579-000.

39. *Ibid.*

40. Blohm & Voss diagrams 407, 408, 409; Items 10, 11, 12 in list of drawings.

41. The 16,960-ton CLEVELAND, 1909, was the largest Blohm & Voss ship built up to then.

42. These ships were 463 feet long, compared to the 550 feet of the superstructure. The combined width of Ballin's first two express steamers was 112 feet, compared to the 100-foot width of Hull #212.

43. See Note 13.

44. Blohm & Voss career summary.

45. *Hapag Specifications Book #2, Adams translation, 15.*

46. *Ibid.*

47. *Marine Engineering and Shipping Age, Nov. 1922, "The Reconditioning of the Steamship LEVIATHAN—Newport News Shipbuilding and Dry Dock Company Converting the World's Second Largest Vessel Into the Finest Transatlantic Liner Afloat," pp. 673-685; profusely illustrated. (Hereafter referred to as Marine Engineering Reconditioning article, 1922), 675.*

48. *Hapag house organ, 1914, 115.*

49. *Loc. cit., 123.*

50. Fletcher, *op. cit.*, 79. Also see 12-page pamphlet published by Frahm entitled "Advantages of the Anti-Rolling Tank" (London, 1913).

51. The ship's surgeon was a Dr. Joseph E.J. King, who became a lifelong friend of Capt. Hartley's, later operating on him for a stomach blockage. Letter from Dr. King to author, Feb. 6, 1970, and interview between Dr. King and Dr. E.C. Braynard, the author's father, in March, 1970.

52. Kurt F. Innecken, whose father had worked for years for Blohm & Voss, was a passenger on this same voyage. See letter to author June 8, 1970.

53. *N.Y. Herald, March 23, 1913.*

54. *The author is indebted to Hamburg historian Arnold Kludas for this explanation of the VATERLAND's name—see his letter of Jan. 19, 1970.*
55. *Buell, op. cit., 11. The Red Star Line, a part of I.M.M., had a ship named the VADERLAND at this time. She was of 12,000 tons. See Bonsor, op. cit., 317. Several ships have been named VATERLAND since this date. In 1926 Count Felix von Luckner had a sailing ship with this name (see Sea Breezes, June, 1948, 360). Hapag started to build a large liner with this name during World War II, but she was destroyed by bombs (Sea Breezes, Feb., 1961, 87). At this writing there is a Rheir River passenger steamer of 1,865 tons named VATERLAND.*

NOTES — Chapter III

1. *Hapag house organ, 1914, 111.*
2. *Hayes, Sir Bertram, Hull Down, Reminiscences of Wind-jammers, Troops and Travellers, MacMillan Co. (New York, 1925), 164.*
3. *International Marine Engineer, June, 1914; see also Hapag house organ 1914, 117.*
4. *Hamburg-Amerika Linie, Summer Number 1913, house organ, 350 pp., illustrated, English edition, Hamburg, Germany. Hereafter referred to as Hapag house organ, 1913.*
5. *This was the painting that as time passed was continually being mistaken for a painting of Kaiser Wilhelm II.*
6. *Hamburg-American Line, "Across the Atlantic—Photographic Reproductions of the Company's Various Types of Steamers Comprised in the Transatlantic Passenger Service," 80-page pamphlet (N.Y., 1907), referred to hereafter as Hapag 80-page brochure. Also see Morton Allan Directory of European Passenger Steamship Arrivals for the Years 1890 to 1930 at the Port of N.Y., Bernard Pub. Co. (N.Y., 1931). Also see Eugene W. Smith's Passenger Ships of the World, Past and Present, George H. Dean Co. (Boston, Mass., 1963), 32.*
7. *Hapag house organ, 1913, 46.*
8. *Marine Review, Cleveland, Ohio, June, 1910.*
9. *Vernon Gibbs, Commander C.R., The Western Ocean Passenger Lines and Liners, 1934-1969, Brown, Son & Ferguson, Ltd. (Glasgow, 1970), 100.*
10. *Her cousin, Mrs. Margaret Atkinson, lives in Rye, N.Y., at this writing. She overhead LEVIATHAN veteran John Carrothers talking about this book in a restaurant on Dec. 2, 1969, and identified herself to him.*
11. *Hapag house organ, 1913, 48,49.*
12. *Marine Engineering and Shipping Age, Sept., 1922, 585.*
13. *N.Y. Herald, Apr. 4, 1913.*
14. *International Marine Engineering, June, 1913, 247.*
15. *Hapag house organ, 1914, 117.*
16. *Contemporary clipping from British magazine about shipping in author's files. The magazine is not identified and no date is shown on the clipping.*
17. *Fletcher, op. cit., xv, 241.*
18. *Shipping World, Apr. 9, 1913.*
19. *R.H. Schmidt to author Jan. 12, 1971.*
20. *G.F. Weber to author Mar. 25, 1970.*
21. *Shipping World, June 25, 1913.*
22. *Grattidge, op. cit., 127. Captain Grattidge in his autobiography says five were killed, although this may be an exaggeration, as Captain Grattidge never liked this ship. "She was a ship of gloomy panelled majesty, hard to handle, clumsy and Teutonic, a creation of industry without pretensions to beauty." He served as her master when she was the BERENGARIA. Also see Bonsor, op. cit., 121.*
23. *Isherwood, op. cit., 121.*
24. *Working drawings of this early Sperry gyro-compass were provided the author by Sperry Gyroscope Co. executive Fred Braddon, May 26, 1970. E. Wulff interview Apr. 9, 1970.*
25. *A feature article on Commodore Ruser was published in the newspaper Hamburger Abendblatt, Nr. 104, Seite 9, 1970.*
26. *Walker, op. cit.*
27. *See unpublished ms. of autobiography of Captain George Seeth II, son of the Captain Seeth referred to here. The author is editing this work.*
28. *Isherwood, op. cit., 330.*
29. *N.Y. Herald, June 20, 1913.*
30. *N.Y. Times, June 19, 1913.*
31. *Photos in author's collection from the N.Y. Herald Tribune picture file.*
32. *Hapag house organ, 1914, 111.*

33. Ibid, 149.

34. Loc. cit.

35. Ibid, 141-143.

36. Cecil, op. cit., 110.

37. Many Hapag folders and passenger lists of 1913 and 1914 carry company advertisements about these zeppelin cruises. Had the war not intervened, it is likely that Hapag would have pioneered in transatlantic lighter-than-air service.

38. From unpublished ms. entitled "Seven O'Clock Cutter," by William Seabrook, whose experience includes work for White Star Line in the early 1920s, for the International Mercantile Marine during the LEVIATHAN period, and for many other ship lines.

39. Data on total passengers carried by ship, by class and by voyage, eastbound and westbound, are available in the "Report of the Trans-Atlantic Passenger Movement," published each year for private circulation by the Trans-Atlantic Passenger Conference, Brussels. Copies of most of these reports from 1899 to 1958 are in the author's files, loaned by Kenneth Gautier, Passenger Traffic Manager, U.S. Lines.

40. It was seen by G.F. Weber, newly arrived from Germany, who had been a passenger on IMPERATOR; see his letter to author dated Apr. 19, 1970.

41. Interview with Captain Schultz Apr. 7, 1970.

42. Trans-Atlantic Passenger Conference, Report of the Trans-Atlantic Passenger Movement, 1913, 34-35. Hereafter referred to as T.A. Conference Passenger Movement Report (with year of issue).

43. His grandson, F.G. Schreiber, made available the Willy Schreiber scrapbook and other family records. Hereafter referred to as Schreiber scrapbook.

44. See Blohm & Voss side elevation Plan #408; also Isherwood VATERLAND article, 410 ff.

45. Interview with Marcus P. Iverson, Jan. 26, 1971.

46. Shipbuilder, June, 1914, 351.

47. Hamburg-American Line, "VATERLAND—The World's Largest Ship," 32-page pamphlet, illustrated, published in 1914 in New York. Hereafter referred to as N.Y. VATERLAND brochure.

48. International Marine Engineering, June, 1914, 263.

49. Shipbuilder, June, 1914, 351.

50. Loc. cit.

51. Hapag house organ, 1914, 129.

52. Schreiber scrapbook.

53. British maritime author Colin Sorensen informed the author of this secret panel. He learned of it from a handwritten note on the back of a photo of the Social Hall. The note called attention to a white inked "X" on the photo, marking the panel. Sorensen got the photo from a London picture agency; he called it to the author's attention in a letter dated Oct. 19, 1970. Also see Hapag house organ 1914, 131.

54. The author has failed to find anything about the early history of these four paintings. All four were destroyed in 1939 when the Middleton Tower Holiday Centre, at Morecambe, near Blackpool, burned down. They had been bought by Mr. N. Kamiya when the LEVIATHAN was scrapped. See the author's ms. entitled "Art on the VATERLAND." C.J. Gumbrell, of Hants, England, uncovered this sad ending to a quartet of paintings that would probably have brought more than the 1938 scrap value of the LEVIATHAN herself if they had survived up to this writing. Also see N.Y. Times, Jan. 11, 1938.

55. Letter from Institut fur Auslandsbeziehungen, Stuttgart, Feb. 24, 1972. The Institute's Director, Mr. Halft, asked the author for word on the present location of this Houdon statue.

56. Photos from the Gibbs & Cox LEVIATHAN file.

57. This piano was found in a Norfolk, Va., piano store in 1919 by Mrs. Edna E. Sheldon, who played it and marveled at its resonant chords. Letter to author Apr. 10, 1970.

58. A piece of this rug was bought at auction in 1917 by Lt. Cdr. Ray Clifton Shepherd and kept in the family many years. Interview Mar. 9, 1970.

59. Saturday Review of Literature, June 18, 1932. An article entitled "Drawing Out the LEVIATHAN," by W.S.H., 795, gives the name of the sculptor.

60. Gilbert, O. Rundel, Public Auction Catalogue—Estate of Herman Goldman, 96 pp., June, 1968, Plandome Manor, N.Y. Hereafter referred to as Goldman Auction Catalogue.

61. One is owned by the Mariners Museum, Newport News, Va.; one is in the law offices of Kirlin, Campbell & Keating; one is in the marine insurance offices of Johnson & Higgins; and the fourth, from the Goldman estate, is on display at Marshall's ship supply store in Port Washington, N.Y.

62. Hapag house organ, 1914, 133.

63. Shipbuilder, Midsummer, 1911, Fig. 14.

64. Hapag house organ, 1914, 133.

65. Clapp, Edwin J., The Port of Hamburg, Yale Univ. Press (New Haven, Conn., 1912), 82.

66. The knockers for cabins 101 and 202 are part of the door knocker collection owned by Jerome Dukoff, of Brooklyn, who sent the author a photo of them Aug. 25, 1970.

67. One is owned by Leslie Stratton, and two others were part of the household of Herman Goldman, director of U.S. Lines. See Item 710 in Goldman Auction Catalogue.

68. One cabin had two prints from paintings by British artist F. Wheatley, R.A. Both had captions in English and French. Both have been preserved by W. Norman Zippler, of Gibbs & Cox, and were shown the author Dec. 9, 1969.

69. Various contemporary Hapag folders and p. 29 of a 1914 passenger list for the KAISERIN AUGUSTE VICTORIA.

70. "Preliminary First Cabin Plan of the Quadruple Screw Steamship VATERLAND", loaned to the author by Vincent Messina. Published by the Hamburg-American Line, 1914.

71. This piano was also in the Norfolk, Va., piano store in 1919 and was seen by Mrs. Sheldon.

72. By the time the BISMARCK came out, immigration restrictions made such huge dormitories useless. See International Marine Engineering, June, 1913, 247; also Shipbuilder, June, 1914, 347-359.

73. International Marine Engineering, June, 1914, 263.

74. Hamburg-American Line, "Steerage and Third Cabin Circular No. 1," published by John C. Rankin Co., Jan. 1, 1914 (24 pages).

75. Hapag house organ, 1914, 117.

76. N.Y. VATERLAND brochure, 5.

77. Wulff, interview, Apr. 9, 1970.

78. Hapag house organ, 1914, 121.

79. Loc. cit.

80. Loc. cit.

81. Fellowes-Wilson, V.S., The Largest Ships of the World, Crosby Lockwood and Son (London, 1929).

82. Marine Engineering, June, 1922, 396.

NOTES — Chapter IV

1. Cecil, op. cit., 199.

2. Hamburg-American Line "Facts and Figures Showing the Remarkable Development of the World's Largest Steamship Co.," 8 pp., published by N.Y. office, 1914.

3. Cecil, op. cit., 61.

4. N.Y. Herald, Feb. 24, 1914. The two companies were actually forced to join under Hitler, separating after World War II only to join again in 1970.

5. N.Y. VATERLAND brochure.

6. Grandfather of Howard Nielson and Irving Miller, of Moran Towing & Transportation Co.

7. Shipbuilder, June, 1914, 347.

8. Hapag house organ, 1914, 139.

9. Op. cit., 147.

10. Her funnels were to have been 80 feet high, as were those on IMPERATOR, but after the top heavy problem developed in the earlier ship they were re-designed 16 feet shorter.

11. A picture of the VATERLAND entering this "schwimmdock" is shown on p. 4 of the Foerster-Sutterlin 1918 paper on her design and construction referred to in Chapter II.

12. Much of this information has been developed from a study of Blohm & Voss photos and others provided by Gibbs & Cox. Also see N.Y. World, May 3, 1914.

13. N.Y. Times, March 20, 1914.

14. Cary, Alan L., Famous Liners and Their Stories, D. Appleton-Century (New York, 1937), 30. Hereafter referred to as Cary, Famous Liners.

15. Interview with C. Rosner, Mar. 16, 1970.

16. N.Y. Herald, Apr. 26, 1914.

17. Interview with E. Wulff, Apr. 9, 1970.

18. N.Y. Journal of Commerce, May 2, 1914.

19. Angus, op. cit., xii.

20. Blohm & Voss Career Summary.

21. N.Y. Journal of Commerce, May 2, 1914.

22. A diagram showing this illustrates that the initial curve of a ship's righting movement dips below the line and then rises gradually, but much less pronouncedly than does a ship with a positive g.m. Interview with James Gordon, M.I.T., formerly of Marine Engineering, Apr. 6, 1970.

23. Hart, Frank A., "List of Radio Stations of the World (1916)" Marconi Wireless Co. of America, N.Y., 1916.

24. *N.Y. Times, May 2, 1914.*
25. *N.Y. Times, May 3, 1914.*
26. *N.Y. Journal of Commerce, May 2, 1914.*
27. *"Shipping Gazette Weekly Summary," May 15, 1914, from files of American Merchant Marine Institute, author's collection.*
28. *N.Y. Herald, May 15, 1914.*
29. *T.A. Conference Passenger Movement Report, 1914, 30, and a Hapag passenger list for this May 14, 1914, crossing, loaned by R. Lincoln Hedlander, Secretary, LEVIATHAN Veterans Association.*
30. *Hapag VATERLAND passenger list for May 14, 1914, crossing.*
31. *Hapag sepia-toned VATERLAND postcards—see one entitled "Sonnedeck III. Klasser."*
32. *N.Y. Times, May 15, 1914, front-page story.*
33. *Ibid.*
34. *N.Y. Tribune, May 15, 1914.*
35. *N.Y. Sun, May 15, 1914.*
36. *N.Y. Times, May 15, 1914.*
37. *Hapag 'Information Booklet for Passengers—Steamship VATERLAND," first 40 pages in German, remainder in English. Cardboard-thick covers. Indexed. 1,000 printed Apr. 29, 1914. Loaned by LEVIATHAN Veterans Association.*
38. *Much of this detail comes from two outstanding photos taken by Beken, famed Cowes photographer of ships, and sent to the author by Philip J. Fricker, of Cowes, July 31, 1970.*
39. *Hartley, Herbert, as told to Cliff Bonner, Home Is the Sailor, Vulcan Press (Birmingham, Ala., 1955), 2-3. The un-sailorlike language suggests that ghost-writer Bonner was putting words into Hartley's mouth here.*
40. *J. Reynard in letter to author Mar. 18, 1971. Reynard was always known as "Shaver" because of his short stature. Also Reynard letter dated May 19, 1971.*
41. *Records of the Schreiber family loaned by F.G. Schreiber, Apr. 26, 1970.*
42. *This music program loaned by LEVIATHAN Veterans Association. It was found aboard the ship in 1917.*
43. *Loaned by LEVIATHAN Veterans Association.*
44. *Third Officer Archie Horka, in letter to author Feb. 17, 1970.*
45. *N.Y. Times, Nov. 28, 1965. Mr. Hecker remained in the U.S. and for many years was a waiter at Luchow's, one of New York's best-known German restaurants.*
46. *Mrs. Levine ran a newspaper store in the author's hometown until her death in 1969. She told him all about her VATERLAND experiences on Oct. 31, 1967.*
47. *Fellowes Wilson, op. cit., 40.*
48. *Votau, W.A., "Postal Union Mails and Sea-Post Service," manuscript article by former Assistant Director, International Postal Service, U.S.A., New York, 1923. 5 pp. Loaned by author.*
49. *N.Y. World, May 17, 1914. One of these Pittoni works was spotted in a Bristol wine merchant's office by Sir Kenneth Clark. Lord Clark confirmed this in a letter to the author dated Jan. 21, 1972. The other has also survived and is in New York in the Chrysler Collection. See letters from Ross Watson, Museum Curator, National Gallery of Art, in author's file.*
50. *All three stories have just one single line in the N.Y. Times Index: "Maiden voyage a great success." N.Y. Times, May 18, May 19, and May 20, 1914.*
51. *N.Y. Herald, May 20, 1914.*
52. *Ibid.*
53. *Here the editor is unconsciously reflecting the typical American attitude that most new ships are foreign liners coming from Europe to America. In the years between the Civil War and this writing, only eight new liners of first-class stature have been built in the U.S. for U.S.-flag North Atlantic passenger service: ST. LOUIS, ST. PAUL, FINLAND, KROONLAND, MANHATTAN, WASHINGTON, AMERICA, and UNITED STATES.*
54. *N.Y. Times May 22, 1914.*
55. *N.Y. World, May 21, 1914.*
56. *N.Y. Times, May 22, 1914, and N.Y. World, May 21, 1914.*
57. *N.Y. World, May 21, 1914.*
58. *Ibid.*
59. *VATERLAND's official ship's document, seized in April, 1917, by R. Lincoln Hedlander. Entitled: "Schiffs-Mes ? Brief," and identified at the bottom right as Nr. A. 42. This document is on parchment and measures 9½" x 17". It has a green tint, with black printing and some green overprinted by black. Many spaces have been filled in in ink.*
60. *Bensor, op. cit. 582.*

61. *Letter dated Dec. 17, 1969, written one week before Captain Madigan died; also see Allen, E.L., Pilot Lore—From Sail to Steam, United New York and New Jersey Sandy Hook Pilots Benevolent Association (New York, 1922). Pilot McCarthy belonged to the New Jersey Association.*

62. *Alfred Miller, leading marine photographer in New York, has provided many reproductions for this work at no cost. This story came from an interview with him Jan. 16, 1968.*

63. *N.Y. Times, May 22, 1914.*

64. *Mr. Nernoff was 87 in 1969 and in good health when his son John Jr. told the author this happening.*

65. *N.Y. Tribune, May 22, 1914.*

66. *Letter from G.F. Weber, March 25, 1970.*

67. *Seabrook, op. cit. Mr. Seabrook is a Briton by birth.*

68. *This was not the first time that the VATERLAND was called a "leviathan." It would be interesting to make a study as to how the casual nickname became the real name. See N.Y. Herald, May 22, 1914.*

69. *N.Y. Tribune, May 22, 1914.*

70. *One of these Hapag tugs lasted down until this writing as part of the Moran fleet. She was built in 1913 as Hamburg-American Line No. 3, becoming the MICHAEL MORAN. See Palmer, Capt. Earl C., Moran Fleet List, 1861-1965 (New York, 1965), 11 (manuscript).*

71. *N.Y. Herald, May 20, 1914.*

72. *N.Y. Times, May 22, 1914.*

73. *N.Y. Times, May 22, 1914.*

74. *Interview with Admiral Edmond J. Moran, Chairman of Moran Towing & Transportation Co., Sept. 17, 1969.*

75. *Miss Schaetz married and became Mrs. Stemi Stemitakis.*

76. *N.Y. Herald, June 21, 1923.*

77. *N.Y. Times, May 22, 1914.*

78. *Ibid.*

79. *Milwaukee Germania-Herold, May 21, 1914.*

80. *Cecil, op. cit., 200.*

NOTES — Chapter V

1. *Interview with Vice Admiral Harry Manning (U.S.M.S.), Nov. 30, 1969.*

2. *See advertisement of the DeMayo Engineering Co. with a picture and caption in Marine Engineering, June 1920, 20. In the ad the caption incorrectly calls the VATERLAND the IMPERATOR.*

3. *N.Y. Tribune, May 24, 1914.*

4. *Gleaves, Vice Admiral Albert, A History of the Transport Service, George H. Doran Co. (New York, 1921), 189.*

5. *Phelps, Capt. William W., "Handling Biggest Ship Afloat in War Time by Her Captain," The N.Y. World, June 22, 1919.*

6. *Interview with Ralph Pontifex, Jan. 19, 1970.*

7. *N.Y. Tribune, May 26, 1914.*

8. *N.Y. Times, N.Y. Sun, N.Y. Herald, N.Y. Tribune, May 25, 1914.*

,9. *N.Y. Tribune, May 26, 1914.*

10. *Seabrook, op. cit.*

11. *N.Y. Herald, May 27, 1914. Captain G.J. Madigan, Sandy Hook Pilot, is the source of this reference to the FREEPORT. See his letter dated Dec. 17, 1969.*

12. *N.Y. World, May 26, 1914.*

13. *Ibid.*

14. *N.Y. Tribune, May 27, 1914.*

15. *Seabrook, op. cit.*

16. *John Carrothers, engineer, has been of as great help with this story as anyone, and is the source of a variety of the VATERLAND/LEVIATHAN artifacts in the author's collection, including a lamp from the Kaiser's suite, engine room signs, and a large "E Deck" sign.*

17. *N.Y. Herald, May 27, 1914, and Seabrook, op. cit.*

18. *Interview with electrician Charles A. Ward, April 11, 1970. An explanation of the problem and how it was eventually solved on the LEVIATHAN will be found below.*

19. *N.Y. Times, Nov. 15, 1919. The author has been unable to find any evidence of what actually happened to the engines in the Hapag files in Hamburg. See Anderson, Ernest H.B., "Propelling Machinery of the LEVIATHAN, Jan., 1920, International Marine Engineering, 51 ff. Also see Jessop, Commander E.P., "Repairing German Vandalism on Interned Vessels by Electric Welding," Journal of the American Society of Naval Engineers, March, 1918, 124.*

20. The sailor was R. Lincoln Hedlander, who gave it to the author 53 years later.
21. N.Y. Times, May 28, 1914.
22. Letter from Pilot Captain G.J. Madigan, Dec. 17, 1968.
23. N.Y. Herald, June 2, 1914; see also Baarslag, Karl, SOS to the Rescue, Cadmus Books (Chicago, 1935), 79-97.
24. The Sphere, May 23, 1914, 243.
25. Fishguard was Cunard's regular express stop at this time, and is located just east of St. David's Head. It is a ferry terminal for three lines from southeastern Ireland. See Cunard time schedules and folders for the period in author's collection.
26. U.S. Atlantic Fleet, Cruiser & Transport Forces, History of USS LEVIATHAN, Brooklyn Eagle Job Dept. (Brooklyn, N.Y., 1914), 152. Hereafter referred to as Navy LEVIATHAN History.
27. N.Y. Tribune, June 2, 1914.
28. N.Y. Times, June 4, 1914.
29. N.Y. Sun, June 5, 1914; also letter dated Feb. 21, 1970, from Captain Jens Nilsen, who was in New York at the time.
30. Seabrook op. cit. When the AQUITANIA was scrapped in 1950 it was the author's privilege to write the editorial used by the Herald Tribune honoring her for her long career, for which he received $11.
31. Reade to author, Apr. 8, 1970.
32. N.Y. Tribune, June 14, 1914.
33. N.Y. Tribune, June 7, 1914.
34. N.Y. Tribune, June 17, 1914; also see T.A. Conference Pass. Movement Report, 1914, 30.
35. N.Y. Tribune, June 17, 1914.
36. Interview with Mrs. Sarah Sadowsky, Aug. 12, 1970.
37. Mrs. Sarah Sadowsky's photo album has a faded print.
38. N.Y.Herald Tribune, May 27, 1934; N.Y. Times, June 21, 1914.
39. If the real Herr S.A. Goldschmidt is still living or if his relatives see this work the author would like to hear from them.
40. The passenger lists printed for the VATERLAND for her westbound crossings differed substantially from those done for the eastbound trips. The former were printed in Germany and had considerably less English. The layout was different and the cover paintings of the VATERLAND were also different. The eastbound lists had a misty, greenish painting of the VATERLAND emerging from a fog, with Hapag's first steamship shown like a small, tiny tug in the foreground. The westbound lists had the VATERLAND-at-her-pier painting mentioned above. The full list of officers is given with titles in English in the eastbound list, but in German in the list offered for westbound crossings.
41. This photograph was later released by Hapag's publicity department.
42. Letter from Felix J. Tomei, Jr., Jan. 7, 1970.
43. VATERLAND electrician E. Wulff loaned the author the list for this voyage. All Mr. Tomei had been sure of was that it was the trip during the course of which the Archduke had been killed.
44. N.Y. Times, July 5, 1914.
45. Letters from Mrs. Helen Fleming Kawaters, dated Aug. 3 and Aug. 11, 1970.
46. N.Y. Tribune, June 8, 1914. T.A. Conference Passenger Movements, 1914, 30.
47. Hapag "List of Cabin Passengers of the New Quadruple Turbine Mail and Express Steamer VATERLAND," Tuesday, July 7, 1914, printed by John C. Rankin Co., N.Y.; loaned by Herbert Frank, Jr., whose uncle made the trip.
48. Interview with Captain E.O. Zohe, Apr. 15, 1970.
49. U.S. Archives, LEVIATHAN file, letter from C.D. Guthrie, then Radio Supervisor of the U.S. Shipping Board, to R.W. Watkins, dated Nov. 1, 1923.
50. While the author was interviewing Captain Schultz about his time on the VATERLAND, the veteran mariner, still bluff and rosy-cheeked, did his best to persuade the author to write a book about the POTOSI instead of the VATERLAND, March 20, 1970.
51. See the author's article "Unidentified Floating Objects," June 4, 1970, Proceedings, U.S. Naval Institute for RHAETIA story.
52. Both Mr. Wulff and Captain Schultz remained in America and became American citizens after staying with the ship for her period of internment in New York.
53. Hapag, "Steerage and Third Cabin Circular No. 5," July 23, 1914.

NOTES — Chapter VI

1. After World War I Mr. Dunn could see the LEVIATHAN from his lower Hudson office windows. He watched her coming and going, he saw her during her long stretches of idleness, and he was there watching when she sailed for the scrapyard "wearing the largest Red Ensign I have ever seen." See letter dated Aug. 13, 1970.

2. *Votau, op.cit.; and N.Y. Journal of Commerce, July 5, 1923.*

3. *N.Y. Times, Aug. 1, 1914.*

4. *Navy LEVIATHAN History, 33, 34.*

5. *Ibid.*

6. *N.Y. Times, Aug. 3, 1914.*

7. *N.Y. Times, Aug. 5, 1914.*

8. *N.Y. Tribune, Aug. 5, 1914.*

9. *N.Y. Times Nov. 28, 1965.*

10. *N.Y. Times, Aug. 6, 1971.*

11. *N.Y. Tribune, Aug. 6, 1914.*

12. *N.Y. Times, Aug. 7, 1914; N.Y. Tribune, Aug. 7, 1914.*

13. *Hayes, op. cit., 165-166.*

14. *Ibid.*

15. *Navy LEVIATHAN History, 34.*

16. *N.Y. Times, Aug. 9, 1914.*

17. *N.Y. Times, Aug. 11, 1914.*

18. *N.Y. Times, Aug. 15, 1914.*

19. *N.Y. Times, Aug. 16, 1914.*

20. *N.Y. Times, Aug. 17, 1914.*

21. *N.Y. Times, Sept. 20, 1936, feature article signed by Charles A. Finn.*

22. *Harms, W.L., "Speed Ratings Held by Ocean Liners Are Not Always Stated Accurately," Marine Review, Oct. 1932, 10-11.*

23. *Navy LEVIATHAN History, 152.*

24. *Interview with Eberhardt Wulff, Apr. 19, 1970.*

25. *N.Y. Tribune, Sept. 27, 1914.*

26. *N.Y. Tribune, Oct. 28, 1914.*

27. *Ibid, N.Y. Times, Oct. 28, 1914.*

28. *N.Y. Times and N.Y. Tribune, Nov. 8, 9, and 10, 1914.*

29. *N.Y. Times, Dec. 12, 1914.*

30. *N.Y. Times, Jan. 16, 1915.*

31. *Bonsor, op. cit., 122.*

32. *Wulff, interview, Apr. 9, 1970.*

33. *N.Y. Times, Jan. 26, 1914.*

34. *N.Y. Times, Feb. 3, 1915.*

35. *N.Y. Times, Feb. 7, 1915.*

36. *See folder in author's collection with photos of this fine display. The liner was building in Belfast at the time and the folder said she would be added to the company's service "in due course of time." Actually she would never fly the Holland-American Line's houseflag, as will be seen below.*

37. *N.Y. Times, Mar. 7, 8, and 10, 1915.*

38. *N.Y. Times, Mar. 12, 1915.*

39. *N.Y. Times, Apr. 18, 1915.*

40. *N.Y. Times, May 13, 1915.*

41. *N.Y. Times, May 27, 1915.*

42. *N.Y. Times, May 30, 1915.*

43. *N.Y. Tribune, July 8, 1915.*

44. *N.Y. Times, July 10, 1915.*

45. *N.Y. Times, Aug. 24, 1915.*

46. *N.Y. Times, Sept. 1, 1915.*

47. *N.Y. Times, Oct. 23, 1915. Ralph Whitney, steamship historian, is writing a book about this fleet of interned German liners which he has tentatively entitled "The Hohenzollerns of Hoboken."*

48. *N.Y. Times, Nov. 24, 1915.*

49. *N.Y. Times, Dec. 14, 1915.*

50. *N.Y. Times, Dec. 26, 1915.*

51. *Schultz, interview, Apr. 7, 1970.*

52. *N.Y. Times, Dec. 11, 1915.*

53. *Braynard, F.O., "American Shipping on the North Atlantic," M.A. thesis, Columbia University, 1940.*

54. *House Merchant Marine & Fisheries Committee Hearings on H.R. 10500, 1916, and ms. history of United States Lines by Thomas B. Ellsworth, Jr., Yale University Scholar in the House thesis, 1959-1960, Chapter VI, 226-67.*

55. *Cecil, op. cit., 226-230, and Huldermann, op. cit., 230-232.*

56. *Huldermann, op. cit., 229.*
57. *Huldermann, op. cit., 132-133.*
58. *Loc. cit., 248.*
59. *N.Y. Tribune, Jan. 12, 1916.*
60. *N.Y. Times, Jan. 19, Feb. 5, Feb. 19, 1916.*
61. *N.Y. Times, Jan. 23, 1916.*
62. *Cary, Alan L., Giant Liners of the World, D. Appleton-Century (New York, London, 1937), 52. Hereafter referred to as Cary, Giant Liners.*
63. *N.Y. Times, Jan. 24, 1916, and an undated clipping from the Cleveland, Ohio, marine magazine Marine Review in author's files.*
64. *See folder loaned by E. Wulff, entitled "Fuhrer fur die Zeppelin-Bude und Schiffsmodelle."*
65. *N.Y. Tribune, June 14, 1916.*
66. *Navy LEVIATHAN History, 35.*
67. *Schultz, interview, Mar. 20, 1970. The author has one of these VATERLAND artifacts, a gift of the late John Baker of Todd Shipyards Corp.*
68. *The author has one, also the gift of John Baker.*
69. *A copy of this program loaned by E. Wulff.*
70. *N.Y. Times, Oct. 2, 1916.*
71. *N.Y. Times, Oct. 3, 1916.*
72. *N.Y. Times, Oct. 29, 1916.*
73. *N.Y. Times, Nov. 5, 1916.*
74. *Wulff, interview, Apr. 9, 1970.*
75. *Liverpool Journal of Commerce, Feb. 11, 1920.*
76. *Huldermann, op. cit. 229.*
77. *N.Y. Times, Feb. 11, 1917.*
78. *N.Y. Times, Feb. 2, 1917.*
79. *N.Y. Times, Feb. 3, 1917.*
80. *N.Y. American, Feb. 3, 1917.*
81. *N.Y. Times, Feb. 4, 1917.*
82. *Liverpool Journal of Commerce, Feb. 11, 1920.*
83. *N.Y. Times, Feb. 6, 1917.*
84. *N.Y. Tribune, Feb. 6, 1917.*
85. *Schultz, interview, Mar. 20, 1970. Captain Schultz still had his 2nd officer's uniform when he spoke with the author. He offered to give it to him as a memento. Captain Schultz used to wear it in his motorboat on Lake George, when he would fly both the old German and the American flags. At the time of the interview he had a wholesale business importing German knives.*
86. *N.Y. Times, Feb. 7, 1917.*
87. *Liverpool Journal of Commerce, Feb. 11, 1920.*
88. *N.Y. Times, Mar. 13, 1917.*
89. *Cecil, op. cit., 232-233.*
90. *Liverpool Journal of Commerce, Feb. 11, 1920.*
91. *Tittle, Walter, "The Skipper of the LEVIATHAN," World's Work, Apr., 1927, 678-682; illustrated with a fine sketch of Captain Hartley by Tittle.*
92. *Letter dated Mar. 2, 1918, from H.C. Stuart to the Secretary of the Treasury, found in LEVIATHAN file, U.S. Archives.*
93. *N.Y. Tribune, Mar. 23, 1917.*
94. *Braynard, "Floating Objects."*
95. *Baker, Bernard N., Ships, limited edition of 1,000 copies; John Murphy Co. (Baltimore, 1916), 119-121.*
96. *Harris, Lt. Cmdr. Brayton, The Age of the Battleship, Franklin Watts, Inc. (N.Y., 1965), 159.*
97. *Ibid.*
98. *N.Y. Times, April 4, 1917.*
99. *N.Y. Times, April 16, 1917.*
100. *Interview with Commodore John S. Baylis, Sept. 17, 1969.*

NOTES — Chapter VII

1. *Commodore Baylis, interview, Sept. 17, 1969.*
2. *Hartley, op. cit., 77.*
3. *Navy LEVIATHAN History, 39.*

4. Captain Schultz, interview, Apr. 7, 1970.

5. Collector Malone's admiration for Ruser must have played a part in the particularly gentle treatment afforded the Hapag commodore. N.Y. Times, Apr. 7, 1917.

6. James W. Dunne, letter, Feb. 19, 1970. Dunne was one of these guards.

7. Navy LEVIATHAN History, 43.

8. N.Y. Times, Apr. 7, 1917.

9. Smith, Darrell H. and Betters, Paul V., The United States Shipping Board, Its History, Activities and Organization, Brookings Institution (Washington, 1931), 1.

10. Beebe biographical sheet, LEVIATHAN files, U.S. Archives.

11. Riesenberg, Felix, Jr. Yankee Skippers to the Rescue, Dodd, Mead & Co. (New York, 1955), 47.

12. N.Y. Times, Apr. 8, 1917.

13. N.Y. Times, Apr. 11, 1917.

14. N.Y. Times and N.Y. Tribune Apr. 14, 1917. Later the Rusers became American citizens and settled in Morristown, N.J. Hans grew up there and Americanized his name to Henry. He had a sad ending, being killed in a boxing match in Chicago.

15. N.Y.Tribune, Apr. 14, 1917.

16. N.Y. Times, Apr. 20, 1917.

17. N.Y. Times, Apr. 21, 1917.

18. N.Y. Times, Apr. 22, 1917.

19. Harris, op. cit., 159, 161.

20. J. Fedden to W. Denman, Chairman, USSB, dated May 3, 1917–U.S. Archives, LEVIATHAN file.

21. All these things Mr. Hedlander loaned the author.

22. Letter to author from Mr. Holt, Sept. 17, 1970.

23. Letter from P.A. Ford dated Mar. 7, 1972. Mr. Ford changed his name from Frost in 1933 when he married.

24. Letter from R.P. Cochran dated Mar. 20, 1972.

25. N.Y. Times, Nov. 15, 1919.

26. Jessop, op. cit.

27. Hugo Platt, interview, Aug. 10, 1970.

28. N.Y. Times, Nov. 15, 1919. Also Anderson, op. cit., 51ff.

29. Jessop, op. cit.

30. N.Y.Times, July 4, 1923

31. Marine Journal, May 5, 1917.

32. Navy LEVIATHAN History, 140-150.

33. He still had it when interviewed Aug. 8, 1969.

34. Roger McAdam, interview, Dec. 2, 1969. Mr. McAdam has written four books about the Fall River Line.

35. International Marine Engineering, May, 1917, 237.

36. Schultz, interview Apr. 7, 1970.

37. Wulff, interview Apr. 9, 1970.

38. See the U.S. Shipping Board's history of official acts relating to the LEVIATHAN as published Oct. 4, 1920, in the form of a memorandum; U.S. Archives, LEVIATHAN file.

39. Letter from Capt. G. L. Armstrong, 3rd Officer of the MOMUS on this voyage, Jan. 8, 1970.

40. N.Y. Times, May 27, 1917, also p. 190, Volume 51, Braynard scrapbooks on ships.

41. N.Y. World, July 28, 1917.

42. N.Y. Times Apr. 28, 1917.

43. N.Y. World, May 15, 1917.

44. A.F. Van Dyck to author Apr. 14, 1971.

45. Forest L. Carney to author, Nov. 20, 1965.

46. Harry Cunningham, writing in the N.Y. World, Nov. 19, 1925, and N.Y. Journal of Commerce, Jan. 3, 1919, and Apr. 19, 1920.

47. Undated clipping in LEVIATHAN file of the LEVIATHAN Veterans Association.

48. Letter from Henry Dipple to author, Sept. 9, 1970.

49. A.M. Sullivan to author, Sept. 3, 1970.

50. William Schwartz, interview, Mar. 16, 1970.

51. Commodore Baylis, interview, Sept. 17, 1969.

52. H.E. Whittle, Jr., interview, Apr. 3, 1971.

53. Lt. F.K. Harper, memo to Captain Oman, dated Nov. 13, 1917, on LEVIATHAN stationery, from U.S. Archives, LEVIATHAN file; also Navy LEVIATHAN History, 42.

54. Harper, op. cit.

55. *H.C. Stuart to McAdoo, Mar. 2, 1918; and Rowe to Hurley, Mar. 9, 1918, U.S. Archives, LEVIATHAN file.*
56. *Stuart to McAdoo, Mar. 2, 1918; also N.Y. Journal of Commerce, Jan. 1, 1919.*
57. *German clipping from the Tageblatt, Wurtemberg, translation and photo of original in Navy LEVIATHAN History, 39.*
58. *U.S. Shipping Board, 5th Annual Report, 30.*
59. *Howard McKissick to Chester Underhill, Apr. 15, 1934, part of Ray Green LEVIATHAN file loaned to author.*
60. *The North American, Philadelphia newspaper, July 5, 1923.*
61. *Navy LEVIATHAN History, 42.*
62. *Life Magazine published in their Jan. 23, 1970, issue a picture described as being this bust aboard the VATERLAND. The author wrote them suggesting it might be possible to find the bust in a N.Y. cellar and commenting on the strange position it had in the Social Hall. The picture illustrated an article by William Zinsser, whose father had worked for Hapag before World War I in Germany. Two issues later the magazine ran part of the author's letter and right below it a letter from Peter Vetromile, son of Dominic, saying he had the bust.*
63. *Today the floor is still there but the building is an apartment house. Telephone call from P. Vetromile, Feb. 7, 1970.*
64. *The report of the tables came Mar. 18, 1970, from Adolph Priebe, a waiter in this restaurant. It was stimulated by the author's call for LEVIATHAN material over the WEVD Ilse Wagner "German Hour" radio program that evening. Calls from E. Wulff and Capt. C.W. Schultz came in to the studio that same evening. The table story was confirmed by another waiter at the same restaurant, Max Hinkleman.*
65. *Telephone call from Francis Emmott, Aug. 4, 1970. Both he and his father John Emmott were employed repairing the VATERLAND. The telephone is owned by someone they know whose name they would not divulge.*
66. *Letter to author from F. J. Jones, Mar. 22, 1972.*
67. *Both the hobnailed iron cross and the lignum vitae object were given the author by John Baker, whose father, Col. Wm. B. Baker, found them aboard the VATERLAND.*
68. *Anderson, SNAME paper, 59.*
69. *N.Y. Times, June 14, 1917.*
70. *U.S. Shipping Board, Oct. 4, 1920, memorandum, U.S. Archives LEVIATHAN file.*
71. *N.Y. Times, June 24, 1917.*
72. *Ibid., and 2nd Annual Report, U.S. Shipping Board, Dec. 1, 1918, 45.*
73. *Baker, SHIPS, 44.*
74. *Anderson, SNAME paper, 58.*
75. *U.S. Shipping Board memo dated Oct. 4, 1920, 2.*
76. *Ibid.*
77. *The Shipping Board turned the ship over to the Army, which in turn turned her over to the Navy to be operated on the Army's behalf. After the war it was stated she would be transferred to the Army Transport Reserve and allocated to the Shipping Board. See memo from Leroy Lewis, Major, Army Quartermaster Corps., dated Jan. 22, 1920, in the U.S. Archives, LEVIATHAN file.*
78. *W.R.B. Stevens, interview, Apr. 3, 1971.*
79. *Navy LEVIATHAN History, 45.*
80. *J.J. Callahan to author, Mar. 27, 1970.*
81. *N.Y. Herald Tribune, Oct. 8, 1933.*
82. *Charleston (W.Va.) Gazette, June 20, 1951; letters from his cousin Mrs. R.B. Cassady, Aug. 7 and Aug. 18, 1970.*
83. *Clipping without date from newspaper called the Herald Telephone, loaned author by Woodward family; paper must have been published between 1924 and 1928.*
84. *Marine Engineering Weekly News Bulletin, Jan. 17, 1931.*
85. *The strike was on Aug. 6. N.Y. Times, Aug. 7, 1917.*
86. *Gleaves, op. cit., 241.*
87. *Navy LEVIATHAN History, 48.*
88. *Iverson, interview, May 14, 1969; N.Y. Times, Oct. 10, 1937.*
89. *N.Y.Times obituary, Sept. 1, 1944.*
90. *Flowers, Frank, "As the LEVIATHAN Echoed," The International Steward, July, 1938, 7-17.*
91. *Loc. cit., 17.*
92. *J.J. Callahan to author, Mar. 27, 1970.*
93. *N.Y. World, Nov. 19, 1925, and Navy LEVIATHAN History, 45.*
94. *Hartley, op. cit., 78-79.*

95. *J.A. McFadden to author, Sept. 3, 1970.*
96. *A. Cunningham to author, Aug. 13, 1970.*
97. *Webster's New International Dictionary, 2nd Ed., Merriam-Webster, 1422.*
98. *Book I, line 200-9, Milton's Paradise Lost, sent author by David Varas, Aug. 3, 1970.*
99. *While the author was writing this section he heard Ralph Vaughn Williams' Symphony No. 7, which includes a vocal part that mentions "the great LEVIATHAN of the deep."*
100. *Sea Breezes, May, 1957, 400.*
101. *Bonzor, op. cit., 193.*
102. *Sea Breezes, Aug., 1962, 140.*
103. *Anderson, SNAME paper, 58.*
104. *Navy LEVIATHAN History, 48.*
105. *Navy LEVIATHAN History, 45.*
106. *Anderson, SNAME paper, 59.*
107. *Iverson, interview, May 14, 1969.*
108. *N.Y. Tribune, Oct. 20, 1917.*
109. *Ibid.*
110. *See 23-page blue ditto, legal size, document called "U.S.S. LEVIATHAN, SHIP'S ORGANIZA-TION"–from LEVIATHAN Veterans Association files.*
111. *W.F. Engel to author, Mar. 27, 1970.*
112. *Navy LEVIATHAN History, 48-49.*
113. *Navy LEVIATHAN History, 48.*
114. *Anderson, SNAME paper, 60.*
115. *Navy LEVIATHAN History, 49,*
116. *Daniels, Josephus, Our Navy at War, George H. Doran Co. (New York, 1922), 96.*

NOTES — Chapter VIII

1. *The phone book was loaned to the author by the LEVIATHAN Veterans Association.*
2. *Mrs. H. Fleming Kawaters, letters Aug. 3 and Aug. 11, 1970.*
3. *The card loaned to the author by Tom's sister, Mrs. Dorothy Butler, Sea Cliff, L.I. Tom's nephew runs the gas station the author uses.*
4. *The Navy's LEVIATHAN history has a full section on the trial trip, but the author has relied largely on new data he has gathered.*
5. *J.J. Callahan, letter Mar. 27, 1970.*
6. *The Navy history says no one cheered, but in-person reports of crew members dispute this. The Navy book says 18 tugs were used. The Capt. Howell obituary says 22 were used; see undated N.Y. Times clipping given the author by Moran tug captain Bert Prime. See letter from Henry Dipple, Sept. 9, 1970.*
7. *A 10-inch disc, with 360 degrees cut into its rim and with a moving arrow on its face, was given the author by D.W. Hurley, a LEVIATHAN gunner. It was part of the sub-sighting equipment on one of these six-inch guns.*
8. *E.F. Engel, letter Mar. 27, 1970.*
9. *Navy LEVIATHAN History, 50-51.*
10. *Hugh Platt, interview, Aug. 10, 1970, and Jan. 10, 1972 letter.*
11. *Van Dyck to author, Apr. 14, 1971.*
12. *James V. Shand's son told the author this story Dec. 2, 1969. He is Jean Shand and was working for Gibbs & Cox. Also see Navy LEVIATHAN History, 54.*
13. *W.F. Engel to author, Mar. 27, 1970.*
14. *Anderson SNAME paper, 60.*
15. *J.W. Thomas to author, Apr. 21, 1970.*
16. *N.Y. Journal of Commerce, Nov. 24, 1917.*
17. *See letter from R.E. Cropley to Secretary McAdoo, dated Dec. 6, 1917, a part of the LEVIATHAN file, U.S. Archives. Referred to hereafter as Cropley letter.*
18. *Cropley letter. In the 1940s the author knew "Doc" Cropley, who at that time was a purser on United Fruit banana boats. Later he worked for the Maritime Commission. His newspaper clipping file, of 100-plus volumes, is a widely used Smithsonian Institution source. At his death he was librarian of the Seamen's Church Institute Museum in New York.*
19. *N.Y. Times, July 6, 1923.*
20. *Mackay, W.H., International Marine Engineering, Dec. 1919, 830.*
21. *Booklet loaned to author by LEVIATHAN Veterans Association.*
22. *"U.S.S. LEVIATHAN, Embarkation Instructions, signed by A. Staton, LEVIATHAN file, U.S. Archives.*

23. *Navy LEVIATHAN History, 219, and 2-page mimeographed summary.*

24. *Navy LEVIATHAN History, 57-59; letter from William Oman, son of Captain Oman, to author, dated Oct. 25, 1971.*

25. *Flowers, op. cit., 16.*

26. *J.W. Thomas to author, Apr. 21, 1970.*

27. *M. Iverson, interview, May 14, 1970.*

28. *LEVIATHAN file, U.S. Archives, no date.*

29. *W. Oman to author, Oct. 25, 1971.*

30. *Hedlander to author, Feb. 26, 1970.*

31. *W. Stevens, interview, Apr. 3, 1971.*

32. *W.F. Engel to author, Mar. 27, 1970.*

33. *Bliss memo for Sec. of War, Dec. 18, 1917, entitled "The Efficient Application of Am. Military Power in the War," Pershing Papers (Library of Congress), Box 355, Item 3. Sent to the author by Fr. Don Smythe, S.J., writing a life of General Pershing.*

34. *Fuchs, interview, Apr. 11, 1970.*

35. *M. Iverson, letter, Jan. 18, 1970.*

36. *Henry Whittle, Jr., interview, Apr. 3, 1971.*

37. *Iverson, letter, Dec. 18, 1969.*

38. *Loaned to the author in Jan., 1970, by Iverson.*

39. *Iverson, interview, Jan. 28, 1970.*

40. *J.J. Callahan, letter, May 12, 1970.*

41. *Letters from John Oman, Oct. 25, 1971 and Mar. 14, 1972; also see Elting Morison in his biography of Admiral Sims and the American Navy (Houghton Mifflin, Boston, 1942, p. 308) where he speaks of Sims as a stormy petrel, impulsive and irascible, who played favorites.*

42. *Navy LEVIATHAN History, 106-113; also Iverson interview, Apr. 11, 1970.*

43. *His son loaned it to the author.*

44. *J.J. Callahan, letter, Mar. 27, 1970.*

45. *Iverson, letter, Dec. 18, 1969.*

46. *O. McFarlane, interview, Apr. 11, 1970.*

47. *Popular Mechanics, Dec. 1918, 219.*

48. *Swift, Otis Peabody, "How a N.Y. Artist, With Top Ships, Worked Out Camouflage to Foil U Boats," Evening World, N.Y. Mar. 6, 1919. Only 7 out of the 749 American vessels camouflaged according to Mackay's plans were sunk. The Shipping Board's camouflage specialist, Alton Bement, had the title "Camoufleur." See also Bement, Alton, "Principles Underlying Ship Camouflage," International Marine Engineering, Feb. 1919, 90-93.*

49. *Murphy, Robert C., "Marine Camouflage," Sea Power, Jan. 1919, 28-32.*

50. *Admiral Oman's son prepared a review of the Sims-Oman affair based on Elting Morrison's biography of Sims, referred to above, and Secretary Daniels history of the Navy at war, also mentioned above.*

51. *Undated, unattributed newspaper clippings in U.S. Archives, LEVIATHAN file.*

52. *N.Y. Times, Jan. 31, 1918,*

53. *A copy of the program was found in the U.S. Archives, LEVIATHAN file.*

54. *Navy LEVIATHAN History, 112.*

55. *Ibid., 66.*

56. *Interview with Herbert R. Radunz, Sept. 24, 1971. Mr. Radunz was a member of that crew.*

NOTES — Chapter IX

1. *Hoertz went on to become perhaps the best-known steamship company artist in the 1920s and 1930s.*

2. *The 15 booklets mentioned here are listed in the bibliography among LEVIATHAN "Documents."*

3. *Ward, interview, Apr. 11, 1970; Navy LEVIATHAN History, 138.*

4. *Mackay, W.H., The International Marine Engineer, Dec., 1919, 830.*

5. *Letter from William Oman dated Oct. 25, 1971. Also see Navy LEVIATHAN History, 13; also J.J. Callahan letter, Mar. 27, 1970.*

6. *Blackburn order, Mar. 3, 1918, LEVIATHAN file, U.S. Archives.*

7. *Towne, Jackson E., letter, Aug. 2, 1970.*

8. *Rohr, Col. F.A., letter, Aug. 10, 1970; interview, Oct. 8, 1970.*

9. *13 March 1918, C.R.R. Dept., U.S.S. LEVIATHAN Memo from First Lt. to Ex. Officer, LEVIATHAN file, U.S. Archives.*

10. *Engel, W.F., letter, Mar. 27, 1970.*

11. *McFadden, J.A., letter, Sept. 3, 1970.*

12. *Mar. 3, 1918, Cdr. Blackburn to all deck officers, LEVIATHAN file, U.S. Archives.*
13. *Mar. 3, 1918, Cdr. Blackburn, to all deck officers, LEVIATHAN file, U.S. Archives.*
14. *Navy LEVIATHAN History, 67.*
15. *McKissick to Chet Underhill, letter Apr. 15, 1934.*
16. *Towne, letter, Aug. 2, 1970.*
17. *Mar. 8, 1918, Gunnery Office Order No. 2-10, LEVIATHAN file, U.S. Archives.*
18. *Mar. 10,1918 Ex. Officer Memo to Watch Officers, LEVIATHAN file, U.S. Archives.*
19. *Badger, Mrs. Oscar, interview, Feb. 8, 1970.*
20. *Towne, letter, Aug. 2, 1970.*
21. *Navy LEVIATHAN History, 68.*
22. *Rohr, Col. F., interview, Oct. 8, 1970.*
23. *Towne, letter, Aug. 2, 1970. Mr. Towne went on to become Librarian of Michigan State Univ.*
24. *Navy LEVIATHAN History, 68.*
25. *Gleaves, op. cit., 190.*
26. *Iverson, Marcus P., interview Jan. 28, 1970.*
27. *Iverson, interview, Jan. 2, 1970.*
28. *Callahan, J.J., letter, Mar. 27, 1970.*
29. *Iverson, interview, Jan. 28, 1970.*
30. *N.Y. Tribune, Mar. 16, 1918.*
31. *N.Y. Times, Mar. 28, 1918.*
32. *International Marine Engineering, Apr., 1918, 178.*
33. *Boucher, C.H., "Organization for Submarine Defense," from LEVIATHAN Veterans Association file.*
34. *Letter from Sec. Daniels to Rear Adm. Oman Nov. 29, 1920. Cited to author in letter from Wm. Oman dated Dec. 13, 1971.*
35. *Letter from Sec. Daniels to Rear Adm. Oman Dec. 1, 1920. Cited in letter from Wm. Oman dated Dec. 13, 1971, which also lists 11 other letters on the matter.*
36. *Navy LEVIATHAN history, 69.*
37. *Loc. cit.*
38. *Apr. 10, 1918, Order 2-7, LEVIATHAN File, U.S. Archives.*
39. *Ward, C., interview, Apr. 11, 1970.*
40. *Navy LEVIATHAN History, 70.*
41. *Badger, Mrs. O., interview, Feb. 8, 1970.*
42. *"Our New Troopship," The Wireless Age, April, 1918, 550.*
43. *Carroll, J.T., interview, Jan. 25, 1970.*
44. *Foster, Lawrence H., "On Board the USS LEVIATHAN," History of the 306th Field Artillery, Knickerbocker Press (N.Y., 1920), 12-13.*
45. *Carroll, J.T., interview, Feb. 12, 1970.*
46. *Carroll, J.T., interview, Jan. 25, 1970.*
47. *Navy LEVIATHAN History, 72.*
48. *Carroll, J.T., interview, Mar. 27, 1970.*
49. *Hawkins, Anna L., letter to author Apr. 22, 1972*
50. *N.Y. Times, Apr. 28, 1918.*
51. *May 1, 1918, U.S.S. LEVIATHAN, Memo, "Recapitulation All Persons on Board," LEVIATHAN file, U.S. Archives.*
52. *May 2, 1918, Bateman, Lt. A.H., order to watch officers, LEVIATHAN file, U.S. Archives.*
53. *Engel, W.F., letter, Mar. 27, 1970.*
54. *Carroll, J.T., interview, Jan. 25, 1970.*
55. *May 2, 1918, Blackburn, J.H., to all officers, LEVIATHAN file, LEVIATHAN Veterans Association.*
56. *Wilson, Capt. John F., interview, Mar. 27, 1970. Capt. Wilson is the son of Admiral Wilson. The latter, who lived to be 92, died in 1957.*
57. *Berens, George, letter, Feb. 22, 1963.*
58. *Hirzel, Wm., letter, Aug. 3, 1970; and many other similar letters.*
59. *Engle, W.F., letter, Mar. 27, 1970.*
60. *May 9, 1918, U.S.S. LEVIATHAN, Cleaning Bill, LEVIATHAN Veterans Association files.*
61. *Navy LEVIATHAN History, 75.*

NOTES — Chapter X

1. *R.A. Blauvelt, Jr., interview, Jan. 30, 1970.*
2. *May 12, 1918, typed memo to 1st Lt.'s Office from Executive Officer's U.S.S. LEVIATHAN.*

3. Gleaves, op. cit., graph on p. 95.
4. May 28, 1918, memo from Commanding General, Headquarters, U.S. Troops, On Board U.S.S. LEVIATHAN.
5. D.R. Stringham letters, Aug. 2, 1970, and Aug. 17, 1970.
6. Ralston Hayden, Jr., son of Lt. J.R. Hayden, interview, Sept. 3, 1970.
7. Adams, James A., to author, July 30, 1970. This took place near where the LEVIATHAN went aground in Dec. 1923.
8. Dipple, Henry, letter, Sept. 9, 1970. Mr. Dipple, a wood pattern maker, later built a 17-inch model of the LEVIATHAN in her troopship colors.
9. Navy LEVIATHAN History, 76.
10. Navy LEVIATHAN History, 78.
11. Hayden, Ralston, Jr., interview, Sept. 3, 1970.
12. Baltimore Sun, June 10, 1918.
13. June, 1918, clipping from some New York paper, undated and unidentified; from file of LEVIATHAN Veterans Association.
14. Conversation at LEVIATHAN Veterans dinner, N.Y., Apr. 11, 1970.
15. Engle, W.F., letter, Mar. 27, 1970; also May 30, 1918, order from Commander Blackburn entitled "Officers' Coaling Bill."
16. Gleaves, op.cit., 248.
17. Navy Lt. A.B. Randall had charge of the LINCOLN's lifeboat and the passenger was W.W. Hoffman.
18. Callahan, letter, May 12, 1970; Navy LEVIATHAN History, 80.
19. June 3, 1918, memo to gunnery umpires from Capt. H.F. Bryan, U.S.S. LEVIATHAN.
20. June 3, 1918, "Battle Practice at Submarine Target," Lt. A.H. Bateman, U.S.S. LEVIATHAN.
21. June 5, 1918, "Order," U.S.S. LEVIATHAN at sea, Lt. A.H. Bateman.
22. Mr. Hurley gave this disc to the author.
23. International Marine Engineering, June, 1918, 26.
24. Iverson, letter, Apr. 6, 1970.
25. June 4, 1918, Commander Blackburn, "Order, Order, Order," U.S.S. LEVIATHAN.
26. Keane, J.D., interview, Apr. 11, 1970.
27. U.S.S. LEVIATHAN, "Army Organizations Carried (Casuals Excluded)," undated but going through Dec. 1918, and including all voyages as a troopship before the war's end, from LEVIATHAN file, U.S. Archives. Hereafter referred to as "Army Organizations Carried".
28. Adams, James A., letter, July 30, 1970.
29. June 15, 1918, story from International News Service, out of Washington, from U.S. Archives, LEVIATHAN file.
30. The author was a guest on Isadore's radio program called "Bertrand's Belfry Tower" Aug. 22, 1970. Mr. Bierman had changed his name in later years to Lewis Bertrand.
31. One of Webber's proudest possessions was a painting of the LEVIATHAN done on velvet by the artist Will Princh. Mr. Webber died in 1944. See letter from Eileen Webber, his daughter, Mar. 21, 1971; and interview with M. Iverson, Apr. 3, 1971.
32. June 18, 1918, Blackburn memorandum from Executive Officer's Office, U.S.S. LEVIATHAN.
33. Navy LEVIATHAN History, 82.
34. June 30, 1918, "Memorandum for All Officers," from Ex. Officer's Office, U.S.S. LEVIATHAN.
35. Callahan, letter, Mar. 27, 1970; also Flowers, op. cit. 16, and W.F. Engel, letter, Mar. 27, 1970.
36. June 20, 1918, "Coaling Bill," U.S.S. LEVIATHAN, from J.H. Blackburn, Commander, Ex. Officer.
37. June 21, 1918, "Officer's Coaling Bill," U.S. LEVIATHAN, from J.H. Blackburn, Commander, Ex. Officer.
38. Phelps, op. cit.
39. Callahan, letter, Mar. 27, 1970.
40. A. Engel, letter, Apr. 5, 1971.
41. Newark Sunday Call, June 30, 1918.
42. Navy LEVIATHAN History, 83.
43. June 28, 1918, "Order" from Ex. Officer's Office, U.S.S. LEVIATHAN, J.H. Blackburn, Commander, U.S. Navy, Ex. Officer.
44. July 8, 1918, unsigned carbon of letter from an unidentified 1st Lt. on U.S.S. LEVIATHAN, Port of Embarkation, Hoboken, N.J.
45. June 30, 1918, "Memorandum to Commander," U.S.S. LEVIATHAN.
46. The other liners were the little American coastwise liner LENAPE, Clyde Line; the trans-Pacific Matson Line's WILHELMINA; the Holland-America Line's RIJNDAM; the PRINZESS ALICE, of Hapag; the

NGL's GEORGE WASHINGTON; the Italian DANTE ALEGHIERI; and the DE KALB, formerly the PRINZ EITEL FRIEDRICH. See Gleaves, op. cit., 125.

47. July 2, 1918, "Memorandum to All Officers," from J.H. Blackburn, U.S.N., Ex. Officer, U.S.S. LEVIATHAN.
48. W.F. Engel, letter, Mar. 27, 1970.
49. Bogart, Tunis G., The Bogart Story (N.Y., 1959), 171; Iverson letter Apr. 6, 1970, W.F. Engel letter Mar. 27, 1970.
50. Army Organizations Carried.
51. R.L. Hedlander, interview, Apr. 11, 1970.
52. July 9, 1918, memo from Commander Blackburn, "To All Division Officers," U.S.S. LEVIATHAN.
53. July 12, 1918, "Memorandum for All Division Officers, from Commander Blackburn, U.S.S. LEVIATHAN.
54. July 12, 1918, "Sea Routine and Port Routine" memo from Commander Blackburn, U.S.S. LEVIATHAN. See Appendix for these two routines in full.
55. July 15, 1918, "Memorandum for All Officers," from Milton H. Anderson, Secretary Naval Officers Mess, Brest, France.
56. Undated memo, File 724, U.S. Naval Forces Operating in European Waters—Forces in France, U.S.S. PROMETHEUS, Flagship Brest—From: Commander, U.S. Naval Forces in Europe to Commanding Officer, U.S.S. LEVIATHAN.
57. Wilson, Colin, review in New York Times, Book Review section, Aug. 8, 1971, p.3, of book by Stanley Weintraub, The Crucible Years of Bernard Shaw, 1914-1918, Weybright & Talley (N.Y., 1971).
58. July 17, 1918, "General Order No. 31, Engineering Dept., U.S.S. LEVIATHAN, from Lt. Cmdr. V.V. Woodward.
59. Navy LEVIATHAN History, 84.
60. Ibid, 85; also July 23, 1918, "Memorandum to Commander, Summary of Passengers Voyage No. 6 Westbound," U.S.S. LEVIATHAN.
61. Iwaniki, Felix, interview, Apr. 11, 1970.
62. Hamburger Fremdenblatt, Hamburg, Germany, July 23, 1918 morning edition.
63. Ibid, evening edition.
64. July 25, 1918, "To Whom It May Concern," letter from Lt. R.H. Jones, Senior Assistant Engineering Officer, U.S.S. LEVIATHAN; also Iverson, letter to author, July 20, 1971.
65. Fellowes Wilson, op. cit., 176.
66. Many articles have been written about these two fine vessels. See the author's chapter on the GREAT NORTHERN in his book Famous American Ships, published by Hastings House (N.Y., 1957), 149 ff.

NOTES — Chapter XI

1. N.Y. Times, July 27, 1918.
2. July 26, 1918, "Memorandum for First Lieutenant," Executive Officer's Office, U.S.S. LEVIATHAN.
3. July 29, 1918, "Memorandum to All Officers," from Commander Blackburn, U.S.S. LEVIATHAN.
4. Aug. 2, 1918, "Memorandum," from First Lieutenant Haltnorth, U.S.S. LEVIATHAN.
5. Aug. 2, 1918, "General Memo to All Officers," from First Lieutenant Haltnorth, U.S.S. LEVIATHAN.
6. Vaugh H. Woodward, letter, Feb. 8, 1971.
7. Aug. 11, 1918, "Memorandum for Commander," U.S.S. LEVIATHAN.
8. This snapshot, so faded and yellow it can not be reproduced, was given the author by the late Fred Fellendorf, who took it.
9. Charles, R.W., Troopships of World War II, Army Transportation Ass'n (Wash., D.C., 1947), 30 — an excellent review of GREAT NORTHERN's service in Second World War. The NORTHERN PACIFIC burned shortly after World War I ended.
10. Aug. 5, 1918, "Memo Re Permission Slips," Commander Blackburn, U.S.S. LEVIATHAN.
11. Navy LEVIATHAN History.
12. Ibid, 178.
13. N.Y. Times, Aug. 9, 1918.
14. Aug. 8, 1918, "Debarkation Bill," from Commander Blackburn, U.S.S. LEVIATHAN.
15. Rutherford remembers the time of the search as being only 20 minutes; the Navy's LEVIATHAN History says it was an hour and a half. See Rutherford letter, Aug. 8, 1970.
16. Navy LEVIATHAN History, 86.
17. Aug. 9, 1918, "Gunnery Practice Averages," memo in file of LEVIATHAN Veterans Association; also see Navy LEVIATHAN History, 129-130.

18. *Aug. 10, 1918, separate memos from Commander Blackburn.*
19. *Robert Bolger, Tom's brother, interview, June 4, 1970.*
20. *W.F. Engel, letter, Mar. 27, 1970.*
21. *M. Iverson, letter, Dec. 23, 1969.*
22. *Aug. 18, 1918, "Summary of Passengers Aboard," Memo to Commander, U.S.S. LEVIATHAN.*
23. *W.F. Engel, letter, Mar. 27, 1970.*
24. *Aug. 14, 1918, "Order," from A.H. Bateman, U.S.S. LEVIATHAN.*
25. *Navy LEVIATHAN History, 128.*
26. *Aug. 16, 1918, "Battle Practice at Sub. Target," from A.H. Bateman, U.S.S. LEVIATHAN.*
27. *W.F. Engel, letter, Mar. 27, 1970.*
28. *Aug. 15, 1918, "Memorandum for Commander, from J.H. Blackburn, U.S.S. LEVIATHAN.*
29. *A copy of this program was found in the LEVIATHAN file, U.S. Archives.*
30. *Cunningham newspaper biographies were published in N.Y. Herald Tribune, Sept. 3, 1945; Brooklyn Eagle, Jan. 29, 1928; and the Herald Tribune, Dec. 12, 1930.*
31. *Navy LEVIATHAN History, 85.*
32. *Aug. 20, 1918, "Watch Officers Sheet Schedule," LEVIATHAN Veterans Association.*
33. *Aug. 22, 1918, "To All Officers," from Commander Blackburn, U.S.S. LEVIATHAN.*
34. *Aug. 30, 1918, "List of officers – U.S.S. LEVIATHAN."*
35. *Sept. 1, 1918, "To All Officers," from Commander Blackburn, U.S.S. LEVIATHAN.*
36. *Sept. 8, 1918, "Memorandum for Commander: Numbers on Board," U.S.S. LEVIATHAN.*
37. *"Army Organizations Carried."*
38. *W.F. Engel, letter, Mar. 27, 1970; also Navy LEVIATHAN History, 87-88.*
39. *Nutting, W.W., "The Mysterious Paravane," International Marine Engineering, Apr., 1919, 289-292.*
40. *Navy LEVIATHAN History, 88.*
41. *R.B. Sickles letter, July 13, 1970.*
42. *Thomas Lindquist's copy of this souvenir photo album was loaned the author by his niece, Mrs. Howard Butler, of Sea Cliff.*
43. *Sept. 3, 1918, "To All Officers," from Lt. Haltnorth.*
44. *R.B. Sickles, letter, July 13, 1970.*
45. *Gleaves, op. cit., 143.*
46. *Navy LEVIATHAN History, 89.*
47. *Navy LEVIATHAN History, 89-90.*
48. *Dr. G.J. Schoelles, letter, Sept. 18, 1967.*
49. *Sept. 8, 1918, "Memo to First Lieutenant," from Commander Blackburn.*
50. *Sept. 8, 1918, "Memo to All Officers," from Commander Blackburn.*
51. *Sept. 9, 1918, "Memo to All Officers," from Commander Blackburn.*
52. *Sept. 10, 1918, "Memo on Uniforms," from Commander Blackburn.*
53. *Navy LEVIATHAN History, 91.*
54. *Sept. 11, 1918, "Memo to Commander: Numbers on Board," U.S.S. LEVIATHAN.*
55. *Sept. 11, 1918, "Memo to All Officers," from Commander Blackburn.*
56. *Navy LEVIATHAN History, 91.*
57. *Ellis, Edward Robb, "The Epic of New York City," Coward-McCann (New York 1967).*
58. *Sept. 20, 1918, "To All Officers," from Commander Blackburn.*
59. *Sept. 20, 1918, "War Loan Memo," from Commander Blackburn.*
60. *Sept. 25, 1918, "Treasury Certificate Memo," from Commander Blackburn.*
61. *Sept. 25, 1918, "Cameras Authorized," from Cmdr. Blackburn.*
62. *Sept. 25, 1918, "To All Officers," from Cmdr. Blackburn.*
63. *R.D. Zucker, letter, May 7, 1971.*
64. *"Army Organizations Carried."*
65. *J.J. Callahan letter, May 12, 1970; also see Navy LEVIATHAN History, 93, 162-163.*
66. *Undated, unidentified newspaper clipping loaned by Richard Zucker May 8, 1971.*
67. *Kenneth Harder, interview, Apr. 17, 1971.*
68. *Flowers, op. cit., 16.*
69. *Oct. 1, 1918, "To All Officers," memorandum on paper work, from Captain Phelps.*
70. *Oct. 1, 1918, two other memos—U.S.S. LEVIATHAN—one re battle practice, the other re umpires.*
71. *Undated memo from Executive Committee LEVIATHAN Naval Ball, LEVIATHAN file, U.S. Archives.*
72. *Oct. 10, 1918, "Notice Notice Notice," from Commander Blackburn, U.S.S. LEVIATHAN.*
73. *R.D. Zucker, letter, May 7, 1971.*
74. *Ibid.*
75. *See April 4, 1938, The Newport Daily Express, and Mar. 20, 1972 letter from R.P. Cochran. When the LEVIATHAN was scrapped Cochran appealed to Gibson, then a Senator, asking for the ship's wheel. He got it.*

76. *Interview with son-in-law of Mr. Hollings, James Gordon, Mar. 22, 1970.*
77. *Navy LEVIATHAN History, 93.*
78. *J.J. Callahan, letter, May 12, 1970.*
79. *Navy LEVIATHAN History, 94.*
80. *J.J. Callahan, letter, May 12, 1970.*
81. *R. Sickles, letter, July 13, 1970.*
82. *Navy LEVIATHAN History, 162-163.*
83. *Ibid, 94.*
84. *Oct. 10, 1918, "Memo to Commander, numbers on board," U.S.S. LEVIATHAN.*
85. *Phelps, op. cit.*
86. *Oct. 9, 1918, issue of "The Red Watch Mark," loaned by LEVIATHAN Veterans Association.*
87. *Navy LEVIATHAN History, 94.*
88. *Author's collection, AMERIKA/AMERICA file clippings, notes, photographs of this historic ship's sinking.*

NOTES — Chapter XII

1. *"The Red Watch Mark," Oct. 16, 1918.*
2. *Oct. 17, 1918, "Memo from First Lt. to Commander, C & R Dept., U.S.S. LEVIATHAN.*
3. *J.J. Callahan, letter, May 12, 1970.*
4. *"The Red Watch Mark," Oct. 23, 1918.*
5. *Ibid, 3.*
6. *Ibid, 4.*
7. *"Army Organizations Carried".*
8. *R.M. Safford, son of Maurice, letter, Aug. 6, 1970.*
9. *Handwritten notes on copy of "Rules Governing Censorship of Private Correspondence" issued Oct. 26, 1918, by Commander Blackburn, U.S.S. LEVIATHAN.*
10. *Phelps, op. cit.*
11. *Navy LEVIATHAN History, 152.*
12. *Charles Wood, interview, Apr. 3, 1971.*
13. *Sea Cliff is the author's home, and many of the author's friends knew Chaplain McDonald. See letter from Dr. George J. Schoelles, Sept. 18, 1967.*
14. *"The LEVIATHAN Press," Nov. 1, 1918, 2.*
15. *Phelps, op. cit.*
16. *Navy LEVIATHAN History, 95.*
17. *A.F. Dappert, letters, Mar. 5, 1970, and Mar. 11, 1970.*
18. *Ibid.*
19. *M. Iverson, letter, Feb. 14, 1970.*
20. *W.F. Engel letter, Mar. 27, 1970.*
21. *Navy LEVIATHAN History, 95.*
22. *"The LEVIATHAN Press," Nov. 3, 1918.*
23. *Nov. 4, 1918, Commander J.H. Blackburn, Memo 11418-2.*
24. *"The Red Watch Mark," Nov. 6, 1918.*
25. *Ibid.*
26. *Bonsor, op. cit., 122-123.*
27. *Cecil, op. cit., 333-346.*
28. *M. Iverson interview, May 14, 1969.*
29. *Ibid.*
30. *Congressional Record, Nov. 7, 1918, 12617.*
31. *Havgaard, Prof. William, "Buoyancy and Stability of Troop Transports," read Nov. 14, 1918, before Society of Naval Architects & Marine Engineers, N.Y., published in two parts—in Jan. and Feb. issues of International Marine Engineering, 1920.*
32. *Statement by P.S.A. Franklin before Shipping Board hearing Oct. 4, 1921, published in Marine Journal, Nov. 12, 1921.*
33. *N.Y. World, Nov. 27, 1918.*
34. *"The Red Watch Mark," Nov. 13, 1918.*
35. *"The Red Watch Mark," Nov. 20, 1918.*
36. *"The Red Watch Mark," Dec. 4, 1918.*
37. *Navy LEVIATHAN History, 95.*
38. *"The Red Watch Mark," Nov. 27, 1918.*

39. Gleaves, op. cit., 94. The story of what happened to the IMPERATOR during the war years would make a most interesting study.
40. "The Red Watch Mark," Dec. 11, 1918.
41. Ibid.
42. Tibbetts, Lt. N.L., Acting Chaplain, "Homeward Bound," from a printed war history sent the author by Stanley D. Day, Liverpool historian. The book's title and publisher were not shown on the Xerox copies sent.
43. Dec. 4, 1918, "To All Officers," Commander Blackburn, U.S.S. LEVIATHAN.
44. W.F. Engel, letter, Mar. 27, 1970, with additional comments from others of the crew.
45. Tibbetts, op. cit.
46. Godfrey, Mrs. Mary Robinson, letter dated Jan. 10, 1972.
47. N.Y. Globe, Dec. 5, 1918.
48. N.Y. Daily Mail, Dec. 9, 1918.
49. R.M. Armistead, letter, Aug. 10, 1970.
50. Dec. 8, 1918, "Numbers of Passengers Aboard," Voyage No. 10, Westbound, U.S.S. LEVIATHAN.
51. W.F. Engel letter, March 27, 1970.
52. Bludworth, T. Franklin, "U.S.S. LEVIATHAN," from same unidentified war history mentioned in Tibbetts note.
53. Ibid.
54. "The LEVIATHAN Press," Dec. 10, 1918.
55. H. McKissick, letter to Chester Underhill, Apr. 15, 1934.
56. L. Hammond, interview, Dec. 14, 1969.
57. "The LEVIATHAN Press," Dec. 14, 1918.
58. "Debarkation" booklet published aboard LEVIATHAN, no date, from files of LEVIATHAN Veterans Association.
59. Dec. 15, 1918, clipping from unidentified N.Y. paper from LEVIATHAN Veterans Association file.
60. N.Y. Sun, Dec. 16, 1918.
61. N.Y. Tribune, Dec. 16, 1918. Also see N.Y. Sun, Dec. 16, 1934.
62. N.Y. Tribune, Dec. 16, 1918.
63. N.Y. Tribune, Dec. 16, 1918.
64. N.Y. Evening Post, Dec. 14, 1918.
65. N.Y. Times, Dec. 17, 1918.
66. N.Y. World, Dec. 17, 1918.
67. N.Y. Evening Mail, Dec. 16, 1918.
68. N.Y. Evening Mail, Dec. 16, 1971.
69. N.Y. Sun, Dec. 17, 1918.
70. Mrs. R.B. Cassady, letter, Aug. 18, 1970.
71. N.Y. Sun, Dec. 17, 1918.
72. N.Y. Times, N.Y. Tribune, N.Y. Herald, N.Y. Sun.
73. N.Y. Sun, Dec. 17, 1918.
74. R.M. Safford, letter, Aug. 6, 1970.
75. N.Y. Sun, Dec. 17, 1918; see also N.Y. Tribune, Dec. 17, 1918, feature article.
76. R. Sickles to author, July 13, 1970.
77. N.Y. Sun, Dec. 17, 1918.
78. Photos loaned by LEVIATHAN Veterans Association.
79. R.M. Armistead, letter, Aug. 10, 1970.
80. Original two-page typed "Brief Record of the U.S.S. LEVIATHAN from the ship's files, saved in the archives of the LEVIATHAN Veterans Association.

NOTES — Chapter XIII

1. Jack Lawrence's famous book about his career as a ship news reporter is a classic, although filled with exaggerated stories and overdrawn anecdotes. It is entitled When the Ships Come In. See also The Evening World, Dec. 19, 1918.
2. Several volumes of scrapbooks relating to the LEVIATHAN and other ships in the archives of Gibbs & Cox.
3. From Woodward papers, loaned by Mrs. Oscar Nelson.
4. "The Red Watch Mark," Dec. 18, 1918.
5. Statement by P.A.S. Franklin made Oct. 4, 1921, at Shipping Board hearing, reported in the Marine Journal of Nov. 12, 1921. See Chapter 12.

6. *N.Y. Times, Dec. 23, 1918.*
7. *Interview with George Griffiths, Apr. 3, 1971.*
8. *Program loaned by R. L. Hedlander.*
9. *Western Newspaper Union photo loaned by R.L. Hedlander.*
10. *Navy LEVIATHAN History, 98-99.*
11. *. Interview with Mr. Jean Shand, Dec. 2, 1969.*
12. *Letter from Mrs. Mary R. Godfrey, Jan. 10, 1972.*
13. *Navy LEVIATHAN History, 152.*
14. *N.Y. Times, Dec. 31, 1918, and interview with David W. Hurley, Oct. 10, 1971.*
15. *Jan. 2, 1919–Engineering Dept., Op. Order No. 33.*
16. *Jan. 3, 1919, Memo for all officers.*
17. *Jan. 4, 1919, Commander J. H. Blackburn to all officers.*
18. *Jan. 6, 1919, lst Lt. Haltnorth to his officers.*
19. *Jan. 7, 1919, Commander Blackburn to all officers.*
20. *Jan. 9, 1919, Captain Phelps to all officers.*
21. *N.Y. Tribune, Jan. 12, 1919.*
22. *"The Red Watch Mark," Jan. 15, 1919.*
23. *Ibid.*
24. *"The Red Watch Mark," Jan. 22, 1919.*
25. *Jan. 27, 1919, memo for commander.*
26. *Navy LEVIATHAN History, 101-105.*
27. *"The LEVIATHAN Press," Jan. 28, 1919.*
28. *"The LEVIATHAN Press," Jan. 29, 1919.*
29. *"The Red Watch Mark," Jan. 22 and Jan. 29, 1919.*
30. *"The Red Watch Mark." Jan. 29, 1919.*
31. *"The Transport Ace," Jan. 30, 1919.*
32. *Feb. 7, 1919, memo for commander; "The LEVIATHAN Press," Feb. 8, 1919.*
33. *"The Red Watch Mark," Feb. 5, 1919.*
34. *Ibid.*
35. *Ibid.*
36. *Photo loaned by J.W. Thomas.*
37. *Interview with Wm. Weston, Jan. 24, 1970.*
38. *"The LEVIATHAN Press," Feb. 10, 1919.*
39. *Feb. 15, 1919 letter from Mary Robinson to Mrs. J.W. Robinson; Mary R. Godfrey to author Jan. 10, 1972.*
40. *Feb. 18, 1919, Kunz to commander.*
41. *J.J. Callahan, letter Mar. 27, 1970.*
42. *Mrs. Harold J. Raynor, letter Mar. 10, 1971.*
43. *Miss E.S. Favor, letter, July 6, 1970.*
44. *Mrs. Harold J. Raynor, letter, Mar. 10, 1971. See Appendix for this poem.*
45. *Miss E.S. Favor, letter, July 6, 1970.*
46. *Ibid.*
47. *"The LEVIATHAN Press," Feb. 19, 1919.*
48. *Ibid.*
49. *"The LEVIATHAN Press," Feb. 20, 1919; also see letter from Mary R. Godfrey, Mar. 7, 1972.*
50. *Feb. 20, 1919, letter from Mary Robinson to her mother; also see Mary R. Godfrey's letter to author, Mar. 7, 1972.*
51. *See program for Feb. 21-22 and "The LEVIATHAN Press," Feb. 22, 1919.*
52. *"The LEVIATHAN Press," Mar. 4, 1919.*
53. *Mar. 3, 1919, memo for the commander.*
54. *"The LEVIATHAN Press," Feb. 27, 1919.*
55. *"The LEVIATHAN Press," Feb. 28, 1919.*
56. *"The LEVIATHAN Press," Mar. 2, 1919.*
57. *Ibid.*
58. *Mar. 2, 1919, Engineering Dept., Op. Order No. 46.*
59. *"The LEVIATHAN Press," Mar. 3, 1919.*
60. *"The LEVIATHAN Press," Mar. 4, 1919.*
61. *"The LEVIATHAN Press," Mar. 5, 1919.*
62. *N.Y. Tribune, Mar. 6, 1919.*
63. *Ibid.*

64. *John Carrothers, letter, Apr. 4, 1970.*
65. *Midweek Pictorial, N.Y., Mar. 13, 1919.*
66. *Mar. 6, 1919, letter from Mary Robinson to her mother; and letters from Mary R. Godfrey to author dated Jan. 10, 1972 and Feb. 10, 1972.*

NOTES — Chapter XIV

1. *Mar. 6, 1919, "Brief Record of the U.S.S. LEVIATHAN, LEVIATHAN Veterans Association document.*
2. *Mar. 11, 1919, Staton to all officers.*
3. *Osmond McFarlane, interview, Apr. 11, 1970.*
4. *W.F. Engel letter Mar. 27, 1970.*
5. *Mar. 17, 1919, "Memorandum for Commander, Office of the Transport Personnel Adjutant."*
6. *"The Red Watch Mark," Mar. 22, 1919.; also letter from Mrs. Mary Robinson Godfrey, Jan. 10, 1972.*
7. *"The LEVIATHAN Press," Mar. 20, 1919.*
8. *Mar. 21, 1919, "Memo for all Officers—A. Staton."*
9. *Mar. 21, 1919, "Request approval—memo from Commander Staton. 12221."*
10. *Mar. 22, 1919, "Memo Passage Hoboken to Brest—to All Heads of Depts re Liberty at Brest."*
11. *Mar. 22, 1919, "Coaling Bill Brest; W.W. Phelps."*
12. *"The Transport Ace." Apr. 23, 1919.*
13. *Mar. 22, 1919, "Troop Compartments and Capacity."*
14. *Mar. 29, 1919, "Memo for Commander."*
15. *Chester C. Nash, letter, Feb. 25, 1970.*
16. *"The LEVIATHAN Press," Mar. 28, 1919.*
17. *"The LEVIATHAN Press," Mar. 29, 1919.*
18. *Mar. 30, 1919, letter from Nurse Robinson to her mother.*
19. *"The LEVIATHAN Press," Mar. 30, 1919.*
20. *"The LEVIATHAN Press," Mar. 31, 1919.*
21. *"The LEVIATHAN Press," Apr. 10, 1919.*
22. *Mar. 31, 1919, "Bill of Fare for the General Mess."*
23. *Interview with Butcher Shand's son, of Gibbs & Cox, Dec. 2, 1969. The brig lock and key, with other choice Gibbs items, were turned over to the Mariners Museum, Newport News, Va., as this volume was being completed.*
24. *Statement by Franklin before Oct. 4, 1921, U.S.S.B. Hearing; Marine Journal, Nov. 12, 1921.*
25. *W.F. Engel, letter, Mar. 27, 1970.*
26. *N.Y. Times, Apr. 4, 1919.*
27. *G. Cogswell, interview, Apr. 3, 1971.*
28. *Apr. 4, 1919, letter from Nurse Robinson to her mother.*
29. *"The LEVIATHAN Press," Apr. 12, 1919.*
30. *"The LEVIATHAN Press," Apr. 8, 1919.*
31. *"The LEVIATHAN Press," Apr. 9, 1919. (It was a straw vote by this same magazine, predicting a Landon landslide victory over Roosevelt, that killed the publication.)*
32. *"The LEVIATHAN Press," Apr. 10, 1919.*
33. *"The LEVIATHAN Press," Apr. 13, 1919.*
34. *"The LEVIATHAN Press," Apr. 14, 1919.*
35. *Navy LEVIATHAN History, 218.*
36. *"The Transport Ace," Apr. 23, 1919.*
37. *"The Transport Ace," Apr. 19, 1919.*
38. *"The Transport Ace," Apr. 21, 1919.*
39. *"The Transport Ace," Apr. 23, 1919.*
40. *"The Transport Ace," May 7, 1919.*
41. *"The Transport Ace," May 8, 1919.*
42. *"The Transport Ace," May 9, 1919.*
43. *N.Y. Tribune, May 23, 1919.*
44. *"The Transport Ace," May 10, 1919.*
45. *"The Transport Ace," May 11, 1919.*
46. *"The Transport Ace," May 13, 1919.*
47. *"The Transport Ace," May 16, 1919.*
48. *"The Transport Ace," May 16, 1919.*
49. *From Victor R. Talbot collection.*

50. "The Transport Ace," May 16, 1919.
51. "The Transport Ace," May 17, 1919.
52. "The Transport Ace," May 18, 1919.
53. Ibid.
54. "The Transport Ace," May 19, 1919.
55. Ibid.
56. N.Y. Tribune, May 23, 1919.

NOTES — Chapter XV

1. Fred Hoertz continued to paint liners, becoming one of the best-known ship artists in America.
2. Albums loaned by Mrs. Dorothy Butler, Sea Cliff, the late Mr. Lindquist's sister.
3. "The Transport Ace," May 28, 1919.
4. Benny Southstreet is the famous gambler in Frank Loesser's musical Guys and Dolls, based on a story by Damon Runyon.
5. Interview with David Hurley, Oct. 10, 1971.
6. "The Transport Ace," June 7, 1919.
7. P.A.S. Franklin, statement Oct. 4, 1921, before Shipping Board, as reported in Marine Journal, Nov. 12, 1921.
8. June 10, 1919; U.S.S.B. "To the Congress," 12-page mimeographed report signed by Hurley and Commissioner John A. Donald.
9. June 12, 1919; R.B. Stevens "To the Congress."
10. Shipping Board 2-page mimeographed record of "Voyages made by the LEVIATHAN during her transport period."
11. Interview with E. DeSchamps, Apr. 11, 1970.
12. Marc Iverson, letter, Dec. 21, 1969.
13. U.S. Shipping Board personnel record file for Capt. Bowen.
14. N.Y. World, June 22, 1919.
15. Letter from Mary Robinson to mother dated July 1, 1919, original loaned to author 3,7,72.
16. June 27, 1919, Troop Movement Officer, Pier No. 3, Embarkation Order #315 (Revised).
17. Capt. Amsden's diary, sent to the author by his son John Page Amsden, Aug. 3 and 11, 1970.
18. Letter from J.G. McCue to Col. Leo H. Malley, Apr. 22, 1971.
19. Frank Tooker, letter Aug. 13, 1970.
20. N.Y. Tribune, July 6, 1919.
21. N.Y. Tribune, July 7, 1919.
22. "The Marine Review," July 1919.
23. Letter from Mary Robinson Godfrey, Jan. 10, 1972.
24. "The Transport Ace," July 14, 1919.
25. "The Transport Ace," July 16, 1919.
26. "The Transport Ace," July 18, 1919.
27. "The Transport Ace," July 19, 1919.
28. "The Transport Ace," July 20, 1919.
29. N.Y. Tribune, Aug. 1, 1919.
30. Oct. 4, 1920, "Memo for Col. Goff, U.S. Shipping Board by Edward M. Hyzer, Assistant General Counsel," 13 pages.
31. "The Transport Ace," Aug. 5, 1919.
32. Letter from Miss Robinson to her mother, Aug. 12, 1919.
33. N.Y. Times, Aug. 14, 1919.
34. "Marine Journal," Aug. 30, 1919.
35. Letter from Albert Engel, Apr. 29, 1971.
36. Letter from Mary Robinson Godfrey, Jan. 10, 1972.
37. Interview with D.W. Hurley, Oct. 10, 1971.
38. Interview with A.W. Weston, Apr. 6, 1969.
39. "Downeast Magazine," Nov. 1964, 32.
40. N.Y. Herald, Sept. 8, 1919.

INDEX

(Ships, Shipyards, Ship Lines, Ports and People Included)

287

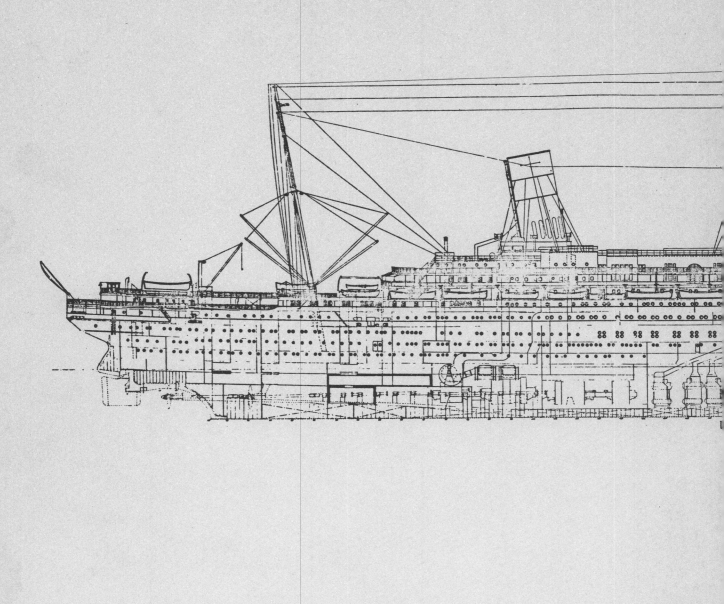
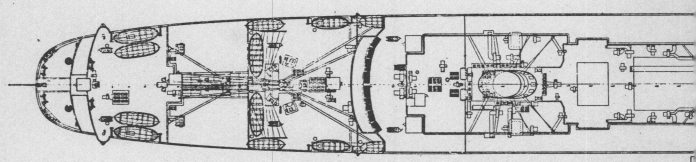